SOCIAL IMPACT ASSESSMENT
AND MANAGEMENT

APPLIED SOCIAL SCIENCE BIBLIOGRAPHIES
(General Editor: H. Russell Bernard)
Vol. 3

GARLAND REFERENCE LIBRARY
OF SOCIAL SCIENCE
Vol. 205

APPLIED SOCIAL SCIENCE BIBLIOGRAPHIES

General Editor: H. Russell Bernard

SOCIAL IMPACT ASSESSMENT AND MANAGEMENT
An Annotated Bibliography

F. Larry Leistritz
Brenda L. Ekstrom

with
Robert A. Chase
Ronald Bisset
John M. Halstead

GARLAND PUBLISHING, INC. · NEW YORK & LONDON
1986

Library of Congress Cataloging-in-Publication Data

Leistritz, Larry, 1945–
  Social impact assessment and management.

  (Garland reference library of social science ;
vol. 205. Applied social science bibliographies ; vol. 3)
  Bibliography: p.
  Includes indexes.
  1. Economic development projects—Evaluation—
Bibliography. 2. Economic development projects—
Social aspects—Bibliography. 3. Evaluation research
(Social action programs)—Bibliography. I. Ekstrom,
Brenda L. II. Title. III. Series: Garland reference
library of social science ; v. 205. IV. Series:
Garland reference library of social science. Applied
social science bibliographies ; vol. 3.
  Z7164.E15L44 1986 [HD47.4] 016.3389'0068 83-48219
  ISBN 0-8240-9047-0 (alk. paper)

Printed on acid-free, 250-year-life paper
Manufactured in the United States of America

In memory of...
Marie Gedney Leistritz
Sigred H. Silsand Engel
C. Harry Anderson
Robert E. Halstead, Sr.

Contents

SIA AND SPECIFIC DEVELOPMENT TYPES--CASE STUDIES

Series Foreword

This volume on social impact assessment is the latest in the series of bibliographies on "applied social science." There is some confusion about what "applied social science" is. From my perspective, social science is applied in three activities: in advocacy, in management, and in research. Persons who are trained as social scientists are quite often called upon these days to work as advocates for constituent groups: mental health patients, recipients of public housing, ethnic minorities, and so on. They may testify in court cases, or they may prepare grant proposals on behalf of certain groups.

Other social scientists make their careers in the day-to-day management of programs that deliver services, usually to the public, but increasingly within large corporations. Managers and advocates have something important in common: they are *consumers* of social research. The primary audience for this volume, however, are the *producers* of social research--the third group, whose activities are central to all applied social science. Applied social research is, simply, *the conduct of social research in the context of someone else's need to make a data-based decision (or justify one that has already been made) about the distribution of some resources* (money for day-care centers, for salary raises, etc.). This kind of research is variously called "needs assessment," or "evaluation research," or "social impact assessment." The compilers of this volume concentrate on the area of social impact assessment, but researchers in all these allied fields will find this volume useful.

The *Bibliographies in Applied Social Science* series has been designed to meet the needs of new researchers in particular fields. Scholars confronting for the first time such topics as those treated in this volume run into thousands of titles very quickly. Where to begin? The compilers in this series have been selected because they have already gained considerable experience in their fields of study; they know "where to begin."

New researchers in social impact assessment should not expect to find exhaustive lists of references here. Dr. F. Larry Leistritz and Ms. Brenda Ekstrom offer instead a truly useful, critical intro-duction to the most important sources, the *essential* literature on the various aspects of social impact research. Researchers may work backwards from the sources in this book; or, perhaps more impor-tantly, they may work forward in time by using the *Social Science Citation Index* (SSCI) to see who has cited, since 1969, any of the works annotated in this volume. All compilers in this series are asked to keep this technique in mind as they select works for inclu-sion in their bibliographies. They are asked to "choose works that, for better or worse, are likely to be cited by other researchers in the field."

Until very recently, building bibliographies on highly
specialized topics, like impact assessment of energy development in
the Third World, was a formidable task.   Published bibliographies
were useful, but tended to become out of date quickly.   The advent
of such tools as the SSCI and on-line data bases have made good,
annotated bibliographies like this one indispensable to researchers
who need an overview of a field so that they can begin a biblio-
graphic search in depth.   Thus, rather than becoming out of date,
this bibliography by Leistritz and Ekstrom will become more and more
valuable as the number of references in social impact assessment
grows in the future.   This bibliography will provide the essential
entry to that growing body of literature for years to come.

H. Russell Bernard
Gainesville, Florida

Acknowledgments

Is there a special place in heaven for bibliographers?   One can only hope, but there is certainly a place for our word processor operator!   Not only did she accurately type hundreds of annotations and format them into final book form, but she also coerced a stubborn word processor into sorting thousands of index items. Needless to say, without Lori Cullen's outstanding job performance this book would have taken much longer to become a reality.

We would also like to acknowledge the assistance of the staff of the Interlibrary Loan system at North Dakota State University, particularly Deb Sayler, Connie Kreps, Julie Albrecht, and Lorrettax Mindt.   They succeeded in securing hundreds of works for us in a very timely manner.

A special thanks also goes to Steve H. Murdock and H. Russell Bernard for reviewing the manuscript and to Carolyn Thoms for her assistance in printing and copying the manuscript.

Finally, we extend our appreciation to the Department of Agricultural Economics and the North Dakota Experiment Station at North Dakota State University for their support in completing this effort.

As always, our gratefulness to these individuals and entities does not implicate them for any remaining errors or omissions.

Introduction

The purpose of this book is to present a guide to the literature on social impact assessment and management. The literature
examines social and economic effects of policies, programs, and
projects, discusses alternative methods for anticipating these
effects, and describes measures to ameliorate impacts which are
generally deemed undesirable and/or to accentuate effects that are
considered beneficial.

In order to provide the reader with a frame of reference for
understanding the literature reviewed, we will first clarify some
commonly used terms in the field and identify problems associated
with reviewing the literature, then briefly discuss the scope,
methodology, and organization of the book, before examining the
current status of social impact assessment as it is reflected in the
literature. Following the introduction, the reader will also find a
list of acronyms and models commonly used in the field of impact
assessment.

The Problem

The social and economic effects of policies, programs, and
projects have become an issue of increasing concern to policymakers,
planners, and citizen groups. The process of anticipating the
nature and magnitude of these effects has been described most
frequently as *social impact assessment* (SIA) or *socioeconomic impact
assessment*. Many authors use these terms interchangeably to
describe evaluations which include economic, demographic, public
service, fiscal, and social effects. Others, however, use the term
socioeconomic impact assessment to denote all but the social
effects, and use the term *sociocultural* impact assessment to denote
evaluations of effects on social organization and structure, social
institutions, social perceptions and attitudes, and processes of
interaction. In general, however, social impact assessment (SIA)
has become accepted as the general term for analyses of the entire
spectrum of effects on individuals, families, communities, and local
governments.

Impact management is a term that typically describes efforts
to alter the effects of a project or program. Socioeconomic impact
management may include measures designed to enhance a project's
local benefits, to provide for various forms of compensation to
local interests, and/or to reduce or eliminate negative effects.
Impact mitigation is another term sometimes used to describe such
efforts, but many authors view mitigation in the narrower context of

merely reducing or eliminating negative impacts. Impact management, on the other hand, generally encompasses procedures and programs aimed at ensuring both equitable and timely distribution of project-related benefits and the avoidance and/or amelioration of negative socioeconomic effects.

While social impact assessment draws heavily on traditional social science methods (for example, those of regional economics, public finance, and sociology), two major characteristics set it apart as a distinct field of interdisciplinary knowledge and application. Perhaps the most important of these is that the focus of SIA is on *anticipatory* research, attempting to evaluate the social effects of a policy, program, or project while it is still in the planning stage. SIA can thus be contrasted with *evaluation* research which attempts to measure the effectiveness of programs already in operation. A second salient characteristic of SIA is its emphasis on providing "use knowledge" for impact mitigation and management. SIA does not seek knowledge for its own sake alone but more importantly as a guide to public decisionmaking. Public officials may use assessment findings as one of the bases for project approval (or rejection) or may order modification of a proposed program or project to achieve more desirable social and economic effects.

Although the intellectual and research traditions of SIA reach back more than 40 years, extensive development of the field did not occur until after the enactment of the National Environmental Policy Act of 1969 in the United States and after similar manifestations of increased concern for policy and project evaluation in other countries, which largely occurred early in the 1970s. Thus, the literature relating to social impact assessment and management has expanded rapidly during the last decade. Several factors, however, have made this literature difficult to access rapidly.

The first major difficulty arises from the multidisciplinary nature of impact assessment, which results in SIA-related articles appearing in a large number of journals representing a wide variety of disciplines. For example, the compilers of this bibliography found more than fifty journals which at least occasionally contain articles dealing with SIA-related topics. Although numerous journals representing disciplines as diverse as law, planning, economics, geography, sociology, and anthropology as well as inter-disciplinary journals dealing with a variety of environmental and development issues contain SIA articles on occasion, only a handful of journals are devoted primarily to the subject. The *Social Impact Assessment Newsletter* is devoted solely to SIA, and the *Impact Assessment Bulletin* and the *Environmental Impact Assessment Review* include a substantial percentage of SIA articles, but most other social science journals and periodicals only infrequently contain such articles and contributions. A major challenge for those scholars, practitioners, or decisionmakers interested in obtaining a working knowledge of SIA principles and procedures, then, is simply to identify relevant literature.

A second major problem for those seeking an understanding of social impact assessment and management is that much of the relevant literature is not found in readily available professional journals or commercially published texts. Rather, many of the most relevant

works in the field consist of reports prepared for agencies or firms
concerned with social impacts of specific projects or programs,
proceedings of conferences devoted to selected impact assessment
topics, or unpublished papers presented at such conferences.   Such
documents can be very difficult to identify, and obtaining a
physical copy of such works sometimes can be even more difficult.
Thus, scholars and practitioners alike could benefit from a single-
source reference work which would help them readily identify key
works which relate directly to specific issue areas (for example,
financing community infrastructure) or to particular types of
development (for instance, offshore oil and gas exploration).
    This book is an attempt to meet the needs of (1) students of
social impact assessment; (2) teachers and researchers in the
academic community; and (3) government agency personnel, representatives of development firms, and consultants who may be required to
prepare or review social impact assessments or to design and imple
ment impact management plans.   The specific elements of its focus
and scope are discussed below.

Scope

    The focus of this book is on the assessment and management
of social (or socioeconomic) impacts of development programs and
projects.   The geographical scope is international, and the authors
have attempted to identify salient studies undertaken in developing
countries as well as in the more industrialized nations.   The
preponderance of annotations, however, are drawn from the English-
speaking nations of the industrialized world.   This is partially a
reflection of the compilers' familiarity with the literature of the
United States, Canada, and the United Kingdom.   In addition, it
results from the fact that a high percentage of the SIA studies to
date have been directed at large-scale resource development or
construction projects, and particularly at such projects when they
are located in rural and/or remote areas.   Many of these projects
have been developed in remote areas of the western United States,
Canada, Australia, and Scotland and have provided the impetus for a
large volume of SIA literature.
    The subject matter categories of primary interest are (1)
economic, (2) demographic, (3) public service, (4) fiscal, and (5)
social impacts.   *Economic* impacts include changes in local employment, business activity, earnings, and income which result from
project development.   *Demographic* impacts refer to changes in the
size, distribution, and composition of the study area population.
Public service impacts refer to changes in the demand for and in the
availability and quality of public services and facilities while
fiscal impacts relate primarily to changes in revenues and costs of
local governmental jurisdictions.   *Social* impacts include project-
induced changes in patterns of interaction, formal and informal
relationships resulting from such interactions, and the perceptions
of such relationships among various groups in a social setting.
These impact categories have become relatively standard in works on
SIA methodology.

Several topics that are closely related to social impact assessment are not included in this work. For example, the literature on *technology assessment*, which focuses on long-range, society-wide effects of new technologies, is extensive and is not covered in this book. A few items from this literature have been included, however, because they deal with concerns particularly germane to SIA (see, for example items 3, 37, and 40). Similarly, *cultural resource assessment* is the subject of a substantial and growing body of literature which was deemed to be beyond the scope of this work. An excellent introduction to this area of applied archeology is provided by Dickens and Hill (item 15).

To summarize the scope of this work, it deals with the anticipation and management of socioeconomic impacts of development projects. It provides a guide to the literature on techniques for impact projection and on methods for managing the effects of rapid community change.

Methodology

This bibliography concentrates on the period 1970 through 1984, but some salient works published prior to 1970 have been included. It is based on a review of journals, books, and selected reports and government documents. In addition, the compilers personally contacted more than 50 SIA practitioners and solicited their suggestions concerning relevant literature.

In deciding which references to include, the major criteria were methodological or empirical contribution, timeliness, and availability. When several reports or articles addressed similar topics, the more recent or extensive works were generally selected for inclusion. Likewise, works which were commercially published and widely available were given preference over those whose availability appeared uncertain. However, because SIA is an applied field, much useful material was found in governmental and/or consultants' reports. Such references were included when it appeared that the information they contained was important and was not available in more accessible sources.

Organization of the Bibliography

The bibliography proper is divided into five broad areas: (1) Overview of SIA, (2) Methodology of SIA, (3) Impact Management, (4) Case Studies, and (5) Reference Works. If a citation was relevant to two or more categories, it was cited in full in the most relevant section and cross-referenced as an unnumbered item in secondary categories.

The author index includes all authors and/or editors and lists the citation numbers (not page numbers) of annotations for which the person is an author or co-author. Likewise, the subject index includes major subjects and their citation numbers.

Findings

The findings from the literature review reflect the recent history and current status of social impact assessment and management. Perhaps the most important of these findings is that the field of SIA has matured considerably in recent years. For example, a review and comparison of several recent books and review articles dealing with impact assessment methods indicates that general agreement appears to be emerging concerning the key impact dimensions to be considered and the basic steps in the assessment process.

A major debate in SIA circles in the recent past concerned the role of such analysis in the policy- and decision-making process. One view perceived SIA as primarily an exercise in social research, with its major goal being to provide information to enlighten decisions. The other viewpoint saw SIA as primarily a mechanism for mobilizing public involvement in the decision process. A perspective which is increasingly being embraced attempts to combine the social research and participatory roles of SIA. Impact assessment and management are becoming increasingly institutionalized in development and planning processes, and the importance of SIA-derived data and analyses in providing a more objective basis for political decisionmaking is becoming more widely accepted.

Another recurring theme in the SIA literature is a concern for more detailed analysis of the distribution of impacts—geographically, over time, and among groups within the affected communities. This concern is not surprising; dissatisfaction regarding the inability of such project evaluation techniques as benefit-cost analysis to reflect the distribution of costs and benefits was one of the factors leading to the rise of SIA. The development of methods for more effectively analyzing the distribution of impacts, however, remains a priority research need.

Reviews of the methodology of SIA lead to several general conclusions. First, in each major assessment area (such as economic, fiscal, or social), SIA draws heavily on the concepts and techniques of traditional social science disciplines. Further, in each area, the basic methodological alternatives appear to be relatively well-established and the bases for choosing among alternative models or techniques are also generally accepted. Finally, the review of SIA methods suggests several substantial limitations. The most serious of these appear to be (1) insufficient conceptualization of key relationships, (2) inadequate data bases, and (3) insufficient validation of models and methods.

Inadequate conceptualization of key relationships, although apparent to some degree in all major assessment dimensions, is most evident in the integration of major components. In fact, it appears that no clear conceptual premises have been established to provide a basis for interfacing many key socioeconomic dimensions. Even for the economic-demographic interface, which appears to be the most highly developed, the specific procedures employed are often *ad hoc* in nature, and their reliability under a variety of contextual conditions has not been adequately assessed.

Insufficient data bases pose limitations to socioeconomic impact analysis which are at least as severe as those resulting from inadequate conceptualization. Whatever the limitations in model

conceptualization, it still appears that our capacity to design
highly sophisticated modeling systems has far outrun our ability to
implement them, given the primitive nature of available data and
data-gathering techniques. In nearly all dimensions of SIA, limitations in data bases are major barriers to the development of more
comprehensive and reliable assessment models.

Finally, greater attention to the validation of impact
assessment models and techniques is urgently needed. Despite the
extensive resources devoted to impact assessments and the development of increasingly sophisticated assessment techniques, the
validity and reliability of different assessment methods have not
been adequately evaluated.

These limitations of current SIA techniques have led many
observers to suggest that greater emphasis on model validation and
ex post facto auditing of impact predictions are essential to the
advancement of the field and that impact monitoring during the
course of development is essential to informed impact management.
The recent increase in such monitoring and validation studies should
augur well for the overall progress of SIA.

Impact management, though long suffering relative neglect, is
now seen as extremely significant. Measures to modify project
effects in order to achieve a more desirable balance of benefits and
costs for area residents are increasingly being mandated through
requirements imposed by facility siting permits, mineral leases, and
community-developer impact agreements. Further, recent shutdowns of
a number of large-scale facilities have led to increased emphasis on
moderating the impacts of project closure on workers and affected
communities. Impact management has also received increased attention in the SIA literature recently; this attention appears to have
followed, rather than preceded, greater emphasis on mitigation and
management by decisionmakers and SIA practitioners.

Despite the increasing awareness that socioeconomic impacts
are important and must be addressed, however, the field of impact
management is in need of additional development. In particular, the
need for substantial systematization, conceptual development, and
empirical analysis is readily apparent. There are simply few
analyses that identify the relative advantages and disadvantages of
different types of public participation processes, different forms
of financing, or different types of public service provision. In
like manner, there has been virtually no conceptual guidance
provided for understanding or interpreting the impact management
process. Much of the literature in the area has simply involved a
chronicling of actions taken to resolve the problems occurring in
diverse locations. The skills of academicians, policy analysts, and
planners must thus be brought to bear to ensure that the critical
decisions that must be made during the impact management process are
theoretically and methodologically sound.

In closing, it should be noted that the development of SIA
has been influenced substantially by the fact that most impact
analysts have had to be more concerned with the immediate needs of
policy-making than with methodological development. This fact,
together with the time and budget constraints associated with most
impact studies, has tended to inhibit conceptual and methodological
development. Thus, it has frequently been noted that project-
oriented SIAs need to be complemented by longer-term academic

research. Recently, however, increasing numbers of social
scientists appear to be interested in pursuing impact-related
research as a legitimate research area with scientific merit.   If
such interest can be maintained, the outlook for the advancement of
the state-of-the-art in SIA should be bright.

Acronyms

Following is a list of acronyms cited frequently in this book.

AID   Agency for International Development
CD   community development
CI   cumulative impact
EIA   environmental impact assessment (analysis)
EIS   environmental impact statement
FEIS   Final Environmental Impact Statement
FES   Final Environmental Statement
FIA   family impact analysis
IIA   integrated impact assessment
IPP   Intermountain Power Project
MAP   Man-in-the-Arctic Program
MBPP   Missouri Basin Power Project
NEPA   National Environmental Policy Act
NRC   Nuclear Regulatory Commission
OCS   Outer Continental Shelf
OECD   Organisation for Economic Co-Operation and Development
PADC   Project Appraisal for Development Control
ROSA   Rest of State Area
SIA   social (socioeconomic) impact assessment
SMSA   Standard Metropolitan Statistical Area
TA   technology assessment
TMI   Three Mile Island
TVA   Tennessee Valley Authority
UIA   urban impact analysis
UNEP   United Nations Environmental Programme
UNIDO   United Nations Industrial Development Organization
WIPP   Waste Isolation Pilot Project

Models

Following is a list of model acronyms cited frequently in this book and in other literature.

AFSEM   Air Force System Evaluation Model

ATOM   Arizona Trade-Off Model

BASS   Bay Area Simulation Study

BREAM   Bureau of Reclamation Economic Assessment Model

CLIPS   Community-Level Impacts Projection System

EIFS   Economic Impact Forecast System

MAP   Man-in-the-Arctic Program (model)

MASTER   Metropolitan and State Economic Regions (model)

NEDAM   North Dakota Economic-Demographic Assessment Model

NRIES   National Regional Impact Evaluation System

PDM   Purdue Development Model

RAM   Rural Alaska Model

RED   REAP* Economic-Demographic model
           (*Regional Environmental Assessment Program)

RIMS   Regional Industrial Multiplier System

RIMS II   Regional Input-Output Modeling System

SCIMP   Small Community Impact (model)

SEAM   Social and Economic Assessment Model

SEARS   SocioEconomic Analysis of Repository Siting

SIAM   Strategic Impact and Assumptions-Identification Method

SIMS   Social Impact Management System

TAMS   Texas Assessment Modeling System

UPED   Utah Process Economic and Demographic Impact Model

General Review of SIA

SIA in "Industrialized" Countries

NORTH AMERICA

1. Alston, Richard M. "Socio-economic Considerations in Environ-
    mental Decisionmaking." *Humboldt Journal of Social Relations*
    2, No. 2 (1974): 58-66.

    Presents a generalized overview of the nature of benefit-cost
    models used for evaluating natural resources allocation,
    particularly the implications with respect to the special
    problems of the resource manager. The paper also examines
    legislation which forms the basis on which agency decision-
    making models must be based. The last section is a discussion
    of structuring conflict and building it directly into decision
    systems currently being used in Forest Service analysis.

2. Ballard, Steven C., Allyn R. Brosz, and Larry B. Parker.
    "Social Science and Social Policy: Roles of the Applied
    Researcher." *Policy Studies Journal* 8 (1980): 951-57.

    Outlines four roles taken by policy researchers which have
    helped to increase the potential usefulness of research on
    policy impact: substantive expert, information processor,
    change agent, and scholar. Specific implementation strategies
    are suggested.

3. Ballard, Steven C., Michael D. Devine, Thomas E. James, and
    Michael A. Chartock. "Integrated Regional Environmental
    Assessments: Purposes, Scope, and Products." *Impact Assess-
    ment Bulletin* 2, No. 1 (1982): 5-13.

    Explores integrated regional environmental assessment as it
    relates to two major assessments: Energy from the West and An
    Integrated Assessment of the Sunbelt.

4. Bardach, Eugene, and Lucian Pugliaresi. "The Environmental-
    Impact Statement Versus the Real World." *The Public Interest*
    49 (Fall 1977): 22-38.

    Presents the strengths and shortcomings of the environmental
    impact statement (EIS) process. The authors contend that while
    the process insures that federal agencies take some look at

environmental issues, it has also insured that they do not take
a hard look because the EIS process exposes the preparing agency
to a good deal of legal harassment. The article closes with
several suggestions for improving the process.

5. Beanlands,   Gordon E., and Peter N. Duinker.   *An Ecological
    Framework for Environmental Impact Assessment in Canada.*
    Halifax, Nova Scotia: Dalhousie University, Institute for
    Resource and Environmental Studies, and Federal Environmental
    Assessment Review Office, 1983. 132 pp.

    Reports that environmental impact assessment in Canada has
    evolved into a complex sociopolitical phenomenon involving
    extensive administrative support systems.   However, there is a
    growing concern within the assessment community that the scien-
    tific requirements and implications of such highly developed
    administrative procedures have not received similar attention.
    This report presents results of a two-year project designed to
    address this concern in the Canadian context. A major recommen-
    dation of the study is that monitoring be formally recognized as
    an integral part of the assessment process.

6. Bever,   Michael B., and Lawrence E. Susskind, eds.   "Special
    Issue on Assessing the Environmental Impacts of Offshore Oil
    and Gas Exploration and Development." *Environmental Impact
    Assessment Review* 4, Nos. 3 and 4 (December 1983): 265-613.

    Focuses on impact assessment methods specific to the oil and
    gas industry in the United States and other countries (Norway,
    United Kingdom, Canada) that have begun to explore and develop
    oil and gas resources in offshore areas, namely the North
    Atlantic, Central California, Beaufort Sea, and the North Sea.
    The review reveals that (1) decision-makers often have not used
    EISs as decision aids; (2) "worst case" approaches to impact
    assessment typical of most oil and gas exploration EISs have
    undermined the credibility of many impact assessments; (3) fore-
    cast models in projecting oil and gas impacts have been less
    than convincing due to incomplete understanding of the natural
    systems involved; (4) most EISs devote very little attention to
    mitigation; and (5) the requirement to prepare EISs has spurred
    as much conflict as consensus building.

7. Bissett,   Ronald.   "Methods for Environmental Impact Analysis:
    Recent Trends and Future Prospects." *Journal of Environmental
    Management* 11 (1980): 27-43.

    Reviews recent developments in impact analysis methods and
    examines their ability to meet criteria developed to assess
    their utility.   It is shown that none of the methods meet all
    the criteria.   Changes in the perception of the role of impact
    analysis in project planning in the United States are also
    discussed.

8. Bowles, Roy T. *Social Impact Assessment in Small Communities.* Toronto, Ontario: Butterworth, 1981. 129 pp.

Focuses on socioeconomic impacts of large-scale developments in rural Canadian communities and on the characteristics of communities which affect their capacity to mediate and control these impacts while maintaining a vital community social life, a viable local economy, and internal political efficacy. After examining literature about SIA methodology and community processes, Bowles concludes that (1) public participation in decision making is possible if governmental bodies and corporations recognize community claims as legitimate, provide total information, and include community members early in the decision-making process; (2) communities are permitted and encouraged to encounter changes as a collective unit; and (3) local residents have access to employment and entrepreneurial opportunities of large-scale development.

9. Branch, Kristi, Douglas A. Hooper, James Thompson, and James Creighton. *Guide to Social Impact Assessment: A Framework for Assessing Social Change.* Boulder, Colorado: Westview Press, 1984. 322 pp.

Aims to assist agency field staff in conducting social assessments in such a way that they are dependable and useful decision-making tools, so that they can deliver useful information to managers. This means integrating the assessment smoothly and effectively into the planning and policy-setting procedures of federal natural resources agencies and complying with relevant federal legislation and policy. First, general principles of social assessment are described. Then, a framework for social assessment is developed, including discussions of scoping the assessment effort, formulating alternatives, describing the existing environment, forecasting and evaluating the project's social effects, and mitigation, monitoring, and plan selection. The final section discusses methods and techniques, including organizing a field trip, sampling, surveying, interviewing, data analysis, and use of secondary data.

10. Brown, M. P. Sharon. *Eastern Arctic Study Annotated Bibliography.* Kingston, Ontario: Queen's University, Institute for Local Government and Centre for Resource Studies, 1984. 69 pp.

Provides a partially annotated listing of documents assembled by the Eastern Arctic Study. The purpose of the study was to examine the potential impact of the settlement of land claims of Inuit Tapirisat of Canada, and of constitutional changes in the Northwest Territories (NWT), on both local government and regulation of the mineral industry of the NWT, with special emphasis on the interface between local governments and mining companies. A subject index is included.

11. Burkhardt,   Dietrich F.,   and William H. Ittelson, eds.
     Environmental Assessment of Socioeconomic Systems. New York:
     Plenum Press, 1978. 597 pp.

     Has as an objective to increase the knowledge of the
     relationship between the social, economic, and technical
     subsets of environmental assessments. The book is divided into
     two parts: methodology (planning, prediction, and assessment)
     and case studies (technology and social systems, and social
     impacts).   Case studies used are from the United States,
     Canada, the United Kingdom, France, and West Germany.

*   Carley, Michael J., and Eduardo Bustelo. *Social Impact Assess-
     ment and Monitoring: A Cross-Disciplinary Guide to the
     Literature.* Cited below as item 974.

*   Chalmers, James A., and E. J. Anderson.   *Economic/Demographic
     Assessment Manual: Current Practices, Procedural Recommenda-
     tions, and a Test Case.* Cited below as item 97.

12. Couch,   William J., ed.   *Environmental Assessment in Canada:
     1983 Summary of Current Practice.* Ottawa, Ontario: Canadian
     Council of Resource and Environmental Ministers, 1983.   41
     pp.

     Provides an overview of environmental impact assessment
     legislation, regulations, and current practice at the federal
     and provincial levels in Canada.

13. Couch,   William J.,   J. F. Herity, and R. E. Munn.
     "Environmental Impact Assessment in Canada." *Environmental
     Impact Assessment.*   Edited by Project Appraisal for Develop-
     ment Control (PADC) Environmental Impact Assessment and
     Planning Unit. (Item 58), pp. 41-59.

     Presents an examination of Canadian approaches to environ-
     mental impact assessment (EIA). First, the factors existing in
     the late 1960s that led to the formal adoption of an EIA
     process in Canada in 1973 are examined.   Then the nature of
     Canadian governmental structures and the evolution of various
     procedures are discussed. This leads into a discussion of the
     key features of Canadian EIA processes (from project screening
     to formal public review), the relationship of EIA to planning
     and regulatory activity, the status of scientific method, and
     the related issues of social impact assessment and public
     participation.

14. Cramer,   James C., Thomas Dietz, and Robert A. Johnston.
     "Social Impact Assessment of Regional Plans: A Review of

Methods and Issues and A Recommended Process." *Policy Sciences* 12 (1980): 61-82.

Introduces SIA as a form of policy analysis, similar to other analytical techniques as cost-benefit analysis and systems analysis. Various SIA methods are identified and evaluated for their probable effectiveness in assessing regional plans with particular attention directed to regional planning conditions and the constraints and demands placed upon SIA. The authors propose a strategy for SIA where public input along with expert analysis is utilized during cyclical planning iterations for efficiently identifying and assessing the most important social impacts.

15. Dickens, Roy S., Jr., and Carole E. Hill, eds. *Cultural Resources: Planning and Management*, Boulder, Colorado: Westview Press, 1978. 204 pp.

Includes sixteen of an original twenty-four papers presented at a two-day symposium. The authors, representing academia, private industry, and governmental agencies, address the following topics: definition of the cultural resource, the legal process, expectations of agencies and contractors, and methods and public participation.

16. Erickson, Paul A. *Environmental Impact Assessment: Principles and Applications*. New York: Academic Press, Inc., 1979. 395 pp.

Presents a comprehensive set of guidelines and suggestions for conducting multidisciplinary environmental impact assessments. A general background on the bureaucratic and legal aspects of the National Environmental Policy Act (NEPA) process is provided in addition to separate guidelines for assessing the physical and social environments and for integrating procedures into an assessment of the total human environment.

17. Federal Environmental Assessment Review Office. *Revised Guide to the Federal Environmental Assessment and Review Process*. Ottawa, Ontario: Minister of Supplies and Services, Canada, 1979. 12 pp.

Describes the Federal Environmental Assessment and Review Process from the time a project is conceived to the time a decision is made on its environmental acceptability. Social consequences of a project are specifically included among the environmental factors that must be considered under the process.

18. Finsterbusch, Kurt. *Methods for Evaluating Non-market Impacts in Policy Decisions with Special Reference to Water Resources*

Development Projects. Fort Belvoir, Virginia: U.S. Army
Engineer Institute for Water Resources, December 1977. 46
pp.

Reviews nineteen comparative techniques most applicable to
the planning tasks of problem identification, formulation of
alternatives, impact assessment, and evaluation. It explores
the problem of accounting for nonmarket impacts in policy
decisions. The social impacts of water resource projects are
reviewed and related to the nineteen comparative techniques.

19. Finsterbusch,   Kurt, Lynn G. Llewellyn, and C. P. Wolf, eds.
     Social Impact Assessment Methods. Beverly Hills, California:
     Sage Publications, 1983. 318 pp.

     Attempts to go beyond previous works on social impact assess-
     ment methodology   by systematically inventorying   a broad
     spectrum of techniques and methods with proven utility. Its 14
     chapters provide an overview and, where appropriate, a critique
     of major techniques and procedures by researchers who have used
     them in a variety of settings. The book is organized into four
     major sections: (1) frameworks and methodological approaches,
     (2) primary data collection methods, (3) secondary data collec-
     tion methods, and (4) special methodologies

     Contains items 213, 214, 246, 250, 288, 307, 329, 346.

20. Finsterbusch,   Kurt, and C. P. Wolf, eds.   *Methodology of*
     Social Impact Assessment. 2d ed. Stroudsburg, Pennsylvania:
     Dowden, Hutchinson, and Ross, Inc., 1981. 386 pp.

     Contains thirty-five original articles which   explore a
     variety of aspects of SIA. The articles are organized into six
     major sections: (1) the role of SIA in instituting public
     policies, (2) methodological approaches, (3) profiling, (4)
     projecting, (5) assessment, and (6) evaluation. The book thus
     provides a very useful cross section of SIA approaches and
     experiences.

21. Freudenburg,   William R.   "An Overview of Social Science
     Research." *Paradoxes of Western Energy Development: How Can*
     We Maintain the Land and the People If We Develop? Edited by
     Cyrus M. McKell, Donald G. Browne, Elinor C. Cruze, William
     R. Freudenburg, Richard Perrine, and Fred Roach.   AAAS
     Selected Symposium 94. (Item 290), pp. 221-45.

     Suggests that the social (or socioeconomic) impacts of
     development can be usefully grouped into three categories: (1)
     demographic and economic impacts (including public service
     requirements and fiscal implications), (2) sociocultural
     impacts, and (3) biophysical impacts (the human consequences of
     projects' direct and indirect impacts on the biophysical

environment). The author points out that biophysical impacts have received much less emphasis to date than those in the other two categories.

22. Freudenburg, William R. "Social Impact Assessment." *Rural Society in the U.S.: Issues for the 1980s.* Edited by Don A. Dillman and Daryl J. Hobbs. (Item 236), pp. 296-303.

    Examines the scientific competence of social impact assessment and offers recommendations to improve the quality of social assessments. The discussion centers on two aspects of SIA: (1) data and methods and (2) the proper role of the researcher.

23. Gray, John A., and Patricia J. Gray. "The Berger Report: Its impact on Northern Pipelines and Decision Making in Northern Development." *Canadian Public Policy* 3, No. 4 (1977): 509-14.

    Summarizes and analyzes the Berger Report on the proposed Mackenzie Valley pipeline. This report is hailed as the most comprehensive and thorough contribution to public decision making ever achieved in Canada.

24. Grimes, Michael D., Jeanne J. DeVille, and Elizabeth G. Leonard. "Critical Issues in the Analysis of Social, Economic, and Cultural Impacts of Energy Extraction and Development of Local Areas." *Journal of the Community Development Society* 15, No. 1 (1984): 45-58.

    Discusses critical conceptual and methodological issues in the analysis of social, economic, and cultural impacts of energy extraction and development on the local communities and surrounding areas. The paper presents and discusses three groups of issues: (1) site-specific issues--choice of a unit of analysis, choice of variables to represent the environment(s), the "timeliness" of the indicators, and the problem of using data from different sources; (2) technology-specific issues--characterizing the scope of the energy development, estimating the pace of the development, and estimating the impact of different energy development technologies; and (3) the impact parameter problem--the problem of determining the parameters within which the impacts are to be assessed and compared. Policy implications and suggestions for improving the quality of impact assessment are presented.

25. Hart, Stuart L., Gordon A. Enk, and William F. Hornick, eds. *Improving Impact Assessment: Increasing the Relevance and Utilization of Scientific and Technical Information.* Boulder, Colorado: Westview Press, 1984. 440 pp.

Considers ways in which the development and evaluation of scientific and technical information for environmental impact statements can be improved. Addressing key legal, social, political, and ecological issues, the authors explore ways to facilitate communication between researchers and policymakers, evaluate the need for an Environmental Impact Assessment Network, and review case-study applications of new approaches.

26. Hollick, Malcolm. "Who Should Prepare Environmental Impact Assessments?" *Environmental Management* 8, No. 3 (May 1984): 191-96.

Reviews the practice of environmental impact assessment (EIA) in a number of states so as to avoid bias, integrate the EIA with project design, and make the proponent pay. The author concludes that the best arrangement may be to make the proponent responsible for EIA preparation subject to a number of constraints designed to improve the quality of studies and reduce bias. First, the proponent should be required to select a consultant from a register of those known to be technically competent, honest, unbiased, and capable of working with the project team. Second, two steering committees should be established to identify key issues; specify data collection, modeling progress and methodology; and ensure that the study remains on course.

27. *Impact Assessment Bulletin.* Special Issue: *Teaching and Learning Impact Assessment.* Organized by Sally Lerner. Vol. 3, No. 2 (Spring 1984). 85 pp.

Focuses on the educational aspects of teaching people how to perform impact assessments. Contributors consider impact assessment both as a general interdisciplinary, policy-related activity and as a more specialized activity focused on particular needs or perspectives.

28. James, Thomas E., Jr., Steven C. Ballard, and Michael D. Devine. "Regional Environmental Assessments for Policymaking and Research and Development." *Environmental Impact Assessment Review* 4, No. 1 (March 1983): 9-24.

Contends that there are a number of inherent weaknesses which characterize the traditional environmental assessment research and suggests using the integrated regional assessment approach to help redress some of these deficiencies. The integrated approach (1) provides the big picture of environmental problems and issues; (2) suggests several mechanisms for selecting key problems and issues; (3) facilitates analysis of cumulative impacts; (4) pays specific attention to problem solutions; and (5) reduces the barriers between users and producers of knowledge.

29. Knetsch, Jack L., and Peter H. Freeman. "Environment and Economic Assessments in Development Project Planning." *Journal of Environmental Management* 9 (1979): 237-46.

Argues to change the usual strategy of an impact assessment to provide greater incentive not only to identify environmental impacts but also to supply information on their implied values, and consequently increase the likelihood that these are more appropriately reflected in planning judgements.

30. Lang, Reg, and Audrey Armour. *The Assessment and Review of Social Impacts.* Ottawa, Ontario: Federal Environmental Assessment Review Office, March 1981. 184 pp.

Seeks to clarify the nature of, and identify procedural options for dealing with, social and community impacts in relation to the kinds of major federal projects that have undergone or are likely to be subject to the Environmental Assessment and Review Process in Canada, and to document relevant examples of recent experience in the United States and Canada.

31. Leistritz, F. Larry, and Steve H. Murdock. *The Socioeconomic Impact of Resource Development: Methods for Assessment.* Boulder, Colorado: Westview Press, 1981. 286 pp.

Attempts to (1) describe the conceptual and methodological approaches and specific techniques for assessing the major economic, demographic, public service, fiscal, and social impacts of resource development and the patterns of interrelationships among these impact categories; (2) delineate the policy considerations and information needs related to each type of impact; and (3) present the state-of-the-art of impact assessment for projecting each of the types of impacts and their integration. An extensive bibliography is included.

32. McEvoy, James III, and Thomas Dietz. *Handbook for Environmental Planning: The Social Consequences of Environmental Change.* New York: John Wiley and Sons, 1977. 323 pp.

Addresses the measurement of social consequences of environmental change in American society in seven thematic chapters: law, demography, land use, economics, transportation, sociocultural, and social impact information. Many of the chapters include data sources, methods of analysis, case studies, and evaluation of impacts.

* McKell, Cyrus M., Donald G. Browne, Elinor C. Cruze, William R. Freudenburg, Richard Perrine, and Fred Roach, eds. *Paradoxes of Western Energy Development: How Can We Maintain the Land*

and the People If We Develop? AAAS Selected Symposium 94.
Cited below as item 290.

33. Mason, Peter F. "Theory and Practice of Environmental Impact
    Analysis." *The Journal of Environmental Education* 6, No. 2
    (1974): 40–44.

    Reviews the origin and nature of environmental impact
    analysis (particularly the importance of activity in
    California), attempts to identify the position environmental
    impact analysis occupies in land use planning, and reviews the
    theory and practice of environmental impact analysis since
    1969.

34. Merrill, Frederick, Jr. "Areawide Environmental Impact
    Assessment Guidebook." *EIA Review* 2, No. 2 (1981): 204–7.

    Outlines the methodology behind the Areawide Environmental
    Impact Assessment Guidebook prepared by the Department of
    Housing and Urban Development to assist in assessing the
    impacts of alternative patterns of urban development and
    redevelopment in metropolitan-scale impact study areas.

35. Murdock, Steve H., and F. Larry Leistritz. *Energy Development
    in the Western United States: Impact on Rural Areas.* New
    York: Praeger Special Studies, 1979. 363 pp.

    Explores the nature and range of socioeconomic impacts
    associated with western energy development, and the policies
    and programs for impact alleviation. It attempts to draw
    together the highly diverse literature on the socioeconomic
    impacts of rural energy development, to cumulate and compare
    actual data from impact sites across the West, and to formulate
    tentative generalizations about the nature of such impacts.
    Also, it provides an overview of the major research issues and
    research priorities requiring additional analyses and
    emphases.

36. Ozawa, Connie. "Targeting the NEPA Process: Critics Heard at
    CEQ Meeting." *EIA Review* 3, No. 1 (1982): 102–8.

    Excerpts from eight commentaries submitted to the Council on
    Environmental Quality (CEQ) prior to its public meeting in
    August 1982 regarding whether the CEQ guidelines were effecting
    their intended purpose.

37. Porter, Alan L., Frederick A. Rossini, Stanley R. Carpenter,
    and A. T. Roper. *A Guidebook for Technology Assessment and
    Impact Analysis.* Series Volume 4. New York: Elsevier North
    Holland, 1980. 510 pp.

Describes the conceptual and practical facets of technology assessment (TA) and environmental impact analysis (EIA). To this end, TA and EIA are described in a societal context, general strategies and essential steps are presented, and methodology provided. Issues involving managing and evaluating assessments are then discussed, and TA and EIA are critiqued.

38. Rau, John G. "Socioeconomic Impact Analysis." *Environmental Impact Analysis Handbook*. Edited by John G. Rau and David C. Wooten. New York: McGraw-Hill Book Company, 1980. pp. 2-1 to 2-78.

Outlines the types of impacts generally examined within the socioeconomic sections of environmental impact statements and the basic steps in performing the socioeconomic impact assessment. As such, it offers a useful introduction to the field for potential practitioners. Numerous tables provide useful data on service standards and typical costs of common governmental functions.

39. Robertson, Andrew. "Introduction: Technological Innovations and Their Social Impacts." *International Social Sciences Journal* 33 (1981): 431-46.

Reviews literature concerning the social impacts of technological innovations. The author contends that technological innovations should be accompanied by social innovations if irreparable damage is not to be done to industrialized societies.

40. Rossini, Frederick A., and Alan L. Porter, eds. *Integrated Impact Assessment*. Boulder, Colorado: Westview Press, 1983. 320 pp.

Attempts to establish intellectual cohesiveness for impact assessment, including technology assessment, environmental impact assessment, and social impact assessment. Integrated impact assessment (IIA) involves the study of the full range of impacts of the introduction of a new technology, project, or program and emphasizes the policy options available for mitigating the impacts. This work contains twenty-two articles which present a variety of perspectives on means of achieving the goals of IIA.

41. Schweitzer, Martin. "The Basic-Questions Approach to Social Impact Assessment." *EIA Review* 2, No. 3 (1981): 294-99.

Presents basic questions in thirteen major issue areas of social impact assessment based on a set of guidelines developed by Oak Ridge National Laboratory's Social Impact Analysis Group.

42. Selby,   John, and Lambert Wenner.   *Social Analysis Bibliography
     for Forest Service Programs*. Washington, D.C.: U.S. Depart-
     ment of Agriculture, Forest Service, 1984.   49 pp.

     Annotates   selected   recent   publications   concerning   social
     impact analysis.   Items selected for inclusion were chosen on
     the basis of availability, currentness, and relevance to the
     current state of Forest Service SIA activity.   Each entry is
     indexed by author and subject.

 *   Summers,   Gene   F.,   and Arne   Selvik, eds.   *Energy   Resource
     Communities*.   Cited below as item 61.

43. Summers,   Gene   F.,   and Arne Selvik,   eds.   *Nonmetropolitan
     Industrial   Growth   and   Community   Change*.   Lexington,
     Massachusetts: Lexington Books, 1979.   269 pp.

     Is a four-part collection of fifteen original articles
     summarizing current   research in   Poland,   Great   Britain,
     Scandinavia, the United States, and continental western Europe.
     Part I provides an overview of contemporary research emphases
     in each region.   Part II includes three discussions of the
     nonmetropolitan industrial growth process which together offer
     some explanations of the phenomena of industrial decentraliza-
     tion and suggest some implications for rural communities.   Part
     III draws attention to critical dimensions of community change
     produced by the inmigration of industry and the associated
     modification of the community economic base.   Part IV includes
     four empirical assessments of community change.

44. Tester,   F. J.   "Social Impact Assessment: Coping With the
     Context   of Our Times."   *Social Impact Assessment* No. 53/54
     (1980):   2-19.

     Discusses social impact assessment in the context of its
     historical development and relationships to other policy
     sciences.   It is argued that social impact assessment should be
     concerned with examining fundamental assumptions about the
     objectives and ends pursued by society.   A number of different
     definitions of social impact assessment are discussed.   From
     these it is argued that the main two divergent views of social
     impact assessment hinge on whether it is seen as "process" or
     "product."   In the former, social impact assessment is seen as
     a means of bringing about fundamental social change by
     encouraging informed public participation.   In the latter it is
     part of incremental, bureaucratic decision making in which a
     social impact assessment is a "product" to be used in decision
     making.

45. Tester, Frank J., and William Mykes, eds. *Social Impact Assessment: Theory, Method, and Practice.* Calgary, Alberta: Detselig Enterprises Ltd., 1981. 380 pp.

    Contains twenty-four original papers treating various aspects of social impact assessment. Authors from academic, government, and private sector entities of Canada and the United States provide a cross section of current thinking on social impact assessment.

    Contains items 215, 261, 330.

46. Torgerson, Douglas. *Social Impact Assessment: Moving Toward Maturity.* Toronto, Ontario: York University, 1980. 200 pp.

    Offers a thought-provoking introduction to a set of issues of central concern to SIA theorists and practitioners. Foremost among these perhaps is the question of whether the field should evolve in a "technocrat" or "participatory" direction. The author's treatment of this question within the context of the evolution of the policy sciences in recent decades leaves no doubt about his own preference for an explicitly participatory approach.

47. University of Alberta. *Abstract of Papers, The Human Side of Energy: Second International Forum.* Edmonton, Alberta: The University of Alberta, 1981. 108 pp.

    Contains abstracts of sixty-five papers presented at this international conference. The papers cover a wide range of topics including growth management planning; future energy sources; implications of energy development for the elderly, women, and Native peoples; social service provision; and community involvement. A listing of conference participants together with their areas of interest also is included.

48. Vlachos, Evan. "Cumulative Impact Analysis." *Impact Assessment Bulletin* 1, No. 4 (1982): 60-70.

    Outlines an approach to the study of cumulative impacts (CIs), defines CIs in the context of existing legal mandates, builds on current practices of CI assessment, and offers some pragmatic strategies of CI assessment and evaluation.

49. Waiten, Cathy M. *A Guide to Social Impact Assessment.* Ottawa, Ontario: Indian and Northern Affairs Canada, Research Branch, Corporate Policy, 1981. 120 pp.

    Provides an overview of social impact assessment (SIA) with the objective to demystify SIA both as a process and as a

research technique.   After presenting a working definition and
characteristics   of   SIA,   the   roles   and   responsibilities   of
various   actors   involved   in   SIA   are   outlined.   The legislative
(or policy)   framework   in   which   SIA operates   in   Canada   is
discussed, along with the operational phase of SIA.

* Weber, Bruce A., and Robert E. Howell, eds. *Coping with Rapid
  Growth in Rural Communities.* Cited below as item 592.

50. Wolf,   C. P.   "Social   Impact   Assessment: The State   of the
     Art." *Environmental Impact   Assessment.*   Edited by Project
     Appraisal for Development Control (PADC) Environmental Impact
     Assessment and Planning Unit. (Item 58), pp. 391–401.

     Is a brief state-of-the-art survey of social impact assess-
     ment (SIA), including a review of topics and concerns in the
     field, an appraisal of successes and failures to date, and some
     suggestions for further improvement.

* Yarie, Sally, ed.   *Alaska Symposium   on the   Social, Economic,
  and Cultural Impacts of Natural Resource Development.*   Cited
  below as item 593.

                              OVERSEAS

51. Ahmed,   Yusef   J.,   and   Frank   G.   Muller,   eds.   *Integrated
     Physical,   Socio-Economic,   and   Environmental   Planning.*
     Dublin, United Kingdom: Tycooly International, 1982.   199
     pp.

     Represents   the   tenth volume   in   the   Natural   Resources and
     Environment Series published for the United Nations Environment
     Program (UNEP).   The first   part of the work discusses the
     environmental impact of socioeconomic activities in a general,
     descriptive manner; it outlines the initiatives and activities
     of the Economic Commission for Europe along with the topics of
     environmental management, institutional aspects, and inter-
     active learning models. The second part of the volume consists
     of seven case studies in six countries—France, Mexico, Poland,
     Sweden, USSR, and the USA—on such subjects as public partici-
     pation, national physical planning, pollution control, economic
     reform, and environmental conservation.

52. Armstrong,   Anona   F.   *First Directory   of Australian   Social
     Impact Assessment: Practice and   Practitioners.*   Victoria,
     Australia: University of Melbourne, Program in Public Policy
     Studies, 1982. 71 pp.

Provides a comprehensive register of projects dealing with social impact assessment. Information for each project includes commencement date, responsible organization, project leader, and objectives. Indexes identify project leaders and organizations with projects.

53. Bisset, Ronald. "A Critical Survey of Methods for Environmental Impact Assessment." *An Annotated Reader in Environmental Planning and Management.* Edited by Timothy O'Riordan and R. Kerry Turner. Oxford: Pergamon Press, 1983. pp. 169-86.

Discusses the following methods: matrices, networks/systems diagrams, quantitive/index methods, manuals, and models.

54. Hall, Peter, ed. "Environmental Impact Analysis." *Built Environment* 4, No. 2 (June 1978): 85-160.

Is a special issue devoted to the state of EIA in Britain, Europe, and the United States. Particular emphasis of the issue is a review of EIA methodology and its effectiveness relative to project appraisal and planning. The issue is composed of ten articles on EIA methodology; EIA in Britain, United States, and Europe; case studies of EIA in Britain; and EIA in the planning process.

55. Morgan, R. K. "The Evolution of Environmental Impact Assessment in New Zealand." *Journal of Environmental Management* 16 (1983): 139-52.

Traces the changes in the form of the environmental impact assessment (EIA) system in New Zealand since its introduction in 1974. The modifications to the administration of the system, and to the procedures that form the basis of the system, are examined in the context of the original intentions of the EIA process. The main pressure for change seems to have come from government departments, because of concern about public interference in detailed planning. The overall trend has been from a National Environmental Policy Act style EIA system to, first, a project-specific, development-controlling Environmental Impact Report process for application to major projects, and second, an informal impact assessment process for other proposed actions.

56. Newton, P. W. "The Problems and Prospects of Remote Mining Towns: National and Regional Issues." *Urban Australia: Living in the Next Decade.* Papers presented at symposium on Macro-Economic and Social Trends in Australia. Canberra: Australian Institute of Urban Studies, 1983. pp. 95-104.

Explores factors that have produced the patterns of economic development in present-day Australia, and the implications for the country's resource regions and society. Author discusses several characteristics of the mineral industry that illustrate its orientation to the world economy rather than regional or national economies. Town and regional issues are presented, and contrasts between new and old mining towns are drawn. Newton suggests that flying workers to new mining centers is an alternative to the major investments by industry and government needed to house workers and their families.

57. O'Riordan, Timothy, and W. R. Derrick Sewell, eds. *Project Appraisal and Policy Review.* Chichester, United Kingdom: John Wiley and Sons, 1981. 304 pp.

Discusses the role of environmental impact assessment as it affects project appraisal and policy review in a number of different countries. The editors place EIA in perspective with other project assessment techniques, such as cost-benefit analysis; planning, programming and budgeting; and risk analysis. In spite of definitional shortcomings, the authors have advanced the field especially as EIA relates to policy analysis. The book represents one of the first volumes on comparative EIA with case studies of United States, Canada, United Kingdom, West Germany, Australia, Japan, and selected developing countries.

58. Project Appraisal for Development Control (PADC) Environmental Impact Assessment and Planning Unit. *Environmental Impact Assessment.* Boston: Martinus Nijhoff Publishers, 1983. 439 pp.

Contains twenty-two papers presented at the NATO Advanced Study Institute on Environmental Impact Assessment held in Toulouse, France, in 1981. Areas of emphasis are (1) institutions and procedures of environmental impact assessment (EIA) in various countries, (2) the role of EIA in the planning process, (3) EIA methods, (4) assessment of specific types of impacts, and (5) postdevelopment audits. Several articles address social impacts directly.

Contains items 13, 50, 497.

59. Scott, Anthony, and Harry Campbell. "Policies Toward Proposals for Large-Scale Natural Resource Projects: Attenuation Versus Postponement." *Resources Policy* 5, No. 2 (June 1979): 113-40.

Examines the problem of assessing the environmental impact of uranium mining in Australia and considers its wider implications. The government, faced with unknown environmental and social damage from the initiation of uranium mining in northern

Australia, has begun an environmental impact analysis procedure. This requires the company to provide information about the proposed project and its alternatives, and often the company's proposal is followed by "postponement." This is contrasted with an alternative procedure of "attenuation," allowing the project to proceed albeit at a reduced scale in order to obtain further, more complete information. Comparisons are made between impact information which might be obtained by the two alternative procedures and the expected relative benefits and costs derived from postponed and attenuated projects.

60. Shopley, J. B., and R. F. Fuggle. "A Comprehensive Review of Current Environmental Impact Assessment Methods and Techniques." *Journal of Environmental Management* 18 (1984): 25–47.

Identifies the strengths and weaknesses of individual methods and techniques which can be incorporated into environmental impact assessment procedures. Methods and techniques developed and used on several continents are analyzed for the role they could play if combined with others in an adaptive approach. The review does not attempt to evaluate procedures as complete systems for environmental impact analysis, but seeks to highlight the unique contributions of each method and technique. Several methods and techniques not previously reviewed in the environmental impact assessment literature are included along with an extensive bibliography.

61. Summers, Gene F., and Arne Selvik, eds. *Energy Resource Communities.* Bergen, Norway: The Institute of Industrial Economics, 1982. 228 pp.

Consists of ten original articles addressing economic, demographic, public service, fiscal, and social impacts of large-scale energy resource development. Authors from Canada, Norway, the United Kingdom, and the United States examine various dimensions of community impacts.

Contains items 299, 368.

SIA in "Developing" Countries

62. Allen, C., and G. Willams, eds. *Sub-Saharan Africa.* London: Macmillan, 1982. 217 pp.

Provides an introduction to class and society in Africa in the twentieth century. The articles by various contributors examine colonialism and class formation; gender, production and politics; peasants, poverty and patrons; prophets, priests and

rebels; the urban poor; and African bourgeoisies. The articles
concentrate on empirical studies of general and theoretical
importance and cover most countries in the region.

63. Appasamy,   Paul   P.   "Impact   Assessment   of International
     Development Projects."   *Impact Assessment Bulletin* 2, No. 2
     (1983): 173-86.

     Identifies in broad terms the assessment processes of impacts
     that result from international development project-related aid.
     Two classes of impacts are examined: those on the natural and
     physical environment, and those on the human environment.

64. Boden,   Roger.   "Resource   Development   and Conservation
     Conflicts in Developing Countries." *Third World Planning
     Review* 4, No. 3 (August 1982): 265-80.

     Argues that developing nations should place greater emphasis
     on evaluating the environmental implications of development
     projects.   The suitability of various environmental impact
     assessment   techniques and   who should execute   them are
     reviewed.

65. Bowonder,   B.   "Impact Analysis of the Green Revolution in
     India."   *Technological Forecasting and Social Change* 15
     (1979): 297-313.

     Offers a useful, comprehensive summary of a wide range of
     direct and indirect effects resulting from the introduction of
     a new technology in a developing country.   The socioeconomic
     effects of the agricultural green revolution in India are
     examined using a network-type approach.   The green revolution
     has had a significant effect on increasing agricultural
     production, but has produced a number of negative social
     impacts.   Other   impacts examined   include   demographic,
     political, and environmental consequences.   In particular it
     has enhanced existing rural economic disparities and favored
     rich farmers.   It is argued that proper comprehensive technol-
     ogy assessment coupled with government-initiated mitigating
     actions might have avoided these harmful effects and led to a
     better distribution of the benefits from the green revolution.

66. Center   for Integrated Rural Development for Asia and the
     Pacific (CIRDAP). *Rural Urban Balance Study.* Overview paper
     and a summary of the country papers presented at the regional
     workshop on rural urban balance held at CIRDAP, Kotbari,
     Comilla, 2-6 November, 1981. Kotbari, Bangladesh, 1981.   144
     pp.

     Undertook the study of six countries (Bangladesh, India,
     Malaysia, Nepal, Pakistan, and the Philippines) in order to:

(1) document the nature and magnitude of rural-urban differentials that exist in the countries in terms of various socioeconomic dimensions; (2) describe some of the development trends and socioeconomic phenomena that appear to have aggravated the differentials; (3) examine the nature of the problems that confront the rural sector; and (4) assess and evaluate the major development policies and programs that have been undertaken to redress the rural-urban imbalance.

67. Cochrane, Glynn. *The Cultural Appraisal of Development Projects*. New York: Praeger Publishers, 1979. 138 pp.

Is directed toward those with responsibility for the identification, design, and implementation of Third World development projects--projects whose benefits are intended to reach the poorest in those countries. The focus is on the role of the project manager in the public and private sectors and on the relationships among participants, social scientists, and nonproject officials.

68. Conyers, Diana. *An Introduction to Social Planning in the Third World*. Chichester, England: John Wiley and Sons, 1982. 224 pp.

Adopts a practical approach to social planning in third world countries. Topics include the nature of social planning, policy, and reform; planning social services; role of social planning in project planning and national development planning; participatory planning; data collection; and social planning organization and methods.

69. Derman, William, and Scott Whiteford, eds. *Social Impact Analysis and Development Planning in the Third World*. Boulder, Colorado: Westview Press, 1985. 250 pp.

Examines many of the social issues of development planning from the perspective of social impact analysis. Drawing on case material from socialist and capitalist countries located primarily in Africa and Latin America, the authors differ on how sociocultural factors should be incorporated into the planning process, but agree that these factors are seldom adequately understood by development project planners.

70. Eicher, Carl K., and John M. Staatz, eds. *Agricultural Development in the Third World*. Baltimore: Johns Hopkins University Press, 1984. 491 pp.

Presents different views about what has been learned theoretically and empirically about agricultural development in the Third World since the early 1970s. Topics include the role of agriculture in economic growth, intersectoral linkages,

mechanisms of agricultural growth, institutional reform,
functioning of factor markets, choice of technique, and the
generation and social impact of technical change. Case studies
from China and Africa end the book.

71. Freeman, Howard E., Peter H. Rossi, and Sonia R. Wright.
     Evaluating Social Projects in Developing Countries. Paris:
     Development Centre of the Organisation for Economic Co-
     operation and Development, 1980. 239 pp.

     Has as its purpose to provide a contemporary introduction to
     the evaluation of projects designed to ameliorate adverse
     conditions and problems in our social and human environments,
     particularly in developing countries. Topics include use of
     evaluations, project planning research, evaluation of project
     implementation, assessing impacts of social projects, measuring
     efficiency through resource allocation techniques, and decision
     making.

 *   Garcia-Zamor, Jean-Claude, ed. *Public Participation in
     Development Planning and Management: Cases from Africa and
     Asia.* Cited below as item 667.

72. *(The) Journal of Development Studies.* Special Issue:
     Measuring Development. Guest Editor: Nancy Baster. Vol. 8,
     No. 3 (1972). 182 pp.

     Explores development indicators in developing countries since
     World War II. Topics include income distribution and social
     stratification, welfare measurement, development models,
     indicators of political development, and industrialization.

     Contains item 289.

73. Mollett, J. A. *Planning for Agricultural Development.*
     Published by Croom Helm, London, and St. Martin's Press, New
     York, 1984. 355 pp.

     Is a guide to program formulation and implementation in
     developing countries. Some of the topics are demand and supply
     projections, stocktaking and diagnostic survey analysis,
     financing, and monitoring.

74. Morss, Elliott R., and David D. Gow, eds. *Implementing Rural
     Development Projects: Lessons from AID and World Bank
     Experiences.* Boulder, Colorado: Westview Press, 1985. 243
     pp.

     Examines the problems frequently encountered by agencies,
     managers, and technicians who try to implement large-scale

development projects. Specifically, it focuses on implementation problems of projects sponsored by the U.S. Agency for
International Development (AID) and t.ie World Bank in
developing countries. Topics include political, economic,
environmental, personnel, and institutional constraints;
institutional and organizational realities; shortcomings of
technical assistance; implementing decentralization and participation strategies; timing; information systems; differing
objectives of development; and sustaining project benefits.

75. Moy, P. J. "Environmental Impact Assessment Consultants: The
     Case Against Self-regulation." *Journal of Environmental
     Management* 18 (1983): 393-401.

     Examines the performance of EIA consultants, a topic which
     has received little attention in the literature. Examination
     of EIA market structure indicates that characteristics, such as
     monopoly power, "thin" markets, lack of information, and
     inadequate third-party review, provide environments in which
     market forces are more likely to sanction than eliminate
     unethical behavior. Analysis of professional self-regulation
     as a policy option for controlling unethical behavior by
     consultants suggests that such a policy is likely to favor the
     profession's own vested interests rather than the public
     interest. An alternative of improved market performance
     achieved through measures designed to open the EIA process to
     third-party scrutiny and to provide incentives for ethical (and
     professional) behavior is suggested. These measures include
     expanded provision for public participation and judicial review
     of administrative actions. Such policy has potential benefits
     greater than has the alternative of self-regulation without the
     potential social costs of cartel behavior.

76. Munn, R. E. "Environmental Impact Assessment: A Useful
     Tool?" *Mazingira* 6, No. 2 (1982): 66-73.

     Discusses some of the problems associated with performing an
     environmental impact assessment in industrialized and develop-
     ing countries. The author highlights a need to consider inter-
     national EIAs wherever there are spillover effects, such as the
     acid rain problem in Scandinavia and North America, desertifi-
     cation in northern Africa, and environmental management in
     Antarctica. Munn recommends that the United Nations Environ-
     mental Programme (UNEP) devise frameworks for EIAs, appealing
     to the example of the World Bank as being successful in
     utilizing EIAs in developing countries.

77. Muqtada, M. "Agrarian Structure, Growth, and Equity Consider-
     ations." *Journal of Social Studies* 19 (1983): 45-75.

Advances a number of essential points for a structural framework for analyzing stagnation and poverty: (1) The agricultural sector has to be viewed according to its own merits and
needs; (2) Inequality is not a given state for an underdevelop-
ed country, but has emerged within a given system of growth and
production; (3) The agrarian structure with its 'relevant'
institutions in the present agricultural sector are integrally
related to the state of production; and (4) Within the peasant
system there is a distinct differentiation of the persons
involved in production.

78. Niehoff,   Arthur H.   *Planned Change in Agrarian Countries.*
     Alexandria, Virginia: Human Resources Research Organization,
     Division No. 7, December 1969. 147 pp.

     Presents results of an analysis of 203 case descriptions of
     projects in developing countries. A taxonomy of factors that
     exerted positive or negative influences on the progress of
     innovative efforts was developed and studied.

79. Patnaik, S. C. *Economics of Regional Development and Planning
     in Third World Countries.*   Atlantic Highlands, New Jersey:
     Humanities Press, 1982. 177 pp.

     Examines   growth   theories,   concepts,   techniques,   and
     strategies   in the   context of   Third   World development
     situations.   Specific chapters discuss techniques of regional
     analysis and planning.

80. Robock,   Stefan H.   "Are There Development Lessons From
     Brazil?"   *International Development Review (Revista Del
     Desarrollo Internacional)* 18, No. 1 (1976):   16-22.

     Summarizes   the positive and negative aspects of Brazil's
     development strategies and programs that have been shaped by
     the   cultural, political, and physical setting.   The author
     reviews Brazil's development model and special development
     techniques.

81. Sammy,   G. K., and Larry W. Canter.   "Environmental Impact
     Assessment in Developing Countries: What are the Problems?"
     Impact Assessment Bulletin 2, No. 1 (1982):   29-43.

     Delineates some of the problems associated with the conduct
     of EIA studies in developing countries, particularly with
     reference to selection of methodologies.

82. Schwartz,   Hugh, and Richard Berney, eds.   *Social and Economic
     Dimensions of Project Evaluation.*   Washington, D.C.:   Inter-
     American Development Bank, 1977. 338 pp.

Presents the proceedings and papers of the Symposium on the Use of Socioeconomic Investment Criteria in Project Evaluation held in 1973. Included are comments on the United Nations Industrial Development Organization's (UNIDO) approach to benefit-cost analysis, UNIDO's guidelines for project evaluation, an economic appraisal of an investment project in a developing country, the social value of investment, and the shadow wage rate.

83. Swanberg, K. G. *Evaluative Research for Agricultural Development Projects.* Development Discussion Papers No. 127. Cambridge, Massachusetts: Harvard University, Harvard Institute for International Development, 1982. 47 pp.

   Demonstrates the use of an analytical framework to structure an evaluation system for an agricultural development project in Mexico, and in so doing develops a technique which can be applied to a general model of integrated rural development projects. The structural framework is described and is then applied to the evaluation system developed for the Rainfed Agricultural Districts Programme in Mexico.

84. Waller, R. A. "EIA Guidelines for the United Nations Environment Programme." *Impact Assessment Bulletin* 2, No. 1 (1982): 44-52.

   Discusses the development, content, recommendations within, and response to the guidelines for assessing industrial environmental impact and environmental criteria for siting industry in developing countries. The guidelines were drafted by Atkins Research and Development in 1978 for the United Nations Environment Programme (UNEP).

Methodology of SIA

Impact Assessment

ECONOMIC

85. Amin, Galal A. "Project Appraisal and Income Distribution."
    World Development 6, No. 2 (1978): 139-52.

    Critiques the equity and employment objectives of development
    projects, contending that these objectives continue to be
    sacrificed to the objective of increasing aggregate income.
    The commonly accepted justifications for the neglect of income
    distribution are criticized along with the recent attempt of
    incorporating income distribution weights in social cost-
    benefit analysis. Argues that blame rests on the persistent
    tendency to aggregate costs and benefits accruing to highly
    heterogeneous social groups, as well as the tendency to replace
    unquantifiable phenomena by quantifiable ones.

86. Baster, Jeremy. "Stability of Trade Patterns in Regional
    Input-Output Tables." *Urban Studies* 17 (1980): 71-75.

    Points out that applications of input-output tables generally
    involve an assumption of the stability over time of trade
    patterns, although evidence supporting this is thin, especially
    at the regional level. Data from Strathclyde, Scotland, at the
    level of the individual establishments over the two-year period
    1974-76 indicate a high level of stability, especially when
    aggregated at the industry level. It also gives some support
    to the hypothesis that instability is concentrated in products
    with a high value-to-weight ratio.

*   Batey, Peter W. J., and Moss Madden. "The Modeling of
    Demographic-Economic Change within the Context of Regional
    Decline: Analytical Procedures and Empirical Results."
    Socio-Economic Planning Sciences. Cited below as item 336.

87. Bendavid-Val, Avrom. *Regional and Local Economic Analysis for
    Practitioners.* 2d ed. New York: Praeger Publishers, 1983.
    292 pp.

    A rudimentary book intended to serve as a reference guide for
    persons engaged in local and regional economic development
    planning. Beginning with a review of the basic economic

concepts involved in regional development analysis, the author
discusses a wide range of regional economic analytical methods
including economic base, input-output, income and product
accounts, and cost-benefit analysis. The concluding chapters
place these analytical methods within a discussion of the
general planning process.

88. Bender, Lloyd D. *Differences in the Timepaths of Service
     Employment Responses: Rapid Growth and Local Planning.* ERS
     Staff Rpt. AGES 841201. Washington, D.C.: U.S. Department
     of Agriculture, 1984. 12 pp.

     Describes annual adjustments of nonbasic employment in
     response to different hypothetical changes in basic income.
     The results illustrate findings of a regression analysis of
     data from 1971-79 of thirty rural counties that had experienced
     rapid growth. The analysis produced significant lags in annual
     nonbasic employment changes in relation to basic income
     changes. The timing of changes in nonbasic and basic sectors
     and consequently of population in rapidly growing local
     economies is a critical element in local fiscal planning.

89. Bender, Lloyd D., and Larry C. Parcels. "Structural Differ-
     ences and the Time Pattern of Basic Employment." *Land
     Economics* 59, No. 2 (May 1983): 220-34.

     Tests whether economic structures differ significantly among
     rural counties and whether these differences are related to the
     time pattern of basic employment growth and decline. Signifi-
     cant structural differences are found with respect to the ratio
     of service to basic employment and the ratio of employment to
     population.

90. Bezdek, Roger H., and Arlene K. Shapiro. "Empirical Tests of
     Input-Output Forecasts." *Socio-Economic Planning Sciences* 12
     (1978): 29-36.

     Analyzes previous studies of the accuracy of input-output
     forecasts as compared with projections derived from alternative
     forecasting techniques. The problem of constructing appro-
     priate tests of input-output forecasts is discussed. Major
     tests of the interindustry approach and alternative techniques,
     such as final demand blowup, GNP blowup, and multiple
     regression, conducted in the past four decades are reviewed,
     and the major findings summarized. It is shown here that,
     contrary to the belief of some economists, the input-output
     forecasting model performs as well as and usually better than
     any of the alternatives considered.

91. Billings, R. Bruce. "The Mathematical Identity of the
     Multipliers Derived from the Economic Base Model and the

Input-Output Model." *Journal of Regional Science* 9, No. 3 (1969): 471-73.

Demonstrates that the aggregate personal income multiplier derived from input-output analysis is identical to the economic base multiplier. The author believes that the identity of the multipliers lends credence and theoretical backing to the economic base model results. He acknowledges, however, the limitations associated with any aggregate multiplier.

* Blomquist, Glenn. "The Effect of Electric Utility Power Plant Location on Area Property Value." *Land Economics.* Cited below as item 919.

92. Boehm, William T., and Martin T. Pond. "Job Location, Retail Purchasing Patterns, and Local Economic Development." *Growth and Change* 7, No. 1 (1976): 7-12.

Considers the effects of changing local employment patterns on the development potential of the local economy. Projects designed to stimulate local economic development may adversely affect rural retail trade sectors which provide local employment and local business property tax revenues. This is due to the interrelationship of employment location and the location of retail purchases, for which the article presents evidence. The authors point out that the location-of-purchase decision of the consumer will determine the fate of individual retailers and groups of retailers.

93. Boisvert, Richard N., and Nelson L. Bills. *A Non-Survey Technique for Regional I-O Models: Application to River Basin Planning.* A.E. Res. 76-19. Ithaca, New York: Cornell University, Department of Agricultural Economics, 1976. 95 pp.

Reviews existing methods for developing regional input-output models from secondary data (i.e., nonsurvey methods) and develops an improved procedure. The two important improvements are (1) use of a highly disaggregate table (such as a four-digit SIC classification) as the basis for estimating regional technical coefficients, and (2) more explicit identification of noncompetitive regional imports. The procedure is illustrated through analysis of water development in the Hudson River Basin.

94. Boster, Ronald S., and William E. Martin. "The Value of Primary Versus Secondary Data in Interindustry Analysis: A Study in the Economics of Economic Models." *The Annals of Regional Science* 6, No. 2 (1972): 35-44.

Compares the accuracy and costs of primary and secondary approaches to constructing regional input-output models. Two models developed for the state of Arizona are compared. Statistical tests reveal that the coefficients of the two models are quite similar but that the time and cost requirements of the secondary data approach are much less. The authors conclude that models based on secondary data are probably quite adequate for most policy analyses.

* Brady, Guy, Jr. "The Economic Impact of Industrialization on a Rural Town Economy: Wynne, Arkansas." Master's Thesis. Cited below as item 942.

95. Braschler, Curtis. "A Comparison of Least-Squares Estimates of Regional Employment Multipliers with Other Methods." *Journal of Regional Science* 12, No. 3 (1972): 457-68.

Considers the relationship between multipliers generated by state interindustry models and multipliers that can be generated by the use of a single-equation model. Reports the results of an empirical test of the single-equation model using a cross-sectional observation matrix on county employment as the basic data input.

* Brownrigg, Mark. "Industrial Contraction and the Regional Multiplier Effect: An Application in Scotland." *Town Planning Review.* Cited below as item 836.

96. Cartwright, Joseph V., and Richard M. Beemiller. *The Regional Economic Impact of Military Base Spending.* Washington, D.C.: U.S. Department of Commerce, 1980. 55 pp.

Attempts to develop a methodology that can analyze the local impacts of the realignment of military bases. The Regional Industrial Multiplier System (RIMS) is utilized to estimate gross output, earnings, and employment multipliers associated with military base realignments. The RIMS methodology is applied to assess the probable impacts of closing three military bases.

97. Chalmers, James A., and E. J. Anderson. *Economic/Demographic Assessment Manual: Current Practices, Procedural Recommendations, and a Test Case.* Denver, Colorado: Bureau of Reclamation, 1977. 300 pp.

Is focused on the problems associated with projecting the population, employment, and income impacts of both the construction and the operation phases of water resource development projects. The manual consists of three sections.

(1) *Survey of Current Practices.* A large number of environmental assessments and planning reports are reviewed. Methods
currently being used for economic and demographic analysis are
described. (2) *Procedural Recommendations.* Based partly on
current practices and partly on the professional social
science literature, a set of procedural recommendations are
made for carrying out economic-demographic assessments.
Methodological options are identified and evaluated as they
apply to the different steps in the projection and assessment
process. (3) *Test Case.* The procedural recommendations are
demonstrated by applying them to a proposed desalting plant
near LaVerkin, Utah. The organization of the assessment
follows the procedural recommendations and illustrates the way
in which many of the practical problems of an actual assessment can be met.

98. Chalmers, James A., Eric J. Anderson, Terrance Beckhelm, and
    William Hannigan. "Spatial Interaction in Sparsely
    Populated Regions: An Hierarchical Economic Base Approach."
    International Regional Science Review 3, No. 1 (1978): 75-
    92.

    Applies ideas from central place theory to the problem of
    describing the economic interaction among centers in sparsely
    settled regions. A method is proposed to trace the impact of
    an exogenous change in income or employment through the
    functional economic hierarchy.

99. Clayton, E. "Agricultural Development and Farm Distribution
    in LDC's." *Journal of Agricultural Economics* 34, No. 3
    (1983): 349-59.

    Contends that the dominant development objective in develop-
    ing countries should be to encourage the enterprise ability
    and energy of small farmers and their families. Such a
    strategy produces a degree of unequal distribution of benefits
    which reflects the distribution of personal qualities and
    endowments and acts as an incentive to their exercise. To
    keep disparities within bounds, agricultural policies relating
    to pricing, extension, credit, research, and so on should aim
    at widening the number of small farmer beneficiaries of agri-
    cultural development.

100. Collier, P. "Oil and Inequality in Rural Nigeria." *Agrarian
     Policies and Rural Poverty in Africa.* Edited by D. Ghai and
     S. Radwan. Geneva, Switzerland: International Labour
     Office, 1983. pp. 191-217.

     Explores the unequal distribution between rural and urban
     populations of the benefits of Nigeria's oil boom since 1968.
     There were also shifts in income distribution within the rural
     community as a result of oil revenues. The paper reiterates

the view that rapid growth at a national level does not
automatically benefit a country's rural poor.

101. Conopask, Jeff V. *A Data-Pooling Approach to Estimate
     Employment Multipliers for Small Regional Economies.* Tech.
     Bull. No. 1583. Washington, D.C.: U.S. Department of
     Agriculture, 1978. 31 pp.

     Demonstrates a procedure for estimating disaggregated and
     lagged economic base multipliers for short- to intermediate-
     term forecasting models. A covariance model and an error
     components model are demonstrated by an application of pooled
     cross-sectional time-series data for northern Great Plains
     coal development.

102. Davis, H. Craig. "A Synthesis of Two Methods of Estimating
     Regional Sector Multipliers." *Growth and Change* 9, No. 2
     (1978): 9-13.

     Argues that two nonsurvey methods of input-output model
     construction can be combined in such a way that savings in
     data collection costs may be obtained with little loss in
     accuracy in estimating multipliers for the various sectors.
     The Technique for Area Planning (TAP) and the Rectangular
     Matrix Method (RMM) are applied independently and in combina-
     tion with an input-output model of Vancouver, British
     Columbia, and the results are discussed.

103. Davis, H. Craig, and Douglas R. Webster. "A Compositional
     Approach to Regional Socio-Economic Impact Assessment."
     Socio-Economic Planning Sciences 15, No. 4 (1981): 159-63.

     Presents a methodological discussion which argues for a more
     integrated approach to socioeconomic impact assessment.
     Economic and social impact assessments of resource develop-
     ments are often undertaken by independent analysts, and rarely
     is an integrated approach adopted. A case is made that
     economic impact assessment can facilitate social impact
     assessment and simultaneously improve the accuracy of employ-
     ment estimation by distinguishing between various sociodemo-
     graphic groups. In turn, the assessment of sociodemographic
     composition of the local community has direct implications for
     the accuracy of the economic impact assessment. The approach
     is illustrated by an empirical study concerning the employment
     impact of a fisheries enhancement program on two Vancouver
     Island, British Columbia, settlements.

104. Davis, R. M., G. S. Stacey, G. I. Nehman, and F. K. Goodman.
     "Development of an Economic-Environmental Trade-Off Model
     for Industrial Land-Use Planning." *The Review of Regional
     Studies* 4, No. 1 (1974): 11-26.

Describes a methodology developed to help planners address the trade-offs between environmental quality and economic development. The methodology consists of a Regional Analysis Submodel (based on an expanded input-output model incorporating land use, resource inputs, and waste-emission outputs) and a Site Analysis Submodel. The methodology is applied to a case-study area centered on Charleston, South Carolina.

105. Deaton, Brady J., and Maurice R. Landes. "Rural Industrialization and the Changing Distribution of Family Incomes." *American Journal of Agricultural Economics* 60, No. 5 (1978): 950-54.

Reports that obtaining employment at new plants resulted in a shift toward equality of family incomes of manufacturing workers in rural Tennessee. Much of this shift resulted from female workers' taking jobs in the new plants.

* Doeksen, Gerald A., John Kuehn, and Joseph Schmidt. "Consequences of Decline and Community Economic Adjustment To It." *Communities Left Behind: Alternatives for Development.* Edited by Larry R. Whiting. Cited below as item 842.

106. Doeksen, Gerald A., and Dean F. Schriner. *Interindustry Models For Rural Development Research.* Tech. Bull. T-139. Stillwater, Oklahoma: Oklahoma Agricultural Experiment Station, 1974. 57 pp.

Presents four models used in rural development research. The four models include input-output, from-to, dynamic input-output, and simulation. Input-output and from-to analyses are static models used to measure interindustry effects in the short-run. Dynamic input-output is introduced to measure interindustry effects over time. Simulation is a model which can be used for short- and long-run analyses. The bulletin is intended to present the models in a nonmathematical manner for researchers and students who have not had previous experience with the models. The mathematical appendixes are presented for those who are more mathematically inclined and for those who desire deeper knowledge of the underlying theory.

107. Emerson, Craig. "Mining Enclaves and Taxation." *World Development* 10, No. 7 (1982): 561-71.

Examines certain macroeconomic effects of major mining projects in developing countries, with special attention to the mining developments of Bougainville and OK Tedi in Papau, New Guinea. The paper assesses the contribution of these projects to economic development through their generation of government revenues. Emerson reviews existing evidence on the linkage effects of foreign investment in mining projects in developing countries along with empirical results of a study on the macroeconomic effects of major mining projects on Papau, New Guinea. Considerable support is found for the proposition that such projects tend to perform as enclaves, having only weak direct links with the host national economies.

108. Erickson, Rodney A. "Sub-Regional Impact Multipliers: Income Spread Effects from a Major Defense Installation." *Economic Geography* 53, No. 3 (1977): 283-94.

Presents a framework for estimating total income that accrues to peripheral communities from a specific income source. Key elements of the framework include a gravity model formulation for replicating commuting patterns and community trade multipliers for estimating indirect income effects.

* Findeis, Jill L., and Norman K. Whittlesey. "The Secondary Economic Impacts of Irrigation Development in Washington." *Western Journal of Agricultural Economics.* Cited below as item 935.

109. Fishkind, Henry H., Jerome W. Milliman, and Richard W. Ellson. "A Pragmatic Econometric Approach to Assessing Economic Impacts of Growth or Decline in Urban Areas." *Land Economics* 54, No. 4 (1978): 442-60.

Describes an econometric model developed for the Gainesville, Florida SMSA. Three unique features of the model are (1) it is the first small area model that incorporates monetary and financial variables, (2) it includes a number of environmental variables which are functionally linked to economic activities, and (3) the model is developed entirely from secondary data. Application of the model is illustrated by analyzing the potential impacts of (1) a firm's entering the community and (2) a no-growth policy for the area's leading employer.

110. Fowler, John M., Jeff M. Witte, and Jerry G. Schickedanz. *Oil and Gas Interactions with the Ranching Industry in New Mexico.* Bulletin 715. Las Cruces, New Mexico: New Mexico Agricultural Experiment Station, 1985. 32 pp.

Addresses the economic impacts on the ranching industry that result from the introduction of oil and gas development. Monetary and nonmonetary benefits and costs were examined to determine long-run net gain or loss resulting from oil and gas development. The results show that when the rancher does not share in royalty payments, the compensation received from developers is generally not adequate to offset development-related costs. This is the case on public lands and in other ownership situations where subsurface mineral rights are severed from surface rights.

* Funk, Herbert Joseph. "Effects of a New Manufacturing Plant on Business Firms in an Eastern Iowa Community." Ph.D. Dissertation. Cited below as item 943.

111. Gamble, Hays B., and Roger H. Downing. "Effects of Nuclear Power Plants on Residential Property Values." *Journal of Regional Science* 22, No. 4 (1982): 457-78.

Uses hedonic price equations to test the hypothesis that residential property values are directly related to distance from nuclear power plants. Property values in areas surrounding four nuclear power plants in the Northeast were examined before the March 1979 Three Mile Island (TMI) incident; no significant positive or negative effects were found on 540 properties. Property values near TMI were also examined after the incident; no effects were observed through 1979 when the net effects on 695 properties were examined.

112. Gamble, Hays B., Roger H. Downing, and Owen Sauerlender. "Community Growth Around Nuclear Power Plants." *American Real Estate and Urban Economics Association Journal* 8, No. 3 (1980): 268-80.

Analyzes growth rates of sixty-four municipalities around four nuclear power plants in the Northeast, as reflected by changes in equalized total real property market values from 1960 to 1976. From 1960 to 1970 (years prior to operational plants), growth rates were directly related to distance from the site. However, from 1970 to 1976 when plants were operational, growth rates were inversely related to distance from the plant. Two conclusions were drawn: (1) apparently the presence of a nuclear plant did not inhibit the growth of the communities nearby, although it was not possible to isolate the specific effects of nuclear power plants on growth rates; and (2) the presence of a nuclear power plant may have served as a stimulus to growth because the growth rate was higher for the host communities than for the region.

See also item 111.

113. Garrison, Charles B. "The Impact of New Industry: An Application of the Economic Base Multiplier to Small Rural Areas." *Land Economics* 48 (1972): 329-37.

Presents findings of a study which relies upon economic base theory to estimate the employment and income multiplier effects of new industry in rural areas. Case studies were conducted for five small towns in Kentucky which attracted new

manufacturing plants during the period 1958-1963. The average
income multiplier for the new plants was 1.62, and the average
employment multiplier was 1.08. The small size of the employment multiplier was attributed in large part to a substantial
underutilization of labor and capital in the nonbasic sectors
of these small communities.

114. Gerking, Shelby D., and Andrew M. Isserman. "Bifurcation and
      the Time Pattern of Impacts in the Economic Base Model."
      Journal of Regional Science 21, No. 4 (1981):   451-67.

      Examines the question whether secondary economic response to
      a change in basic activity is a short-run or long-run
      phenomenon.   The authors find that the method used to
      bifurcate total activity into basic and nonbasic components
      plays a major role in determining whether empirical estimates
      support the long- or short-run hypothesis. Their findings for
      three areas suggest that secondary response occurs quite
      rapidly.

115. Goddard, N. J.   *The Impact of a Power Project on Local
      Service, Transport and Construction Firms.* Working Paper 4.
      Hamilton, New Zealand: University of Waikato, School of
      Social Sciences, 1977. 81 pp.

      Describes the impact of the Huntly Power Project on a sample
      of those Huntly firms directly involved with the construction
      project, and appraises the method of research in order to aid
      future study.   Overall, the impact has not been significant;
      profits have not been greatly increased, and capital and
      material resources have not been extended.   Labor resources,
      however, have been stretched, and the attraction of skilled
      workers to the project has affected several firms.

116. Gordon,   John,   and David Mulkey.   "Income Multipliers For
      Community Impact Analyses--What Size Is Reasonable? *Journal
      of Community Development Society of America* 9, No. 1 (1978):
      85-93.

      Reports that personal income multipliers are extremely
      useful in community impact analyses but that insight is needed
      concerning reasonable income multiplier size.   The authors
      demonstrate that multipliers for small- to medium-sized
      communities are likely to be within the range of 1.1 to 1.5
      and that a community income multiplier over 2.5 should be
      critically evaluated.

117. Greytak,   David.   "A Statistical Analysis of Regional Export
      Estimating Techniques."   *Journal of Regional Science* 9, No.
      3 (1969):   387-95.

Presents what is apparently the first statistical evaluation
of the nature and source of estimation error associated with
the location quotient and minimum requirements techniques of
regional export estimation. The author also investigates the
possibility of improving the export estimates by means of a
linear correction.

118. Hageman, Ronda K. "Nuclear Waste Disposal: Potential
Property Value Impacts." *Natural Resources Journal* 21
(1981): 789-810.

Presents a theoretical analysis of potential property value
impacts resulting from the proximity of a nuclear waste
repository site or transportation route. Findings from a
Delphi survey of experts in seventeen states with nuclear
facilities support the theoretical view that property value
loss may result from the proximity of potential nuclear
hazards but that such losses may be overshadowed by enhanced
local economic activity.

* Halstead, John M., and F. Larry Leistritz. "Energy Develop-
ment and Labor Market Dynamics: A Study of Seven Western
Counties." *Western Journal of Agricultural Economics.*
Cited below as item 729.

119. Harmstron, Floyd K., and Richard E. Lund. *Application of an
Input-Output Framework to a Community Economic System.*
University of Missouri Studies Volume XLII. Columbia,
Missouri: University of Missouri Press, 1967. 124 pp.

Describes the input-output technique and compares it with
alternative methods of economic base analysis. The essential
steps for applying the input-output framework at the community
level are described, including industry and sector delineation
and data collection and analysis. Practical uses of the
input-output method are also discussed.

120. Harvey, Andrew S. "Spatial Variation of Export Employment
Multipliers: A Cross-Section Analysis. *Land Economics* 49
(1973): 469-74.

Examines the significance of a number of factors related to
employment multiplier variation among Canadian cities.
Regression analysis of data from 115 Canadian cities with
populations of 10,000 and over revealed that larger multiplier
values could be attributed to high rates of female labor force
participation, high rates of population growth, high per
capita income levels, a high ratio of nonlabor to labor
income, a large population, and/or a diversified industry mix.
For small cities, geographic isolation also contributed to

larger multiplier values.   Economic dependence   on mining was
associated with lower multiplier values.

121.   Henry, Mark S.   "The Spatial and Temporal Economic Impact of
       a Nuclear Energy Center—A Methodological Discourse and
       Application to a Southern Regional Site." *Socio-Economic
       Planning Sciences* 15, No. 2 (1981):   59–64.

       Proposes to integrate several socioeconomic modeling tech-
       niques with various demographic assumptions in developing a
       framework for estimating the economic impact of a nuclear
       energy ce.1ter site in South Carolina consisting of twelve
       potential 1200 Mw nuclear energy plants clustered in a single
       location. A regional nonsurvey input-output model and spatial
       allocation model are utilized to allocate the direct and
       indirect employment, population, and income impacts to the
       county level within a twelve-county impact region.

122.   Henry, Mark S., Arlen Leholm, Glenn Schaible, and James
       Haskins. "A Semi-Survey Approach to Building Regional
       Input-Output Models: An Application to Western North
       Dakota." *North Central Journal of Agricultural Economics* 2,
       No. 1 (1980):   17–24.

       Describes an input-output data collection methodology that
       uses a combination of primary and secondary data sources. The
       method's strong points are a uniform data base between
       sectors, a relatively low cost when compared to traditional
       approaches of gathering primary input-output data, and an
       ability to incorporate data on new firms or expansion by
       existing firms in a timely and inexpensive manner.

123.   Henry, Mark S., and J. C. O. Nyankori.   "The Existence of
       Short-Run Economic Base Multipliers: Some New Empirical
       Evidence." *Land Economics* 57, No. 3 (1981):   448–57.

       Tests for the existence and structure of a short-run
       relationship between basic and nonbasic employment. Results
       obtained from analysis of data for the Greenville–Spartanburg,
       South Carolina, SMSA indicate a strong short-term relationship
       between basic and nonbasic employment.

124.   Hirschl, Thomas A., and Gene F. Summers.   "Cash Transfers and
       the Export Base of Small Communities." *Rural Sociology* 47,
       No. 2 (1982):   295–316.

       Proposes an export base model of local employment growth.
       Basic sectors considered were agriculture, manufacturing,
       intergovernmental transfers, and cash transfers to
       individuals. The findings and hypotheses are discussed in
       relation to the population turnaround of nonmetropolitan

communities, the growth of social welfare payments, the
economic significance of cash transfers to local communities,
and the Keynesian macro approach to economic growth.

125. Huskey, Lee, Will Nebesky, Bradford Tuck, and Gunnar Knapp.
     Economic and Demographic Structural Change in Alaska. Tech.
     Rpt. No. 73. Anchorage: U.S. Bureau of Land Management,
     Alaska Outer Continental Shelf Office, 1982. 292 pp.

     A collection of five papers which analyze a number of
     aspects of structural change associated with economic growth
     and offshore petroleum development in Alaska. The first paper
     addresses local economic response in the form of support
     sector expansion as additional basic employment is
     "multiplied." The second paper addresses local labor force
     response to additional employment opportunities The third
     paper examines residency patterns of outer continental shelf
     workers in Alaska. The final two papers address statewide
     patterns of structural change which occur with economic growth
     in general and with oil development in particular.

126. Hyman, Eric L. "The Valuation of Extramarket Benefits and
     Costs in Environmental Impact Assessment." *EIA Review* 2,
     No. 3 (1981): 227-58.

     Examines the validity, reliability, and freedom from
     systematic bias of specific techniques in each of the
     following categories: economic surrogates, supply-side
     approaches, hypothetical valuation, tradeoff analysis,
     valuation of human lives, and threshold analysis.

127. Isserman, Andrew M. "A Bracketing Approach for Estimating
     Regional Economic Impact Multipliers and a Procedure for
     Assessing Their Accuracy." *Environment and Planning A* 9
     (1977): 1003-11.

     Presents a bracketing approach whereby upper and lower
     bounds of the economic impact multiplier are estimated. It
     also presents and applies a procedure that can be used to test
     the accuracy of alternative methods for estimating economic
     base multipliers.

128. Isserman, Andrew M. "The Location Quotient Approach to
     Estimating Regional Economic Impacts." *Journal of the
     American Institute of Planners* 43, No. 1 (1977): 33-41.

     Presents a theoretical rationale for the use of location
     quotients in estimating regional economic impacts. Then it
     suggests a number of procedural modifications which are
     consistent with that underlying rationale. Two of the modifi-
     cations are implemented and are shown to improve the accuracy

of the multiplier. Previous empirical work, often cited as
evidence of the inaccuracy of the location quotient approach,
is found to be questionable itself. The paper concludes, in
part, that the location quotient approach can be a useful
planning tool.

129. Jacobs, James J., Edward B. Bradley, and Andrew Vanvig.
     Coal-Energy Development and Agriculture in Northeast
     Wyoming's Powder River Basin. RJ-178. Laramie, Wyoming:
     Wyoming Agricultural Experiment Station, 1982. 77 pp.

     Provides information on the type and magnitude of agricul-
     tural impacts associated with coal development. Principal
     objectives are (1) to determine the nature and magnitude of
     coal-mineral and surface-land transactions that have occurred
     between agricultural operators and coal-energy companies, (2)
     to estimate the benefits and costs of coal mine land
     reclamation, (3) to identify the potential impact of coal
     mines on surrounding groundwater aquifers, (4) to estimate the
     cost of increasing the supply of water to anticipated water
     demand points in the region, and (5) to estimate the impact of
     coal-energy development on agricultural operators.

130. Johnson, Kenneth M. *Population and Retail Services in*
     Nonmetropolitan America. Boulder, Colorado: Westview
     Press, 1985. 250 pp.

     Examines the effects of rural-urban population shifts on the
     business infrastructure that supplies goods and services to
     rural areas, and finds that a decrease in population may not
     lead to the demise of the local business community.

131. Johnson, M. H., and J. T. Bennett. "An Input-Output Model of
     Regional Environmental and Economic Impacts of Nuclear Power
     Plants." *Land Economics* 55, No. 2 (1979): 236-52.

     Assesses the potential for expanding input-output models to
     include environmental variables. A model which incorporates
     air and water pollution and ecological effects in addition to
     economic impacts is proposed. It is argued that the model is
     more advanced than previous models because it copes with the
     nonlinearity of environmental relationships. The model is
     applied to the construction and operation of a nuclear power
     plant, and its results reviewed.

132. Jones, Lonnie L., Thomas L. Sporleder, and Gholam Mustafa.
     "Estimation Bias in Regional Input-Output Models Using
     Secondary Data." *Canadian Journal of Agricultural Economics*
     20 (1972): 10-17.

Illustrates the nature of inaccuracy that may result when national coefficients are used in conjunction with secondary data to estimate regional input-output models. Because the most widely used estimation techniques estimate regional exports and imports on a net or residual basis, the resulting input-output multipliers will tend to be overestimated. Methods for improving the accuracy of regional estimates are suggested.

133. Kresge, David T., Daniel A. Seiver, Oliver S. Goldsmith, and Michael J. Scott. *Regions and Resources: Strategies for Development.* Cambridge, Massachusetts: The MIT Press, 1984. 257 pp.

Reports results of the Man in the Arctic Program (MAP), a long-term research project to determine economic impacts of petroleum development in Alaska. MAP's general objectives were to (1) define patterns of Alaska's growth and development, (2) identify the critical forces of economic growth and project possible changes in those forces, and (3) use these findings to analyze specific problems and policy alternatives. Computer models of the Alaskan economy and related demographic change developed by MAP are being used actively to assist in policy planning in Alaska.

134. Kuehn, John A., and Lloyd D. Bender. "Nonmetropolitan Economic Bases and Their Policy Implications." *Growth and Change* 16, No. 1 (1985): 24-29.

Reports a first step in attempting to establish a rational basis for classifying the nonmetropolitan counties in the nation into groups which have differing characteristics related to policy objectives.

135. Kuehn, John A., Michael H. Procter, and Curtis H. Braschler. "Comparisons of Multipliers from Input-Output and Economic Base Models." *Land Economics* 61, No. 2 (1985): 129-35.

Presents empirical comparisons of multipliers for three different models. First, multipliers from a simple nonsurvey I-O model are compared with a more complex semisurvey model. Second, the nonsurvey model is used to estimate earnings multipliers for Missouri's nonmetropolitan counties in 1977-79, and these multipliers are then compared with economic base multipliers for nonmetropolitan counties in a Midwestern region.

136. Leigh, Roger. "The Use of Location Quotients in Urban Economic Base Studies." *Land Economics* 46, No. 2 (1970): 202-5.

Examines the accuracy of the location quotient technique in estimating exports and basic employment for an urban area. The author finds that the location quotient technique systematically underestimates exports and thus would result in an overestimate of the export multiplier.

* Leistritz, F. Larry, and Steve H. Murdock. *The Socioeconomic Impact of Resource Development: Methods for Assessment.* Cited above as item 31.

137. Leistritz, F. Larry, Steve H. Murdock, and Arlen G. Leholm. "Local Economic Changes Associated with Rapid Growth." *Coping with Rapid Growth in Rural Communities.* Edited by Bruce A. Weber and Robert E. Howell. (Item 592), pp. 25-61.

Describes changes which may occur in the local economy as a result of rapid population growth, examines factors that influence their nature and extent, and briefly reviews research findings aimed at quantifying local economic effects of large-scale resource development projects.

138. Lewis, W. Cris. "Export Base Theory and Multiplier Estimation: A Critique." *Annals of Regional Science* 10 (1976): 58-70.

Shows that the various alternatives commonly used at each step in the process of an export-base analysis (i.e., to specify one or more equations and estimate an indirect-direct employment multiplier) generate widely varying estimates of that multiplier. A recommendation is made that regional scientists turn their attention to other methods, including input-output frameworks and case studies, for determining appropriate multiplier values.

139. Little, R. L., and S. B. Lovejoy. "Energy Development and Local Employment." *The Social Science Journal* 16 (April 1979): 28-45.

Examines the distribution of benefits that accrue from rural industrialization and concludes that, in terms of employment opportunity, at least, local rural residents do not tend to receive benefits (jobs, higher incomes) commensurate with their expectations. Based on a study of residents living near the proposed Kaiparowits Generating Station in southeastern Utah, the authors conclude that (1) there is a mismatch between locally available job skills and those required by the project and (2) local residents were reluctant to be trained in needed skills.

140. Longbrake, David, and James F. Geyler. "Commercial Development in Small, Isolated Energy Impacted Communities." *The Social Science Journal* 16, No. 2 (1979): 51-62.

     Points out that many energy-impacted communities, especially those that are small and geographically isolated, suffer from inadequate development of their local retail and service sectors. A case study of Rangely, Colorado, was conducted to determine (1) the degree to which local residents obtain large percentages of their needs from firms located in other towns, (2) the general categories of goods and services most affected, (3) citizens' attitudes concerning the retail services offered, and (4) what citizens feel is needed to improve the local commercial base.

141. Lonsdale, Richard E., and H. L. Seyler, eds. *Nonmetropolitan Industrialization*. Washington, D.C.: V. H. Winston and Sons, 1979. 196 pp.

     Provides a survey and assessment of the growth in manufacturing in nonmetropolitan areas of the United States. Twelve articles examine (1) forces leading manufacturing firms to locate plants in rural areas and (2) the impact of industrialization on affected communities.

142. Lovejoy, Stephen B. "An Examination of the Direct Employment Gains to Rural Residents from Energy Development." Station Bulletin No. 286. West Lafayette, Indiana: Purdue University, Agricultural Experiment Station, Department of Agricultural Economics, August 1980. 44 pp.

     Examines the question of how many of the new jobs from an energy development will be captured by local residents. Data utilized to examine the direct local employment effects were obtained from a large-scale survey of the residents of southern Utah and northern Arizona conducted in 1974. Interviews were conducted with rural residents in southern Utah and Page, Arizona, many of whom were employed with the construction of the Navajo Generating Station, a coal-fired power plant. Though present predictive models suggest that local residents will receive significant direct employment from energy development, the evidence suggests that the incorporation of other characteristics of local residents, namely desire for such type of employment, skills, education, and union affiliation, are important determinants that would improve the model's predictive power.

143. Macarthur, J. D. "Appraising the Distributional Aspects of Rural Development Projects: A Kenya Case Study." *World Development* 6, No. 2 (1978): 167-93.

Demonstrates different approaches for the weighting of income changes attributable to a project, based on a case study of alternative farming systems for settlement projects in Kenya.

144. McGuire, A. "The Regional Income and Employment Impacts of Nuclear Power Stations." *Scottish Journal of Political Economy* 30, No. 3 (1983): 264-74.

Attempts to quantitatively assess the income and employment impacts associated with two nuclear power stations, Dounreay and Torness, in Scotland. The effects, analyzed at a subregional level, resulted in employment multipliers ranging between 1.2 and 1.7 and income multipliers of 1.06 for construction and 1.2 for operation. With the assumption of a relatively small level of local labor recruitment, the amount of inmigration becomes a significant factor in the estimation of the subregional multiplier. The impacts associated with the construction and operation of nuclear power stations on the subregional economies arise largely from employee expenditures. The high degree of leakage (85% of construction expenditures and 45% of operational expenditures) is indicative of localities which do not have specialized capital goods sectors necessary to meet the construction and maintenance demands of nuclear power plants. A concluding discussion addresses the difficulty of subregional-level modeling when data are scarce.

145. McKusick, Robert, Nelson Bills, Richard Clark, Clifford Jones, Robert Niehaus, Charles Palmer, Sterling Stipe, John Wilkins, and Linda Zygadlo. *Regional Development and Plan Evaluation: The Use of Input-Output Analysis.* Agr. Handbook No. 530. Washington, D.C.: U.S. Department of Agriculture, Economic Research Service, 1978. 128 pp.

Examines the use of input-output (I-O) analysis in the plan evaluation process for water and related land resources by the federal government. An I-O model depicts the supply and demand relationships of an economy in equilibrium and estimates the indirect economic changes which would occur if a plan were implemented. The authors attempt to provide guidance to resource planners concerning the economic information needs associated with resource development and the most appropriate quantitative methods to use in developing this information.

146. McMenamin, David G., and Joseph E. Haring. "An Appraisal of Nonsurvey Techniques for Estimating Regional Input-Output Models." *Journal of Regional Science* 14, No. 2 (1974): 191-205.

Has the objectives of (1) reviewing and criticizing several nonsurvey techniques, (2) presenting a new nonsurvey method for building a regional input-output table, (3) performing accuracy comparisons among several nonsurvey methods, and (4) evaluating the usefulness, cost effectiveness, and accuracy of nonsurvey regional tables.

147. McNulty, James E. "A Test of the Time Dimension in Economic Base Analysis." *Land Economics* 53, No. 3 (1977): 359-68.

Describes a test of the export base theory of regional growth which is designed to produce both short-run and long-run estimates of regional income multipliers using cross-sectional data. The economic base theory of regional growth was found to fit the facts very well in the long run but to provide a very poor explanation of short-run regional economic developments.

148. Mahler, V. A. "Mining, Agriculture, and Manufacturing: The Impact of Foreign Investment on Social Distribution in Third World Countries." *Comparative Political Studies* 14, No. 3 (1982): 267-97.

Focuses upon the impact of foreign-owned, private, direct investment holdings on the distribution of power and wealth within countries of the Third World. It finds that hypotheses relating extensive foreign investment holdings to inequitable income distribution, extensive unemployment, and low levels of demonstrated social welfare in Third World countries were generally borne out.

149. Mehmet, Ozay. "Manpower Planning and Labour Markets in Developing Countries: A Case Study of West Malaysia." *Journal of Development Studies* 8, No. 2 (1972): 277-89.

Argues that disaggregated manpower research, focussed on current problems and conditions of employment markets, would be more useful to economic development policies than abstract macro-planning aimed at forecasts of long-term manpower requirements. Mehmet discusses three insulated labor markets with practically no mobility.

150. Mellor, Patricio, and Manuel Marfan. "Small and Large Industry: Employment Generation, Linkages, and Key Sectors." *Economic Development and Cultural Change* 29, No. 2 (1981): 263-74.

Analyzes the relevance of the small and large industry dichotomy in relation to the problem of employment generation in a developing country. The authors empirically examine (1) relative importance of direct employment within the total

employment generated by large and small industry output
variations, (2) backward and forward employment linkages, and
(3) key sectors for employment generation within the Chilean
industrial sector.

151. Miernyk, William H. "Comments on Recent Developments in
     Regional Input-Output Analysis." *International Regional
     Science Review* 1, No. 2 (1976): 47-55.

     Reviews efforts to produce regional, industry-specific
     multipliers with less-demanding data requirements than those
     of the traditional input-output analysis. Nonsurvey methods
     for estimating regional input-output tables and short-cut
     techniques for estimating regional industry multipliers are
     found to be substantially less accurate than survey-based
     input-output models. Such methods likely will continue to be
     used as the basis for many impact assessments and policy
     analyses, however, because of the prohibitive data require-
     ments for constructing survey-based tables. The author
     believes that the greatest future need is not for more
     elaborate or refined methods to handle presently available
     data but rather for better data collected on a uniform basis.

152. Miernyk, William H. *The Elements of Input-Output Analysis.*
     New York: Random House, 1965. 158 pp.

     Is a basic reference on the development and use of input-
     output analysis, one of the basic methods for economic impact
     assessment. Major emphasis is placed on explaining how an
     input-output system works and how it can be applied in
     regional forecasting and impact analysis, rather than on the
     statistical problems involved in the construction of an input-
     output table. The essentials of input-output analysis are
     presented in simplified terms.

153. Miernyk, William H. "Local Labor Market Effects of New Plant
     Locations." *Essays in Regional Economics.* Edited by J. F.
     Kain and J. R. Meyer. Cambridge, Massachusetts: Harvard
     University Press, 1971. pp. 161-85.

     Examines the effects of new plant locations on local employ-
     ment and unemployment. Characteristics of employees in the
     new plants are compared with those from random samples of
     local labor forces and with those of rejected applicants.

154. Miernyk, William H. "Long-Range Forecasting with a Regional
     Input-Output Model." *Western Economic Journal* 1, No. 3
     (1968): 165-76.

     Discusses problems inherent in forecasting changes in
     regional economic activity and alternatives for resolving

them. Attention is focused on (1) estimating regional input-output coefficients and (2) projecting changes in these coefficients over the forecast period.

155. Milliman, Jerome W. "Large-Scale Models for Forecasting Regional Economic Activity: A Survey." *Essays in Regional Economics.* Edited by J. F. Kain and J. R. Meyer. Cambridge, Massachusetts: Harvard University Press, 1971. pp. 309-51.

    Discusses general problems of developing regional economic projections and then concentrates upon developments in regional model building in the United States. A survey of seven important regional forecasting models is presented with a catalogue of important differences and a comparative analysis of alternative approaches. The seven models reviewed are the (1) New York Metropolitan Region Study, (2) Upper Midwest Economic Study, (3) Ohio River Basin Study, (4) California Development Model, (5) Oahu, Hawaii Model, (6) Lehigh Basin simulation model, and (7) Susquehanna Basin simulation model. Suggestions for further research and appraisal conclude the paper.

156. Moore, Craig L. "The Impact of Public Institutions on Regional Income: Upstate Medical Center as a Case in Point." *Economic Geography* 50 (1974): 124-29.

    Examines the special problems associated with measuring the impact that public institutions have on regional income. This is followed by an empirical analysis of the income which accrues to Syracuse, New York, from the operation of the Upstate Medical Center, a large state institution.

157. Morrison, W. I., and P. Smith. "Nonsurvey Input-Output Techniques at the Small Area Level: An Evaluation." *Journal of Regional Science* 14, No. 1 (1974): 1-14.

    Attempts to integrate previous work on nonsurvey input-output methods at the regional level by comparing the results of the application of the most promising of the nonsurvey methods with an empirically derived input-output model for the City of Peterborough, England. The results of the analysis suggest that some nonsurvey techniques are quite promising but that at least some survey data likely will be required if accurate simulations of small area economic systems are to be made.

158. Northeast Regional Center for Rural Development. *Evaluating Impacts of Economic Growth Proposals: An Analytical Framework for Use with Community Decision-Makers.* Publication 8. Ithaca, New York: Cornell University, April 1975. 180 pp.

Contains papers presented at a conference designed to aid individuals and communities achieve better decision making when dealing with questions of growth. The underlying purpose is to aid communities in asking the right questions about growth at the right times. Three case studies are also included.

159.   Pearce,   D.   W.   "Social Cost-Benefit Analysis and Nuclear Futures." *Energy Economics* (April 1979):   66-71.

Considers the usefulness of cost-benefit analysis in making nuclear power investment decisions. Pearce concludes that the cost-benefit approach is of limited value in the nuclear power case because of its inapplicability to such issues as the liberty of the individual and nuclear weapons proliferation.

160.   Pfister,   R. L.   "On Improving Export Base Studies." *Regional Science Perspectives* 6 (1976):   104-16.

Suggests procedures to alleviate some of the shortcomings of the export base model and thus improve the quality of export base studies.   The author feels that such models have considerable potential and points out that time and cost constraints rule out alternative models in many cases.

161.   Pleeter,   Saul, ed.   *Economic Impact Analysis: Methodology and Applications.*   Boston: Martinus Nijhoff Publishing, 1980.   196 pp.

Contains nine original papers dealing with both methodology and applications of economic impact assessment.   Topics covered include alternative economic base bifurcation techniques, nonsurvey input-output methods, and applications of regional econometric models in impact assessment.   An extensive bibliography is included.

  *   Porter,   Ed, and Lee Huskey.   "The Regional Economic Effect of Federal OCS Leasing: The Case of Alaska." *Land Economics.* Cited below as item 909.

162.   Pratt,   Richard T.   "An Appraisal of the Minimum-Requirements Technique." *Economic Geography* 44, No. 2 (1968):   117-24.

Considers the assumptions, structure, and conclusions of the minimum requirements technique for economic base estimation. The author feels the minimum requirements technique is inferior to the location quotient method because (1) averages are more meaningful than minimums, (2) both techniques require the same assumptions, and (3) the minimum requirements technique is more subject to error from improper aggregation.

163. President's Economic Adjustment Committee. *Boom Town Business Opportunities and Development Management.* Washington, D.C.: U.S. Department of Defense, Office of Economic Adjustment, 1981. 133 pp.

Examines local business opportunities and community growth management in five communities, each of which experienced population growth greater than nine percent annually sometime between 1971 and 1978. The five counties included two that were affected by defense facilities (Liberty County, Georgia, and Cavalier County, North Dakota) and three that were affected by energy development (Mercer County, North Dakota; Moffat County, Colorado; and Platte County, Wyoming).

164. President's Economic Adjustment Committee. *Modeling the Regional Economic Impacts of Major New Military Bases.* Washington, D.C.: U.S. Department of Defense, Office of Economic Adjustment, 1983. 78 pp. plus appendix.

Discusses the modeling of the regional economic impacts of new military bases and presents case studies for three bases. The impacts estimated in the case studies are based on (1) base-specific information supplied by the U.S. Department of Defense, (2) regional economic models derived from the Regional Input-Output Modeling System (RIMS II) and the National Regional Impact Evaluation System (NRIES), both developed at the Bureau of Economic Analysis (BEA), U.S. Department of Commerce, and (3) additional methodology developed especially for taking into account the unique characteristics of military bases with respect to regional economic activity. The major focus of this monograph is on how the direct regional impacts of opening (or significantly expanding) a military base can be integrated with existing BEA regional macroeconomic impact models to identify indirect impacts in terms of changes in industry-specific employment and gross inmigration at the multicounty or state level.

165. Pulver, Glen C., Arne Selvik, and Ron Shaffer. "The Impact of a Major Economic Development Event on Community Income Distribution." *Resource Communities: A Decade of Disruption.* Edited by Don D. Detomasi and John W. Gartrell. Boulder, Colorado: Westview Press, 1984. pp. 71-83.

Summarizes the empirical literature on the impact of major economic development on community income distribution. It covers a number of studies dealing with capital control, profit taking, wages, other income, property taxes, and living costs with specific emphasis on their distribution within the community. In this paper, a community is defined as the immediate trade area of a development project. The first part of the paper outlines a general framework for looking at the question of the distributional effect of major economic developments. The second part is a presentation of the

results extracted from previous research. Finally, conclusions regarding the adequacy of current knowledge about the
distributional effects of development are presented.

166. Radetski, Marian. "Regional Development Benefits of Mineral
      Projects." *Resources Policy* 8, No. 2 (September 1982):
      193–200.

      Discusses the development impact of mining and mineral
      processing on the regions in which they are situated. The
      long-run changes in mining and mineral processing technology
      defined in a broad sense are then explored, in order to
      clarify why the regional development impacts of mineral
      resource projects may be muted over time. The concluding
      discussion identifies some policies that would increase the
      regional development impact of mineral activities and presents
      the appropriateness of such policies from a national viewpoint
      of a developing country.

167. Rathge, Richard W., and F. Larry Leistritz. "Shifts in
      Indicators of Inequality Associated With Energy Resources
      Development." *Impact Assessment Bulletin* (item 278), pp.
      54–71.

      Examines the effects of energy development on local
      residents in impacted areas and analyzes shifts in the distri-
      bution of income and education, two important indicators of
      mobility and well-being. Changes in aggregate measures of
      median income and median education between impacted and
      corresponding nonimpacted counties in North Dakota are
      analyzed, controlling for population growth, then shifts in
      inequality are illustrated utilizing Lorenz curves.

168. Reinschmiedt, Lynn, and Lonnie L. Jones. "Impact of
      Industrialization on Employee Income Distribution in Rural
      Texas Communities." *Southern Journal of Agricultural
      Economics* 9, No. 2 (1977): 67–72.

      Addresses the effects of industrial development on incomes
      and income distribution of rural industrial workers in Texas.
      Data from nine industrial plants in six Texas communities with
      populations less than 15,000 indicated that 80% of all workers
      increased or maintained their previous earnings when they took
      jobs at the plants. The analysis also indicated a slight
      increase in the equality of overall income distribution among
      these workers. Individuals in the lowest income categories
      prior to taking jobs with the plant experienced the greatest
      income gains, partly because 27% of the workers had previously
      been unemployed.

169. Roberts, Kenneth J., and R. Bruce Rettig. *Linkages Between the Economy and the Environment: An Analysis of Economic Growth in Clatsop County, Oregon.* Bulletin No. 618. Corvallis, Oregon: Oregon Agricultural Experiment Station, 1975. 32 pp.

Analyzes some of the linkages between economic growth and environmental change in a rural community. An input-output model of the local economy is augmented by adding rows representing key input requirements of, or residuals discharged by, the various economic sectors. This model is then used to estimate indirect, as well as direct, environmental effects resulting from a new aluminum plant.

170. Rogers, David L., Brian F. Pendleton, Willis J. Goudy, and Robert O. Richards. "Industrialization, Income Benefits, and the Rural Community." *Rural Sociology* 43, No. 2 (1978): 250-61.

Examines the equality of individual income distribution for all residents of Iowa towns of 2,500 to 10,000. A positive, but weak, relationship was observed between the percentage of the community's labor force employed in manufacturing and the equality of income distribution. In general, these authors conclude that the relationship between changes in manufac turing activity and changes in income distribution may be inconsequential in smaller towns that do not experience large changes in manufacturing activity.

171. Romanoff, Eliahu, and Stephen H. Levine. *Implications of a Nuclear Facility in South County, Rhode Island.* Vol. 4. *Economic Impact Dynamics.* Cambridge, Massachusetts: Regional Science Research Center, 1980. 72 pp.

Presents results of projections of the dynamic economic impact of the Charlestown Nuclear Power Plant on the coastal communities of South County, Rhode Island. A sequential interindustry model, a form of input-output model, is used to develop impact projections.

172. Rose, Adam, Stahrl Edmunds, and Everard Lofting. "The Economics of Geothermal Energy Development at the Regional Level." *Journal of Energy and Development* 4, No. 1 (Autumn 1978): 126-52.

Examines the viability of geothermal energy illustrated by a case study of a proposed geothermal power plant in Imperial County, Califoria. By utilizing an input-output modeling framework, the economic impacts associated with developing the geothermal energy resource are examined. Most of the economic impacts are favorable under the normal market conditions supplemented by a modicum of general planning. More stringent policies could be implemented to avoid the negative impacts, although there remain policy questions to be answered regarding interregional equity and irreversible effects.

173. Sabot, R. H., ed. *Migration and the Labour Market in Developing Countries.* Boulder, Colorado: Westview Press, 1982. 254 pp.

Clarifies the linkages among income distribution, migration, surplus labor, and poverty in developing countries. It reviews models of unemployment, discusses the difficulty of testing hypotheses and accurately projecting regional population growth, and treats the issue of defining income and prices when comparing laborers in different localities.

174. Schwartz, Harvey. *A Guide to Regional Multiplier Estimation.* Prepared for the Project Assessment and Evaluation Branch, Department of Regional Economic Expansion. Ottawa, Ontario: Minister of Supply and Services Canada, 1982. 186 pp.

Provides a step-by-step approach to the mechanics of multiplier estimation and application in policy analysis and project appraisal. The economic base model is utilized to introduce the derivation of employment multipliers for small, subprovincial regions. Employment multipliers are stressed because the labor force data requirements for estimation are the most easily obtained data at the small-region level in Canada. After the model is introduced, the nature of the employment created by a large-scale project is investigated. An equally important question is how to select the appropriate region for which the multiplier effects are to be measured. Empirical examples are used throughout with particular emphasis on the multiplier's role in the appraisal of a project, on the analysis of the project's regional impact, and on the analysis of national welfare change.

175. Schwinden, Cynthia J., and Jay A. Leitch. *Regional Socioeconomic Impact of the Devils Lake Fishery.* Agr. Econ. Rpt. No. 191. Fargo: North Dakota Agricultural Experiment Station, 1984. 24 pp.

Reports findings of a survey of anglers who fished Devils Lake, North Dakota, during the 1983-84 season and of subsequent analysis to estimate direct and secondary impacts on the Devils Lake local economy.

176. Shaffer, Ron, and Luther Tweeten. "Estimating Net Economic Impact of Industrial Expansion." *Journal of Community Development Society* 5, No. 2 (1974): 79-89.

Addresses the issue of how to evaluate the economic impact of industrial expansion in the community through a study of 12 industrial plants in eastern Oklahoma. The model developed measures the net economic impact of industry on three sectors of the community: private, municipal government, and school district. The model measures the additional income and tax revenues generated by industry as well as the costs incurred by the community as a result of development. Results confirm that industrial expansion has a substantial income effect on the private sector; however, only minor or negative effects on the municipal government and school districts may result. The authors urge communities to use caution if industrial expansion is sought solely for the purpose of lowering taxes for its citizens.

177. Oluhldsuless, Oluhlu, William Olllls, and Ron Oluffer. "Community Characteristics and Employment Multipliers in Nonmetropolitan Counties, 1950-1970." *Land Economics* 59, No. 1 (1983): 84-93.

Presents results of a systematic examination of community characteristics which condition the magnitude of local secondary employment impacts (i.e., determine the size of the multiplier). Data from 264 nonmetropolitan counties were used to estimate the relationship.

178. Stoloff, David, and Rebecca Kemmerer. "Site Screening to Minimize Socioeconomic Impacts of Power Facilities." *Social Impact Assessment* 33 (September 1978): 2-18.

Presents a rationale for impact assessment in utility plant siting and, in particular, for the fact that socioeconomic impacts are being given greater consideration as an area of environmental effects. The article describes the development of a computer-assisted socioeconomic screening method; the technique draws upon and refines the existing technique developed by the Tennessee Valley Authority.

179. Summers, Gene F., and Frank Clemente. "Industrial Development, Income Distribution, and Public Policy." *Rural Sociology* 41, No. 2 (Summer 1976): 148-68.

Examines the public policy implications of industrial development and its effects on the income status of weak competitors in a community system. Age, sex, education, and labor force status were regarded as resources which indicate the competitive capacity of individuals. Income differences between strong and weak competitors are found to increase over time. However, there is no evidence that the changes are due to industrial development. Finally, it was found that sex and labor force status have a stronger net effect on income than either age or education.

180. Tiebout, Charles M. *The Community Economic Base Study.*
     Supplementary Paper No. 16. New York: Committee for
     Economic Development, December 1962. 84 pp.

     Is the seminal work on the economic base study method for
     local economic analysis. This highly readable book describes
     what an economic base study is, explains the utility of such
     studies, and presents guidelines for conducting economic base
     studies in local communities.

181. Ullman, Edward L., and Michael F. Dacey. "The Minimum
     Requirements Approach to the Urban Economic Base." *Papers
     and Proceedings of the Regional Science Association* 6
     (1969): 175-93.

     Introduces the minimum requirements method, a procedure for
     understanding the urban employment structure. This technique
     estimates the minimum percentage of a labor force required in
     various sectors of an economy to maintain the viability of an
     urban area. The area's employment which is greater than this
     minimum requirement is called excess employment. The minimum
     requirement closely approximates the service or internal needs
     of a city, and the excess employment approximates the export
     or basic employment.

182. Watkins, G. C., and J. Fong. "Comparisons in Economic
     Development: Alberta and Texas." *Journal of Energy and
     Development* 6, No. 1 (Autumn 1980): 1-24.

     Reveals the key role of agriculture and petroleum in the
     economies of Alberta (Canada) and Texas, along with other
     similarities. Employing an input-output model of the two
     economies, the resultant multipliers reveal the prominance of
     agricultural and petroleum processing sectors. High indices
     of both backward and forward linkages in economic sectoral
     interdependence are also discussed.

183. Weiss, Steven J., and Edwin C. Gooding. "Estimation of
     Differential Employment Multipliers in a Small Regional
     Economy." *Land Economics* 44 (1968): 235-44.

     Describes a partially disaggregated economic base multiplier
     model, whereby it is possible to derive differential multi-
     plier estimates for distinct sectors of export activity. The
     model is applied to a case study of the economy of Portsmouth,
     New Hampshire, and differential multipliers are estimated for
     three export sectors. The employment multipliers of the three
     sectors are found to differ substantially.

184. Wyche, Mark C., Theodore D. Browne, Edward F. Harvey, and
     Ford C. Frick. *Impacts of Coal Development Upon the*

Billings Urban Area. Denver, Colorado: Brown, Bortz and Coddington, 1980. 121 pp.

Examines the direct and secondary impacts caused by regional coal development on Billings, Montana, by measuring economic change over recent years, evaluating proposed and present coal development, and estimating impacts associated with regional coal activity.

SOCIAL

185. Abonyi, George. "SIAM: Strategic Impact and Assumptions-Identification Method for Project, Program, and Policy Planning." *Technological Forecasting and Social Change* 22 (1982): 31-52.

Presents a method, called SIAM, for assessing the "social soundness" of projects, programs, and policies (with emphasis on the first two). It is vital to assess not only a project's technical and economic viability, but also its strategic viability involving sociopolitical considerations. A project embodies certain expectations about the present and future behavior of a variety of interests. These assumptions are implicit in the technical design and projected impacts, including the estimated benefits. The success of the project hinges on the validity and stability of these assumptions. SIAM provides a procedure to comprehensively identify relevant stakeholders and stakeholder-project linkages, and to identify the critical assumptions implicit in the technical design of the project and in its economic assessment. SIAM was applied initially as one part of a computer-assisted framework for the socioeconomic assessment of highway infrastructure plans. It has since proven useful in a wide range of projects and programs.

186. Abumere, Sylvester I. "People's Choice: Resettlement Preferences of Displaced Persons from Nigeria's New Federal Capital Territory." *Ekistics* 48(1981): 476-80.

Discusses the resettlement choices of the 26,000 heads of households in 845 villages and hamlets displaced by the creation of Nigeria's new Federal Capital Territory. The degree of attachment for their original homes and the preferred area of resettlement were examined.

187. Aiken, Michael, and Paul E. Mott, eds. *The Structure of Community Power.* New York: Random House, 1970. 538 pp.

Contains forty-three articles dealing with various aspects of community power. These articles are organized into six

major sections: (1) the meaning of power, (2) historical
perspective and community power structure, (3) factors influencing configurations of power, (4) locating centers of power,
(5) interaction among centers of power, and (6) comparative
studies of community power.

188. Albrecht, Stan L. "Paradoxes of Western Energy Development:
     Socio-Cultural Factors." *Paradoxes of Western Energy Devel-
     opment: How Can We Maintain the Land and the People If We
     Develop?* Edited by Cyrus M. McKell, Donald G. Browne,
     Elinor C. Cruze, William R. Freudenburg, Richard Perrine,
     and Fred Roach. AAAS Selected Symposium 94. (Item 290),
     pp. 247-63.

     Argues that western energy development has created an impor-
     tant paradox for area residents. The benefits it brings in
     the form of new employment and income opportunities have long
     been sought after; however, the changes in local lifestyles
     that accompany project-induced growth are viewed with skepti-
     cism and anger by many long-time residents.

189. Albrecht, Stan L. "Socio-cultural Factors and Energy
     Resource Development in Rural Areas in the West." *Journal
     of Environmental Management* 7 (1978): 78-90.

     Points out that most of the rural areas that are likely to
     experience future energy-induced growth and change tend to be
     isolated and to have experienced little change in the past.
     Against this background, projected rapid population growth
     almost insures that these communities will have difficulty
     responding efficiently and effectively. This study emphasizes
     the importance of integrating the newcomers into the life of
     the community in order to reduce apathy, alienation, and the
     great potential for conflict between newcomers and oldtimers.
     Energy development is described as "a form of domestic
     colonialism." Rural communities need to be provided more of
     the benefits of this development and protected from the loss
     of the rural way of life that they value.

190. Alexander, K. C. "Agricultural Development and Social Trans-
     formation: A Study in Ganganagar, Rajasthan." *Journal of
     Rural Development, India* 1, No. 1 (1982): 1-71.

     Relates results of a study based on a sample survey of 600
     respondents in two areas of Ganganagar district in Rajasthan,
     India. The production system, organization of production and
     occupational structure, income and level of living, market
     development, farmers' beliefs, and values are studied in turn.
     Conclusions are drawn regarding any change from subsistence to
     commercial agriculture, increases in commercial activities,
     changes in the division of labour in agriculture, changes in

occupational structure, and any modernization in beliefs or values.

191. Allcock, John B. "Tourism and Social Change in Dalmatia." *The Journal of Development Studies* 20, No. 1 (1983): 34-55.

Raises some general problems relating to the role of tourism in social and economic change through an examination of the case of Yugoslavia. The prosperity of the region was found to be more closely associated with its general level of economic development (especially with urbanization) than with the specific impact of the tourist industry.

192. Ament, Robert H. "Comparison of Delphi Forecasting Studies in 1964 and 1969." *Futures* 2 (March 1970): 35-44.

Compares the results and reviews the consistency of two Delphi forecasting sessions that considered prospective developments in physical and biological technologies. Results indicated that there was (1) a relative consistency in the forecasts, (2) a shift to earlier median dates of many biological forecasts and to later dates of several space forecasts, and (3) similar forecasting behavior, at least in terms of the spread of opinion, as a function of median time in the future.

193. Anderson, Charles H. *The Sociology of Survival: Social Problems of Growth.* Homewood, Illinois: The Dorsey Press, 1976. 299 pp.

Is intended to provide the framework for an understanding of the dangers and threats posed by growth to the existence and quality of human and biological life. Among the topics addressed are (1) the relationship of economic growth to human welfare and to equality; (2) the effects of economic growth on the natural environment; and (3) the implications of economic and population growth for availability of nonrenewable natural resources, such as fossil fuels.

194. Appelbaum, Richard P. *Theories of Social Change.* Chicago: Markham Publishing Company, 1970. 151 pp.

Reviews theories of social change according to what are felt to be the dominant paradigms in the field. Four broad categories are identified: evolutionary theories, equilibrium theory, conflict theory, and "rise and fall" theories.

195. Arensberg, Conrad M., and Arthur H. Niehoff. *Introducing Social Change: A Manual for Community Development.* 2d ed. Chicago: Aldine · Atherton, Inc., 1971. 263 pp.

Focuses on guided change in developing countries and among
ethnic groups in industrialized countries. Topics include the
concept of culture, cultural change, motivation for change,
adaptation techniques, secondary strategies, and field
procedures.

196. Aspelin, Paul Leslie. "Social Impact Assessment in Hydro-
     electric Power Development in Southern Brazil." *Indian SIA:
     The Social Impact Assessment of Rapid Resource Development
     on Native Peoples.* Edited by Charles C. Geisler, Rayna
     Green, Daniel Usner, and Patrick C. West. Monograph No. 3.
     (Item 260), pp. 338-70.

     Presents initially a discussion of the institutional context
     within which Indian-related social impact assessments take
     place in Brazil. Then, a case study of one recent social
     impact assessment regarding Indian areas in Brazil is
     presented, followed by an analysis of how it was conditioned
     by this particular institutional context.

197. Babbie, Earl R. *Survey Research Methods.* Belmont,
     California: Wadsworth Publishing Company, 1973. 384 pp.

     Is a practical guide for undergraduates and beginning survey
     researchers. Babbie focuses on the logic and skills involved
     in sampling and survey design, and discusses data collection
     and processing, pretesting, and analysis. The book closes
     with a discussion of the ethics and uses of survey research
     and of the use of survey research in social and scientific
     perspectives.

198. Baldwin, Thomas E., and Roberta Poetsch. *An Approach to
     Assessing Local Sociocultural Impacts Using Projections of
     Population Growth and Composition.* ANL/EES-TM-24. Argonne,
     Illinois: Argonne National Laboratory, 1977. 126 pp.

     Demonstrates a methodology for assessing sociocultural
     impacts. There are two basic aspects: (1) projecting the
     size and composition of local population based on natural
     growth trends and inmigration induced by industrial develop-
     ment; and (2) identifying problems that can be assessed using
     these demographic projections.

199. Baring-Gould, Michael, and Marsha Bennett. *Social Impact of
     the Trans-Alaska Pipeline Construction in Valdez, Alaska,
     1974-1975.* Juneau: Alaska Office of Coastal Management,
     1975. 51 pp.

     Reviews social impacts associated with construction of the
     Trans-Alaska Pipeline. A series of survey interviews with
     household heads together with informal participant observation

and interviews with key informants provided the principal data base for the study.

200. Baxter, Judith. "Changing Stages of Development: Consequences for Community Change." Unpub. Master's thesis. Denver, Colorado: University of Denver, 1981. 97 pp.

Examines the effects of construction and subsequent abandonment of a large military installation on the town of Langdon, North Dakota. The research emphasizes the social changes which have resulted from the changing economic situation and thus attempts to increase understanding of the long-range implications of the boom-bust cycle. An ethnographic research approach is utilized.

* Bennett, Marsha Erwin, Susan D. Heasley, and Susan Huey. *Northern Gulf of Alaska Petroleum Development Scenarios: Sociocultural Impacts.* Tech. Rpt. No. 36. Cited below as item 882.

201. Berkes, F. "Some Environmental and Social Impacts of the James Bay Hydroelectric Project, Canada." *Journal of Environmental Management* 12, No. 2 (1981): 157-72.

Is a retrospective analysis of the LaGrande complex of the James Bay hydroelectric development project in Quebec on the Cree Indian tribe. Paper identifies prior environmental and social impact studies and concludes that the development process accompanying the project has resulted in an incremental erosion of the land and resource base of the Cree Indian people. Author recounts a large number of unanticipated secondary impacts, many of which are due to a lack of understanding of the Cree Indian lifestyle, local economy, and cultural practices, and a considerable number of unanticipated social impacts resulting from the construction of a road network in a previously roadless area. A concluding section critiques the agreement made between the governmental developers of the project and the Cree Indians in the area.

202. Bernard, Harvey Russell, and Pertti J. Pelto, eds. *Technology and Social Change.* New York: The Macmillan Company, 1972. 354 pp.

Contains ten case studies of the effects of the adoption of modern Western technology in stimulating social and cultural changes. Cases examined include development of a new industrial city in Mexico, construction of a large dam in Africa, development of a hydroelectric power complex in Peru, adoption of snowmobiles in Arctic regions of Canada and Scandinavia, governmental provision of modern housing for native peoples in the Canadian Arctic, and the decline of the sponge fishing industry in Greece.

Contains items 933, 938, 946, 950.

203.   Bertrand, Alvin L. "Rural Social Organizational Implications of Technology and Industry." *Rural U.S.A.: Persistence and Change.* Edited by Thomas R. Ford. (Item 251), pp. 75–88.

Points out that recent developments in agricultural technology and rural industrialization help account for the growth and redistribution of the United States population. The behavior of rural people (and urban people as well) is undergoing constant adjustment and alteration as a partial consequence of these developments in rural technology and industry. Further, the rate of adjustment varies from one region to another. The contemplation of this change phenomenon and of what it portends highlights this chapter.

204.   Boothroyd, P. "Issues in Social Impact Assessment." *Plan Canada* 18, No. 2 (1978): 118–34.

Suggests solutions to some difficult issues involved in social impact assessment. These issues are related to the definitions of the term "social impact assessment" and to the evolution, role, and future of social impact assessment. In the discussion of the term "impact," different causal relations between developments and impacts are examined. The characteristics of impacts are discussed and the differences between unique, inevitable, and/or contingent impacts are considered. Also, the problem of the extent to which secondary and tertiary impacts should be traced, before a decision is made on where an impact assessment should cease, is discussed. An extensive checklist of factors to be considered in social impact assessments is provided. This is based on sociopsychological research on conditions required for the satisfaction of human needs. In addition, a checklist of the different types of individuals and social groups which may be affected is provided for use with the checklist of sociopsychological factors. It is recommended that social impact assessment should be integrated into the planning and design of major developments.

205.   Bowles, Roy T., ed. *Little Communities and Big Industries: Studies in the Social Impact of Canadian Resource Extraction.* Toronto, Ontario: Butterworth & Co., 1982. 220 pp.

Collects twelve previously published articles on the impact of large industrial enterprises on social and economic development in small Canadian communities. Emphasis in the compilation is on case studies of resource communities and industrial towns. Articles center on social characteristics of one-industry towns in Canada; historical perspective of Canadian resource towns; resource town policy in British Columbia; and case studies of Cobalt, Ontario; Flin Flon, Manitoba; Coal Branch, Alberta; Asbestos, Quebec; Drummondville, Quebec; Elliot Lake, Ontario; Coppermine, Northwest Territories; and coastal Labrador.

206. Bradbury, J. H. "Class Structures and Class Conflicts in 'Instant' Resource Towns in British Columbia--1965-1972." *BC Studies* 37 (Spring 1978): 3-18.

Focuses on the meaning and derivation of class, class relations, and class conflict in both resource frontier areas and society as a whole.

* Brealey, T. B., and P. W. Newton. *Living in Remote Communities in Tropical Australia: The Hedland Story.* Cited below as item 764.

207. Bronfman, B. H. *A Study of Community Leaders in a Nuclear Host Community: Local Issues, Expectations, and Support and Opposition.* ORNL/TM-5997. Oak Ridge, Tennessee: Oak Ridge National Laboratory, 1977. 27 pp.

Summarizes a study of community leaders undertaken in Hartsville, Tennessee, site of the Tennessee Valley Authority (TVA) Hartsville Nuclear Power Plant then under construction. Leaders were found to be extremely supportive of the plant and of TVA's efforts to mitigate impacts expected to result from construction. Like their citizen counterparts, leaders expect economic benefits and some growth-related disruption to occur as a result of the plant, while environmental impacts are seen as extremely unlikely to occur. Plant-related issues, such as housing availability and traffic congestion, dominate leaders' thinking about current issues.

208. Bulmer, M. I. A. "Sociological Models of the Mining Community." *Sociological Review* 23 (1975): 61-92.

Examines four models of a mining community: archetypal proletarian, isolated mass, industrial homogeneity and the sociocultural setting, and occupational communities. The final section describes the ideal type of the traditional mining community with the following characteristics: physical isolation, economic predominance of mining, the nature of work (physical, dangerous, uncertain), social consequences of occupational homogeneity and isolation (little contact with outside social groups), leisure activities (formal and informal community activities), the concept of family (sharply segregated marital roles), economic and political conflict, and the whole society (overlapping social ties that form close-knit and interlocking locally based collectivities of actors).

209. Burch, Jr., William R., and Donald R. DeLuca. *Measuring the Social Impact of Natural Resource Policies.* Albuquerque, New Mexico: University of New Mexico Press, 1984. 216 pp.

Discusses the social dimensions of energy and natural resource systems, seeking to link the applied needs of impact assessment to several bodies of well-developed theory and data including time budget, life cycle, adoption, community, regional, social survey, and social indicators approaches. Contends that the underlying thrust of social assessment research is the measurement of social well-being which complements the approaches of economics and engineering.

210. Burvill, P. W. "Mental Health in Isolated New Mining Towns in Australia." *Australian and New Zealand Journal of Psychiatry* 9 (1975): 77-83.

Contends that it is not the environment of isolated boom towns that is the prime etiological factor in the production of mental illness there, but the individual's personality and his or her prior life experiences. Burvill discusses some of the factors that affect the onset of psychiatric illness, namely, the characteristics of the town and the individual.

* Campbell, W. J. *Hydrotown.* Cited below as item 766.

211. Canan, Penelope, and Michael Hennessy. "Community Values as the Context for Interpreting Social Impacts." *Environmental Impact Assessment Review* 3, No. 4 (1982): 351-65.

Describes an SIA data collection process that uses community values as the basis for collecting, organizing, reporting, and interpreting social impact materials. A method is demonstrated for comparing the value structures of two or more groups which might affect the course of a development project in a given community. This procedure provides a focus for organizing SIA data and a basis for assisting members of the impacted community to articulate their value positions.

212. Canan, Penelope, Michael Hennessy, Kathleen K. Miyashiro, Michael Shiroma, Lee Sichter, Debra Lewis, David C. Matteson, Lynette Kono, William Dendle, and Jeffrey M. Melrose. *Moloka'i Data Book: Community Values and Energy Development.* Honolulu: University of Hawaii, Urban and Regional Planning Program, 1981. 435+ pp.

Describes a project conducted for the Hawaii Natural Energy Institute to provide baseline data from which public and private officials and community residents can determine which modes of alternate energy production will enhance the quality of life on Moloka'i. Report contains information on social and economic trends, results of a values and attitudes survey, a description of existing public facilties and services, and the planning and management capabilities pertinent to the island.

213. Carley, Michael J. "A Review of Selected Methods." *Social Impact Assessment Methods*. Edited by Kurt Finsterbusch, Lynn G. Llewellyn, and C. P. Wolf. (Item 19), pp. 35-54.

Outlines guidelines for methodological development in SIA and factors to be considered in developing or evaluating assessment methods. Then, a number of comprehensive or general procedures for assessing social impacts are evaluated. Methods evaluated fall into two categories: (1) numerically oriented SIA methodologies and (2) participatory and combination SIA methodologies.

214. Carley, Michael J. "Social Indicators Research." *Social Impact Assessment Methods*. Edited by Kurt Finsterbusch, Lynn G. Llewellyn, and C. P. Wolf. (Item 19), pp. 151-67.

Defines some important aspects of social indicators; explores quality of life studies, community monitoring systems, and public service delivery measurement; and concludes with a discussion of some methodological issues in social indicators research.

215. Carley, Michael J., and Anna Walkey. "Exploring Some Key Elements in SIA." *Social Impact Assessment: Theory, Method, and Practice*. Edited by Frank J. Tester and William Mykes. (Item 45), pp. 13-22.

Discusses the basic elements of SIA. A perspective is proposed which describes SIA in terms of a rational problem-solving process which is common to a variety of project appraisal techniques. The nature of the social environment, which is the focus of SIA, is examined; it consists of the social setting and the social condition--the former character-ized by various objective measures and the latter by percep-tual indicators. Finally, the problems of measuring the social setting and social condition are examined.

216. Carlson, John E., Marie L. Lassey, and William R. Lassey. *Rural Society and Environment in America*. New York: McGraw-Hill Book Company, 1981. 425 pp.

Attempts to (1) offer a description of the contemporary
status of rural society, (2) develop an environmental perspective from which to examine social issues in rural regions, (3)
examine the more profound and possibly enduring impacts which
are occurring, (4) suggest specific procedures which may
assist the satisfactory resolution of major issues while
productively dealing with profound impacts, and (5) reflec-
tively consider what the future might hold if public policies
and procedures can effectively respond to contemporary and
emerging social and environmental opportunities.

217. Clemente, Frank, Dean Rojek, and E. M. Beck. "Trade Patterns
      and Community Identity: Five Years Later." *Rural Sociology*
      39, No. 1 (1974): 92-95.

Examines the arguments that such technologically based
variables as improved highways and mass communication have
vitiated the utility of defining *community* in terms of
economic interaction, and that changing facets of rural life
are rendering trade patterns irrelevant to community identity.
Results indicate that the relationship between the locus of
economic activity and community identification was weak but
did not diminish over time, nor did industrial development
have any substantial effect upon that relationship.

218. Clemente, Frank, and Gene F. Summers. "Industrial Develop-
      ment and the Elderly: Longitudinal Analysis." *Journal of
      Gerontology* 28, No. 4 (1973): 479-83.

Analyzes the impact of industrial development in nonmetropolitan regions upon the economic status of the aged. Data
from a five-year study (1966-1971) of the construction of a
large manufacturing facility in rural Illinois are compared to
parallel data from a control region. Results suggest that
industrial development accelerates the decline in the economic
status of the elderly, especially retirees. Because many
older people are concentrated in small towns which may be
actively seeking large industry, the financial well-being of
the elderly may be negatively affected.

219. Cluett, Christopher, Marjorie Greene, and Linda Radford.
      *Individual and Community Response to Energy Facility Siting:
      A Review of the Literature.* Seattle, Washington: Battelle
      Human Affairs Research Centers, 1979. 83 pp.

Reviews selected literature areas, including the boom town
studies, that focus primarily on the social, economic, and
political effects of energy development, and specifically on
the impacts of coal extraction and processing on rural
communities. Abstracts of selected studies within this literature are appended to this report as an annotated
bibliography. The abstracts are intended to summarize

research findings that pertain to the process of community development, social change, and public reaction to rapid energy development in rural areas.

220. Cluett, Christopher, and Frederic A. Morris. "The Transportation of Radioactive Materials Through Urban Areas: Social Impacts and Policy Implications." *The Southwestern Review of Management and Economics* 2, No. 2 (1982): 207-21.

Assesses the social impacts that have occurred or may occur due to transportation of radioactive materials through densely settled urban areas. Although the number and severity of transportation incidents have been small, psychological, political, legal, and organizational impacts have occurred. The political and legal attention given such transportation may escalate the general controversy surrounding nuclear power. The burden of proof of nuclear power safety may fall more heavily on transportation than on other components. The article suggests several ways of achieving a better integration of technical and social analysis into environmental impact statements.

221. Cohen, Anthony P. "Oil and the Cultural Account: Reflections on a Shetland Community." *The Scottish Journal of Sociology* 3, No. 1 (1978): 129-41.

Examines impacts of oil development on the way of life in the Shetland Islands community of Whalsay. Cohen suggests that analysis of the effects of oil-related developments on indigenous cultures must recognize (1) the diffuse character of such consequences, (2) the pervasiveness and empirical ramifications of a culture, and (3) that oil-related development or any other form of rapid industrialization is difficult to separate from the host of other pressures and influences on a culture.

222. Copp, James H. *Social Impacts of Oil and Gas Developments on a Small Rural Community.* CEMR-MS8. College Station, Texas: Texas A&M University, Center for Energy and Mineral Resources, 1984. 51 pp.

Describes the effects of an oil and gas exploration boom during the period 1979 through 1981 on the community of Caldwell, Texas. The study is intended to (1) give oil and gas industry managers a better understanding of the impact their industry may have on local communities, and (2) give community leaders and rural development advisors a better idea of what to prepare for when energy developments are proposed.

223. Cortese, Charles F. "The Impacts of Rapid Growth on Local Organizations and Community Services." *Coping with Rapid*

Growth in Rural Communities. Edited by Bruce A. Weber and Robert E. Howell. (Item 592), pp. 115-35.

Provides a review of literature on the sociological effects of rapid growth on local organizations, including schools, health and social services, local business organizations, local government, and churches. An interpretation follows of the changes, stresses, and strains occurring in rapid-growth communities, and generalizations are made which cut across community organizations and across communities in similar rapid growth situations. The conclusion provides suggestions about what local organizations might do to assist the community as a whole in coping with rapid growth.

224. Cortese,   Charles F.   "The Social Impacts of Energy Development   in the West: An Introduction."   *The Social Science Journal* 16, No. 2 (April 1979):   1-7.

Defines the socioeconomic impact process as consisting of five major factors: (1) extra-local context--policies and perspectives outside the affected area that help set the tone and pace for development projects; (2) impacting element--the nature and type of energy development projects being introduced into the area; (3) local context--characteristics of the local community; (4) social impact--social and cultural changes that occur as the new project enters the area, and (5) modes of response--ways in which local people and their institutions react to social and cultural change.

225. Cortese,   Charles F.,   and Bernie   Jones.   "The Sociological Analysis of Boom Towns."   *Western Sociological Review* 8, No. 1 (1977):   76-90.

Indicates that major changes are occurring in the social structure and cultural systems of previously stable rural communities which are experiencing rapid growth resulting from energy development. Evidence is presented to illustrate both changes in the role structure and a cultural shift toward increasing impersonalization, bureaucratization, and specialization. Patterns of personal response to these changes also are discussed.

226. Cottrell,   William   F.   "Caliente."   *Technology, Man, and Progress.* Authored by William F. Cottrell.   Columbus, Ohio: Charles E. Merrill Publishing Company, 1972.   pp. 67-86.

Re-examines a small western desert town which lost its primary income, the railroad, in 1951. Earlier predictions by the author included diminishing population and social disorganization. However, selective emigration occurred; those remaining were devoted to the preservation of the town through collective efforts to maintain city services and to prevent inmigration and criminal deviation. Caliente (a ficticious name) has changed from an economy based on transportation to one based on services--educating their children (the school system was not lost), rehabilitating juvenile girls (residents lobbied for a girls' training center), housing and providing amenities for the elderly, providing parks and free services to travelers, and maintaining law and order. They have exchanged their dependency on one outsider (the railroad) for another outsider (the voters).

See also item 227.

227. Cottrell, William F. "Death by Dieselization: A Case Study in the Reaction to Technology Change." *American Sociological Review* 16, No. 3 (1951): 358-65.

Examines changing attitudes and values of residents in a one-industry railroad town faced with the replacement of the steam engine by the diesel and subsequent termination of railroad activities. The town initially lost about three-fifths of its total tax assessments. Many men had only local job seniority; others had skills no longer needed. Loss of income and personal demoralization resulted. Property devaluation affected both local merchants and homeowners. In short, those who assumed the greatest family and community responsibilities were the greatest losers. Attitudes changed from viewing the railroad company as an employer concerned with the community to one concerned only with the bottom line. Collective action became the key to survival. Unions and communities joined together to ensure retention of existing union rules and adoption of new rules and government regulations--rules which operated for their benefit rather than for the public good or general welfare.

See also item 226.

228. Craig, F. E., and Frank J. Tester. "Indigenous Peoples: Reassessing Directions for SIA." *Indian SIA: The Social Impact Assessment of Rapid Resource Development on Native Peoples.* Edited by Charles C. Geisler, Rayna Green, Daniel Usner, and Patrick C. West. Monograph No. 3. (Item 260), pp. 16-40.

Concerns institutional analysis and SIA. The authors feel that institutional analysis, as a component of SIA, can serve to clarify the relationship between philosophical principles or values, development decisions, the more general social and institutional context within which development takes place, and the social costs and consequences of specific projects. Such clarification is seen as essential if, in fact, SIA is conducted with a view to implementing mitigative measures and providing compensation for unavoidable impacts.

229. Cram, John M. "Differential Need Satisfactions of Mine
      Workers in Northern Canada." *Canadian Journal of Behavioral
      Science* 4 (1972): 135-45.

      Reports the following results of an eighteen-item adaptation
      of L. W. Porter's needs satisfaction questionnaire which was
      administered during individual interviews of 228 workers in
      five geographically isolated mining camps in the Canadian sub-
      Arctic: (1) a consistent hierarchy of need importance exists
      across camps; (2) fulfillment and dissatisfaction of lower
      needs vary with actual camp conditions; (3) high social
      fulfillment and low dissatisfaction are universal; (4)
      different autonomy perceptions might discriminate between
      Porter's and E. E. Lawler's managers and rank-and-file
      workers; and (5) low fulfillment and high dissatisfaction in
      the higher order needs of esteem and self-actualization form
      consistent patterns in each camp and could contribute to high
      turnover in northern mines.

230. Dahrendorf, Ralf. *Class and Class Conflict in Industrial
      Society*, Stanford, California: Stanford University Press,
      1959. 336 pp.

      Is one of the basic works in the area of conflict theory.
      The book consists of eight chapters divided into two parts:
      (1) The Marxian Doctrine in the Light of Historical Changes
      and Sociological Insights, and (2) Toward a Sociological
      Theory of Conflict in Industrial Society.   From the conflict
      perspective, life involves a struggle for control of limited
      resources.   Individuals come together to form interest groups
      to more effectively compete for resources.   The major groups
      between which conflict occurs include social classes and
      economic ownership groups.

231. D'Amore, Louis J. "An Executive Guide to Social Impact
      Assessment." *The Business Quarterly* (Summer 1978): 35-44.

      Considers several dimensions of SIA in the context of use in
      and by the business sector and in the context of "community
      ecology." The author first describes the evolution of SIA in
      terms of societal trends and legislation, then examines state-
      of-the-art concepts and methodologies.   Finally, the author
      considers the issues involved in the proponent-
      community-consultant relationship.

232. D'Amore, Louis J., and Sheila Rittenberg. "Social Impact
      Assessment: A State of the Art Review." *Urban Forum* 3, No.
      6 (March-April 1978): 8-15.

      Examines the background and evolution of SIA, considers
      approaches to conducting assessments, presents a theoretical

framework, and discusses future directions for the state of the art.

233. Daneke, Gregory A., and Jerry Delli Priscoli. "Social Assessment and Resource Policy: Lessons from Water Planning." *Natural Resources Journal* 19, No. 2 (1979): 359-75.

Illustrates the significance of social accounting in policy formulation and evaluation by tracing the development of social accounting and outlining its potential with special reference to water development policy. Three goals for social assessment are presented: to display and help adjudicate conflicting claims, to design socially useful projects and programs which produce minimal social disruptions, and to explore means of enhancing the general quality of life.

* Davenport, Joseph, III, and Judith Ann Davenport. *The Boom Town: Problems and Promises in the Energy Vortex.* Cited below as item 787.

234. De'Ath, Colin. "Social Impact Assessment: A Critical Tool in Land Development Planning." *International Social Science Journal* 34, No. 3 (1982): 441-50.

Argues that the primary purpose of SIA is as a reflexive examination of socially cohesive communities in the context of the natural resources on which they depend and the forecasting of the likely effects of contemplated change. Using a small community on a densely populated island in the Philippines as an illustration, the author proposes ways in which an SIA team could assist local people in their problems. He applies SIA to such issues as extensive or intensive land use for agricultural, mining, and urban development. A general approach to utilizing appropriate development models is described, and some common hidden biases are underscored.

235. Delbecq, Andre L., Andrew H. Van de Ven, and David Gustafson. *Group Techniques for Program Planning: A Guide to Nominal Group and Delphi Processes.* Glenview, Illinois: Scott, Foresman and Company, 1975. 174 pp.

Explains in detail the Nominal Group Technique (NGT) and Delphi Technique as tools to increase the creative productivity of group action, facilitate group decision, help stimulate generation of critical ideas, give guidance in the aggregation of individual judgments, and save human effort and energy. In addition to explaining the two techniques, the authors discuss the use of NGT in planning exploratory research, involving citizens, identifying multidisciplinary experts, and reviewing project proposals.

236. Dillman,   Don A., and Daryl J. Hobbs, eds.   *Rural Society in*
      the U.S.:   Issues for the 1980s.   Boulder, Colorado:
      Westview Press, 1982.   437 pp.

      Contains 41 original articles which examine a variety of
      issues affecting rural communities during the 1980s.   Areas
      examined   include   industrialization,   housing,   community
      services, community development, social impact assessment, and
      social indicators.

      Contains items 22, 320.

237. Dixon, Mim. *What Happened to Fairbanks?*   Boulder, Colorado:
      Westview Press, 1978.   337 pp.

      Examines the social and economic effects of the trans-Alaska
      oil pipeline on the town of Fairbanks.   Fairbanks served as a
      transport, employment, and supply center for the pipeline, and
      it was generally thought that the effects of the pipeline
      would benefit the community.   However, many of the expected
      impacts never occurred.   Community response to the effects of
      the pipeline is recorded, and the unplanned negative effects
      were found to outweigh the beneficial impacts.   The population
      influx severely affected Fairbanks' ability to provide social
      services.   The major problems of the community arose from
      inflation, decreasing family cohesiveness, and increasing
      crime.

238. Donohue,   Marian, Sallie Edmunds, Ruby Edwards, Jan Hiranaka,
      Robey Lal, Raymond Oshiro, Harry Partika, Rik Scarce, James
      Schweithelm, Colleen Wallace, and Jan Yamamoto.   *Exploring*
      the Social Impacts of a General Aviation Airport at Waipio.
      DURP No. 831402.   Honolulu: University of Hawaii, Depart-
      ment of Urban and Regional Planning, 1983.   60 pp.

      Provides   basic   information   for   politicians,   community
      leaders and members, and government officials to use in
      discussing the social effects of siting a general aviation
      airport at Waipio.   Consideration was given to technical,
      economic, environmental, and social issues.   Recommendations
      include finding a mechanism for grouping parties with common
      interests, formulating a policy and procedures statement,
      integrating the SIA into the policymaking   process, and
      performing a Community Interaction Program to address the
      degree of controversy associated with siting.

239. Duncan,   Otis D., Howard Schuman, and Beverly Duncan.   *Social*
      Change in a Metropolitan Community.   New York: Russell Sage
      Foundation, 1973.   126 pp.

      Assesses social change in the Detroit, Michigan, metropol-
      itan area by comparing results of a survey conducted in 1971

with those from similar studies in the mid 1950s. Changes in attitudes and values were assessed in a number of areas including marriage, women and work, rearing children, social participation, religious participation, communal involvement, religious beliefs, political orientations, and racial attitudes.

240. Dunlap, Riley E. *Environmental Sociology: A Bibliography of Conceptual, Methodological and Theoretical Readings.* Monticello, Illinois: Vance Bibliographies, 1983. 10 pp.

Introduces readers to a core body of literature involved in the sociological study of societal-environmental interactions, such as environmentalism, natural hazards, housing, social impact assessment, and energy.

241. Dunlap, Riley E., and William R. Catton, Jr. "Environmental Sociology: A Framework for Analysis." *Progress in Resource Management and Environmental Planning*, Vol. 1. Edited by T. O. Riordan and R. C. d'Arge. Chichester, England: John Wiley, 1979. pp. 57-85.

Presents an analytical framework that can integrate the diverse interests of environmental sociologists and perhaps provide impetus for the field's further development on a systematic basis. The framework is based on an ecological perspective. The chapter includes a brief history of the emergence of the field, an explanation of the framework and its use, and a discussion of various types of environment and levels of interaction.

242. Eadington, William R. "Quality of Life in the Growing Community." *Annals of Regional Science* 9, No. 2 (1975): 61-71.

Develops a model of individual migration based on the assumption that individuals or households will locate in communities which maximize their perception of the quality of life. When aggregated, the model can be used to describe how the attractiveness of different communities adjusts relative to one another. The influence of economic factors and the industrial base on population growth and community attractiveness are examined; the tradeoffs between economic and noneconomic components of a community's quality of life are discussed, and implications are presented.

243. Elkind-Savatsky, Pamela D., ed. *Differential Social Impacts of Rural Resource Development.* Boulder, Colorado: Westview Press, 1985. 175 pp.

Assesses the social impact of rural development projects, develops a cultural model based on theories of political economy, and applies that model to a consideration of such factors as geography, language, economics, religion, and cultural patterns of domination. The authors focus on the interrelationship between cultural factors and social stratification. Their model serves as a means for moving from abstract discussions of political economy toward a practical application of social impact assessment.

* England, J. Lynn, and Stan L. Albrecht. "Boomtowns and Social Disruption." *Rural Sociology.* Cited below as item 790.

244. Faris, Robert E. *Social Disorganization.* 2d ed. New York: The Ronald Press Company, 1955. 664 pp.

Designed to be a college text. The primary concern is with those basic processes that are to some extent fundamental causes of many of the troubles studied under the terms *social problems* and *social pathology.* Topics include social organization and disorganization; personal disorganization; reactions to economic disorganization and poverty; crime; vices; suicide; mental abnormality; disorganization of family, religious institutions, and political systems; mass behavior and mob violence; reorganization processes; and prospects of stability.

245. Finsterbusch, Kurt. "Psychological Impact Theory and Social Impacts." *Impact Assessment Bulletin* 1, No. 4 (1982): 70-89.

Attempts to redress the deficiency among social impact analysts regarding their understanding of how individuals experience adversity. Stress and life satisfaction theories are explored and applied to SIA.

246. Finsterbusch, Kurt. "Survey Research." *Social Impact Assessment Methods.* Edited by Kurt Finsterbusch, Lynn G. Llewellyn, and C. P. Wolf. (Item 19), pp. 75-94.

Discusses the uses of surveys in social impact assessment and outlines the essential steps in conducting a survey. Specific survey steps that are discussed in some detail include selection of survey method (e.g., telephone, mail), sampling design, and questionnaire construction.

247. Finsterbusch, Kurt. *Understanding Social Impacts: Assessing the Effects of Public Projects.* Vol. 110. Sage Library of

Social Science. Beverly Hills, California: Sage Publications, Inc., 1980. 309 pp.

Summarizes existing knowledge in the field of social impact assessment. Attention is focused on population changes, employment changes, displacement and relocation, neighborhood disruption, noise impacts, leisure-recreation impacts, stressful community growth, and community decline. In each area the book summarizes the available and relevant knowledge base for social impact assessors, discussing the impacts of projects and explicating the more general phenomena involved in each impact area.

* Finsterbusch, Kurt, Lynn G. Llewellyn, and C. P. Wolf, eds. *Social Impact Assessment Methods.* Cited above as item 19.

* Finsterbusch, Kurt, and C. P. Wolf, eds. *Methodology of Social Impact Assessment.* 2d ed. Cited above as item 20.

248. Flynn, Cynthia B. "The Local Impacts of the Accident at Three Mile Island." *Public Reactions to Nuclear Power: Are There Critical Masses?* Edited by William R. Freudenburg and Eugene A. Rosa. (Item 794), pp. 205-32.

Summarizes what happened at the Three Mile Island nuclear power plant and briefly reviews the effects of the accident on individuals, the local economy, and organizations in the area surrounding the plant. The effects of the accident on requirements for equipment modification, additional training programs, and emergency planning at other nuclear power plant sites also are described.

249. Flynn, Cynthia B., and James H. Flynn. "The Group Ecology Method: A New Conceptual Design for Social Impact Assessment." *Impact Assessment Bulletin* 1, No. 4 (1982): 11-19.

Describes an integrated chain of social and economic causation that links functional groups in the local study area to the project-induced effects.

250. Flynn, Cynthia B., James H. Flynn, James A. Chalmers, David Pijawka, and Kristi Branch. "An Integrated Methodology for Large-Scale Development Projects." *Social Impact Assessment Methods.* Edited by Kurt Finsterbusch, Lynn G. Llewellyn, and C. P. Wolf. (Item 19), pp. 55-72.

Describes the design of an integrated approach to social impact assessment that covers the whole range of social effects, including public response. The authors indicate that such an approach is extremely useful in siting projects and in the design of mitigation plans and monitoring programs. In addition, it allows for the identification of the objective changes due to the project, the distribution of those effects to functional social groups, the determination of the groups' evaluation of those effects, and an overall evaluation of the significance of the proposed action.

251. Ford, Thomas R., ed. *Rural U.S.A.: Persistence and Change.* Ames, Iowa: Iowa State University Press, 1978. 255 pp.

Contains thirteen original essays dealing with changes that are occurring in different segments of rural society. The authors deal with changes in such areas as land use, population, technology, values, social organization, public services, the status of minorities, the role of women, and the incidence of poverty.

Contains items 203, 327, 397

252. Freeman, D. M. "A Sociological Method for Assessing Resource Management Alternatives in Land Use Planning." *Environmental Impact Analysis: Emerging Issues in Planning.* Edited by R. K. Jain and B. L. Hutchings. Urbana, Illinois: University of Illinois Press, 1978. pp. 153-70.

Discusses various problems encountered in determining and measuring "social well-being." It is argued that "social well-being" can be linked directly with the context and number of environmental options open to decision makers. One way of looking at the effects of developments is to examine "futures" or options likely to be foregone if a particular development alternative were to proceed. There are three measurable attributes to the "social well-being" concept: (1) the scope of lost options—the proportion of people or things losing an option, (2) the intensity of loss—the significance of lost options, and (3) the duration of a lost option—the length of time before a lost option is restored. The Delphi technique is used to make judgements on quantifying lost options.

253. Freeman, David M., R. Scott Frey, and Jan M. Quint. "Assessing Resource Management Policies: A Social Well-Being Framework with a National Level Application." *EIA Review* 3, No. 1 (1982): 59-73.

Provides a framework for assessing the nonmarket social impacts of alternative natural resource programs or projects prior to their actual implementation. The proposed framework allows one to rank management strategies from most to least desirable according to their social effects so that results can be integrated with economic and technical analyses.

Framework is applicable to land use plans, forest service plans, water policies, or energy plant siting.

254. Freudenburg, William R. "Boomtown's Youth: The Differential Impacts of Rapid Community Growth on Adolescents and Adults." *American Sociological Review* 49 (1984): 697-705.

Reports that when adolescents from a rapidly growing community are compared to counterparts in three nearby communities that are expecting growth of their own, the young persons in the rapidly growing community have significantly lower evaluations of their community, more negative attitudes toward growth, lower levels of satisfaction, and higher levels of alienation. None of these differences are found when adults from the growing communities are compared to adults in the same three control communities, and none can be explained by sociodemographic background factors (including length of community residence).

255. Freudenburg, William R. "The Impacts of Rapid Growth on the Social and Personal Well-Being of Local Community Residents." *Coping with Rapid Growth in Rural Communities.* Edited by Bruce A. Weber and Robert E. Howell. (Item 592), pp. 137-70.

Examines the impacts of rapid growth on human well-being. The first section provides an overview of research on social and personal well-being in rapid-growth communities; it includes an interpretation of available boomtown statistics and a brief discussion of the measurement of "well-being." The second section summarizes the basic background information available on the characteristics of the new people who move into rapid-growth communities. The third and longest section reviews researchers' findings and propositions about the impacts of rapid growth on identifiable subgroups within local communities.

* Freudenburg, William R. "An Overview of Social Science Research." *Paradoxes of Western Energy Development: How Can We Maintain the Land and the People If We Develop?* Edited by Cyrus M. McKell, Donald G. Browne, Elinor C. Cruze, William R. Freudenburg, Richard Perrine, and Fred Roach. AAAS Selected Symposium 94. Cited above as item 21.

* Freudenburg, William R. "Social Impact Assessment." *Rural Society in the U.S.: Issues for the 1980s.* Edited by Don A. Dillman and Daryl J. Hobbs. Cited above as item 22.

*   Freudenburg,   William   R.   "Women   and   Men   in   an   Energy
     Boomtown: Adjustment, Alienation, and Adaptation."   *Rural
     Sociology.*   Cited below as item 793.

256.   Freudenburg,   William,   Linda   M.   Bacigalupi,   and   Cheryl
       Landoll-Young.   "Mental   Health   Consequences   of   Rapid
       Community Growth: A Report   from the Longitudinal Study of
       Boomtown   Mental Health   Impacts."   *Journal   of   Health and
       Human Resources Administration* (Winter 1982):   334-52.

       Reports   findings   from   an   ongoing study   of   mental health
       consequences   of   rapid growth in one northwestern Colorado boom
       town.   Two   hypotheses   are   tested: (1)   some   newcomers
       (especially   young   males)   are   disproportionately   likely   to
       experience mental   health and   other   social   problems—having
       brought their problems with them; and (2) if a change is found
       in the level of mental health problems in a community, it will
       also   reflect   significant   changes   in   the   behaviors   and   percep-
       tions of long-time residents.

257.   Freudenburg,   William R.,   and Kenneth M. Keating.   "Increasing
       the Impact of Sociology on Social Impact Assessment: Toward
       Ending the Inattention."   *The American   Sociologist* 17 (May
       1982):   71-80.

       Examines the existing lack of sociological expertise   in the
       impact statement process and makes the   following suggestions:
       (1) focus on human and social well-being, (2) consider mitiga-
       tion   strategies which   include possible   alterations   in   the
       proposed projects, (3) focus on longitudinal research, and (4)
       seek cooperation   between academic   and   applied sociologists.
       The paper concludes that improved impact assessments   not only
       could exert an increased influence on policy outcomes, but can
       hold the potential to contribute to basic sociology.

*   Freudenburg,   William R.,   and Eugene   A. Rosa, eds.   *Public
     Reactions   to Nuclear Power.*   Cited below as item 794.

258.   Fuguitt,   Glen V.,   and John D. Kasarda.   "Community Structure
       in Response   to Population Growth and Decline: A Study   in
       Ecological Organization."   *American Sociological   Review* 46
       (1981):   600-15.

       Assesses   how three key components of   community structure—
       managerial, clerical, and professional and technical support—
       respond to   population size, growth, and decline.   A positive
       association   existed between   both population size   and growth
       and the   proportion of   workers employed   in   professional and
       clerical occupations, for metropolitan areas that grew between
       1960 and 1970, and   a negative   association was found   for the
       managerial component.

* Galginaites, Michael, Claudia Chang, Kathleen M. MacQueen, Albert A. Dekin, Jr., and David Zipkin. *Ethnographic Study and Monitoring Methodology of Contemporary Economic Growth, Socio-Cultural Change, and Community Development in Nuiqsut, Alaska.* Tech. Rpt. No. 96. Cited below as item 890.

259. Gartrell, John W., Harvey Krahn, and Tim Trytten. "Boom Towns: The Social Consequences of Rapid Growth." *Resource Communities: A Decade of Disruption.* Edited by Don D. Detomasi and John W. Gartrell. Boulder, Colorado: Westview Press, 1984. pp. 85-100.

Examines the social effects of rapid population growth in the context of experiences in Canadian resource communities. The authors (1) examine several Canadian case studies in an effort to broaden the empirical basis of discussion; (2) place this evidence within a conception of stages of development, and (3) develop a research agenda designed to focus the boom-town debate on issues of broader sociological significance.

260. Geisler, Charles C., Rayna Green, Daniel Usner, and Patrick C. West, eds. *Indian SIA: The Social Impact Assessment of Rapid Resource Development on Native Peoples.* Monograph No. 3. Ann Arbor: University of Michigan, Natural Resources Sociology Research Lab, 1982. 448 pp.

Contains nineteen original articles divided into four sections: (1) Adapting SIA to Unique Indian Circumstances, (2) Indian-SIA Case Studies in the United States, (3) Indian-SIA Case Studies in Canada, and (4) Indian-SIA Case Studies in Latin America.

Contains items 196, 228, 282, 315.

261. Goldstein, Joan. "The Pine Barrens: A Case Study of the Social Impact of Urban Development Upon Rural Communities." *Social Impact Assessment: Theory, Method, and Practice.* Edited by Frank J. Tester and William Mykes. (Item 45), pp. 327-33.

Outlines a theoretical framework through which conflicts associated with development activities may be analyzed. The framework is illustrated by examining the polarity of views with respect to unbanization and associated land use changes in the Pine Barrens region of New Jersey.

262. Gould, L. "Social Science Research on the Energy Boomtown." *Social Science Energy Review* 1, No. 1 (1978): 8-30.

Reviews social science literature on boom towns. It reports that there is often a political struggle between old and new

residents and that local governments are asked to perform
duties for which they have no experience. Inter-
jurisdictional conflicts and basic social structure changes
are also reported.

263. Greider, Thomas, and Richard S. Krannich. "Neighboring
      Patterns, Social Support and Rapid Growth: A Comparison of
      Three Western Communities." *Sociological Perspectives* 28,
      No. 1 (1985): 51-70.

      Tests empirically the assertion that rapid community growth
      has various disruption consequences, including a deterioration
      of the importance of neighboring as a source of both primary
      interaction and localized informal social support. Authors
      examine data on neighboring phenomena from three small commun-
      ities (the boom town of Evanston, Wyoming; the energy resource
      town of Delta, Utah; and the regional retailing center of
      Tremonton, Utah) in the Intermountain West that in recent
      years have experienced substantially different rates of
      population growth.

264. Gribbin, C. C., and T. B. Brealey. "Social and Psychological
      Well-Being and Physical Planning in New Towns: How Closely
      Are They Related?" *Man-Environment Systems* 10 (1980): 139-
      45.

      Questions the assumption made by architects and planners
      that, within acceptable design criteria, physical planning can
      positively and directly influence the social and psychological
      well-being of residents in a new community. To test the
      assumption, existing data on social ties and mental health in
      a new remote mining community in northern Australia were
      analyzed in light of statements of planning philosophy.

265. Griffith, Carl R. "Assessing Community Cohesion Impact
      Through Network Analysis." *Journal of Environmental Systems*
      9, No. 2 (1979-80): 161-67.

      Presents a new descriptive method for assessing changes to
      community cohesion via network analysis, a project-
      independent method with relative analytical simplicity that
      allows events to be "frozen" in a convenient form and subse-
      quently interrogated from several angles. Selected results
      from a test application for the proposed Glengowan Dam and
      Reservoir in Ontario, Canada, indicated that community
      cohesion would be adversely affected.

266. Hawley, Amos H. *Human Ecology: A Theory of Community
      Structure.* New York: The Ronald Press Company, 1950. 456
      pp.

Aims to develop a full and coherent theory of human ecology. The argument begins with the contributions of plant and animal ecologists and seeks to elaborate the logical implications of general ecological theory. This leads to investigation of the nature and development of community structure.

267. Hawley, Willis D., and Frederick M. Wirt, eds. *The Search for Community Power.* 2d ed. Englewood Cliffs, New Jersey: Prentice-Hall, Inc., 1974. 390 pp.

Contains twenty articles about the power structures of American communities. Definitions, findings, methods, problems, and future research directions are addressed. The articles were selected to provide a comprehensive survey of the nature, quality, potential, and problems of community power research.

268. Helmer, Olaf. "Problems in Futures Research: Delphi and Causal Cross-Impact Analysis." *Futures* 9 (1977): 17-31.

Discusses two methods of futures research and presents the causal cross-impact analysis model as one that avoids the criticisms that have been leveled at correlational cross-impact analysis.

269. Hill, Kim Quaile, and Jib Fowles. "The Methodological Worth of the Delphi Forecasting Technique." *Technological Forecasting and Social Change* 7 (1975): 179-92.

Discusses the problems of reliability and validity of the Delphi technique. Reliability problems often arise from ill-considered procedural variations and lack of standardization; validity problems arise principally from pressures for convergence of predictions. Article closes with a discussion in support of its continued use in spite of its shortcomings, as well as with comments on alternative approaches.

270. Himelfarb, Alex. *The Social Characteristics of One-Industry Towns in Canada.* Royal Commission on Corporate Concentration Report No. 30. Ottawa, Ontario: Minister of Supply and Services Canada, 1977. 43 pp.

Attempts to summarize what is known about the social characteristics of single-industry communities in Canada. Himelfarb focuses on community structure, community institutions, and interpersonal relations.

271. Hitchcock, Henry. *Analytical Review of Research Reports on Social Impacts of Water Resources Development Projects.* IWR Contract Report 77-3. Fort Belvoir, Virginia: U.S. Army

Corps   of Engineers,   Institute for   Water   Resources, March
1977.   203 pp.

Is an analytical review on three levels of summary:
individual studies, study characteristics (e.g., research
objectives, general methodology), and impacts identified
through all the studies.   An analysis of patterns formed by
the characteristics and impacts further highlights research
gaps.   Research questions to address in the future are
suggested, and a bibliography of the research reports is
included.

272.   Hobart,   Charles W.   "Impact of Resource Development Projects
       on Indigenous People."   *Resource Communities: A Decade of
       Disruption.* Edited by Don D. Detomasi and John W. Gartrell.
       Boulder, Colorado: Westview Press, 1984. pp. 111-24.

       Examines the effects of resource development projects on
       native peoples in northern Canada.   The article begins with a
       brief   review of industrial work experiences   of native
       Canadians prior to 1965.   Then, three alternative resource
       development scenarios are examined, and their consequences for
       native communities and people are discussed.   These scenarios
       are (1) the work site in the home community, (2) relocation of
       workers and   families to work sites, and   (3) rotation
       employment.

273.   Hobbs,   Daryl J.   "Rural Development: Intentions and Conse-
       quences." *Rural Sociology* 45, No. 1 (1980):   7-25.

       Describes a frame of reference for   rural development
       research by emphasizing the identification and assessment of
       consequences for people and communities of programs and
       policies   undertaken in the name of   rural development.
       Researchers must be aware that development is political and
       concerned with values.   Many of the features of prevailing
       developmental   ideology   have   produced   nondevelopmental
       outcomes.   Hobbs urges a greater integration of knowledge
       around major policy and development issues.

274.   Hoinville,   Gerald, and Roger Jowell.   *Survey Research
       Practice.* London: Heinemann Educational Books, 1977.   228
       pp.

       Focuses on the methods and procedures by which survey theory
       should be applied.   Topics include unstructured design work,
       questionnaire construction, sampling, interviewing, organizing
       fieldwork, postal survey procedures, data preparation, and
       classifying respondents.

275. House, J. D. "Big Oil and Small Communities in Coastal Labrador: The Local Dynamics of Dependency." *Canadian Review of Sociology and Anthropology* 18, No. 4 (1981): 433-52.

     Assesses the likely effects of offshore Labrador petroleum development upon coastal communities. To date, there has been little impact and practically no benefits for native Labradorians. The underlying structural reason for this is a contradiction between the principles by which the international oil industry operates and those of the local social economy. In the absence of governmental intervention, tensions between the two systems are reconciled in favor of the dominant party, the oil companies.

276. House, J. D. "Oil Companies in Aberdeen· The Strategy of Incorporation." *The Scottish Journal of Sociology* 3 (1978): 85-102.

     Argues that in adapting to a new area that is already developed--in the sense of having a high degree of industrialization, mass literacy, and the kinds of skills acquired through formal education, and a basic cultural similarity to the Western home countries of the multinational corporations-- the oil companies pursue a general strategy of *incorporation* rather than simply *exploitation* toward the local population. Despite local suspicions and various adjustment problems on both sides, this strategy (in the short term) has proven quite compatible with local interests and aspirations in northeastern Scotland.

277. *Impact Assessment Bulletin.* Special Issue: *Impacts of the Arms Race.* Organized by Elizabeth Moen. Vol. 2, No. 4 (Fall 1983). 71 pp.

     Focuses on the impacts of ongoing planning and preparation for nuclear war. Articles are as follows: "Ethical Implications of Planning for War;" "Impact Assessment of National Defense;" "Value of Crisis Relocation;" "Nuclear War and Crisis Relocation Planning: A View from the Grassroots;" "Impacts on Local Communities of Planning for Peace;" "Impact of War Policy Planning: the Role of the Expert in Decision-Making;" and "Planning and Preparing for Nuclear War: Implications for Impact Assessors."

278. *Impact Assessment Bulletin.* Special Issue: *Social Impact Assessment.* Edited by F. Larry Leistritz and Steve H. Murdock. Vol. 3, No. 1 (Winter 1984). 84 pp.

     Addresses the need for both further refinement in SIA theory and methods and for enhancement of the knowledge base concerning socioeconomic impacts. The articles in this volume

focus on several major trends in the development of SIA: (1)
development of integrated and flexible systems for performing
socioeconomic impact assessments; (2) development of a better
understanding of the economic, demographic, and social changes
which occur under conditions of rapid growth; and (3) application of the basic approach and methods of social impact
assessment to new issues and in new settings.

Contains item 167.

*   Johnson, Sue, and Esther Weil. *Social Aspects of Power Plant
     Siting.*   Ohio River Basin Energy Study, Vol. III-D.   Cited
     below at item 925.

279. Jones,   Grant R., Ilze Jones, Brian A. Gray, Bud Parker, and
      Jon C. Coe.   "A Method for the Quantification of Aesthetic
      Values   for   Environmental Decision   Making."   *Nuclear
      Technology* 25 (1975):   682-712.

      Offers a method for quantitatively evaluating the visual
      quality resulting from the introduction of a nuclear facility
      into a landscape setting, as viewed from the surrounding area.
      Three methods were tested on a group of landscape architects,
      environmental planners,   and urban designers.   The most
      reliable results were obtained when the viewscape was divided
      into major visual components (landforms, sky, etc.) and each
      rated for memorability of scene, wholeness of scene, and
      harmony of its parts.

280. Jorgensen,   Joseph G.   "Energy Developments in the Arid West:
      Consequences for Native Americans." *Paradoxes of Western
      Energy Development: How Can We Maintain the Land and the
      People If We Develop?*   Edited by Cyrus M. McKell, Donald G.
      Browne, Elinor C. Cruze, William R. Freudenburg, Richard
      Perrine, and Fred Roach.   AAAS Selected Symposium 94.
      (Item 290), pp. 297-322.

      Reports that Native American persons and   communities have
      been affected in a number of unanticipated ways by existing
      and proposed energy developments.   One of the clearest trends
      is an increase in conflicts, often between tribal members and
      their elected leaders. In addition, reciprocity-based kinship
      networks have been affected, and expectations have been
      changed.

281. Jorgensen,   Joseph G.   "Native Americans and Rural Anglos:
      Conflicts and Cultural Responses to Energy Developments."
      Human Organization 43, No. 2 (1984):   178-85.

      Briefly analyzes the importance of land, technology, labor,
      economic distribution, and kinship in the formation and the

persistence of cultural ideologies, and hence provides a
plausible explanation for conflicts and cultural responses to
rapid, large-scale energy development. Data are from several
primary field investigations conducted since 1974 among
Indian, Eskimo, ranching, and farming communities in Alaska
and the American West.

* Jorgensen, Joseph G., and Jean A. Maxwell. *Effects of Renew-
  able Resource Harvest Disruptions on Socioeconomic and
  Sociocultural Systems Impact Analysis: Unalakleet, Norton
  Sound.* Tech. Rpt. No. 90. Cited below as item 896.

282. Justus, Roger, and JoAnne Simonetta. "Oil Sands, Indians and
     SIA in Northern Alberta." *Indian SIA: The Social Impact
     Assessment of Rapid Resource Development on Native Peoples.*
     Edited by Charles C. Geisler, Rayna Green, Daniel Usner, and
     Patrick C. West. Monograph No. 3. (Item 260), pp. 238–57.

     Reports on an evaluation of social, cultural, political, and
     economic impacts of oil sands plants and associated develop-
     ment on native communities in the Fort McMurray area. The
     effectiveness of impact mitigation measures also was
     evaluated.

283. Krahn, Harvey, and John W. Gartrell. "Labour Market Segmen-
     tation and Social Mobility in a Canadian Single-Industry
     Community." *Canadian Review of Sociology and Anthropology*
     20, No. 3 (1983): 322–45.

     Examines occupational mobility opportunities in a Canadian
     resource development community by analyzing the status attain-
     ment of a 1979 sample of male residents of Fort McMurray,
     Alberta. Although the labor force of this single-industry
     community appears to have experience only marginally greater
     than Canadian labor forces as a whole, frequent and large
     socioeconomic status changes accompanied the move to this
     community. This migration involved substantial mobility from
     periphery into core sector (oil, in this case) firms.

* Krahn, Harvey, John Gartrell, and Lyle Larson. "The Quality
  of Family Life in a Resource Community." *Canadian Journal
  of Sociology.* Cited below as item 772.

284. Krannich, Richard S., and Thomas Greider. "Personal Well-
     Being in Rapid Growth and Stable Communities: Multiple
     Indicators and Contrasting Results." *Rural Sociology* 49,
     No. 4 (1984): 541–52.

     Addresses the possibility that success or failure at coping
     with the changes which accompany boom growth will vary

substantially across distinct subpopulations in rapid growth
communities. Using three distinct indicators of personal
well-being, the authors examined differences and similarities
between boom town mobile home residents, boom town residents
in conventional homes, and residents of a stable comparison
community. Results provide evidence of disruption on only one
of the well-being indicators and also indicate the importance
of disaggregating boom town populations into distinct
subpopulations when attempting to assess the effects of rapid
growth.

285. Krawetz, N. M. *Implications for Development Planning.* Final
      Report Paper No. 8. (Item 524), 31 pp.

      Outlines a generic set of parameters which are useful to
      consider in assessing the social consequences of a project on
      the community in which it is to be located. These parameters
      are based not only on the Huntly Monitoring Project findings
      but also on overseas research. The parameters are organized
      into three groups: (1) community characteristics, (2) project
      characteristics, and (3) social processes affecting and
      affected by the interaction of community and project charac-
      teristics. In general, the social consequences of a
      particular project in a particular community depend on the
      degree of fit or consistency between the characteristics of
      the two.

  *   Leistritz, F. Larry, and Steve H. Murdock. *The Socioeconomic
      Impact of Resource Development: Methods for Assessment.*
      Cited above as item 31.

286. Lewis, Cris, and Stan L. Albrecht. "Attitudes Toward
      Accelerated Urban Development in Low-population Areas."
      Growth and Change 8 (1977): 22-28.

      Reports the attitudes toward rapid economic development held
      by members of two communities with very different economic
      characteristics. The two areas are Caribou County, Idaho,
      (growing, low unemployment) and Beaver County, Utah (stagnant,
      high unemployment). Both are facing energy development,
      although Beaver County's development is at a much more massive
      scale. A majority of respondents in both areas agreed that
      positive changes would occur in their communities as a result
      of industrial development; however, for a range of items a
      higher percentage of the Beaver County residents agreed that
      positive changes would occur.

287. Little, Ronald L., and Richard S. Krannich. "Organizing for
      Local Control in Rapid Growth Communities." *Coping with
      Rapid Growth in Rural Communities.* Edited by Bruce A. Weber
      and Robert E. Howell. (Item 592), pp. 221-41.

Has three major objectives: (1) to present several community organization models and strategies which can be used to better organize communities under conditions of rapid development-induced change; (2) to describe factors in the local community that must be understood prior to assembling a community organization strategy, and (3) to outline roles and approaches which could be adopted by a community organizer or change agent when helping a community undergoing rapid growth to organize so as to enhance local control over the nature and rate of community change.

288. Lounsbury, John W., Kent D. Van Liere, and Gregory J. Meissen. "Psychosocial Assessment." *Social Impact Assessment Methods,* Edited by Kurt Finsterbusch, Lynn G. Llewellyn, and C. P. Wolf. (Item 19), pp. 215-39.

Reviews the conceptual issues and empirical findings of psychosocial assessment and discusses the prospects for advancing knowledge and practice in this area. The authors consider psychosocial assessment to be any type of social assessment that focuses on individual subjective states and that attempts to relate them to structural conditions or processes. Their focus is on attitudes, beliefs, values, intentions, and behavioral responses.

* Lucas, Rex A. *Minetown, Milltown, Railtown: Life in Canadian Communities of Single Industry.* Cited below as item 773.

289. McGranahan, Donald. "Development Indicators and Development Models." *The Journal of Development Studies* (item 72), pp. 91-102.

Is concerned with the semantics of indicators and the concepts of development. Procedures for selection and validation of indicators are discussed. The system model, which underlies the United Nations Research Institute for Social Development's measure of development, is contrasted with other approaches.

290. McKell, Cyrus M., Donald G. Browne, Elinor C. Cruze, William R. Freudenburg, Richard Perrine, and Fred Roach, eds. *Paradoxes of Western Energy Development: How Can We Maintain the Land and the People If We Develop?* AAAS Selected Symposium 94. Boulder, Colorado: Westview Press, 1984. 327 pp.

Contains fifteen original articles which evaluate the energy resources of the western United States and then discuss the consequences of development on the region's physical and social environments. Among the questions considered are, Who

will reap the economic benefits of development, and who will
bear the environmental costs?, What will be the effects on
the social structure and on the quality of life?, and, given
the recent trend of western states-rights militancy and shifts
of population to the Southwest, What impact will new federal
and state policies have on resource management?

Contains items 21, 188, 280.

291. Micklin, Michael, ed. *Population, Environment, and Social
      Organization: Current Issues in Human Ecology.* Hinsdale,
      Illinois: The Dryden Press, 1973. 509 pp.

      Contains twenty-one articles that examine various aspects of
      the population-environment conflict both in the United States
      and worldwide. The book consists of eight chapters organized
      into three major sections: (1) ecological adaptation, (2)
      organizational aspects of ecological adaptation, and (3)
      critical issues in ecological adaptation. Each chapter has a
      short introduction, followed by two or three short articles
      dealing with major issues.

292. Mitchell, R. B., J. Tydeman, and R. Curnow. "Scenario
      Generation: Limitations and Developments in Cross-Impact
      Analysis." *Futures* 9 (June 1977): 205-15.

      Focuses on the art of scenario generation by reviewing a
      number of existing procedures and noting their limitations.
      Information needs of decision makers are discussed, and three
      alternative approaches are outlined and compared in terms of
      their relative efficiency (linear programming, mixed-integer
      linear programming, and simulation).

293. Moen, Elizabeth. "Women in Energy Boom Towns." *Psychology
      of Women Quarterly* 6, No. 1 (1981): 99-112.

      Points out that, although the negative social consequences
      of rapid community population growth associated with energy
      development have been amply documented, little is known about
      how energy development specifically affects women. Data from
      an exploratory study of women in an energy boom town and a
      preboom town suggest that women do not benefit equally with
      men and are even disadvantaged by energy development.
      Categories of families and employed women are discussed, and
      the findings are related to the broader topic of women and
      development.

294. Moore, Robert. *The Social Impact of Oil: The Case of
      Peterhead.* London, England: Routledge and Kegan Paul,
      1982. 189 pp.

Describes events and conditions in Peterhead, Scotland, a coastal town on the nearest point of land to the North Sea oil and gas fields. Moore discusses land speculation, planning in the midst of uncertainty and technical ignorance, public participation, use and management of harbors, and community structure.

295. Moore, Wilbert E. *The Impact of Industry.* Englewood Cliffs, New Jersey: Prentice-Hall, Inc., 1965.

Examines the effects of industrialization on the social structure, and other aspects of affected communities. The central aim of the book is to explore the social significance of economic transformation (or the industrial revolution). The author seeks to generalize from older and newer experience and to predict the probable course of change in areas just beginning the complex process of modernization. The focus of the work is international.

296. Moore, Wilbert E. "Social Aspects of Economic Development." *Handbook of Modern Sociology.* Edited by Robert E. L. Faris. Chicago, Illinois: Rand McNally and Company, 1964. pp. 882-911.

Argues that the analysis of the social aspects of economic development has come to be a major source of empirically grounded generalizations about the patterns of social change. The author attempts to trace out how the problems presented in the study of modernization of traditional societies have interacted both with the ways sociologists have sought to order social phenomena and with theory, in the restricted sense of a body of predictive propositions.

297. Murdock, Steve H. "The Potential Role of the Ecological Framework in Impact Analysis." *Rural Sociology* 44, No. 3 (1979): 543-65.

Examines the potential role of human ecological theory as a conceptual framework for analyzing socioeconomic impacts. Two major dimensions are studied: (1) the close congruence between the basic premises, concepts, and research processes used in human ecology and those used in impact assessment, and (2) the utility of the human ecological framework for explaining, elaborating, and integrating impact research findings and analyses.

298. Murdock, Steve H., and Eldon C. Schriner. "Structural and Distributional Factors in Community Development." *Rural Sociology* 43, No. 3 (1978): 426-49.

Reports on survey results of nine communities in four
western states that are experiencing pre-, current, and post-
development stages. The authors found that occupational and
industrial changes are those directly reflecting the type of
development taking place (military, mining, etc.). Also, the
findings indicate, if comparative results for communities
accurately reflect patterns over time, that such structural
changes will disappear with the development, and the post-
development stage will not differ significantly from the
predevelopment stage. Impact benefits are clearly disproportionately obtained by new residents, but the findings also
show that longtime residents are no worse off than they might
have been had the development not occurred. In terms of
increased occupational stability, decreased downward mobility,
and increased income, they are perhaps somewhat better off
than residents similar to them who are living in nondevelop-
ment areas.

299. Newby, Howard. "A Sociological Approach." *Energy Resource
      Communities.* Edited by Gene F. Summers and Arne Selvik.
      (item 61), pp. 1-21.

      Outlines an agenda for research in studies focused on energy
      resource communities. The paper also examines some factors
      that have led to a decline in both the quantity and quality of
      community studies in the last decade in order that the same
      mistakes are not repeated in the study of energy resource
      communities.

300. Northern Alberta Development Council. *Community Impact
      Assessment Handbook.* Peace River, Alberta: Northern
      Alberta Development Council, 1982. 55 pp.

      Is a how-to primer written for northern Canadian communities
      for the purpose of conducting their own community impact
      assessment studies. This impact assessment report purports to
      be community based; that is, impact assessment is controlled
      by the community, although the community may involve outside
      interests. The particular focus of the report is a step-
      by-step approach to the impact assessment process.

  *   Olien, Roger M., and Diana Davids Olien. *Oil Booms: Social
      Change in Five Texas Towns.* Cited below as item 907.

301. Ory, Marcia G. "Family Impact Analysis: Concepts and
      Methodologies." *Policy Studies Journal* 8 (1980): 941-49.

      Presents family impact analysis (FIA) as a tool for system-
      atically examining, and thus anticipating, how alternative
      policies, programs, and services impact on different aspects

of family life. The conceptual framework and methodologies of
FIA are presented.

302. *Pacific Sociological Review.* Special Issue. Vol. 25, No. 3
     (July 1982). 376 pp.

     Debates the topic of Social Research on Boom Towns through a
     critical review of literature by Kenneth Wilkinson and
     associates. Responding to their assessment of literature
     concerning social disruption associated with large-scale
     energy development in western states are S. Albrecht, K.
     Finsterbusch, W. Freudenburg, R. Gale, R. Gold, S. Murdock,
     and F. L. Leistritz. K. Wilkinson rebuts.

303. Palinkas, Lawrence A., Bruce Murray Harris, and John C.
     Petterson, eds. *A Systems Approach to Social Impact
     Assessment.* Boulder, Colorado: Westview Press, 1985. 280
     pp.

     Provides two case studies that demonstrate the use of
     systems analysis to forecast the often far-reaching conse-
     quences of government policies and economic development for
     the social relations and cultural values of different commun-
     ities. The case studies examine the potential effects of oil
     development in two rural Alaskan communities, comparing the
     impact of proposed oil-related activities with projected
     changes in the sociocultural and socioeconomic aspects of
     these communities under other sets of assumptions, such as the
     development of a local groundfish industry.

304. Perry, Ronald W., C. Richard Schuller, Michael K. Lindell,
     Marjorie R. Greene, Jeffery T. Walsh, and Timothy Earle.
     *Community Stress and Social and Technological Change: A
     Framework for Interpreting the Behavior of Social Movements
     and Community Action Groups.* Final Report. PNL-3403;
     BHARC-411/80/034; VC-70. Seattle, Washington: Battelle
     Memorial Institute, June 1980. 150 pp.

     Examines the research on organized community response
     relevant to the kind of social and technological changes posed
     by the proposed siting of major nuclear facilities, particu-
     larly nuclear waste facilities. It is concerned with such
     manifestations of organized behavior as social movements and
     community action groups and with their interaction with other
     established organizations in the political areas of a commun-
     ity experiencing social stress. It seeks to present
     principles of organizational response that are firmly grounded
     in both social scientific theory and research.

*   Petterson, John S., Bruce M. Harris, Lawrence A. Palinkas,
     Kathleen Burlow, Will Nebesky, James Kerr, Lee Huskey, Steve

Langdon, and Jeffrey Tobolski. *Socioeconomic/Sociocultural Study of Local/Regional Communities in the North Aleutian Area of Alaska.* Cited below as item 908.

305. Pill,   Juri.   "The   Delphi   Method: Substance, Context, a Critique and an Annotated Bibliography." *Socioeconomic Planning Sciences* 5 (1971): 57-71.

Provides a comprehensive review of the Delphi method for efficiently obtaining consensus from a panel of evaluators on questions which are shrouded in uncertainty and cannot be measured in the classical sense. The historical development is described, and the methodology is placed in context along-side other methods of subjective scaling. A 40-item annotated bibliography is included.

*   Roberts,   Richard, and Judith Fisher. *Debunking the Myths of Canadian Resource Communities.* Cited below as item 780.

306. Rohe,   William M. "Social Impact Assessment and the Planning Process in the United States: A Review and Critique." *Town Planning Review* 53, No. 4 (1982):   367-82.

Reviews the objectives of SIA and presents a list of criteria for evaluating the adequacy of SIA.   Various method-ological approaches are discussed, including informed specula-tion and elicitation techniques; ethnographic techniques, project comparison techniques, and trend projection and modeling. The author addresses the methodological, political, and institutional problems by recommending changes in the current SIA process including conducting SIAs on alternatives at early stages of the planning process, greater community participation, increased emphasis on mitigation strategies, and monitoring of actual impacts.

307. Roper,   Roy.   "Ethnography." *Social Impact Assessment Methods.* Edited by Kurt Finsterbusch, Lynn G. Llewellyn, and C. P. Wolf. (Item 19), pp. 95-107.

Explains ethnography and describes applications of ethnography in social impact assessment. Ethnographers tradi-tionally have studied small-scale societies firsthand by immersing themselves into the daily routine of their members. Ethnographers generally do not sample populations and behaviors in the formal, statistical sense and are more concerned with underlying patterns and issues and less with the generalizability of findings to a larger group of individuals. In social impact assessment, ethnography is seen as particularly useful in the areas of dynamic profiling and identification of differentially affected groups.

308. Ross, Peggy J., Herman Bluestone, and Fred K. Hines.
     Indicators of Social Well-Being for U.S. Counties. Rural
     Dev. Res. Rpt. No. 10. Washington, D.C.: U.S. Department
     of Agriculture, 1979. 19 pp. plus a 71-page statistical
     supplement.

     Develops four composite indexes of social well-being for
     3,097 U.S. counties: socioeconomic, health, family status,
     and alienation. National patterns of these composites are
     depicted by U.S. county maps and through mean index scores of
     counties grouped by metro-nonmetro status and rural-urban
     orientation. Counties and metro-nonmetro county groups vary,
     as do geographic regions, in their basic patterns and degrees
     of well-being, indicating that social and economic development
     programs should be tailored to the needs of each region or
     type of county.

309. Runyan, Dean. "Tools for Community-Managed Impact
     Assessment." *Journal of the American Institute of Planners*
     43, No. 1 (1977): 125-35.

     Evaluates the usefulness of a range of available social
     impact assessment techniques for local groups. The use of
     such techniques by local groups can serve to enhance their
     role in local and regional planning and can provide purposeful
     activity for volunteer lay groups. Twelve techniques are
     discussed: check lists, dialectical scanning, impact assess-
     ment game, Delbecq technique, Delphi technique, scenarios and
     surveys, trend extrapolation, cost-benefit analysis, cost
     effectiveness analysis, cross impact, simulation-modeling, and
     input-output analysis.

310. Schnaiberg, Allan. "Obstacles to Environmental Research by
     Scientists and Technologists: A Social Structural
     Analysis." *Social Problems* 24, No. 5 (1977): 500-20.

     Discusses the key element in the social movement for
     environmental protection--the impact analysis role of scien-
     tists and technologists. Because of the structural positions
     of scientific and technological institutions relative to
     monopoly capital interests, serious constraints exist on
     extensions of these roles. For scientists, the constraints
     include (1) the division of scientific labor and power; (2)
     the control of scientific "missions"; (3) the control of
     publication and communication access; and (4) the direct
     social and economic coercion of scientists. Technologists
     experience four additional constraints: (1) control over
     access to data; (2) control of consultantships; (3) ideology
     of "feasibility"; and (4) nontransferability of specialized
     engineering skills.

311. Schoepfle,   Mark,   Michael   Burton, and Kenneth Begishe.
      "Navajo Attitudes Toward Development and Change: A Unified
      Ethnographic   and Survey Approach to an Understanding of
      Their Future."   *American Anthropologist* 86, No. 4 (1984):
      885-904.

      Reports on the methodology and findings of recent integrated
      ethnographic   and   survey   approaches   that   can   be   used   to
      facilitate   mediation among   the tribe, the   different experts
      serving it, and the local people.

   * Sewel,   J. *Social Consequences of Oil Developments.*   Cited
      below as item 745.

312. Smith,   C., T. Hogg, and M. Reagan.   "Economic   Development:
      Panacea or Perplexity for Rural Areas?"   *Rural Sociology* 36
      (1971):   173-86.

      Evaluates the   dual nature of economic development   in rural
      areas   in   light of   the negative   outcomes   of   overexpansion.
      Anticipation of   a water   resource development project   in the
      vicinity of   Sweet Home,   Oregon, stimulated the   community to
      overextend   its school   and municipal services.   Inflation in
      the   national economy, citizen noninvolvement in   the planning
      process,   and   the   loss   of   community   decision   makers   to
      political   interests with   a suburban   and   urban   orientation
      resulted in a short-term boom followed by decline.

313. Stelter,   Gilbert A.   "Community   Development   in Toronto's
      Commercial Empire: The Industrial Towns of the Nickel Belt,
      1883-1931."   *Laurentian University Review* 6   (June 1974):
      3-53.

      Explores the development of resource-based company   towns in
      north central Canada.   These towns are dependent and colonial
      by   function,   subject to   the vagaries   of   the international
      market in staples, and ruled by far-away government   or board-
      room   decisions.   Although   remote,   these towns   are closely
      associated with   the growing   commercial   and agricultural
      villages of   the Sudbury Basin.   The   article   discusses the
      pattern of settlement and the physical and social landscape of
      the towns surrounding Sudbury.

314. Stinner,   William F., and Michael B. Toney.   *Energy Resource
      Development and Migrant-Native Differences in Composition,
      Community   Attachment and   Satisfaction,   and Migration
      Intentions.* Logan, Utah: Utah Agricultural Experiment
      Station and Population Research Laboratory, 1981.   57 pp.

      Analyzes eight nonmetropolitan Utah communities--four that
      had experienced a high level of energy impacts and four that

had not. The analysis was structured about a conceptual model relating migrant status and various other objectively measured attributes of individuals to community attachment and satisfaction and to migration intentions.

315. Stoffle, Richard W., Merle Cody Jake, Pamela A. Bunte, and Michael J. Evans. "Southern Paiute Peoples' SIA Responses to Energy Proposals." *Indian SIA: The Social Impact Assessment of Rapid Resource Development on Native Peoples.* Edited by Charles C. Geisler, Rayna Green, Daniel Usner, and Patrick C. West. (Item 260), pp. 107-134.

Discusses some of the factors that have characterized more than a hundred years of resource competition between Southern Paiute peoples and invading Euroamericans. The authors then discuss various responses by Southern Paiute Peoples to coal production, coal transportation, and electrical transmission proposals.

316. Stoffle, Richard W., Merle Cody Jake, Michael J. Evans, and Pamela A. Bunte. "Establishing Native American Concerns in Social Impact Assessment." *Social Impact Assessment* 65-66 (1981): 4-9.

Sets out some methodological considerations that emerged during three SIA projects involving the Navajo Nation and the Southern Paiute Peoples. Each project involved energy development.

317. Stoffle, Richard W., Charles R. Smith, Danny L. Rasch, and Anita M. Duschak. "The Scavengers: An Unanticipated Human Impact of a Kentucky Dam." *Social Impact Assessment* 65-66 (1981): 11-16.

Documents an unanticipated adverse human impact resulting from a water impoundment project in central Kentucky. Urban scavengers descended upon a rural "ridge community" immediately after its inhabitants were legally forced to move by the U.S. Army Corps of Engineers. These persons took items of public and private ownership from homes, barns, and fields and destroyed much of what they could not remove.

318. Stout-Wiegand, Nancy, and Roger B. Trent. "Sex Differences in Attitudes Toward New Energy Resource Developments." *Rural Sociology* 48, No. 4 (1983): 637-46.

Examines the differences between men and women in their attitudes toward proposed energy developments, support for environmental protection, and occupational ties to the energy industry. Four hundred eighty-five residents of a northern West Virginia county were surveyed. Results indicate that women's lower level of support for energy developments is due (at least partially) to their greater concern with the negative environmental impacts, while men's higher level of support reflects their concern with positive economic impacts.

319. Summers,   Gene F.   "Industrial Development of Rural America."
      Journal of Community Development Society 8, No.   1 (1977):
      6-18.

      Examines the benefits and costs to nonmetropolitan commun-
      ities that encourage industrial development.   In all, 728
      manufacturing plants in 245 locations from thirty-four states
      were studied; the majority of sites were in the Midwest and
      Southeast.   Results are as follows.   There are new jobs, but
      few are filled by local economically disadvantaged citizens.
      Per   capita income   increases, but gains   are unequally
      distributed.   Population grows,   but largely because of
      inmigration.   Although more people stimulate local markets,
      they also demand more public services;   costs of service
      delivery often exceed gains in the fiscal base of the rural
      area.   Owners of local economic assets receive positive gains,
      but local government and economically disadvantaged citizens
      experience small or negative effects.

320. Summers,   Gene F.   "Industrialization." *Rural Society in the
      U.S.:   Issues for the 1980s.*   Edited by Don A. Dillman and
      Daryl J. Hobbs.   (Item 236), pp. 164-74.

      Examines the effects of industrial development on rural
      communities.   Specific topics addressed include, Who obtains
      the new jobs?, What are the effects on local unemployment, on
      per capita income, and income distribution?,   How extensive
      are the multiplier effects associated with a new plant?,   Does
      industrial development lead to growth in population or in
      retail sales?, and What are the effects on costs and revenues
      of local school districts, municipalities, and counties?
      Future research needs in these areas also are discussed.

321. Summers,   Gene F., and Kristi Branch.   "Economic Development
      and Community Social Change."   *Annual Review of Sociology.*
      Vol. 10.   Palo Alto, California: Annual Reviews Inc., 1984.
      pp. 141-66.

      Extracts and reviews what has been learned from studies of
      communities coping with rural industrialization and natural
      resource development, especially large-scale projects.   The
      findings reveal an underlying tension between the free move-
      ment of capital, on one hand, and community stability and
      worker welfare, on the other.   The authors conclude that local
      social changes are integral elements of external processes of
      economic development and that the changes can be understood by

directing attention to the spatial patterns of social, economic, and political inequality and to the mechanisms that generate and sustain unevenness.

* Tester, F. J. "Social Impact Assessment: Coping With the Context of Our Times." *Social Impact Assessment.* Cited above as item 44.

* Tester, Frank J., and William Mykes, eds. *Social Impact Assessment: Theory, Method, and Practice.* Cited above as item 45.

322. Thompson, James G., and Audie L. Blevins. "Attitudes Toward Energy Development In the Northern Great Plains." *Rural Sociology* 48, No. 1 (1983): 148-58.

    Analyzes attitudes of area residents toward increased mineral extraction and processing in the northern Great Plains. Residents of six counties were surveyed from 1973 to 1976; experience with development ranged from no experience to over five years of activity. Results revealed that residents believe economic benefits as well as negative social changes accompany development; a high degree of environmental concern was also expressed.

323. Thompson, James G., Kristi Branch, and Gary Williams. *The Bureau of Land Management Social Effects Project: Summary Research Report.* BLM-YA-PT-82-008-1606. Washington, D.C.: U.S. Department of the Interior, Bureau of Land Management, 1982. 308 pp.

    Presents a model for assessing social impacts. The model has four major components: (1) direct project inputs, (2) the community's resources, (3) its social organization, and (4) the well-being of individuals in the community and their perception of the community. This analytical framework was used to guide assessments of social effects in ten communities that had experienced substantial energy-related growth during the 1970s.

* Torgerson, Douglas. *Social Impact Assessment: Moving Toward Maturity.* Cited above as item 46.

324. United Nations Educational, Scientific and Cultural Organization (UNESCO). *Socio-economic Indicators for Planning: Methodological Aspects and Selected Examples.* Paris: UNESCO, 1981. 122 pp.

Is a collection of four papers. The first presents a
systemic approach to the formulation and use of social
indicators. The second paper discusses the use of socioeconomic indicators in integrated social and economic planning.
The last two papers focus on development planning in Africa.

325. Vlachos, Evan. "Cumulative Impact Analysis." *Impact Assess-
      ment Bulletin* 1, No. 4 (1982): 60-70.

      Outlines an approach to the study of cumulative impacts
      (CIs) by proposing a definition of CIs in the context of
      existing legal mandates, building on current practices of CI
      assessment, and offering some pragmatic strategies of CI
      assessment and evaluation.

326. Walker, P., W. E. Fraize, J. J. Gordon, and R. C. Johnson.
      *Proceedings of the Workshop on Psychological Stress
      Associated with the Proposed Restart of Three Mile Island,
      Unit 1.* NUREG/CP-0026. Washington, D.C.: U.S. Nuclear
      Regulatory Commission, 1982. 130 pp.

      Summarizes a workshop, sponsored by the Nuclear Regulatory
      Commission, to assess the state-of-knowledge relevant to
      assessing psychological stress. Of particular interest was
      the extent to which existing concepts and studies might be
      used to extrapolate or infer the range of stress responses
      likely to result from the proposed restart of the nuclear
      reactor unit 1 at the Three Mile Island site. Eleven experts
      in the field of psychological stress and related areas
      participated in the workshop.

  *   Wilkinson, Kenneth P. "Consequences of Decline and Social
      Adjustment To It." *Communities Left Behind: Alternatives
      for Development.* Edited by Larry R. Whiting. Cited below
      as item 877.

327. Wilkinson, Kenneth P. "Rural Community Change." *Rural
      U.S.A.: Persistence and Change.* Edited by Thomas R. Ford.
      (Item 251), pp. 115-25.

      Focuses on changes in community interaction. The author
      points out that people within a given locality must interact
      to some degree to meet problems arising out of their common
      life in the area. The range of issues addressed through such
      interaction, the degree of organization of collective action,
      and the level of success achieved in meeting needs and
      resolving issues are subject to much variation over time and
      among communities. The final section of this chapter contains
      an assessment of the future prospects for the rural community
      in an increasingly urban society.

328. Wilkinson, Kenneth P., Robert R. Reynolds, Jr., James G. Thompson, and Lawrence M. Ostresh. "Violent Crime in the Western Energy-Development Region." *Sociological Perspectives* 27, No. 2 (1984): 241-56.

Estimates the effects of population growth, increased mining of fossil fuels, and power-plant construction on violent crime rates in nonmetropolitan counties of the western energy-development region in the United States. Regression results give little evidence of additive effects of recent growth and development on the violent crime rate.

* Wolf, C. P. *Quality of Life, Concept and Measurement: A Preliminary Bibliography.* [-249. Cited below as item 1021.

329. Wolf, C. P. "Social Impact Assessment: A Methodological Overview." *Social Impact Assessment Methods.* Edited by Kurt Finsterbusch, Lynn G. Llewellyn, and C. P. Wolf. (Item 19), pp. 15-33.

Discusses the goals of social impact assessment and outlines the major assessment steps and the analytical operations typically associated with each step. The rationale for each of these steps and operations is briefly discussed.

330. Wood, K. Scott. "Managing Social Impacts from Large Scale Industrial Complexes: Norway's Prospective Oil Exploration North of 62° N." *Social Impact Assessment: Theory, Method, and Practice.* Edited by Frank J. Tester and William Mykes. (Item 45), pp. 269-98.

Presents ideas which have emerged from research in Norway with respect to managing the social impacts that will be associated with the development of the off-shore oil and gas reserves of northern Norway. Major topics addressed include (1) how SIA fits in with planning in Norway, (2) what SIA experience they have with their petroleum sector, (3) what SIA plans exist for the area north of 62° N., and (4) what social impacts are expected from a major discovery. Finally, the elements of a strategy for managing social impacts are presented along with a discussion of costs and benefits associated with SIA.

331. Zehner, Robert B. *Indicators of the Quality of Life in New Communities.* Cambridge, Massachusetts: Ballinger Publishing Company, 1977. 243 pp.

Summarizes the results of a nationwide study and evaluation of the quality of life in new communities in the United States. Assessed were community characteristics, including

the number, accessibility, and quality of facilities and
services available, housing and neighborhood characteristics,
and community service systems. Plans and activities of
developers, governments, and other institutions involved in
the development of new and conventional communities were
examined.

DEMOGRAPHIC

332. American Statistical Association. *Report of the Conference
on Economic and Demographic Methods for Projecting
Population.* Washington, D.C., 1977. 178 pp.

Reports proceedings of a conference that grew out of
concerns within the American Statistical Association (ASA) and
federal agencies about the development and quality of the
national statistical data base. The purpose of the conference
was (1) to summarize population modeling and migration
research to date, (2) to identify migration and projection
research concerns that might advance the social science data
base in general, and (3) to construct specific recommendations
to ASA and the National Science Foundation for further sponsored work.

Contains items 344, 351.

333. Anderson, Theodore R. "Intermetropolitan Migration: A
Comparison of the Hypotheses of Zipf and Stouffer." *American Sociological Review* 20, No. 3 (1955): 287-91.

Compares the migration models of Zipf who proposed that,
when unemployment and income are uniformly distributed over an
area, the variable in the numerator should be the area's
population size, and Stouffer who contended that under unspe-
cified conditions the variable in the numerator should be
"opportunities," or total inmigrants. Zipf and Stouffer also
differ on the method of measuring distance in the model.

334. Arriaga, Eduardo, Patricia Anderson, and Larry Heligman.
Computer Programs for Demographic Analysis. Washington,
D.C.: U.S. Department of Commerce, Bureau of the Census,
1976. 580 pp.

Presents a set of computer programs, or subroutines that are
designed to analyze the quality of population data as well as
to calculate and estimate numerous demographic parameters.
These subroutines can be used for such purposes as estimating
levels and trends of fertility and mortality from census and
survey data, projecting populations by age and sex, constructing model or empirical life tables, and performing stable

population analysis. The subroutines have been written in a
level of FORTRAN language that is acceptable to any computer
with a FORTRAN compiler.

335. Barclay, George W. *Techniques of Population Analysis.* New
      York: John Wiley & Sons, Inc., 1958. 311 pp.

      Is a general introduction to research procedures and their
      purposes. Barclay presents a methodology applicable to
      population data of greatly varying quality and content. By
      emphasizing the logic of a procedure rather than the specific
      technique, he makes the understanding of population analysis
      less formidable.

336. Batey, Peter W. J., and Moss Madden. "The Modeling of
      Demographic-Economic Change within the Context of Regional
      Decline: Analytical Procedures and Empirical Results."
      Socio-Economic Planning Sciences 17, No. 5-6 (1983): 315-
      28.

      Concerned with the modeling of economic-demographic change
      within the Leontief input-output framework. Analytical
      methods are developed to measure the consequences of economic-
      demographic change with particular attention directed to the
      problem of assessing the regional impact of transfer payments,
      such as unemployment compensation and retirement pensions.
      The application of these methods was empirically tested in the
      Merseyside metropolitan county of northwest England.

337. Bender, Lloyd D. "The Effect of Trends in Economic Struc-
      tures on Population Change in Rural Areas." *New Directions
      in Urban-Rural Migration.* Edited by David L. Brown and John
      M. Wardwell. (Item 340), pp. 137-62.

      Discusses the effects of changes in rural economic struc-
      tures on population change. Employment opportunities,
      earnings potentials, and living conditions in rural areas are
      constantly changing. Technological innovations, the organiza-
      tion and optimum size of businesses, the amount and type of
      capital devoted to public and private enterprise, and the
      characteristics of communities all change economic and social
      conditions and thus make locations more or less desirable
      places in which to live. These structural changes have been
      occurring for years in rural economies and are among the
      fundamental determinants of the population patterns observed
      now and in the past.

338. Bizien, Yves. "A Model Relating To The Impact of Rural
      Development Projects on Population Change." *Socio-Economic
      Planning Sciences* 13 (1979): 159-74.

Presents a two-period model which attempts to predict the
subjectively optimal fertility response of peasant households
to parametric changes resulting from rural development
projects and other policies. The seven parameters considered
are the relative price of agricultural capital, the off-farm
wage, the responsiveness of outmigration to economic
incentives, the discount rate, and changes in techniques of
production which fall into three categories: neutral, labor
augmenting, or capital augmenting. Some extensions of the
model under different outmigration assumptions, endogenous
marriage decisions, and a "pension motive" for childbearing
are considered.

339. Bogue, Donald J. *Principles of Demography.* New York: John
      Wiley and Sons, Inc., 1969. 917 pp.

      Is intended to be a comprehensive treatise covering the
      entire field of population study. It was designed to serve
      the dual purpose of textbook and reference work. Four goals
      have been pursued in its preparation: (1) to present
      demography as a systematic discipline, (2) to assemble and
      formulate generalizations and principles, (3) to promote an
      international approach to demography, and (4) to integrate
      demography with the other social sciences. The individual
      chapters of the volume are intended to represent the major
      subfields of demography. Each chapter is designed to be a
      comprehensive treatment of that particular subfield. Wherever
      possible, key data are presented to verify or support general-
      izations or principles stated. The book thus provides a
      source of quick information on almost any topic of
      demography.

*   Bowen, Richard L., and David L. Foster. *A Profile of
      Displaced Pineapple Workers on Moloka'i.* Research Extension
      Series 031. Cited below as item 835.

340. Brown, David L., and John M. Wardwell, eds. *New Directions
      in Urban-Rural Migration.* New York: Academic Press, 1980.
      412 pp.

      Is the first book to deal directly with the resurgence of
      population and economic growth in rural America. The volume
      focuses on the determinants and consequences of this popula-
      tion turnaround, with investigations at the national,
      regional, and local levels. Sixteen original essays demon-
      strate why rural areas figure so prominently in development
      trends and in the formation of both urban and rural policy.

      Contains items 337, 370.

341. Cant,   G., et al.   *People and Plannng in Rural Communities.*
      Studies in Rural Change No. 4.   Christchurch, New Zealand:
      University of Canterbury, 1980. 46 pp.

      Is the second of two volumes of papers from a workshop on
      rural depopulation and development held in New Zealand in May
      1979.   The six papers examine the demographic context and
      economic forces related to rural depopulation; the planning
      process in relation to the needs of rural New Zealand;
      planning for social, economic, and environmental development
      in a specific region (the West Coast); smallholders and part-
      time farmers and rural development; and people in the process
      of research, planning, and decision making.

342. Carrothers,   Gerald A. P   "An Historical Review of the
      Gravity and Potential Concepts of   Human Interaction."
      *Journal of the American Institute of Planners 22, No. 2
      (1956). 94-99.*

      Briefly reviews the gravity and potential concepts of human
      interaction, as developed to that date.   Carrothers explains
      the basic concepts of interaction and their early formula-
      tions, then discusses their formalization, modification, and
      adaptations to measuring population mobility, projecting
      national and regional product, analyzing traffic, and
      measuring market potential.

 *   Chalmers,   J. A.   *Bureau of Reclamation Construction Worker
      Survey.* Cited below as item 719.

343. Clemente, Frank, and Gene F. Summers.   "The Journey to Work
      of Rural Industrial Employees."   *Social Forces* 54, No. 1
      (1975): 212-19.

      Examines the effect of socioeconomic status, age, and length
      of employment upon distance between place of rural residence
      and place of work.   Results indicate the composite effect
      accounts for only one percent of the variation in distance
      traveled and that metropolitan commuting models are not appli-
      cable to rural areas.

344. DaVanzo,   Julie.   "The Desirability of Disaggregation in
      Migration Modeling."   *Report of the Conference on Economic
      and Demographic Methods for Projecting Population.*
      (Item 332), pp. 88-101.

      Points out that people choose to migrate for a number of
      reasons.   Projections that take into account expected changes
      in migration determinants seem preferable to those that simply
      extrapolate past migration trends, implicitly assuming no
      change in explanatory variables or in structural parameters.

The reliability of migration projections based on the former approach is limited, however, by (1) the accuracy of predictions of the explanatory variables and (2) the explanatory and predictive power of the model. The author offers suggestions for improving the accuracy and relevancy of migration models and information bases.

345. Demarest, William J., and Benjamin D. Paul. "Mayan Migrants in Guatemala City." *Anthropology UCLA* 11, Nos. 1 & 2 (1981): 43-73.

Documents the employment problems and progress of Mayan migrants from San Pedro la Laguna to Guatemala City. Data from San Pedro and adjoining settlements suggest that urban migrants tend to come from the richer and more educated communities in the countryside, and from a range of economic as well as educational levels.

346. Dietz, Thomas, and C. Mark Dunning. "Demographic Change Assessment." *Social Impact Assessment Methods.* Edited by Kurt Finsterbusch, Lynn G. Llewellyn, and C. P. Wolf. (Item 19), pp. 127-49.

Reviews recent work on predicting changes in basic demographic variables, such as size, number, and age and sex composition of the population of communities affected by large-scale development projects. The authors review the relationship between demographic changes associated with development activities and other socioeconomic impacts. Then a general outline of the demographic impact assessment process is presented. Finally, several computer models for performing demographic impact assessments are reviewed.

  * Dunning, C. Mark. *Report of Survey of Corps of Engineers Construction Work Force.* Res. Rpt. 81-R05. Cited below as item 725.

347. Easterlin, Richard A., ed. *Population and Economic Change in Developing Countries.* Chicago, Illinois: The University of Chicago Press, 1980. 581 pp.

Consists of nine articles focussing on the relationship between economic development and population change in developing countries. Topics receiving special attention include the effect of economic development on fertility and mortality rates and patterns of internal migration in developing countries.

348. Easterlin, Richard A., Michael L. Wachter, and Susan M. Wachter. "Demographic Influences on Economic Stability:

The United States Experience." *Population and Development Review* 4, No. 1 (1978): 1-22.

Argues that in the present state of demand-oriented public policies, the entrance into the labor force of greatly increased numbers of young people born during the baby boom of the late 1940s and 1950s has caused a sharp increase in the rate of unemployment that is compatible with nonaccelerating inflation. These demographic conditions in the United States may signify the birth of a new type of "long swings" or "Kuznets cycles" that extend over periods that are substantially longer than the four- to eleven-year periods associated with business cycles.

349 Greenberg, Michael R. "Methodology of Forecasting for Small Areas." *Population Forecasting for Small Areas.* CONF-7505142. Oak Ridge, Tennessee: Oak Ridge Associated Universities, 1977. pp. 29-35.

Proposes that mathematical extrapolation methods can play a role in small-area forecasting (1) by checking more sophisticated projection models, (2) by filling in at spatial scales or at times when other techniques are not available, and (3) by providing a structure for playing the "what-if" planning game.

350. Greenberg, Michael R., and Donald A. Krueckeberg. "Demographic Analysis For Nuclear Power Plant Siting: A Set of Computerized Models And A Suggestion For Improving Siting Practices." *Computers and Operations Research* 1 (1974): 497-506.

Reviews some of the safety analysis requirements of the U.S. Atomic Energy Commission for land use and demographic analysis of the plant sites and their surroundings, pursuant to the granting of construction permits and operating permits. A computerized population-projection model is presented along with several other suggestions for upgrading the analytic quality of these siting studies.

351. Greenwood, Michael J. "The Contribution of Migration Models To Subnational Population Projections." *Report of the Conference on Economic and Demographic Methods for Projecting Population.* (Item 332), pp. 63-76.

Focuses on two fairly distinct approaches to migration modeling: (1) modified-gravity models of migration, and (2) simultaneous-equations models of migration and local change. When utilized in the context of subnational population projections, each approach involves certain difficulties, which are discussed. Moreover, problems associated with merging the two approaches are considered.

352. Greenwood, Michael J.   "Research on Internal Migration in the
      United States: A Survey."   *Journal of Economic Literature*
      13, No. 2 (1975):   397-433.

      Emphasizes contributions of economists to the migration
      literature since 1960. Literature is organized into two broad
      categories: (1) studies dealing with factors influencing
      migration and (2) studies dealing with the consequences of
      migration. Includes an extensive list of references.

353. Hamilton,   C. Horace, and Josef Perry.   "A Short Method for
      Projecting Population by Age from One Decennial Census to
      Another."   *Social Forces* 41, No. 2 (December 1962):   163-
      70.

      Discusses the logical basis and mathematical character of a
      short method for making population projections by age from one
      decennial census to another.   The method is based on the
      assumption that age-specific vital rates and migration rates
      of the recent past will continue unchanged into the next
      decade. The method includes techniques for making projections
      of the population under ten years of age at the end of the
      decade ahead.

354. Herzog, Henry W., Jr., and Alan M. Schlottmann. "Moving Back
      vs. Moving On: The Concept of Home in the Decision to
      Remigrate."   *Journal of Regional Science* 22, No. 1 (1982):
      73-82.

      Examines the effects of information and psychic costs on the
      remigration propensity of the U.S. labor force. Specifically,
      the authors investigate how the proximity of a potential
      migration destination to a previous residence, and familiarity
      with this residence, affect information and psychic costs, and
      thus, remigration propensity.

355. Hirschman,   Charles.   "The Uses of Demography in Development
      Planning." *Economic Development and Cultural Change* 29, No.
      3 (1981):   561-75.

      Reviews the practice of development planning before
      presenting two models of how demography might enter into the
      planning or policy framework.   The first model, labeled
      "population planning," stresses the relevance of demographic
      theory and knowledge toward a few selected goals, the chief of
      which is the reduction of fertility.   The second model would
      claim that the greatest utility of demographic science lies in
      empirical population research which would   not prescribe
      certain goals but would measure progress along a variety of
      social and economic dimensions.

* Hooper, Janet E., and Kristi M. Branch. *Big Horn and Decker Mine Worker Survey Report*. Cited below as item 733.

356. Hua, Chang-i, and Frank Porell. "A Critical Review of the Development of the Gravity Model." *International Regional Science Review* 4, No. 2 (1979): 97-126.

Analyzes and criticizes recent work on gravity models with respect to form, structure, derivation, and theoretical and methodological grounds. The evolution of the model is summarized and a general form is defined. Certain structural properties of gravity models are compared--biproportionality, scale, endogeny, consistency, and spatial interaction. The various macro and micro approaches to deriving or interpreting gravity models are reviewed. Problems and limitations of each approach are noted, and their basic theoretical foundations are criticized. Finally, the general trend of gravity model development is discussed.

* Huskey, Lee, Will Nebesky, Bradford Tuck, and Gunnar Knapp. *Economic and Demographic Structural Change in Alaska*. Tech. Rpt. No. 73. Cited below as item 125.

357. Irwin, Richard. *Guide for Local Area Population Projections*. Technical Paper 39. Washington, D.C.: U.S. Department of Commerce, Bureau of the Census, 1977. 84 pp.

Provides material with which to review, evaluate, and prepare projections for local areas. There are three main divisions: (1) a textual discussion of various aspects of projections for local areas; (2) supporting information, such as sources of basic data, a bibliography of pertinent litera-ture, a brief glossary of technical terms, and a list of state agencies to assist in locating and obtaining population projections; and (3) a set of appendixes which provide statis-tical information useful in preparing population projections.

358. Irwin, Richard. "Methods and Data Sources for Population Projections of Small Areas." *Population Forecasting for Small Areas*. CONF-7505142. (Item 373), pp. 15-26.

Discusses five broad categories of projection methodology: mathematical extrapolation, ratio, cohort component, economic based, and land use. Also included is an outline of demographic data sources, including birth and death data, basic population statistics, net migration data, gross migra-tion data, and miscellaneous data.

359. Irwin, Richard. "Use of the Cohort-Component Method in Population Projections for Small Areas." *Population*

Forecasting for Small Areas. CONF-7505142. (Item 373), pp. 37-48.

Explains the methodology, advantages, and limitations of the cohort-component method. Population change is interpreted as resulting from the interaction of three components—births, deaths, and net migration—upon the original population. Computation is done by retaining the identity of each age, sex and/or race group (cohort) through time. Advantages include high levels of detail and accuracy, and adaptability to any area size whose geographical boundaries are fixed and for which basic data can be obtained. Disadvantages include the large amount of data needed as basic input, error because the high levels of detail and accuracy may discourage the introduction of needed adjustments for special populations, difficulty in using the method as the geographical area becomes smaller, and errors of measurement in the basic data.

360. Isserman, Andrew M. "The Accuracy of Population Projections for Subcounty Areas." *American Institute of Planners Journal* 43 (1977): 247-59.

Evaluates the accuracy of a number of commonly used extrapolative methods of population projection. More than 3,500 simulated population projections for 1960 and 1970 were made for most of the methods being tested. The simulated projections were compared to actual populations to measure percentage errors and tendencies to over- or underestimate. The results indicate that extrapolative methods may yield sufficiently accurate projections for many planning purposes.

361. Kendall, Mark C. "Labor-Market Models." *Population Forecasting for Small Areas.* CONF-7505142. (Item 373), pp. 49-58.

Suggests that labor-market models for forecasting interarea migration flows are preferable to extrapolation of historical migration trends because a significant portion of net migration seems to be determined by differential job opportunities. The author, however, states that the efficiency of labor-market models has not been evaluated sufficiently to determine either the value of making joint employment and migration forecasts or the sources of error in forecasting.

362. Keyfitz, Nathan. "On Future Population." *Journal of the American Statistical Association* 67, No. 338 (1972): 347-63.

Discusses the problems inherent in population projection and forecasting. Population projections are distinguished from forecasts in that *projections* are conditional on the underlying assumptions about births, deaths, and migration while *forecasts* are unconditional statements of what the population of a given area will be at some future date. Methods of population projection and the problems in applying those methods to forecasting are discussed.

* Leholm, Arlen G., F. Larry Leistritz, and James S. Wieland. *Profile of North Dakota's Electric Power Plant Construction Work Force.* Agricultural Economics Stat. Rpt. 22. Cited below as item 735.

* Leistritz, F. Larry, and Steve H. Murdock. *The Socioeconomic Impact of Resource Development: Methods for Assessment.* Cited above as item 31.

363. Long, Larry H., and Diana De Are. *Migration to Nonmetropolitan Areas: Appraising the Trend and Reasons for Moving.* CDS 80-2. Washington, D.C.: U.S. Department of Commerce, Bureau of the Census, 1980. 29 pp.

Analyzes the duration and motivational basis of the pattern of net migration to nonmetropolitan areas which emerged early in the 1970s. Issues addressed include the stability of this new migration pattern, the extent to which nonemployment motives (e.g., retirement, recreation) underlie such migration, and how many of the migrants stay close enough to metropolitan areas to allow them to commute for employment.

* Malhotra, Suresh, and Diane Manninen. *Migration and Residential Location of Workers at Nuclear Power Plant Construction Sites.* Vol. 1, *Forecasting Methodology.* Vol 2, *Profile Analysis of Worker Surveys.* Cited below as item 738.

364. Masser, Ian. "Planning with Incomplete Data: Population Growth and Metropolitan Planning in the Third World." *Town Planning Review* 45 (1974): 157-69.

Considers existing methods of population projection and puts forth a minimal method which can be used as an operational tool in situations with incomplete data, especially in situations where intercensal population growth is from 50% to 100%.

365. Metz, William C. "Demographic Analysis and Power Plant Facilities." *Aware Magazine* 94 (1978): 9-15.

Describes the key elements to be considered in estimating the extent of local population growth associated with power plant development. Project manpower requirements for typical

coal-fired and nuclear plants are presented along with recent
experience regarding worker relocation and commuting, factors
affecting the geographic distribution of inmigrating workers,
methods for estimating the secondary employment effects of a
project, and a framework for integrating these factors to
estimate the total project-related population increase.

366. Morrison, Peter A. "Forecasting Population of Small Areas:
      An Overview." *Population Forecasting for Small Areas*.
      CONF-7505142. (Item 373), pp. 3-13.

      Reviews strengths and weaknesses of three population projec-
      tion methods: the mathematical extrapolation, the cohort-
      component, and the labor-market methods. The need for
      informed judgment about the assumptions supporting a projec-
      tion or forecast and for continual appraisal of those assump-
      tions is also discussed.

367. Morrison, Peter A., and Kevin F. McCarthy. *Demographic
      Forces Reshaping Small Communities in the 1980s*.
      N-1887-NICHD. Santa Monica, California: RAND Corporation,
      1982. 31 pp.

      Surveys demographic and socioeconomic changes that are
      reshaping the fortunes of small communities, and some of the
      policy issues they will pose. Local population change has
      always confronted nonmetropolitan communities with problems.
      Such communities, with usually limited facilities and finan-
      cial resources, find it especially difficult to deal with
      rapid growth or decline, or to switch from one to the other.
      With the reduction of federal intervention in local affairs,
      small communities now enjoy greater autonomy, but at the cost
      of reduced federal aid. Each community, freed from federal
      mandates, must depend far more on its own resources to manage
      its own growth or decline.

*   Mountain West Research, Inc. *Construction Worker Profile*.
      Cited below as item 740.

*   Mountain West Research, Inc. *Pipeline Construction Worker
      and Community Impact Surveys*. Cited below as item 741.

368. Murdock, Steve H., Rita R. Hamm, and F. Larry Leistritz.
      "Demographic Effects." *Energy Resource Communities*. Edited
      by Gene F. Summers and Arne Selvik. (Item 61), pp. 61-95.

      Suggests a research agenda to address the need for addition-
      al information on the population-related effects of energy
      developments occurring in a variety of physical and cultural
      settings. Specifically, it attempts to (1) describe the

state of knowledge concerning demographic impacts, (2) delineate key research questions that require analysis through a multination comparative approach, and (3) outline a research approach for use in investigating these research questions.

* Murdock, Steven H., Pamela Hopkins, John de Montel, Rita R. Hamm, Tom Brown, Margaret Bauer, and Richard Bullock. *Employment, Population and Community Service Impacts of Uranium Development in South Texas.* Tech. Rpt. 81-1. Cited below as item 742.

369. Murdock, Steve H., F. Larry Leistritz, and Eldon C. Schriner. "Local Demographic Changes Associated with Rapid Growth." *Coping with Rapid Growth in Rural Communities.* Edited by Bruce A. Weber and Robert E. Howell. (Item 392), pp. 63-96.

Uses available evidence to address (1) the major factors affecting local demographic impacts and research limitations with regard to projections of such impacts, (2) the actual size, distribution, and composition of local population changes in areas affected by large-scale projects, and (3) the policy implications of the local demographic impacts associated with rapid economic development.

370. Murdock, Steve H., F. Larry Leistritz, and Eldon C. Schriner. "Migration and Energy Developments: Implications for Rural Areas in the Great Plains." *New Directions in Urban-Rural Migration.* Edited by David L. Brown and John M. Wardwell. (Item 340), pp. 267-90.

Addresses three key dimensions bearing on migration issues: (1) the characteristics of persons migrating to energy development areas; (2) the effects of such migrants on the social, demographic, and economic structure of affected areas; and (3) the effects of energy-related developments on the social and economic conditions and perceptions of migrants and longtime residents in affected communities. Data are derived from household surveys conducted in five coal development communities located in Montana, North Dakota, and Wyoming.

371. Murdock, Steve H., James S. Wieland, and F. Larry Leistritz. "An Assessment of the Validity of the Gravity Model for Predicting Community Settlement Patterns in Rural Energy-Impacted Areas in the West." *Land Economics* 54, No. 4 (November 1978): 461-71.

Provides an assessment of the accuracy of the gravity model in explaining settlement patterns of workers employed at energy facilities in four western states. Data on community of residence obtained for 2,551 workers at twenty different facilities were used to test the model.

372. Newton, P. W. "Rapid Growth From Energy Projects: Assessing Population and Housing Impacts in the Gippsland Energy Resources Region, Victoria." *The Building Economist* 21, No. 3 (December 1982): 99-107.

Outlines a number of problems, specifically associated with housing, that emerge during periods of rapid population growth in towns linked with major new industrial development. These problems are attributed largely to a lack of knowledge on the part of government and industry about the total impact a major new development will have on local communities, a lack of information about costs of service and infrastructure provision, and a lack of suitable guidelines concerning which sector is responsible for funding additional facilities and infrastructure. A simple model for forecasting population impacts of new resource developments is developed and applied to the Gippsland region to improve the information base for planning.

373. Oak Ridge Associated Universities. *Population Forecasting for Small Areas.* CONF-7505142. Oak Ridge, Tennessee, 1977. 90 pp.

Is a collection of papers examining the state of the art of small-area forecasting as applied to the problems of planning. Topics include data sources; use of mathematical extrapolation methods, cohort-component methods, and labor-market models; and application to the specific areas of energy plant sites, education, transportation, and health care.

Contains items 358, 361, 366.

374. Pittenger, Donald B. *Projecting State and Local Populations.* Cambridge, Massachusetts: Ballinger Publishing Company, 1976. 246 pp.

Is intended to serve as a reference and guide for persons who are charged with developing state and local population projections. Its primary audience is the analyst who actually must create the projections. Beginning with a review of basic demographic measures and concepts, the book discusses a wide range of projection methods including extrapolation, ratio, share, density, and cohort-component techniques. Examples are used throughout to illustrate the various methods.

375. Price, Daniel O., and Melanie M. Sikes. *Rural-Urban Migration Research in the United States.* DHEW Publ. No. (NIH)75-565. Washington D.C.: U.S. Department of Health,

Education, and Welfare, Government Printing Office, 1975.
250 pp.

Designed to help the researcher and policymaker be familiar
with past research in rural—urban migration and guide them in
future research and policy development. Included are over
1,200 annotations (with key items flagged), a synthesis of
research findings, and a listing of research needs.

376. Shryock, Henry S., Jacob S. Siegal, and Associates. *The
Methods and Materials of Demography.* (Condensed edition by
Edward G. Stockwell.) San Francisco, California: Academic
Press, 1976. 577 pp.

Is one of the standard reference works on the techniques of
demographic analysis. It presents a systematic and comprehen
sive exposition, with illustrations, of the methods used by
technicians and research workers in analyzing demographic
data. Chapters treating internal migration and population
projections will be of particular interest to SIA analysts.

377. Tarver, James D., and Therel R. Black. *Making County Popula-
tion Projections—A Detailed Explanation of a Three-
Component Method, Illustrated by Reference to Utah Counties.*
Bull. 459. Logan, Utah: Utah Agricultural Experiment
Station, 1966. 97 pp.

Uses a component cohort survival method for making projections of future populations of each county in Utah by age and
sex group. Data sources and calculation procedures are
explained in detail. The authors believe that the procedures
developed here are applicable to counties in any other state.

378. United Nations. *Computer Software Programs for Demographic
Analysis: Aspects of Technical Co-Operation.*
ST/ESA/SER.E/32. New York: United Nations, Department of
Technical Co-Operation for Development, 1983. 29 pp.

Addresses the capabilities and limitations of available
software packages for demographic analysis. The report is
intended to (1) provide a framework which will help developing
countries choose software packages, (2) guide recommendations
for equipment acquisition, and (3) provide a basis for
installing available software packages on specific pieces of
equipment. The three major software packages examined were
developed by the U.S. Census Bureau, the National Academy of
Sciences, and the United Nations.

  * Wieland, James S., F. Larry Leistritz, and Steven H. Murdock.
Characteristics and Settlement Patterns of Energy Related

Operating Workers in the Northern Great Plains. Agricultural Economics Rpt. No. 123. Cited below as item 747.

PUBLIC SERVICE

379. Bacigalupi, Linda, and William R. Freudenberg. "Increased Mental Health Caseloads in an Energy Boomtown." *Administration in Mental Health* 10, No. 4 (1983): 306-22.

Uses a longitudinal analysis of individual-level mental health caseload data to test the hypothesis that incoming energy workers and their families are predisposed to use agency services of all types because of their "special needs." Findings indicate that their use of mental health services is not disproportionately high nor are their problems more severe than those of their nonenergy counterparts.

380. Bougsty, Tom, Prudy Marshall, and Ernest Chavez. "Prevalence and Prevention of Mental Health Problems in an Energy-Impacted Community." *Administration in Mental Health* 10, No. 4 (1983): 272-87.

Employs a standardized instrument and random sampling in a community needs assessment to document high prevalence of problems in an energy-impacted town which has attempted to plan for the rapid growth. At least 35% of the men and 25% of the women randomly sampled in the community reported elevated levels of psychological distress; 48% of the men admitted to alcohol problems. How the local mental health center utilized the needs assessment results to improve services, obtain funding for needed programs, and generally promote the community's quality of life is described.

*   Braid, Robert B., Jr., and Stephen D. Kyles. *The Clinch River Breeder Reactor Plant: Suggested Procedures for Monitoring and Mitigating Adverse Construction-Period Impacts on Local Public Services.* Cited below as item 715.

*   Branch, Kristi M., Douglas A. Hooper, and James R. Moore. "Decision-Making Under Uncertainty: Public Facilities and Services Provision in Energy Resource Communities." *Resource Communities: A Decade of Disruption.* Edited by Don D. Detomasi and John W. Gartrell. Cited below as item 749.

381. Brookshire, David S., and Ralph C. D'Arge. "Adjustment Issues of Impacted Communities or Are Boomtowns Bad?" *Natural Resources Journal* 20 (July 1980): 523-46.

Outlines one approach for assessing whether communities are harmed by rapid energy development. A preliminary statistical analysis is applied to test the hypothesis that energy-related growth induces higher crime rates.

382. Clark, G. L. "Urban Impact Analysis: A New Tool for Monitoring the Geographical Effects of Federal Policies." *The Professional Geographer* 32, No. 1 (1980): 82-85.

Describes urban impact analysis (UIA) which is designed to assess the impact of all federal actions on urban areas and existing urban policies. It is argued that the reasons for the implementation of UIA requirements are (1) the realization that the activities of the government sector may determine the fate of the urban system, (2) the suggestion that federal agencies with nonurban mandates may have more urban effects than those with such responsibilities, and (3) the knowledge that the government may not be aware of the urban consequences of its actions. It is argued that UIA differs from EIA insofar as UIA is not project oriented and UIA requires a spatial breakdown of impacts into central cities, suburbs, and nonmetropolitan areas.

383. Davenport, Judith Ann, and Joseph Davenport, III eds. *Boom Towns and Human Services.* Laramie, Wyoming: University of Wyoming, Department of Social Work, 1979. 156 pp.

Contains eleven articles exploring various aspects of service provision in rapid growth communities. Services discussed in depth include health care, mental health, education, and housing.

384. Fitzpatrick, John S. *The Impact of Natural Resource Development on the Criminal Justice System.* Helena: Montana Board of Crime Control, 1983. 69 pp.

Is intended to inform state and local government officials, legislators, social service agency personnel, and the general public of the problems and needs of the criminal justice system in development situations ranging from boom to bust. Sources of information included (1) literature review, (2) case studies of five Montana and Idaho counties experiencing some phase of resource development, (3) personal interviews with state and local officials, and (4) statistical reports. Data generally cover the period 1970 through 1982.

* Fox, William F., Jerome M. Stam, W. Maureen Godsey, and Susan D. Brown. *Economies of Size in Local Government: An Annotated Bibliography.* Rural Development Research Report No. 9. Cited below as item 987.

385.   Glickman,   N. J.   "Methodological Issues and Prospects for
       Urban Impact Analysis."   *The Urban Impacts of Federal
       Policies*. Edited by N. J. Glickman. Baltimore: The Johns
       Hopkins University Press, 1979. pp. 3-32.

       Reports that urban impact analysis (UIA) in the United
       States is a procedure for assessing the spatial dimensions of
       federal policies, not federal projects.   Policies are assessed
       for their effects on the different components of urban areas,
       that   is, central cities, suburbs, and nonmetropolitan areas.
       UIAs are submitted to the Office of Management and Budget by
       federal agencies as part of their budgeting procedures.
       Consequently, UIAs are not public documents.   This chapter
       contains detailed discussion of a number of issues   in UIA,
       including the time-scale of impacts, different types   of
       impacts (direct or indirect, qualitative or quantitative), and
       spatial units.   In addition, the type of variables to be
       analyzed and equity considerations (the differential distribu-
       tion of impacts between areas and different social groups) are
       discussed.

   *   Hoffman,   Stephen, and Mary Gray.   *The Socioeconomic Impacts
       of Coal-to-Methanol Plants in Wyoming*.   Report prepared for
       the U.S. Department of Energy, Office of Oil, Gas, and Oil
       Shale   Technology. Cited below as item 924.

386.   Honadle,   Beth Walter.   "Voluntary Interlocal Governmental
       Cooperation: A Big Idea For Small Towns."   *Municipal
       Management Journal* 3 (1980-1981):   152-55.

       Suggests specific ways for neighboring local governments to
       work together to solve shared problems.   It is based on the
       experiences local jurisdictions have actually had with volun-
       tary interlocal governmental cooperation.   These cases are
       used to illustrate the major advantages and disadvantages of
       interlocal service delivery.   The historical role of inter-
       local service delivery in small metropolitan and nonmetropoli-
       tan towns is also considered.

   *   Leistritz,   F. Larry, and Steve H. Murdock.   *The Socioeconomic
       Impact of Resource Development: Methods for Assessment*.
       Cited above as item 31.

387.   Lonsdale,   Richard E., and Gyorgy Enyedi, eds.   *Rural Public
       Services: International Comparisons*.   Boulder, Colorado:
       Westview Press, 1984. 362 pp.

       Chronicles and analyzes the experiences of seventeen nations
       with differing economic systems, levels of development, and
       natural environments.   Authors from or very familiar with
       these countries examine their rural public service problems,

service provision objectives, and specific programs and results. Countries are categorized into one of three groups: advanced capitalist, socialist, and Third World.

388. Lovejoy, Stephen B., Deborah J. Brown, and Janet S. Ayres. "Inmigrants in Nonmetropolitan Communities: More Dissatis- fied with Public Services?" *North Central Journal of Agri- cultural Economics* 5, No. 2 (1983): 39–45.

Examines the issue of whether newcomers to nonmetropolitan communities demand different levels and types of public service provision than long-time residents. Based on a study of nine small communities in Indiana, the article concludes that, in general, newcomers are slightly less satisfied with existing quantity and/or quality of services provided especially in the areas of water, fire, ambulance, and recrea- tional facilities. The authors suggest that this dissatisfac- tion may be more attributable to age structures of the inmigrating population, with younger residents demanding higher levels of public services than older residents.

389. Lovejoy, Stephen B., Ramona Marotz-Baden, and John Baden. *Contracting for Public Service Delivery: An Alternative for Boom Towns.* WRDC Paper No. 14. Corvallis, Oregon: Western Rural Development Center, Oregon State University, February 1982. 13 pp.

Presents "contracting" for public services and goods as an alternative for local governments experiencing rapid growth. The authors explain the advantages and disadvantages of contracting to private firms for the production of public goods and services for residents and provide several examples including those in social services (e.g., data processing, tax assessment, land-use planning), maintenance services (e.g., park maintenance, street and road maintenance), health and security (e.g., hospitals, ambulance services, fire and police protection), and other (e.g., water supply, garbage collection, solid waste landfill).

390. McGinnis, Karen A., and Donald A. West. *Community Impacts of Energy Development Projects: The Case of Public Education at Chief Joseph Dam.* A.E. 80-1. Pullman, Washington: Washington State University, Agricultural Economics Department, 1980. 42 pp.

Examines the problem of providing public education in the impacted communities of Bridgeport and Brewster, Washington, during construction of additional hydropower units at Chief Joseph Dam. Local residents experienced increased tax burdens, particularly early in the construction period, and the quality of education appeared to decline somewhat. Impact mitigation payments provided by the federal government are

described, and recommendations for more effective impact
mitigation at future projects are developed.

391. Matthews, Kathryn M. *Cumulative Impacts Study of the Geysers
      KGRA: Public Service Impacts of Geothermal Development.*
      Sacramento: California Energy Commission, 1983. 248 pp.

      Examines the past and potential impacts of geothermal energy
      development in the Geysers region of Northern California
      (Sonoma, Lake, Mendocino, and Napa counties) on local public
      services and fiscal resources. Each county in the Geysers
      region underwent rapid population growth in the 1970s, some of
      which can be attributed to geothermal development. The report
      identifies the number of workers currently involved in the
      various aspects of geothermal development in the Geysers.
      Using two different development scenarios, projections are
      made for the number of power plants needed to reach the
      electrical generation capacity of the steam resource in the
      Geysers. The report also projects the cumulative number of
      workers needed to develop the steam field and to construct,
      operate, and maintain these power plants. The report then
      examines the administrative and public service costs of
      geothermal development to local jurisdictions and compares
      these costs to geothermal revenues accruing to the local
      governments. Revenues do not cover the immediate fiscal needs
      resulting from increases in local road maintenance and school
      enrollment attributable to geothermal development. Several
      mitigation options are discussed and a framework presented for
      calculating mitigation costs for school and road impacts.

392. Matthiasson, J. S. *Resident Perceptions of Quality of Life
      in Resource Frontier Communities.* Winnipeg, Manitoba,
      Canada: University of Manitoba, Center for Settlement
      Studies, 1970. 41 pp.

      Presents an analysis of responses of a survey of residents'
      perceptions of the relative importance of services and
      facilities in Fort McMurray, Alberta, Canada.

393. Milburn, Lonna, Mary Walker, and Yvonne D. Knudson. *Acute
      Health Delivery, Energy Impact, and Rural Texas.* Austin:
      University of Texas; Texas Rural Health Field Services
      Program, 1985. 157 pp.

      Examines what changes occurred in the acute health care
      delivery systems of rural oil and gas communities in Texas
      during the most recent energy impact cycle. The purpose was
      to identify what changes occurred in the emergency medical
      services, the health care provider offices, and the hospitals
      during the pre-impact, impact, and post-impact stages of the
      energy impact cycle.

394. Miller, Michael K., and Donald E. Voth. "Rural Health Service Programs: Evaluating with Pooled Cross-Section and Time Series Data." *Evaluation Review* 6, No. 1 (1982): 47-59.

Evaluates the impact of community development efforts on rural health services by an analytical procedure which pools cross-sectional and time series data, thus taking advantage of both intercommunity and intertemporal variation. Scales of institutional complexity were developed at six time points. To assess the impact of community development efforts, parameters relating health sector growth or decline to existence and type of community development program were obtained using estimation procedures for pooled cross-sectional and time series data.

395. Murdock, Steve H., and Eldon C. Schriner. "Community Service Satisfaction and Stages of Community Development: An Examination of Evidence From Impacted Communities." *Journal of the Community Development Society* 10, No. 1 (1979): 109-24.

Attempts to establish how the levels and dimensions of community service satisfaction differ with stages of economic development and community population characteristics. This study examines levels of service satisfaction for 1,400 respondents in nine western communities. The analysis indicates that both new and longtime residents in currently developing communities are more dissatisfied with community services than residents in either pre- or post-development communities, that differences in levels of satisfaction are not the result of differences in the characteristics of residents, but are significantly related to the stage of community development, and that the dimensions of service satisfaction also vary with the stage of development.

396. Osborne, J. Grayson, William Boyle, and Walter R. Borg. "Rapid Community Growth and the Problems of Elementary and Secondary Students." *Rural Sociology* 49, No. 4 (1984): 553-67.

Reports results of a study in which a stratified random sample of 686 elementary and secondary public school students in rural Utah areas classed as rapidly or not rapidly growing was administered the Mooney Problem Checklist, a survey of perceived personal problems. Secondary female students in rapidly growing communities reported more problems than secondary female students in slow-growing communities, while in general, secondary female students underlined more problems than secondary male students. The results replicate and extend earlier studies that imply differential effects of community growth on certain population subgroups (e.g., secondary female students and elementary students).

397. Rainey, Kenneth D., and Karen G. Rainey. "Rural Government and Local Public Services." *Rural U.S.A.: Persistence and Change.* Edited by Thomas R. Ford. (Item 251), pp. 126-44.

   Points out that the availability of local government services once created a major distinction between rural and urban communities. The need and demand for services differed markedly from city to country. Today, rural and small-town communities are much closer to urban and suburban areas in their service needs and expectations. Like the more publicized urban crises, rural local governments and public service institutions face many difficulties in funding and providing quality public services.

398. Rojek, Dean G., Frank Clemente, and Gene F. Summers. "Community Satisfaction: A Study of Contentment With Local Services." *Rural Sociology* 40, No. 2 (1975): 177-92.

   Attempts to quantify community satisfaction with fifteen services that fell into four major categories: medical, public, commercial, and educational services. Data were drawn from a 1971 area probability sample survey of 1,166 heads of households in a four-county region of Illinois that was divided into three residential strata.

399. Santini, D. J., E. A. Tanzman, and C. M. Hotchkiss. *Education and Other Financial Problems of Areas Experiencing Energy-Induced Boom Growth.* ANL/AA-25. Argonne, Illinois: Argonne National Laboratory, 1980. 74 pp.

   Presents a retrospective look at the characteristics of communities booming because of coal and electric power developments. It focuses primarily on the changing financial needs and resources used to meet those needs during the boom period. The work is presented in three distinct parts: a theoretical examination of changes in community expenditure needs, an actual examination of changes in expenditures and revenues of seventeen counties that experienced boom growth, and a case study of the changes in revenue-generation mechanisms adopted as a result of local energy development in four states.

400. Stinson, Thomas F., and Andrea Lubov. "Segmented Regression, Threshold Effects, and Police Expenditures in Small Cities." *American Journal of Agricultural Economics* 64, No. 4 (1982): 738-46.

   Discusses why assuming piece-wise continuity may be more realistic than assuming that average costs can be represented by a single, smooth, continuous function. Segmented regression is used to test for discontinuities in local per capita expenditures for police protection in Minnesota, North Dakota, and Wisconsin.

401. Uhlmann, Julie M., and Judith K. Olson. *Planning for Rural Human Services: The Western Energy-Impact Experience.* Washington, D.C.: U.S. Department of Health and Human Services, Government Printing Office, 1983. 184 pp.

Presents results of an assessment of human service needs and delivery systems in energy-impacted communities in the states of Colorado, Montana, North Dakota, Utah, and Wyoming. Services included were social services, mental health services, alcohol and drug abuse services, public health nursing services, and youth and seniors' services. Seven specific communities were also studied.

FISCAL

402. Andrews, Donald R., Steve H. Murdock, and Lonnie L. Jones. "Private and Public Sector Economies of Lignite-Energy Resource Development in Rural Central Texas." *Southern Journal of Agricultural Economics* 15, No. 2 (1983): 55-61.

Presents estimates of the economic and fiscal impacts associated with the construction and operation of five lignite-energy generating stations in the Brazos Valley region of central Texas.

  *   Djorustad, David J. "How Nuclear Reactor Siting Affects Local Communities." *Survey of Business.* Cited below as item 918.

403. Burchell, Robert W., and David Listokin. *The Fiscal Impact Handbook.* New Brunswick, New Jersey: Rutgers University, Center for Urban Policy Research, 1978. 480 pp.

Provides a comprehensive guide to fiscal impact analysis methods. Topics include methods of cost projection, methods of revenue projection, and applicability of fiscal impact analysis to municipal planning. The work also includes sections on demographic multipliers for various housing types, gross income multipliers for residential and commercial properties, and computer models for fiscal impact analysis.

404. Cumberland, John H. "The Impacts of a Nuclear Power Plant on a Local Community: Problems in Energy Facility Development." *Energy and the Community.* Edited by R. J.

Burby and A. F. Bell.   Cambridge, Massachusetts: Ballinger
Publishing Company, 1978.   pp. 95-101.

Explores opportunities for mitigating future damage to local
communities from large energy facilities.   Problems created by
the first nuclear plant to be constructed in Maryland (the
Calvert Cliffs plant) are examined.

405. Cummings,   Ronald G., and Arthur F. Mehr.   "Investments for
      Urban Infrastructure in Boomtowns."   *Natural Resources*
      Journal 17 (1977):   223-40.

      Addresses   the   problem   of   devising   optimum investment
      strategies for communities confronted with the prospect of
      fluctuating   population   levels.   Preliminary   estimates   of
      benefits   from   investment   in community   infrastructure   are
      presented,   and   priority   areas   for   further   research   are
      suggested.

406. Cummings,   Ronald G.,   and William D. Schulze.   "Optimal
      Investment Strategy for Boomtowns: A Theoretical Analysis."
      American Economic Review 68, No. 3 (1978):   374-85.

      Deals   with   problems related   to the   provision   of   social
      infrastructure (for example, streets,   roads,   schools,   and
      public safety facilities) in communities experiencing rapid,
      and probably short-lived, growth associated with construction
      of large-scale projects.   The authors   develop a conceptual
      model wherein the marginal capital costs of excess capacities
      during the postconstruction period are equated with the
      marginal social   costs attributable to deteriorated services
      from somewhat lower levels of social infrastructure during the
      construction phase.

407. Galambos,   Eva C., and Arthur F. Schreiber.   *Making Sense Out*
      of Dollars: Economic Analysis for Local Government. PB 80-
      135668.   Springfield,   Virginia: National   Technical
      Information Service, 1978.   140 pp.

      Provides a how-to guide for economic analysis and planning
      for local government decision makers and staff.   The text
      presents basic economic concepts and methods that   have the
      greatest relevance to local government. Applicable to cities,
      counties,   or special districts of any size, step-by-step
      instructions for each method are provided to enable local
      government staffs to apply principles of economics to local
      problems.   Nine chapters present a selected method of economic
      analysis which is grouped into three problem areas: (1)
      understanding the local economy, (2) getting the most from
      each local government dollar, and (3) what is fair and who
      pays for whom. Each chapter begins by defining and describing
      a method of analysis and the major local government issues to

which the method applies.   The steps   and procedures required
to use the method are demonstrated on typical local government
problems.

408. Gilmore,   John S.   "Boom or Bust: Energy Development in the
      Western United States." *Energy and the Community.*   Edited
      by R. J. Burby and A. F. Bell.   Cambridge, Massachusetts:
      Ballinger Publishing Company, 1978. pp. 103-8.

      Describes some of the problems that have arisen with the
      building of power plants in isolated rural communities in the
      Rocky Mountains and Great Plains.   Problems associated with
      rapid population growth in Rock Springs and Green River,
      Wyoming, are discussed to illustrate the effects which often
      occur when large projects are developed in remote areas.

409. Goodwin,   H. L., and James R. Nelson.   *Changes in Oklahoma
      Municipal Government Costs From Industrial Development and
      Growth.* Bull. B-748. Stillwater, Oklahoma: Oklahoma Agri-
      cultural Experiment Station, 1979. 25 pp.

      Reports on development and testing of econometric models to
      determine the effects of industrial development on community
      expenditures. Eighty Oklahoma communities with populations of
      1,000 to 10,000 were selected for analysis.   None of these
      were located in Standard Metropolitan Statistical Areas
      (SMSAs).   Expenditures were examined for the following
      services: water and sewer, sanitation, streets, police
      protection, fire protection, parks and recreation, and general
      administration.

410. Gulley,   David A.   "Severance Taxes and Market Failure."
      Natural Resources Journal 22, No. 3 (1982):   597-617.

      Seeks an answer to the question, Does the severance tax
      effectively ameliorate market failure due to mining?   Gulley
      discusses the severance tax as a corrective instrument and as
      a political institution.

411. Hirsch,   Werner Z.   "Fiscal Impact of Industrialization on
      Local Schools." *The Review of Economics and Statistics* 46
      (1964): 191-99.

      Develops and tests a conceptual framework for determining
      whether additional school district revenues resulting from
      development of a new industry exceed added school costs.
      Indirect and induced effects, as well as direct effects, of
      the new industry are considered.   Identifies industry charac-
      teristics that are central to determining the nature of local
      fiscal effects.

412. Johnson, Fred. "A Pragmatic Methodology for Measuring Fiscal
      Impacts of Industrial Location." *Review of Regional Studies*
      4 (1974): 67–76.

      Presents a simplified procedure for approximating the
      effects of a new firm on local government costs and revenues.
      Input–output tables constructed for other, similar regions
      provide estimates of secondary employment impacts. Subsequent
      calculations are then used to estimate major public sector
      cost and revenue components.

413. Kee, Woo Sik. "Industrial Development and Its Impact on
      Local Finance." *Quarterly Review of Economics and Business*
      8, No. 3 (1968): 19–24.

      Develops a model for predicting marginal costs and revenues
      (to municipalities and school districts) resulting from
      location of a new industry. Key factors considered in the
      model include work force characteristics (income level,
      average dependents per worker, and residential location),
      industry's capital–labor ratio, and the incremental costs of
      school and town services required by employees.

414. Krutilla, John V., and Anthony C. Fisher. *Economic and
      Fiscal Impacts of Coal Development: Northern Great Plains.*
      Baltimore, Maryland: The Johns Hopkins University Press,
      1978. 208 pp.

      Summarizes results of a study to estimate the extent of
      economic and demographic growth and associated changes in
      costs and revenues of local governments associated with coal
      development in Montana's Powder River Basin. The authors
      conclude that while the state and counties in which coal is
      mined will benefit financially, towns and school districts
      will experience serious difficulties. The authors point to
      the need for transfer and equalization mechanisms that can
      facilitate an equitable distribution of burdens and gains
      among jurisdictions.

   * Lamont, William, George Beardsley, Andy Briscoe, John Carver,
      Dan Harrington, John Lansdowne, and James Murray. *Tax Lead
      Time Study: The Colorado Oil Shale Region.* Cited
      below as item 814.

415. Leholm, Arlen G., F. Larry Leistritz, and Thor A. Hertsgaard.
      "Fiscal Impact of a New Industry in a Rural Area: A Coal
      Gasification Plant in Western North Dakota." *Regional
      Science Perspectives* 6 (1976): 40–56.

      Describes a model for *ex ante* evaluation of the effect of a
      new industry on public sector costs and revenues. The model

considers the indirect and induced effects, as well as the
direct effects, of the new industry. Cost and revenue impacts
are evaluated for both state and local levels of government.

* Leistritz, F. Larry, and Steve H. Murdock. *The Socioeconomic
   Impact of Resource Development: Methods for Assessment.*
   Cited above as item 31.

416. Leistritz, F. Larry, Norman E. Toman, Steve H. Murdock, and
     John DeMontel. "Cash Flow Analysis for Energy Impacted
     Local Governments--A Case Study of Mercer County, North
     Dakota." *Socio-Economic Planning Sciences* 15 (1981): 165-
     74.

     Compares alternative energy resource taxation systems in
     terms of their implications for local governments and local
     planning. A fiscal impact simulation model is utilized to
     evaluate a severance-production tax system and, alternatively,
     an *ad valorem* property tax system. The results indicate that
     the form of taxation system adopted can have a major influence
     on the fiscal outlook for local governments in areas affected
     by large-scale development projects and thus on the welfare of
     area residents. These results also suggest that local fiscal
     considerations should receive careful attention in local
     planning and policy formulation.

417. Morse, George W., and Leroy J. Hushak. *Income and Fiscal
     Impacts of Manufacturing Plants in Southeast Ohio.* Res.
     Bull. 1108. Wooster, Ohio: Ohio Agricultural Research and
     Development Center, 1979. 21 pp.

     Develops and tests a model for examining the income and
     fiscal impacts of new or expanded manufacturing plants in
     rural communities. The income impacts examined are the net
     income to employees at the plant, the net income to other
     employees filling vacancies when plant employees shifted jobs,
     and the net income to local merchants and service sector
     employees. The fiscal impacts studied include changes in net
     revenues for city and county governments and for school
     districts. The distribution of benefits between local commun-
     ities, the county, and the region are also examined.

418. Mountain West Research, Inc. *Mineral Fuels Taxation in the
     Old West Region.* Billings, Montana: Old West Regional
     Commission, 1979. 293 pp.

     Summarizes findings of a comprehensive analysis of mineral
     fuels taxation in the Old West region states of Montana,
     Nebraska, North Dakota, South Dakota, and Wyoming. Major
     objectives of the analysis were to (1) summarize current
     mineral taxes in the five states, (2) describe the theoretical
     basis of mineral fuels taxation in the United States, (3)

briefly analyze and describe the mineral fuels industries of
the five-state region, (4) determine the probable direction
and magnitude of interstate shifting of taxes on coal, (5)
determine the relative importance of interstate shifting of
mineral fuels taxes in the Old West states compared to interstate shifting of other taxes by other states, and (6) investigate the total costs (economic and social) imposed on the
Old West states by mineral fuels development.

419. Murray,   James A., and Bruce A. Weber.   "The Impacts of Rapid
      Growth on the Provision and Financing of Local Public
      Services."   *Coping with Rapid Growth in Rural Communities*.
      Edited by Bruce A. Weber and Robert E. Howell.   (Item 592),
      pp. 97-113.

      Is divided into three major sections.   The first section is
      a review of studies of *expected* impacts of rapid growth on the
      local public sector.   The second section is a review of
      studies of *actual* impacts of rapid growth on local public
      services and finances.   The final section is an assessment
      both of our understanding of fiscal impacts of rapid growth
      and of the fiscal information needs of local decision makers
      in rapid-growth situations.   Some possible uses of fiscal
      impact information in helping local decision makers define and
      implement growth management options are discussed.

420. Peter   C. Nichols and Associates Ltd.   *Description of Munici-
      pal Fiscal Impact Model*.   Edmonton, Alberta: Northeast
      Alberta Regional Commission, 1979.   26 pp.

      Describes a model developed to estimate the private and
      public expenditures necessary to develop a new community in
      the oil sands region of northeast Alberta and to determine the
      fiscal impact to the local municipal and school authorities
      and to local taxpayers, of operating the community.

421. Pierroz,   Elaine N.   *Economic Practices Manual: A Handbook
      for Preparing an Economic Impact Assessment*.   Sacramento:
      State of California, Office of Planning and Research, 1978.
      301 pp.

      Prepared as a guide for local governments in assessing the
      economic efficiency and fiscal impacts of alternative land-use
      proposals. It contains chapters on assessing the impacts of a
      project or proposal on local population, employment, income,
      housing, land use, and the environment. A detailed discussion
      of fiscal impact analysis methods completes the work.

   * Purdy,   Bruce J., Elizabeth Peelle, Benson H. Bronfman, and
      David Bjornstad.   *A Post Licensing Study of Community*

Effects at Two Operating Nuclear Power Plants.
ORNL/NUREG/TM-22. Cited below as item 929.

422. Reeder, Richard J. *Nonmetropolitan Fiscal Indicators: A Review of Literature.* AGES 830908. Washington, D.C.: U.S. Department of Agriculture, Economic Research Service, 1984. 53 pp.

Discusses various types of fiscal indicators, their develop- ment, and their public policy importance. Three types of indicator analyses are then reviewed: comparative stress, effort and capacity, and fiscal trends. Examples are drawn from state and municipal government studies, and applications of the analysis are made to nonmetropolitan areas.

423. Skjei, Stephen S. "Difficulties in Assessing the Socioeco- nomic Impacts of Energy Facilities." *Energy and the Community.* Edited by R. J. Burby and A. F. Bell. Cambridge, Massachusetts: Ballinger Publishing Company, 1978. pp. 111-14.

Discusses effects of constructing nuclear power plants on nearby communities. Three characteristics of these plants which are especially important in determining impacts are their labor force, location, and taxable value.

424. Stinson, Thomas F. "Fiscal Status of Local Governments." *Nonmetropolitan America in Transition.* Edited by Amos H. Hawley and S. M. Mazie. Chapel Hill, North Carolina: University of North Carolina Press, 1981. pp. 736-66.

Contains three major sections. The first and largest presents material from the *1977 Census of Governments* describing local government finance outside the metro areas. Current (1977) expenditures and revenues are also compared with those in 1962 and 1972 to provide a historical perspec- tive and a view of long-term trends. The second section divides nonmetropolitan counties into four groups based on their population growth rates and identifies some special problems that may affect them. The third section discusses the effect of inflation on local government finances.

425. Stinson, Thomas F. "State Severance Taxes and the Federal System." *Mining Engineering* 34, No. 4 (1982): 382-86.

Examines the controversy over state severance taxes and cites implications of two recent U.S. Supreme Court decisions.

* Stinson, Thomas F., Lloyd D. Bender, and Stanley W. Voelker. *Northern Great Plains Coal Mining: Regional Impacts.* Agr. Info. Bull. No. 452. Cited below as item 913.

426. Stinson, Thomas F., and George S. Temple. *State Mineral Taxes, 1982.* RDRR No. 36. Washington, D.C.: U.S. Department of Agriculture, Economic Research Service, 1983. 65 pp.

   Summarizes mineral tax laws in effect in thirty-one states as of January 1983. Revenues from mineral taxes accounted for more than 20% of total state tax revenues in seven states in 1980.

427. Stinson, Thomas F., and Stanley W. Voelker. *Coal Development in the Northern Great Plains: The Impact on Revenues of State and Local Governments.* Agr. Econ. Rpt. No. 394. Washington, D.C.: U.S. Department of Agriculture, 1978. 66 pp.

   Reports detailed estimates of the state and local taxes that would be paid by three different-sized coal mines and their employees in Montana, North Dakota, South Dakota, and Wyoming. The estimates were obtained by using the ENERGYTAX simulation model.

428. Stinson, Thomas F., and Stanley W. Voelker. *Energy Development: Initial Effects on Government Revenues.* WRDC Pub. No. 15. Corvallis, Oregon: Western Rural Development Center, 1982. 43 pp.

   Describes the front-end problems which will accompany coal development and electric generating plant construction in the northern Great Plains. The ENERGYTAX simulation model is used to obtain timepaths for new state and local government revenues from energy projects typical of those being developed in the region. Revenues for each year of construction and startup (three years for the mine, five years for the power plant) and for the new projects' first five years of operation are shown for the state, school district, city, and county governments in Montana, North Dakota, and Wyoming. Tax and aid systems differ considerably among these states, so the individual revenue paths provide useful insights into the advantages and disadvantages of various taxes and aids during periods of rapid growth.

429. Stuart/Nichols Associates. *The Fiscal Impacts of Energy Development on Wyoming's Local Governments.* Denver, Colorado: Stuart/Nichols Associates, 1979. 180 pp.

Reports on the comprehensive analysis of statewide impacts of the development of Wyoming's energy resources, as well as on the ability of the affected local governments to manage that growth. Mitigation measures are also presented.

430. Voelker, Stanley W. *State and Local Taxes Affected by Energy Developments in Selected Western States.* EPA-600/7-81-005. Washington, D.C.: U.S. Environmental Protection Agency and U.S. Department of Agriculture, 1981. 63 pp.

Summarizes and compares the state and local revenue systems of five western states--Colorado, Montana, North Dakota, Utah, and Wyoming. The descriptions are based on the laws in effect on July 1, 1980. This report was prepared primarily for administrators and research workers concerned with assessing the local fiscal impacts of coal mining and energy developments.

431. Woods, Mike D., and Lonnie L. Jones. "Measuring the Fiscal Impacts of New Industry in Small Towns." *Municipal Management: A Journal* 5 (1982-83): 48-56.

Presents an industrial impact model which analyzes the net economic impact of industrial development in a rural community. The authors point out that rising public service costs, water shortages, decreasing federal support, and many other problems are causing communities to examine the case for industrial growth more closely.

Integrated Assessment Modeling

432. Adams, R. C., R. J. Moe, and M. J. Scott. *The Metropolitan and State Economic Regions (MASTER) Model--Overview.* PNL-4749. Richland, Washington: Pacific Northwest Laboratory, 1983. 45 pp.

Describes the Metropolitan and State Economic Regions (MASTER) model, a multiregional economic model that was developed by researchers at Battelle, Pacific Northwest Laboratories. MASTER was designed to forecast regional economic activity and assess the regional economic impacts caused by national and regional economic changes (e.g., interest rate fluctuations, energy price changes, construction and operation of a nuclear waste storage facility, shutdown of major industrial operations). MASTER can be applied to any or all of the 268 Standard Metropolitan Statistical Areas (SMSAs), 48 Rest Of State Areas (ROSAs), counties, and states in the continental United States.

433. Anderson,   Eric,   and   Bill   Hannigan.   *Arizona Economic-*
      Demographic Projection Model: A Summary Report and Techni-
      cal Description.   Phoenix,   Arizona: Office of Economic
      Planning and Development, 1977. 204 pp.

      Describes   an economic–demographic model which is used to
      project changes in economic activity and population for
      counties in Arizona.   The report briefly reviews the history
      of economic modeling in Arizona, describes the process by
      which the   research effort   has been   incorporated   into state
      planning, outlines the model's structure and data bases, and
      presents baseline economic and demographic projections.

434. Armstrong,   J. Scott.   *Long-Range Forecasting: From Crystal*
      Ball to   Computer.   New York: John Wiley and Sons, 1978.
      612 pp.

      Is   a guide to the evaluation of long-range forecasting
      methods.   The   book   includes   discussions   of   problem
      structuring, implementing forecasting methods and getting them
      accepted, selecting the most appropriate method for the
      problem, and evaluating forecasting models. The final section
      is a summary of research from a variety of areas; about 1,300
      books and articles primarily from the social and behavioral
      areas were reviewed.

435. Baldwin,   Thomas E., Diana Dixon–Davis, Erik J. Stenehjem, and
      Thomas D. Wolsko.   *A Socioeconomic Assessment of Energy*
      Development in a Small Rural County: Coal Gasification in
      Mercer County, North Dakota. 2 volumes. Argonne, Illinois:
      Argonne National Laboratory, 1976. 411 pp.

      Presents an assessment of economic, demographic, public
      service, fiscal, and social impacts likely to result from
      development of a large coal conversion complex in a rural
      area.   The assessment (presented in volume 1) delineates major
      socioeconomic effects and attempts to identify and understand
      the character of the underlying causal factors. A methodology
      for conducting future assessments is presented in volume 2.

436. Ballard,   Kenneth P., and Robert M. Wendling.   "The National-
      Regional Impact Evaluation System: A Spatial Model of U.S.
      Economic and Demographic Activity."   *Journal of Regional*
      Science 20, No. 2 (1980):   143–58.

      Discusses the National-Regional Impact Evaluation System
      (NRIES), a methodology developed at the Bureau of Economic
      Analysis, which is comprised of 51 state econometric models
      that are integrated into a model of the U.S. economy.   NRIES
      incorporates explicit interregional   and regional-national
      linkages in a bottom-up approach to regional modeling.

437. Baxter, Jeffrey D., and Mark Evans. "Potential Impacts of Energy Development on Population Growth and the Economy of the Four Corners States." *Energy Development in the South-west: Problems of Water, Fish, and Wildlife in the Upper Colorado River Basin.* Edited by Walter O. Spofford, Jr., Alfred L. Parker, and Allen V. Kneese. Research Paper R-18. Washington, D.C.: Resources for the Future, 1980. pp. 201-99.

Describes an economic-demographic model used to assess impacts of energy development in Arizona, Colorado, New Mexico, and Utah. The modeling system features an inter-regional input-output model linked to a cohort-survival population model. Four energy development scenarios spanning the range of possible future levels of development are evaluated using the model.

438. Beckhelm, Terrance L., James A. Chalmers, and William M. Hannigan. *ATOM3: A Description of ATOM3 and of the Research Related to Its Development.* Washington, D.C.: Four Corners Regional Commission, 1975. 153 pp.

Describes an economic-demographic simulation model developed to support state and substate planning efforts in Arizona. The Arizona Trade-Off Model (ATOM) utilizes an input-output module to estimate economic impacts and a cohort-component model to project population change. Economic and demographic projections are linked through a labor-market simulation module which compares the supply of and demand for labor and estimates the level of net in- or outmigration necessary to balance supply and demand.

439. Bender, Lloyd D., George S. Temple, and Larry C. Parcels. *An Introduction To The COALTOWN Impact Assessment Model.* EPA 600/7-80-146. Washington, D.C.: U.S. Department of Agriculture and U.S. Environmental Protection Agency, 1980. 29 pp.

Describes COALTOWN, a computerized system that simulates future employment, population, wage levels, migration, state and local tax receipts, intergovernmental transfers, and local government expenditures for counties in Montana, Wyoming, and North Dakota.

440. Carlson, John F., and G. Fred Doll. *The North Platte River Basin Economic Simulation Model.* Technical Report and Supplement. Laramie, Wyoming: University of Wyoming, Water Resources Research Institute, 1976. 211 pp.

Describes a regional economic-demographic simulation model developed for the North Platte River Basin area of Wyoming. The model has seven major sectors or modules: (1) demographic module, (2) employment module, (3) labor market module, (4) income sector, (5) agricultural sector, (6) water requirements module, and (7) housing sector.

441.   Chase, Robert A., Randal C. Coon, Connie L. Chase, Carlena F. Vocke, Rebecca J. Vuchetich, F. Larry Leistritz, Thor A. Hertsgaard, William Ransom-Nelson, Steve H. Murdock, Pai-Sung Yang, and Rakesh Sharma. *Expansion and Adaptation of the North Dakota Economic-Demographic Assessment Model (NEDAM) for Montana: Technical Description.* Ag. Econ. Misc. Rpt. No. 61. Fargo: North Dakota Agricultural Experiment Station, 1982. 225 pp.

Describes the structural and data base modifications necessary to adapt an existing computerized socioeconomic impact assessment model (North Dakota Economic-Demographic Assessment Model or NEDAM) for use in Montana. The adapted model projects personal income at the multicounty regional level and estimates employment, population, and public sector costs and revenues at county and community levels.

See also item 466.

442.   Clapham, W. B., Jr., and R. F. Pestel. "On the Scenario Approach to Simulation Modeling for Complex Policy Assessment and Design." *Policy Sciences* 11 (1979): 157-77.

Reviews the major issues posed by scenario-based simulation modeling in the policy process by using agricultural policy as an example of a complex decision arena. Scenario-writing provides a way of ordering understanding and judgment about different phenomena to help users interact most effectively with a model and to insure that the perspectives of the model are most appropriate to the needs of the decision maker.

443.   Clayton, Kenneth C., and David Whittington. "The Economics of Community Growth: An Impact Model." *Southern Journal of Agricultural Economics* 9, No. 1 (1977): 63-69.

Describes a model that permits ex ante evaluation of the economic effects of community growth. The model is structured as four modules which respectively project (1) demographic impacts (e.g., employment, population, housing, school enrollment), (2) private sector economic impacts (e.g., sales, income), (3) public sector impacts (e.g., city and county tax revenues, public service costs), and (4) school district impacts (e.g., changes in tax revenues, operating costs, capital expenditures). Application of the model is illustrated through analysis of a new manufacturing plant at Gainesville, Florida.

444. Cockhead, Peter, and Richard Masters. "Forecasting in Grampian: Three Dimensions of Integration." *Town Planning Review* 55, No. 4 (1984): 473-88.

Points out that integrated forecasting is usually discussed in terms of the modeling of mutual compatibility linkages between forecasts of population, employment, and housing. The authors suggest that this is only one facet of the "integration" procedures which are necessary in meeting the varied population-based forecasting requirements within a local authority. From a description of the forecasting approach and models developed within Grampian Regional Council, three dimensions of integration are identified-- horizontal, vertical, and organizational. One conclusion drawn is that the effectiveness of forecasting within the authority is particularly dependent upon the procedures for vertical and organizational integration whereby forecasts are translated into operational programs.

445. Darling, David L. *An Industrial Impact Model For Indiana Counties.* Station Bulletin No. 229. West Lafayette, Indiana: Purdue University Agricultural Experiment Station, 1979. 59 pp.

Describes a model to assist local decision makers in calculating the expected revenues and expenditures attribut- able to a proposed economic change, such as the construction and operation of a new manufacturing facility. The report includes a description of the model's structure, assumptions inherent in its design, sources and preparation of input data, and an example application.

446. Denver Research Institute and Resource Planning Associates. *Socioeconomic Impacts of Western Energy Resource Develop- ment.* Vol. 1, *Summary and Implications.* Vol. 2, *Assessment Methodologies.* Vol. 3, *Case Studies.* Vol. 4, *Computer Model Documentation.* Denver, Colorado: University of Denver, Denver Research Institute, 1979. 645 pp.

Assesses the state of the art in forecasting economic, demo- graphic, public service, fiscal, and social impacts of energy development in the western United States. Volume 1 contains a general analysis of the state of the art, explores the impli- cations of uncertainty for both preparers and users of impact assessments, and recommends performance and evaluation standards for future assessments. Volumes 2, 3, and 4 are addressed to practitioners in the field. Volume 2 provides detailed analyses of assessment needs and alternative approaches for each component of a typical assessment process. It also provides a step-by-step description of a demonstration methodology for each component. Volume 3 describes the appli- cation of the demonstration methodology in two case study

areas.   Volume 4 documents the computer program that incorporates the demonstration methodology.

447. DeSouza,   Glenn   R.   *System Methods for Socioeconomic and
      Environmental Impact Analysis.*   Lexington, Massachusetts:
      Lexington Books, 1979. 163 pp.

      Provides a description of an   integrated socioeconomic
      assessment model called SIMPACT.   The modeling system was
      developed during preparation of an environmental assessment
      for a steel mill proposed for development by the U.S. Steel
      Corporation.   The system consists of four linked submodels.
      The Economic and Demographic Model is used to predict the
      spinoff economic activity generated by the primary project and
      associated migration.   The Community Planning Model is used to
      estimate   requirements   by   inmigrants for   various types of
      infrastructure.   The Fiscal Model is used to forecast the
      changes in revenues and expenditures that will occur at the
      municipal, school district, county, and state levels.   The
      Environmental Model is used to predict the air emissions and
      water effluent associated with the secondary development.
      Each submodel is described, and some concluding suggestions
      are offered to individuals conducting socioeconomic studies.

448. Dewhurst,   Roger.   "Forecasting in Greater Manchester: A
      Multi-Regional Approach."   *Town Planning Review* 55, No. 4
      (1984): 453-72.

      Outlines the approach adopted by the Greater Manchester
      Council to population, household, and labor-supply fore-
      casting.   An integrated   forecasting framework is used,
      including economic and housing variables as well as demo-
      graphic factors.   The paper begins by describing the main
      considerations in developing the suite of forecasting models,
      and later proceeds to examine two multiregional models in
      detail.   A third section deals with the demographic data base
      used in conjunction with the models and highlights the diffi-
      culties of obtaining consistent information from a wide
      variety of sources.

449. ECOS   Management Criteria, Inc.   *The Validation and Improve-
      ment of Socioeconomic Forecasting Methodologies.*   Prepared
      for U.S. Geological Survey.   Cypress, California: ECOS
      Management Criteria, Inc., 1982. 296 pp.

      Evaluates twenty-seven integrated socioeconomic impact
      assessment models in terms of their internal logic, data
      requirements, types of output information provided, and the
      areal specificity of the analysis.   Three of the models
      (BREAM, COALTOWN, and REAP) were selected through this process
      for a more intensive evaluation, using a case study approach.
      A number of recommendations are offered to improve the

accuracy and usefulness of model forecasts in future applications.

450. Energy Research and Development Administration, Office of Planning, Analysis, and Evaluation. *Models and Methodologies for Assessing the Impact of Energy Development.* ERDA 77-91. Washington, D.C.: Energy Research and Development Administration, 1977. 30 pp.

Identifies models and methodologies relevant to assessing the impact of energy development projects on local communities. The report surveys the major land use, transportation, economic-demographic, and simulation models and methodologies to analyze their performance vis-a-vis data requirements, model validity, and ease of use.

451. Evans, Mark, and Jeffrey Baxter. "Regionalizing National Projections With a Multiregional Input-Output Model Linked to a Demographic Model." *The Annals of Regional Science* 14, No. 1 (1980): 57-71.

Reports that multiregional input-output has long been recognized as a tool that provides an appropriate framework for considering regional growth and development questions, but that implementation problems have impeded utilization of this methodology. The authors discuss how several of these problems have been partially overcome with a multiregional economic-demographic model of the Southwest. The model is used to regionalize projections from a national dynamic input-output model.

452. Extension Committee on Organization and Policy, Task Force on Impact Analysis. *How Extension Can Help Communities Conduct Impact Analyses.* I-04-82-1M-E. Madison, Wisconsin: University of Wisconsin, Department of Agricultural Journalism, 1982. 31 pp.

Is intended to provide guidance to extension agents assisting communities experiencing economic development. The report is divided into five sections examining (1) development impacts on the private sector; (2) development impacts on local government; (3) the usefulness and data requirements of input-output and export base models; (4) nonmarket impacts from economic development; and (5) the role of extension in economic impact analysis. The various sections discuss data needs and implementation considerations for community impact analysis, often cataloging in tabular form the types of questions extension agents will need to answer. The report also includes extensive reference material.

453. Ford,   Andrew.   *Summary Description of the BOOM1 Model.* LA-
      6424-MS.   Los Alamos, New Mexico: Los Alamos Scientific
      Laboratory, 1976.   14 pp.

      Describes the principal features of a computer model, BOOM1,
      designed to simulate the "boom town" impacts that may result
      from locating large energy facilities near small, isolated
      communities.   Model outputs include population, permanent and
      mobile homes, public facilities and municipal debt, local
      property tax rate and state transfer payments, construction
      work force, construction productivity, and retail and service
      facilities. The model can be used to simulate the behavior of
      these variables over a time span covering the preboom,
      construction, operation, and retirement phases of an energy
      project.

454. Gulley,   David A.   "Models and Mitigation in Energy Boom-
      Towns." *Resources and Energy* 4(1982): 87-104.

      Examines the growing use of fiscal impact models to assess
      the effect of major changes in regional economic activity on
      the finances of local governments, and raises issues involved
      in the development and use of assessment models.   The
      conceptual methodology of fiscal impact assessment has become
      well established, but as in all modeling, large practical
      problems remain.   Models are not necessarily used in a
      disinterested fashion, perhaps because many public processes
      are characterized by an adversary mode of analysis.   The rise
      of impact assessment reveals conflicts in public policy, as
      well as the role of social and mathematical sciences in the
      implementation of policy.

455. Hamilton,   H. R., S. E. Goldstone, Jerome W. Milliman, A. L.
      Pugh, E. B. Roberts, and A. Zellner. *Systems Simulation for
      Regional Analysis: An Application to River-Basin Planning.*
      Cambridge, Massachusetts: The MIT Press, 1969. 395 pp.

      Explores applications of systems simulation to regional
      analysis. A model of the Susquehanna River Basin is described
      in detail.   The authors believe that the findings of their
      research and the model developed for the Susquehanna region
      are suggestive of other applications and could serve as a
      starting point for the construction of other regional simula-
      tion models. In fact, the Susquehanna Model has had consider-
      able influence on subsequent regional modeling efforts.

456. Hamm,   Rita R., Steve H. Murdock, F. Larry Leistritz, and
      Robert A. Chase.   "A Socioeconomic Impact Model for
      Assessing the Effects of a High-Level Nuclear Waste Reposi-
      tory Site." *Impact Assessment Bulletin* 3, No. 1 (1984):
      6-19.

Describes the SocioEconomic Analysis of Repository Siting (SEARS) impact assessment model. The SEARS model projects economic, demographic, fiscal, and public service impacts associated with the construction and operation of a high-level nuclear waste repository.

457. Henningson, Durham, and Richardson. *A Generalized Regional Socioeconomic Analysis System.* 2 volumes. Norton AFB, California: U.S. Air Force, 1982. 668 pp.

Describes a comprehensive regional socioeconomic modeling system developed for the U.S. Air Force and used extensively in impact studies for the MX missile system. The model provides analyses of economic, demographic, public services, land use, and public finance impacts of military projects. Data inputs, output formats, and user procedures are described in detail.

458. Henry, Mark S. "On the Value of Economic-Demographic Forecasts to Local Government." *The Annals of Regional Science* 14, No. 1 (1980): 12-20.

Points out that both the relative cost and accuracy of alternative forecasting techniques should be considered by local decision makers. The contention of this paper is that estimates of the benefits of increased accuracy from more expensive economic-demographic forecasting models are necessary prior to making a rational choice over how much to spend on model construction. A case study using western North Dakota coal development and its economic-demographic impacts is used to illustrate a method for evaluating these benefits in the public sector.

459. Huskey, Lee, and Jim Kerr. *Small Community Population Impact Model.* Special Report No. 4. Anchorage: U.S. Bureau of Land Management, Alaska Outer Continental Shelf Office, 1980. 64 pp.

Describes a small community impact model (SCIMP) which can be used to describe the population and employment impacts of outer continental shelf (OCS) petroleum development. An example of the model's applications is provided by analyzing the impact of OCS development in the Norton Sound (Bering Sea) on Nome.

460. Joun, Richard Y. P., and Richard S. Conway, Jr. "Regional Economic-Demographic Forecasting Models: A Case Study of the Washington and Hawaii Models." *Socio-Economic Planning Sciences* 17, No. 5-6 (1983): 345-53.

Presents a case study of two regional economic-demographic models: the Washington Projection and Simulation Model and Hawaii Economic-Population Projection and Simulation Model. *Ex ante* prediction tests demonstrate the models' forecasting capabilities. Simulations with the Washington model are conducted to show more clearly the interaction between economic and demographic activity in a region.

461. Knapp, Gunnar. *The Rural Alaska Model: A Description and Documentation.* Anchorage: University of Alaska, Institute of Social and Economic Research, 1983. 86 pp.

Describes the Rural Alaska Model (RAM), which was developed to project population and employment changes in small communities in Alaska. The model also may be used to examine the impacts of a specific project, such as outer continental shelf oil development, upon population, resident employment, and separate (enclave) employment of nonresidents.

462. Kresge, David T., and Daniel A. Seiver. "Planning for a Resource-Rich Region: The Case of Alaska." *The American Economic Review* 68, No. 2 (1978): 99-104.

Describes an econometric model developed to estimate the regional economic impacts of resource development and, more specifically, to evaluate regional policies designed to deal with those impacts. The model, called Man-in-the-Arctic Program or MAP, is used to analyze the situation confronting Alaska as its petroleum resources are developed to meet the nation's energy needs.

463. Leistritz, F. Larry, and Lloyd D. Bender, eds. *Problems of Modeling Local Impacts of Energy Development.* Great Plains Agricultural Council Pub. No. 96. Lincoln, Nebraska: Great Plains Agricultural Council and U.S. Environmental Protection Agency, 1980. 160 pp.

Contains nine papers dealing with the evaluation and subsequent management of local economic, demographic, public service, fiscal, and social impacts of energy resource development. The papers address the following major topics: (1) current status of socioeconomic impact models and techniques, (2) long-term structural changes in rural economies and their implications for impact modeling, (3) labor market implications of large-scale development, (4) advanced approaches to impact assessment and data analysis, and (5) use of impact models in the policy process.

*   Leistritz, F. Larry, and Steve H. Murdock. *The Socioeconomic Impact of Resource Development: Methods for Assessment.* Cited above as item 31.

464. Leistritz, F. Larry, Steve H. Murdock, and Robert A. Chase.
      "Socioeconomic   Impact   Assessment   Models: Review and
      Evaluation."   *Impact Assessment Bulletin* 1, No. 4 (1982):
      30–43.

      Compares characteristics of four socioeconomic models (BOOM-
      1, BREAM, RED/TAMS, and SEAM), evaluates their suitability for
      impact analysis, discusses factors affecting validity of model
      projections, and recommends ways of improving the accuracy and
      utility of impact assessments.

465. Leistritz,   F. Larry, Steve H. Murdock, Norman E.   Toman, and
      Thor A. Hertsgaard.   "A Model for Projecting Localized
      Economic, Demographic, and Fiscal Impacts of Large-Scale
      Projects." *Western Journal of Agricultural Economics* 4, No.
      2 (1979): 1–16.

      Describes and demonstrates the utility of a computerized
      model for projecting the effects of large-scale developments
      on business activity, personal income, employment, population,
      requirements for selected public and quasi-public services,
      and public sector costs and revenues.   The structure, data
      base, and interrelationships of each of the model's six major
      components are described.   Its validity in simulating economic
      and demographic changes at regional, county, and municipal
      levels is then evaluated.

466. Leistritz,   F. Larry, William Ransom-Nelson, Richard W.
      Rathge, Randal C. Coon, Robert A. Chase, Thor A. Hertsgaard,
      Steve H. Murdock, Norman E. Toman, Rakesh Sharma, and Pai-
      Sung Yang. *North Dakota Economic-Demographic Assessment
      Model (NEDAM): Technical Description.* Agr. Econ. Rpt. No.
      158. Fargo: North Dakota Agricultural Experiment Station,
      1982. 231 pp.

      Describes the structure, capabilities, data base, and user
      procedures of an integrated socioeconomic assessment model.
      The model provides baseline and impact projections at
      regional, county, and municipal levels for such variables as
      type of employment, population by age and gender, school
      enrollments, housing requirements, and public-sector costs and
      revenues by type.

467. Louis Berger and Associates, Inc.   *Forecasting Enclave
      Development Alternatives and Their Related Impacts on
      Alaskan Coastal Communities as a Result of OCS Development.*
      Tech. Rpt. No. 76. Anchorage: U.S. Department of Interior,
      Minerals Management Service, 1982. 269 pp.

      Presents a model designed to assist MMS-OCS planners in
      predicting the socioeconomic and cultural impacts on Alaskan
      communities associated with offshore oil exploration and

development.   The model provides a synthesis of past research
and new Alaskan field work concerning the ways in which these
impacts   will   differ,   given   different   types   of onshore
industrial facilities and different levels of isolation from,
or integration   with,   coastal   and   predominantly native
communities.

468.   McDonald, J. M., ed.   *Computer Models and Forecasting Socio-
       Economic Impacts of Growth and Development.*   Edmonton,
       Alberta: University of Alberta, Faculty of Extension, 1980.
       398 pp.

       Contains thirteen   papers which describe   alternative models
       for projecting local economic, demographic, public service,
       and fiscal impacts of large-scale development projects.   Some
       papers also discuss experiences in using such models to guide
       community and regional planning and offer suggestions for more
       effective utilization of computerized modeling systems.

   *   Milliman,   Jerome W.   "Large-Scale Models for Forecasting
       Regional Economic Activity: A Survey." *Essays in Regional
       Economics.*   Edited by J. F. Kain and J. R. Meyer.   Cited
       above as item 155.

469.   Monts, J. Kenneth.   *BOOMP User's Guide.*   Austin: University
       of Texas, Center for Energy Studies, 1978.   61 pp.

       Describes the   structure and user's procedures of the BOOMP
       model.   Derived from the BOOM1 system, BOOMP incorporates
       additional features which allow public sector impacts to be
       modeled in a more detailed fashion.   The public sector is
       disaggregated into the education, police protection, fire
       protection,   water,   sanitary   sewerage,   and   residual
       subsectors.

470.   Monts,   J. Kenneth, and E. Ray Bareiss.   *CLIPS: Community-
       Level Impacts Projection System.*   Austin: University of
       Texas, Center for Energy Studies, 1979.   164 pp.

       Describes a computerized, interactive system for projecting
       localized impacts of large development projects.   Economic,
       demographic, and public service effects of project development
       are evaluated.   Impacts are projected at county and community
       (town) levels.   The report describes the model's conceptual
       basis, structure, data sources, and operational procedures.

471.   Mountain   West Research, Inc.   *Bureau of Reclamation Economic
       Assessment Model (BREAM):   Technical Description and User's
       Guide.*   Denver, Colorado: U.S. Bureau of Reclamation, 1981.
       196 pp.

Describes an economic-demographic assessment model (BREAM) developed for the Bureau of Reclamation as a tool to analyze the interrelated economic and demographic effects of water resource development decisions. The model's principal purpose is to provide projections of employment, income, and population for county and multicounty areas. The model is based on recognition that economic change and demographic change are interrelated because of the influence of employment opportunities on migration.

472. Murdock, Steve H., and F. Larry Leistritz. "Selecting Socio-economic Assessment Models: A Discussion of Criteria and Selected Models." *Journal of Environmental Management* 10 (1980): 241-52.

Describes criteria appropriate for use in evaluating socio-economic impact assessment models and presents a comparison of twelve widely used models in terms of these criteria. The criteria seen as essential in the evaluation of these models include the information needs of the user, the methodological characteristics of the model, and the user attributes of the system.

473. Murdock, Steve H., F. Larry Leistritz, and Lonnie L. Jones. "Economic-Demographic Impact Assessment Models: Character istics and Considerations in Adaptation and Development." *Proceedings of a Workshop on Community Impact Analysis (University of Kentucky, May 24-26, 1982).* Mississippi State, Mississippi: Southern Rural Development Center, 1982. pp. 13-40.

Provides a partial overview of economic-demographic impact modeling procedures, describes their major characteristics, and suggests factors that should be examined by any user who is considering adapting or developing such a model. Specifically, the authors present a brief history of such models as a means of describing the context of development of such models, examine criteria for evaluating such models, provide an evaluation of several of the most widely used models, and discuss key factors that should be considered in the adaptation and development of such models.

474. Murdock, Steve H., F. Larry Leistritz, Lonnie L. Jones, Donald Andrews, Brenda Wilson, Darrell Fannin, and John de Montel. *Texas Assessment Modeling System (TAMS): Technical Description.* College Station, Texas: Texas A&M University, Department of Rural Sociology and Agricultural Economics, 1979. 120 pp.

Presents a technical description of a computerized model for projecting economic, demographic, fiscal, and social impacts of energy development projects. The model projects the local

142	*Methodology of SIA*

and regional impacts of lignite development projects in
Texas.

475.	Murphy/Williams	Urban	Planning	and	Housing	Consultants.
*Socioeconomic Impact Assessment:	A Methodology Applied to
Synthetic Fuels.*	HCP/L2516-01.	Washington,	D.C.:	U.S.
Department of Energy, 1978.	79 pp.

Presents a methodology for projecting socioeconomic impacts
as part of a programmatic environmental impact statement for
synthetic fuels. The report is designed as a handbook for use
by governmental officials and others concerned with the
economic and social consequences of large-scale projects.

476.	Nelson,	Marlys Knutson.	*Socioeconomic Impact Models:	An
Annotated Bibliography.*	ERS	Staff	Rpt.	AGES	850228.
Washington, D.C.:	U.S. Department of Agriculture, Economic
Research Service, 1985.	37 pp.

Examines recent literature related to socioeconomic impact
assessment and planning models. This bibliography contains
thirty-one references to twenty specific impact models. In
addition, references are listed for other related topics:
survey or summary articles, pertinent quantitative techniques,
economic base or econometric forecasting, fiscal models,
population and settlement patterns, employment, and coal or
energy. It is intended as a research tool for students and
users of impact models for their various purposes, notably
equilibrium planning, estimating impact effects of development
projects, and planning for future contingencies.

477.	North	Central	Regional	Center	for	Rural	Development.
Proceedings of the Ex Ante Growth Impact Models Conference.
Ames, Iowa: Iowa State University, 1979.	253 pp.

Covers three areas:	(1) ex ante estimation of private
sector impacts, (2) ex ante estimation of public sector
impacts, and (3) the extension use of the models. Specifically, topics include distributional issues, estimating local
income multipliers, distribution of labor supply, and definition and estimation of private sector benefits.

478.	Olsen, R. J., G. W. Westley, H. W. Herzog, Jr., C. R. Kerley,
D. J. Bjornstad, D. P. Vogt, L. G. Bray, S. T. Grady,
R. A. Nakosteen.	*MULTIREGION:	A Simulation-Forecasting
Model of BEA Economic Area Population and Employment.*
ORNL/RUS-25.	Oak Ridge,	Tennessee:	Oak Ridge National
Laboratory, 1977.	410 pp.

Documents the development of MULTIREGION--a computer model
of regional and interregional socioeconomic development. The

MULTIREGION model interprets the economy of each BEA economic area as a labor market, measures all activity in terms of people as members of the population (labor supply) or as employees (labor demand), and simultaneously simulates or forecasts the demands and supplies of labor in all BEA economic areas at five-year intervals.

479. Power, G., W. Gillespie, D. Wittkowski, and R. Rink. "Computer Modeling of Boomtown Housing: The Fort McMurray Study." *Canadian Journal of Regional Science* 3, No. 1 (Spring 1980): 29–48.

Reports on the results of adapting a computerized economic-demographic model (BOOMH) for use in the boom town of Fort McMurray, Alberta, during the Syncrude project's planning and construction phase of 1971–1979. The model was found to be reasonably successful in reproducing major features of the construction boom.

480. Robinson, D. P., J. W. Hamilton, R. D. Webster, and M. J. Olson. *Economic Impact Forecast System (EIFS) II: User's Manual, Updated Edition.* Tech. Rpt. N-69 (Revised). Champaign, Illinois: U.S. Army Corps of Engineers, Construction Engineering Research Laboratory, 1984. 201 pp.

Describes the Economic Impact Forecast System (EIFS), a computer system which provides information useful for estimating the socioeconomic impacts caused by new military projects and activities. This report provides information for obtaining and initially interpreting output from current and future versions of EIFS.

481. Sanderson, Warren C. *Economic-Demographic Simulation Models: A Review of Their Usefulness for Policy Analysis.* Population and Agricultural Development Technical Paper 4. Rome: Food and Agriculture Organization of the United Nations, 1978. 161 pp.

Reviews the usefulness for policy analysis of economic-demographic simulation models with emphasis on the relevance of the current state of the art for agricultural development planners in developing countries. Five models are evaluated: (1) the Bachue-Philippines Model, (2) the Tempo II Model, (3) the Simon Model, (4) the Food and Agriculture Organization (FAO) Model, and (5) the Kelley, Williamson, and Cheetham Model.

482. Sandoval, A. David. *A Review and Application of MULTIREGION as a Regional Economic Impact and Projection Model.*

DOE/EIA-0183/7.   Washington, D.C.:   U.S. Department of
Energy, 1979.   44 pp.

Presents an overview of the regional economic projections
developed by the Oak Ridge National Laboratory using their
MULTIREGION model.   The MULTIREGION results are compared with
other economic and demographic projections to help determine
its capability as a regional economic impact and projection
model.

483.   Schussman, Klaus.   "Forecasting Methods and the Munich Infra-
       structure Planning System."   *Town Planning Review* 55, No. 4
       (1984):   435-52.

       Describes and evaluates forecasting methods and tools for
       infrastructure planning with reference to the operation of
       urban planning in Munich.   A set of relevant, more or less
       interrelated models in the fields of population, housing,
       social and technical infrastructure, employment, and location
       of jobs is discussed, and the results of the models are
       compared with actual developments.   Conclusions are drawn
       about the problems of reconciling the models' results, about
       problems of dialogue between politicians and planners, and
       about the prospects for and the scope of strategic urban
       (infrastructure) planning.

484.   Sinz,   Manfred.   "Integrated Population   and Employment
       Projections for National-Regional Planning in the Federal
       Republic of Germany."   *Town Planning Review* 55, No. 4
       (1984):   420-34.

       Presents the concepts, methodological approach, assumptions,
       and results of a long-term forecast for eighty-eight federal
       planning regions in West Germany.   It is emphasized that
       population and employment projections for policy consultation
       purposes must be of an intermediate complexity in order to
       remain transparent and reconstructable.   To facilitate the
       interpretation of the forecasting results, a typology of the
       planning regions along the dimension of forecasted labor
       market developments is presented.   Rural peripheral regions
       with employment problems stemming mainly from demographic
       factors and old industrial regions with severe labor market
       imbalances caused by structural change are found to be the
       actual and future problem regions in West Germany.

485.   South,   David W., and Mark J. Bragen.   *User's Guide: The
       Social and Economic Assessment Model (SEAM)--A County Level
       Energy Facility Impact Assessment Model*. Argonne, Illinois:
       Argonne National Laboratory, 1981.   148 pp.

       Describes   the   logic and structure of   the SEAM modeling
       system and describes procedures for utilizing the model.

Procedures for both interactive and batch processing modes of use are described.

486. Southern Rural Development Center. *Proceedings of a Workshop on Community Impact Analysis (University of Kentucky, May 24-26, 1982).* Mississippi State, Mississippi: Southern Rural Development Center, 1982. 163 pp.

Summarizes presentations by research and extension personnel concerning their experiences in developing and adapting socioeconomic impact projection models and in using such models as tools for planning and policy analysis.

487. Stenehjem, Erik J. *Summary Description of SEAM: The Social and Economic Assessment Model.* ANL/IAPE/TM/ 78-9 Argonne, Illinois: Argonne National Laboratory, 1978. 18 pp.

Provides a brief description of SEAM, an integrated socioeconomic impact assessment system. The SEAM data bases and modules can be used to provide a variety of annual projections for any county or combination of counties in the United States. SEAM outputs include (1) projections of population by age, sex, and race, (2) direct employment requirements for a variety of typical energy facilities, (3) estimated indirect employment requirements, (4) projections of the locally available work force, (5) estimates of the number and characteristics of inmigrating worker households, (6) housing requirements, (7) public service requirements, and (8) costs of providing public services.

488. Stinson, Debra Sanderson, and Michael O'Hare. *Predicting the Local Impacts of Energy Development: A Critical Guide to Forecasting Methods and Models.* Cambridge: Massachusetts Institute of Technology, Laboratory of Architecture and Planning, 1977. 96 pp.

Reviews the various methods which have been used to predict the second-order impacts of energy development. The work begins with a general introduction to predictive models and their uses and discusses the most common techniques used by the studies reviewed. It then critically describes the salient features and underlying assumptions of each forecasting model. For employment projection methods Stinson and O'Hare review multipliers, input-output coefficients, capital/labor ratios, and econometric forecasting. For population projection methods they review employment participation ratios, cohort-survival models, and gravity models. Major methods of public service forecasting and fiscal impact analysis are also discussed.

489. Walter,   G.   R.   "Bay Area Simulation Study: Economic and
      Population Models." *The Annals of Regional Science* 2, No. 2
      (1968):   59-71.

      Describes the economic and population components of the Bay
      Area Simulation Study (BASS) modeling system. The BASS system
      consists of a structural model, a shift model, a population
      model, and a reconciliation phase.   The structural and shift
      models   each make an independent determination of employment,
      the population model provides estimates of the supply of labor
      resulting from natural increase, and the   reconciliation phase
      utilizes migration assumptions to reconcile the demand for
      population (employment) with the supply of population (natural
      increase plus migration).   The outputs which result are
      employment   by   twenty-one   industry   groups,   age-specific
      population, householders, and school-aged children, all fore-
      casted from 1970 to 2020.

490. Weaver,   Rodger, Frank C. Hachman, Anthony S. Wilcox, and T.
      Ross Reeve.   *UPED 79:   Report on Revisions of the Utah
      Process Economic and Demographic Impact Model (UPED).*   Salt
      Lake City: University of Utah, Bureau of Economic and
      Business Research, 1980. 79 pp.

      Describes the Utah Process Economic and Demographic Impact
      Simulation Model (UPED) as of 1980.   The general concept of
      the UPED model was established in 1970 and   remains basically
      unchanged from its initial design.   This   report discusses
      recent refinements in the system.   UPED develops annual
      projections of employment and population for counties and
      multicounty regions.   The system can be used to estimate the
      impacts   of a new project on employment, unemployment,
      migration, and population.

491. White,   T. Kelley, Bruce A. McCarl, David R. Martella, and
      Fredrick W. Obermiller.   *The Purdue Development Model: A
      Systems Approach to Modeling Demographic-Economic Inter-
      action in Agricultural Development.*   Res. Bull. No. 925.
      West Lafayette, Indiana: Purdue University Agricultural
      Experiment Station, 1975. 64 pp.

      Describes the Purdue Development Model (PDM), a conceptual
      and operational structure for modeling agricultural economic
      development within a total systems framework.   Interactions
      between economic and demographic change, and the interdepen-
      dence of agricultural, nonagricultural, and public sectors of
      an economy are explicitly incorporated in the PDM.   An exten-
      sive review of economic development and demographic dynamics
      literature, constituting the conceptual basis for the model,
      is included.

492. Winter, R. C., D. J. Santini, D. W. South, C. M. Hotchkiss, and M. J. Bragen. *Selection of Economic Impact Assessment Models for Use by Communities in the Tennessee-Tombigbee Corridor: Phase I.* ANL/EES-TM-160. Argonne, Illinois: Argonne National Laboratory, 1981. 175 pp.

Evaluates existing computer models for assessing socio-economic impacts and gives the results of a demonstration of one of the models, SEAM, to local government officials in the states of Alabama, Kentucky, Mississippi, and Tennessee. Twelve models are evaluated.

493. Woods, Mike D., Gerald A. Doeksen, and James R. Nelson. "Community Economics: Simulation Model for Rural Development Planners." *Southern Journal of Agricultural Economics* 15, No. 2 (1983): 71 77.

Illustrates how university extension workers can utilize community simulation models to aid local decision-makers. The authors (1) review several community impact models, (2) present an overview of methodology used in a community simulation model, and (3) present an application of the community simulation model.

Postdevelopment Audits and Model Validation

494. Adler, Steven P., and Edmund F. Jansen, Jr. *Hill Reestablishment: Retrospective Community Study of a Relocated New England Town.* IWR Contract Report 78-4. Fort Belvoir, Virginia: U.S. Army Engineer Institute for Water Resources, 1978. 229 pp.

Retrospectively analyzes the 1940 relocation of Hill, New Hampshire. The process and techniques of relocation and the social, political, and economic impacts of the relocation are examined over three time periods: prerelocation, relocation-construction, and postrelocation. Three basic analyses were performed to illustrate the process and impacts of relocation on this rural community: (1) an archival search, (2) a trend analysis of social and economic indicators, and (3) an attitudinal study of the existing community. These methods provide separate yet overlapping conclusions.

495. Ascher, William. *Forecasting: An Appraisal for Policy-Makers and Planners.* Baltimore: The Johns Hopkins University Press, 1978. 239 pp.

Discusses the theory and practice of forecasting. A number of past forecasts and methodologies are reviewed in terms of

their success or failure.   The principal   categories of forecasts considered   are population, economic,   energy, transportation, and technological.   The author   estimates that future
developments will   be   centered   in the   areas   of   modeling,
surprise-sensitive forecasting, and normative forecasting.

496.   Ballard, Chester, and James H. Copp.   "Coping with Change in
       an Oil Boom." *Small Town* 12, No. 6 (1982):   5-8.

       Analyzes the historical   development of an oil boom   town in
       Texas.   Biscayne (pseudonym given to the small town   involved
       in the   change) experienced   rapid growth   resulting   from oil
       development beginning in 1975.   Documented are the changes in
       economic activity,   the pressures on public services,   and the
       effects   on   public morality   in the   aftermath   of   petroleum
       development.

  *   Bezdek,   Roger H., and Arlene K. Shapiro.   "Empirical Tests of
       Input-Output Forecasts."   *Socio-Economic Planning Sciences.*
       Cited above as item 90.

497.   Bisset,   Ronald, and   Paul Tomlinson.   "Environmental Impact
       Assessment,   Monitoring,   and   Post-Development   Audits."
       Environmental Impact   Assessment.   Edited by   PADC Environ-
       mental Impact Assessment and Planning Unit.   (Item 58), pp.
       405-25.

       Describes   a   research   project   designed to   compare   the
       predicted and actual impacts of selected   operational projects
       in the United Kingdom,   and thereby to assess the   accuracy of
       the   predictions.   The   authors   conclude that   environmental
       impact assessment   (EIA) should move away from   its concentra-
       tion on baseline   studies and   impact prediction and   toward a
       concern   for impact management.   EIA should   be an   iterative
       process involving a feedback loop from initial project design,
       predictions, auditing   of predictions, and   impact management,
       to subsequent changes in project design.

  *   Bowles, Roy T.   *Social Impact Assessment in Small Communities.*
       Cited above as item 8.

  *   Browne,   Bortz, and Coddington.   *A Retrospective Analysis of
       the Jim Bridger Complex Socioeconomic Effects.*   Cited below
       as item 718.

498.   Burdge,   Rabel J., and   Paul Opryszek, eds.   *Coping with
       Change: An Interdisciplinary Assessment of the Lake Shelby-
       ville Reservoir.* Urbana, Illinois: University of Illinois,
       Institute for Environmental Studies, 1981.   386 pp.

Summarizes four years of studies of the impacts of Lake Shelbyville, a large multipurpose reservoir in east central Illinois. A variety of environmental, economic, community, and recreation impacts are detailed along with a history of the reservoir project and an overview of the basin area before construction. The study assessed the accuracy of some of the predictions made before construction began. For example, it was found that the level of recreation use and the consequently projected economic benefits had been overestimated considerably in the anticipatory assessment. The last section presents methodological and administrative guidelines for the conduct of an interdisciplinary impact assessment.

499. Chalmers, J., D. Pijawka, K. Branch, P. Bergman, J. Flynn, and C. Flynn. *Socioeconomic Impacts of Nuclear Generating Stations; Summary Report on the NRC Post-Licensing Studies.* NUREG/CR-2750. Washington, D.C.: U.S. Nuclear Regulatory Commission, 1982. 229 pp.

Summarizes case studies of the socioeconomic effects resulting from construction and operation of twelve nuclear power stations. Socioeconomic variables examined included economic, demographic, housing, government, public response, and social organization characteristics. Evaluation of socioeconomic effects by area residents also was determined. This summary report describes the collective findings of the twelve individual case studies, compares the findings across sites to identify possible determinants of the effects, and examines the implications of the findings for future siting decisions and for the methodology most appropriate for projective assessments.

* Chase, Robert A., and F. Larry Leistritz. *Profile of North Dakota's Petroleum Work Force, 1981-82.* Agricultural Economics Rpt. No. 174. Cited below as item 720.

500. Culhane, Paul J., and H. Paul Friesema. *Forecasts and Environmental Decision Making: The Content and Accuracy of Environmental Impact Statements.* Boulder, Colorado: Westview Press, 1985. 250 pp.

Examines the accuracy and descriptive characteristics of EIS forecasts in a sample of twenty-nine nationally representative projects. Using data on actual postproject impacts and evaluating the accuracy of over 200 predictions, the authors found that although most EIS predictions on environmental impacts fall short of the ideal, the outcomes of EIS assessments turn out to be reasonably prescient--that is, few impacts are inconsistent with EIS forecasts and almost no significant impacts are wholly unanticipated by EIS writers. The book concludes with suggested ways of redefining the EIS process so as to diminish false expectations and to enhance

the   practical strengths of the National   Environmental Policy
Act.

*   Fookes,   T. W. *Huntly Power Project:*   *A Description.* Final
     Rpt. Paper No. 2. Cited below as item 726.

501. Gilmore,   John S., D. M. Hammond, Keith D. Moore, J. Johnson,
     and Dean C. Coddington. *Socioeconomic Impacts of Power
     Plants.* EPRI EA-2228. Prepared for Electric Power Research
     Institute, Palo   Alto,   California   by   Denver Research
     Institute and   Browne,   Bortz,   and   Coddington, Denver,
     Colorado, 1982. 240 pp.

     Summarizes the major findings of a two-year study of socio-
     economic impacts resulting from power plant construction and
     operation.   Research findings are based on a review of more
     than 600 documents and on twelve retrospective case studies of
     power plants and their impacts on surrounding communities.
     Actual and projected construction employment were compared and
     were generally found to differ considerably, largely because
     of unplanned circumstances associated with the different
     projects and beyond the control of the project manager.   The
     socioeconomic impacts of plant construction tended to be
     dispersed over a considerably wider area than had been
     predicted in anticipatory impact assessments.   Additional
     findings discussed in the report include effects on housing
     demand and supply, local government costs and revenues,
     traffic, and public perceptions of impacts.

502. House,   Peter W., and John McLeod. *Large-Scale Models for
     Policy Evaluation.* New York: John Wiley and Sons, 1977.
     326 pp.

     Is intended to give policymakers and members of their staffs
     information needed for developing large-scale models that can
     be used for comparing and evaluating alternative policies and
     strategies in long-range planning.   The scope of the work is
     restricted to models that are concerned with social science
     issues (primarily environmental) rather than systems dealing
     with physical or natural phenomena. The models are considered
     from the point of view of theory and methodology, data
     adequacy, capability of programming, validation, and finally,
     utility and transferability.

*   Isserman,   Andrew M. "The Accuracy of Population Projections
     for Subcounty Areas."   *American Institute of Planners
     Journal.* Cited above as item 360.

503. Knapp, Gunnar, and Kathy May MarkAnthony. *Sensitivity of RAM
     Model Projections to Key Assumptions.*   Anchorage:

University of Alaska, Institute of Social and Economic
Research, 1984. 196 pp.

Examines the sensitivity of the Rural Alaska Model's (RAM)
projections to a variety of input assumptions. The study
results provide an indication of the kinds of uncertainties
associated with the model's projections as well as an idea of
which assumptions are relatively more significant as sources
of uncertainty. The results provide a starting point for
planned review and revisions of the RAM model.

504. Krannich, Richard S. "A Comparative Analysis of Factors
Influencing the Socioeconomic Impacts of Electric Generating
Facilities." *Socio-Economic Planning Sciences* 13, No. 1
(1979). 41-48.

Investigates a set of socioeconomic factors that may
influence the extensiveness of local impacts induced by energy
facility development. Krannich uses correlational and
regression analysis on a sample of seventeen U.S. nuclear
power plants. Empirical results suggest that some characteristics of the development and host area (namely facility size,
construction time, total number of construction workers, and
distance to a metropolitan center) are significant in projecting the likely levels of some facility-induced socioeconomic
impacts.

505. Leavey, Ralph. "The Socioeconomic Effects of Power Stations
on Their Localities." *Social Impact Assessment* 51-52
(March-April 1980): 11-18.

Investigates the social and economic effects of major power
station developments in Britain, namely the coal-fired power
station at Drax in North Yorkshire and the nuclear power
station at Sizewell in Suffolk. Five main themes were
analyzed: the local labor market; social and demographic
structure; expenditure; service requirements; and physical
development effects.

506. Leistritz, F. Larry, and Karen C. Maki. *Socioeconomic
Effects of Large-Scale Resource Development Projects in
Rural Areas: The Case of McLean County, North Dakota.* Agr.
Econ. Rpt. No. 151. Fargo: North Dakota Agricultural
Experiment Station, 1981. 103 pp.

Examines the socioeconomic impacts of construction and
operation of a large power plant located in a rural area.
Actual changes in key economic and social indicators are
compared with those projected in impact studies conducted
during the early stages of project development.

507. McNicoll,   I. H.   "Ex-Post   Appraisal   of   an   Input-Output
     Forecast." *Urban Studies* 19 (1982):   397-404.

     Compares oil impact forecasts with actual impacts derived
     from surveys in Shetland, Scotland.   Overall results indicate
     that the   ex ante forecast of oil supply base impact on the
     Shetland economy was revealed ex post to have   been a
     relatively poor estimate.   In particular, the magnitude of
     oil-induced output generation was substantially underestimated
     for most economic sectors.   The single most cost-effective
     improvement in the basic forecast would be attempting to
     accurately estimate changes in the supply base aggregate
     propensity to spend locally.

508. Murdock,   Steve H.,   F. Larry Leistritz, Rita R.   Hamm, and
     Sean-Shong Hwang.   "An Assessment of Socioeconomic Assess-
     ments: Utility, Accuracy, and Policy Considerations."
     Environmental Impact Assessment Review 3, No. 4 (1982):
     333-50.

     Reports the   results of   an analysis of   the methodological
     adequacy and utility of a sample of environmental impact
     statements (EISs).   The accuracy of a sample of population
     projections made as a part of the EIS process is assessed, and
     the likely utility of such statements for local impact area
     decision makers is evaluated.

509. Murdock,   Steve H.,   F. Larry Leistritz, Rita R.   Hamm, Sean-
     Shong Hwang, and Banoo Parpia.   "An Assessment of the
     Accuracy of a Regional   Economic-Demographic Projection
     Model." *Demography* 21, No. 3 (August 1984):   383-404.

     Examines the accuracy of an integrated economic-demographic
     projection model in projecting total populations for 1980,
     using 1970 base data, for 106 counties and 553 places in North
     Dakota and Texas.   Comparisons of the model's projections to
     1980 Census counts reveal mean percentage absolute differences
     of 10% for counties and 14% for places.   In addition, the
     model's accuracy was comparable to that for alternative
     projection systems.

510. Pijawka,   David, and James A. Chalmers.   "Impacts of Nuclear
     Generating Plants on Local Areas." *Economic Geography* 59,
     No. 1 (January 1983): 66-80.

     Summarizes the impacts of constructing and operating nuclear
     power plants.   Data were drawn from case studies of twelve
     nuclear plants in the United States. Economic benefits to the
     local areas near plant sites generally were not large because
     of high levels of commuting by project workers, income leakage
     from the area, and few local purchases of construction
     material.   High levels of commuting also caused project-

related increases in local population and service demands to
be relatively minor.

511. Policy Research Associates. *Socioeconomic Impacts: Nuclear
      Power Station Siting.* NUREG-0150. Prepared for U.S.
      Nuclear Regulatory Commission. Springfield, Virginia:
      National Technical Information Service, 1977. 140 pp.

      Utilizes the literature on rural industrial development to
      gain insights on the socioeconomic effects of nuclear power
      stations. The authors believe that previous studies of large
      industrial facilities located in or near small towns have
      important implications for attempts to understand and antici-
      pate the impacts of nuclear stations. Contains an extensive
      bibliography.

   * Rapp, Donald A. *Uranium Mining and Milling Work Force
      Characteristics in the Western U.S.* LA-8656-MS. Cited
      below as item 744.

512. Summers, Gene F., Sharon D. Evans, Frank Clemente, E. M.
      Beck, and Jon Minkoff. *Industrial Invasion of Nonmetropoli-
      tan America: A Quarter Century of Experience.* New York:
      Praeger Publishers, 1976. 231 pp.

      Attempts to assess the validity of the view that the loca-
      tion of industry in small cities, towns, and rural areas is an
      important tool for solving the twin problems of rural poverty
      and urban crisis. Case studies of industrial plants located
      in nonmetropolitan areas provide the data base for the study.
      A total of 186 case study documents provided information for
      assessing the impact of industrial development on (1) popula-
      tion dynamics, (2) the private sector, (3) the public sector,
      and (4) the quality of individual well-being in the host
      communities.

513. University of Denver Research Institute and University of
      Colorado at Denver, Institute for Urban and Public Policy
      Research. *Impacts of Energy Resource Development on the
      Denver Metropolitan Area.* Golden, Colorado: Colorado
      Energy Research Institute, June 1979. 148 pp.

      Analyzes the effects of energy development on the Denver
      metropolitan area's economy from 1970 to 1978. Results
      indicate that energy-related employment accounts for only 4%
      of the total work force, yet is responsible for nearly a third
      of Denver's employment growth (direct and indirect) since
      1970. An economic base methodology is utilized, and recommen-
      dations for further research are presented, such as monitoring
      key economic variables, refining economic forecasting models,
      and analyzing regional fiscal flows.

514. URS-Berger. *AFSEM Evaluation Report, Version 2.3.* Norton
      AFB, California: U.S. Air Force, AFRCE-BMS DEV, 1984.   188
      pp.

      Reports the results of an extensive empirical evaluation of
      the Air Force System Evaluation Model (AFSEM).   The AFSEM
      system is a detailed socioeconomic impact evaluation tool
      designed for use on Department of Defense (DOD) construction,
      mission change, and other similar projects.   The accuracy of
      the AFSEM system in simulating the processes of economic and
      demographic change was tested by comparing its performance
      against the historic data from two completed projects.

515. Webb,   Stephen, Richard Krannich, and Frank Clemente.   "Power
      Plants in Rural Area Communities: Their Size, Type, and
      Perceived Impacts."   *Journal of the Community Development
      Society* 11, No. 2 (Fall 1980):   81-95.

      Reports analysis of socioeconomic impacts as perceived by
      local informants in 85 communities which had experienced the
      nearby development of electric generating stations.   All
      electric stations produced at least 300 megawatts of power,
      and all were sited east of the Mississippi River. The effects
      of power plant development were perceived as being largely
      positive.   This general pattern of positively perceived
      impacts was maintained across plant types, facility size, and
      community population size.

Monitoring

516. Bankes, Nigel, and Andrew R. Thompson.   *Monitoring for Impact
      Assessment and Management: An Analysis of the Legal and
      Administrative Framework.* Vancouver, British Columbia: The
      University of British Columbia, Westwater Research Center,
      1980.   80 pp.

      Examines the role of monitoring in project assessment and
      the legal and institutional foundations for monitoring in
      Canada.   The experience of the Revelstoke Dam monitoring
      program is reviewed, and conclusions concerning the adequacy
      of legal and institutional foundations for monitoring are
      presented.

517. Briscoe, Maphis, Murray, Lamont, Inc.   *OIA Monitoring System.*
      2 volumes.   Evanston, Wyoming: The Overthrust Industrial
      Association, 1982.   240 pp.

      Presents projections of employment, population, and tax base
      produced by the OIA Monitoring System. To provide the context
      for the projections, and for interested readers, the report

also presents the oil and gas data base and development
simulation model--components which underlie projections of
employment, population, and tax base. The report presents
projections of oil and gas employment in a six-county
monitoring area in Idaho, Utah, and Wyoming. Projections of
total employment, population, and tax base are presented for
Uinta and Lincoln counties, Wyoming.

518. Browne, Bortz, and Coddington. *The 1982 Campbell County
Socioeconomic Monitoring Report.* Denver, Colorado: Browne,
Bortz, and Coddington, 1983. 154 pp.

Is the third in a series of annual reports which summarize
the results of monitoring present socioeconomic conditions and
future prospects for Campbell County, Wyoming. Campbell
County has been affected by the development of a number of
coal mines, a power plant, coal transportation facilities,
uranium mines, and oil and gas resources. The monitoring
program attempts to measure the cumulative effects of these
developments and to project likely future changes in key
economic, demographic, service, and fiscal indicators.

519. Carley, M. J. *Cumulative Socioeconomic Monitoring: Issues
and Indicators for Canada's Beaufort Region.* Ottawa,
Ontario: Northern Economic Planning Branch, Indian and
Northern Affairs, 1984. 167 pp.

Makes the case for a cumulative monitoring program for the
Beaufort region. Primary audiences for information from such
monitoring are identified, and key features of the policy
environment necessary for successful monitoring are
described.

* Carley, Michael J., and Eduardo Bustelo. *Social Impact
Assessment and Monitoring: A Cross-Disciplinary Guide to
the Literature.* Cited below as item 974.

520. Casley, Dennis J., and Denis A. Lury. *Monitoring and Evaluation of Agricultural and Rural Development Projects.*
Baltimore, Maryland: The Johns Hopkins University Press,
1982. 145 pp.

Discusses issues associated with establishment and operation
of monitoring and evaluation mechanisms for development
projects, largely in Third World Counties. The work is
directed primarily to those working within a specific project,
whose task it is to operate the monitoring and/or evaluation
systems, and secondly to those responsible for management of
the project so that they may better assess what they can
expect their monitoring and evaluation operations to provide.
Issues examined include the basic objectives of monitoring and

evaluation, selecting appropriate variables and indicators, identifying sources of data and alternative collection methods, and analyzing and presenting data.

521. Davidson, J. E. "Monitoring and Management of Social and Economic Impacts--The Experience in B.C. on Hydroelectric Dams." *Social Impact Assessment* No. 87-89 (1984): 22-27.

Provides a review of experience in monitoring and management of socioeconomic impacts of hydroelectric projects over the past decade. Because it is difficult to definitively predict socioeconomic impacts, it is also difficult to develop a complete mitigation and compensation proposal prior to project approval. Impact monitoring offers a solution to this problem of uncertainty by providing a record of impacts that allows (1) comparison of predicted and actual impacts, (2) identification of unanticipated impacts, and (3) assessment of the effectiveness of mitigation and compensation measures. The experience of British Columbia Hydro in developing monitoring programs for three hydropower projects is reviewed.

522. Department of the Air Force. *PeaceKeeper Monitoring Program, 1984 Annual Report.* 2 volumes. Washington, D.C.: U.S. Department of Defense, 1985. 357 pp.

Provides information concerning the impacts of the Peace-Keeper strategic missile system development on Cheyenne, Wyoming, and the surrounding area. Information is reported in five major categories: (1) work force characteristics (number, demographic characteristics, migration and settlement patterns), (2) local economy and population, (3) public finance, (4) housing and land use, and (5) public services.

523. Dunn, William N. *Public Policy Analysis: An Introduction.* Englewood Cliffs, New Jersey: Prentice-Hall, Inc., 1981. 388 pp.

Is designed as a text for introductory courses in public policy analysis and introduces technical and conceptual skills necessary for analyzing public policy problems. A chapter devoted to monitoring policy outcomes will be of interest to many. Four approaches to monitoring are discussed: (1) social systems accounting, (2) social experimentation, (3) social auditing, and (4) social research cumulation.

524. Fookes, T. W., Project Coordinator. *Monitoring Social and Economic Impact: Huntly Case Study.* Final Report Series in 13 volumes. Hamilton, New Zealand: University of Waikato, School of Social Sciences, 1981. 532 pages.

Is a series of reports of a six-year research project to monitor the social and economic impacts of a major energy development, the Huntly Power Station. Reports for the general audience are as follows: a description; the social, economic, political, and planning context; monitoring results (expectations and findings, and overseas energy projects); public participation initiatives; generalizations drawn from the project; and monitoring social and economic impacts. Reports for an engineering and planning audience are as follows: implications for development planning; intentions and practice of the project; socioeconomic monitoring information; conclusions; alternative approaches to monitoring; summary statistics; and data retrieval handbook.

Contains items 285, 525, 534, 726.

523. Hookes, T. W. *Monitoring Social and Economic Impacts.* Final Report Paper No. 7. (Item 524), 12 pp.

Describes the objectives, scope, procedures, and general findings of the Huntly monitoring project. The project was conducted from 1974 to 1981 to determine the socioeconomic impacts of the construction of the Huntly Power Station on nearby communities. The author points out that the initial objectives of the program were overly ambitious in light of the resources available. Likewise, provision for improved access to government-held data would expedite future monitoring. Despite the difficulties encountered, however, the monitoring program is seen as having made a valuable contribution to the knowledge base concerning impacts of large-scale projects.

*   Galginaites, Michael, Claudia Chang, Kathleen M. MacQueen, Albert A. Dekin, Jr., and David Zipkin. *Ethnographic Study and Monitoring Methodology of Contemporary Economic Growth, Socio-Cultural Change, and Community Development in Nuiqsut, Alaska.* Tech. Rpt. No. 96. Cited below as item 890.

526. Hancock, Syd, Dave Hardy, Norman Giesbrecht, Diane McKenzie, and Bob Menard. *Community Impact Monitoring Program--Third Annual Report for the Year 1980.* Atikokan, Ontario, Canada: Township of Atikokan and Ontario Hydro, 1981. 45 pp. plus appendix tables.

Summarizes changes in social, economic, and cultural conditions of Atikokan during the 1980 construction period of the Atikokan generating station. Community variables monitored include population change; demands on sewer and water, roads, housing, and health protection; project employment; total employment; housing prices, vacancies, and starts; school enrollment; municipal finances; and alcohol consumption.

527. Harnisch, A. A. *Chief Joseph Dam: Community Impact Report,*
      Update III: Conditions at Peak Impact.   IWR Res. Rpt. No.
      78-R2.   Fort Belvoir, Virginia: U.S. Army Corps of
      Engineers, Institute For Water Resources, 1978. 50 pp.

      Examines how current peak construction social impacts at
      Chief Joseph Dam, Washington, compare with those projected in
      preconstruction phases.   The report examines, in depth, the
      construction workers at   the dam site,   their previous
      employment, current living conditions, and impacts on local
      communities.   The report also generalizes about the methodol-
      ogies for projecting social impacts.

528. Hesling,   Lyulph.   "A Note on Impact Monitoring of Agricul-
      tural Development Projects."   *Journal of Agricultural*
      Economics 35, No. 2 (1984):   279-81.

      Notes that efforts to monitor the impacts of agricultural
      development projects (ADP) in developing countries often
      produce large data sets from which too little information
      emerges too late.   To avoid this problem, the author
      recommends that (1) certain information basic to ADP impact
      monitoring (such as farmer participation and crop production)
      be collected using standardized methodology, (2) reliance be
      placed in some situations on case studies and local knowledge
      of the project staff rather than on massive, though statistic-
      ally valid, sample surveys, (3) clear and detailed objectives
      for impact monitoring be specified in advance to avoid
      unnecessary data collection, and (4) balance be maintained
      between data collection and analytical resources, with no more
      than half of the total resources being allocated to data
      collection.

529. Hollick,   M.   "Environmental Impact Assessment As A Planning
      Tool." *Journal of Environmental Management* 12 (1981):   79-
      90.

      Examines the Environmental Impact Assessment process in the
      light of planning and decision-making theory and finds it to
      have three important shortcomings.   First, it does not
      encourage monitoring and modification of environmental protec-
      tion measures, but relies on uncertain predictions.   Second,
      there is a mismatch between the needs of the proponent and
      those of reviewers.   And, third, land use planning is an
      essential prerequisite for effective EIA.   The Management
      Programme approach used in western Australia,   and the
      integrated planning and assessment legislation in New South
      Wales are described, and proposals for a more satisfactory
      system outlined.

530. Imboden,   Nicholas.   *A Management Approach to Project*
      Appraisal and Evaluation With Special Reference to

Non-Directly Productive Projects. Paris: Organization for
Economic   Co-Operation and Development,   Development Centre,
1978.   172 pp.

Is   addressed   to   government   officials   in   less-developed
countries and aid agencies who are concerned with   the management   of development activities.   The goal   of the book is to
provide   the necessary information to development   managers so
that they can set up their own   appraisal/evaluation framework
in a   technically competent   way.   The book   is based   on the
premise   that   appraisal/evaluation   frameworks   have   to   be
adapted to   the socioeconomic   situation of   a   given country.
Rather than propose   a specific and rigid framework,   the book
discusses   the various   concepts and   frameworks   proposed and
attempts to highlight the   factors that have to be   taken into
account   when choosing and setting up   an appraisal/evaluation
framework.

531.   Imboden,   Nicolas.   *Managing Information for Rural Development
       Projects.*   Paris: Organization for   Economic Co-Operation
       and Development, Development Centre, 1980.   97 pp.

Examines rural   development information   systems   which   are
viewed as   an important   management   tool for   policymakers and
practitioners.   The purpose   of rural development information
systems is to   provide the managers of rural   development with
the   necessary   and   sufficient   information   to   improve   the
selection and   implementation of   rural   development projects,
programs, and policies.   The author   examines the information
needs of rural project management, the process   of determining
indicators to be included, the choice of evaluation design and
data   collection   instruments, data   processing   and   analysis
procedures, and institutional considerations.   Throughout the
report, the author   makes use of experience from   case studies
of   agricultural   and   other   rural   development   projects   in
developing countries.

532.   Intermountain   Power Project.   *IPP Socioeconomic   Monitoring
       Report No. 9, 1983 Annual Report.*   Los Angeles, California:
       City of Los   Angeles, Department   of Water and   Power, 1983.
       206 pp.

Provides   information concerning the   magnitude, demographic
characteristics,   and settlement patterns of the IPP work force
during   1983.   The local   effects of   project development   on
population, local municipal services, and regional   health and
social services also are discussed.   The project sponsors have
committed   to spend in   excess of $48 million to   insure that
adverse conditions   do   not   occur   as   a   result   of   project
development.   Information from the monitoring effort helps to
guide these mitigation activities.

533. Kopas, Paul. "The Structure and Functions of the Revelstoke
Impact Monitoring Program." *Social Impact Assessment* 51/52
(March-April 1980): 3-10.

Retrospective analysis of a monitoring program of the
construction of the Revelstoke Canyon Dam project in British
Columbia. The author describes, in general, the functions and
theoretical basis of monitoring programs and activities and
variables for impact monitoring, specific to the Revelstoke
project.

534. Krawetz, N. M. *Intentions and Practice Reviewed with
Reference to Monitoring Prototypes.* Final Report Paper No.
10. (Item 524), 48 pp.

Examines the role of monitoring within the context of social
impact assessment (SIA). The author's general definition of
monitoring is "a control activity involving the measurement of
change(s) in the light of specific objectives." Important
aspects of monitoring are that (1) it involves the periodic
and systematic measurement of social change, particularly as
it relates to planned development; (2) monitoring is never
neutral, that is, independent of its objectives; (3) it is not
an isolated activity but is part of the management process of
an organization or group; and (4) monitoring involves several
tasks including data collection, analysis, transfer of analytical results to action, and feedback. Monitoring can serve a
variety of purposes including compliance, knowledge, short-
term management, project control, future planning, research
and development, and credibility.

535. Kruse, John, Diddy Hitchins, and Michael Baring-Gould.
*Developing Predictive Indicators of Community and Population
Change.* Tech. Rpt. No. 26. Anchorage, Alaska: Bureau of
Land Management, Alaska Outer Continental Shelf Office,
1979. 502 pp.

Draws upon the oil pipeline impact experiences of Fairbanks
and Valdez, Alaska, to identify the relationships between
community and individual characteristics that can be observed
prior to impact on the one hand, and impact experiences and
assessments on the other. These relationships may be shown in
future studies to apply to communities and individuals,
generally, or at least to apply to a large proportion of the
population which may be affected by such energy developments.
To the extent that the relationships appear to have a general
application, they can be used in combination with observations
of specific community characteristics and development forces
to predict likely patterns of impact.

536. Leistritz, F. L., and R. A. Chase. "Socioeconomic Impact Monitoring Systems: Review and Recommendations." *Journal of Environmental Management* 15 (1982): 333-49.

Reviews the design characteristics and operational procedures of several monitoring systems which have been implemented in connection with major resource development projects. System design features include (1) indicators to be monitored; (2) mechanisms for data collection (e.g., instruments, organizational responsibility); (3) frequency of data collection; (4) frequency and nature of reporting; and (5) number of communities or jurisdictions to be monitored. Major trade-offs in monitoring system design are then discussed, and recommendations concerning successful design and implementation of such systems are presented. The recommendations are based in large measure on the experience of entities which have implemented monitoring systems, as indicated through interviews with representatives of these organizations.

537. Louis Berger and Associates, Inc. *Social Indicators for OCS Impact Monitoring.* Tech. Rpt. No. 77. 3 volumes. Anchorage, Alaska: Minerals Management Service, 1983. 532 pp.

Reports the findings of sociocultural research conducted in the Northwest Alaska Native Association (NANA) and Aleutian-Pribilof Islands regions. The objective of this research was to conduct primary ethnographic and secondary quantitative data research in two dissimilar Alaskan regions that are represented by very different corpora of baseline data, both in quality and quantity, and to ascertain how and in what ways a systematic monitoring of community well-being and stress can be conducted. A research validation and monitoring methodology is proposed, based on the assumption that the social dynamics of Alaskan villages can be captured by a few key indicators and that impacts on social well-being from outer continental shelf (OCS) petroleum development can be observed by measuring these indicators over time. This methodology requires that the indicator system be measured at two additional points in time in a wide variety of villages, including a sample of villages where OCS development is unlikely and villages outside the two study regions. By analyzing the relationships among measurements in three time periods, the indicator system can be refined until it is optimally unbiased and reliable.

538. Marcus, Linda Graves. *A Methodology for Post-EIS (Environmental Impact Statement) Monitoring.* Geological Survey Circular 782. Washington, D.C.: U.S. Department of the Interior, 1979. 39 pp.

Describes a methodology for monitoring the impacts predicted in environmental impact statements (EISs). A monitoring system based on this methodology (1) coordinates a comprehensive, intergovernmental monitoring effort; (2) documents the major impacts that result, thereby improving the accuracy of impact predictions in future EISs; (3) helps agencies control impacts by warning them when critical impact levels are reached and by providing feedback on the success of mitigating measures; and (4) limits monitoring data to the essential information that agencies need to carry out their regulatory and environmental protection responsibilities. The methodology is illustrated using an EIS on phosphate development in southeastern Idaho as a case study.

539. Missouri Basin Power Project. *Socioeconomic Impact Monitoring Report, Final Summary.* Wheatland, Wyoming: Missouri Basin Power Project, 1983. 34 pp.

Provides a final summary of the experience of the Missouri Basin Power Project (MBPP) Monitoring Program. Initiated in 1976, the MBPP Monitoring Program was one of the first monitoring systems in the United States to be developed in response to specific regulatory requirements. Monitoring results were used to guide impact mitigation efforts, including extensive development of temporary housing and loan guarantees for local jurisdictions. The monitoring and mitigation programs were deemed quite effective.

540. Morrison, Peter A. *Different Approaches to Monitoring Local Demographic Change.* P-6743. Santa Monica, California: The RAND Corporation, 1982. 23 pp.

Addresses the problem of how to update demographic variables for small areas in the years following a decennial census. The author reviews conventional approaches to postcensus estimation, such as trend extrapolation, component analysis, and use of symptomatic data. A survey-based approach is then proposed as a complement to these other methods.

541. Old West Regional Commission. *Socioeconomic Longitudinal Monitoring Project, Final Report.* Vol. 1, *Summary.* Vol. 2, *McLean County Profile.* Vol. 3, *Platte County Profile.* Vol. 4, *Wheatland County Profile.* Vol. 5, *Kimball County Profile.* Washington, D.C.: Old West Regional Commission, 1979. 551 pp.

Summarizes findings of a study to compare the actual socioeconomic changes which accompanied construction of two coal-fired electric power plants with those projected in impact statements. Emphasis of the study was on collecting primary data to enable researchers to more accurately estimate social and economic changes which accompany energy development. Data were collected over a two-year period in two "impact counties" and in two counties that were not affected by major projects (control counties).

542. Ontario Hydro and the Proctor and Redfern Group. *A Social and Community Impact Monitoring and Review System.* Rpt. No. 79017. Toronto, Ontario: Ontario Hydro, 1979. 199 pp.

Investigates how community data collection can be used as part of a monitoring system to provide precise, timely, and practical advice on the problems and opportunities which municipalities may experience during construction and operation of generating stations. The study was aimed at providing practical guidelines useful to planners and project management in monitoring community impacts as required by the community impact agreements for the Darlington, Atikokan, and Wesleyville power stations. Three monitoring approaches are discussed: (1) information sponge approach, (2) target tracking approach, and (3) rolling target approach.

* Peelle, Elizabeth, Martin Schweitzer, Phillip Scharre, and Bradford Pressman. *A Study of the Cherokee Nuclear Station: Projected Impacts, Monitoring Plan, and Mitigation Options for Cherokee County, South Carolina.* ORNL/TM-6804. Cited below as item 584.

543. Scott, Wolf. "A Development Monitoring Service at the Local Level." *International Social Sciences Journal* 33 (1981): 82-90.

Presents a scheme for a development monitoring service by using the state of Kerala in India as an example of the need for a system or organization that ensures continuity in data collection, concepts, definitions, and methods and one that ties data collection closely to the uses made of the data.

544. Tennessee Valley Authority. *Hartsville Nuclear Plants Socio-economic Monitoring and Mitigation Report.* HNPSMR-8. Knoxville: Tennessee Valley Authority, 1980. 45 pp.

Provides a summary of the monitoring effort being undertaken by the Tennessee Valley Authority for the Hartsville Nuclear Plants. The monitoring program was initiated in 1976 in response to requirements for mitigation and monitoring imposed by the U.S. Nuclear Regulatory Commission as a condition for project licensing. Monitoring was designed to focus specifically on needs for and effectiveness of mitigation efforts. Work force data, collected through semi-annual surveys of all project workers, included worker origin, demographic characteristics (e.g., number of school-aged children), housing, previous residence, and several other attributes. In

addition, a substantial number of community impact indicators
were monitored.   The Hartsville monitoring program appears to
be one of the most comprehensive undertaken by 1980.

545.   Vincent,   N.   "Field   Actualities   of   an   Impact Monitoring
       Program."   *Social   Impact   Assessment: Theory,   Method,*
       Practice.   Edited by F. J. Tester and W. Mykes.   Calgary,
       Alberta: Detselig Enterprises, 1981. pp. 254-67.

       Summarizes the experience gained from conducting a prototype
       dam impact monitoring program.   (The author   served as Impact
       Monitor of the Revelstoke Dam Project.) The objectives of the
       impact   monitoring   program were   to monitor   the   social   and
       economic effects from the project and to establish a prototype
       design for impact   monitoring programs to be applied   in other
       major   resource development   situations.   The author   reports
       salient   findings   relative   to   each   of   these   objectives.
       Concerning implementation of future monitoring efforts, the
       importance of clarifying the program's objectives to the
       public and to affected local agencies is emphasized.   A frame-
       work for assembly of monitoring information is proposed.

Mitigation and
Management in SIA

Management Overviews

546. Association for University Business and Economic Research. *Socio-Economic Impact of Electrical Energy Construction: Proceedings of the First AUBER Energy Workshop.* Athens, Georgia: University of Georgia, College of Business Administration, 1977. 276 pp.

Contains ten original articles addressing a variety of mitigation and socioeconomic impact assessment issues associated with electric power plant construction.

547. Auger, Camilla, Edward Allen, Sandra Blaha, Virginia Fahys, Charles Franklin, Raymond Maurice, Christine Vestal, and Cynthia Walker. *Energy Resource Development, Socioeconomic Impacts and the Current Status of Impact Assistance: An Eleven State Review.* Boulder, Colorado: TOSCO Foundation, 1978. 241 pp.

Presents an overview of the extent and distribution of current and anticipated socioeconomic impacts in eleven western and eastern states. Major findings are as follows. The more central energy development is to the state's economy, the more prodevelopment it tends to be and the more it views impact assistance as primarily a state responsibility. Major differences in impacts stem more from the type of energy development than from geographic location. Both social disruption and operating costs, as opposed to capital costs under conditions of boom town growth, have been underestimated. Major community development needs in order of priority are housing, road construction and repair, sewer and water systems, schools, and social services. Federal categorical programs were viewed as inadequate and unresponsive to impact needs. Industry participation in community development is widespread and substantial among the large operators; their total contribution constitutes a primary source of impact assistance funding.

548. Barrows, Richard L., and George W. Morse. *Community Growth Policy: Economic Impacts of Growth and Local Policy Choices.* North Central Regional Pub. No. 79. Madison, Wisconsin: University of Wisconsin, 1983. 20 pp.

Is aimed at helping citizens understand the economics of growth and the growth policy alternatives in their local community. It is aimed particularly at communities where

there is debate about local growth policies. For communities
that have already decided to encourage growth, this report may
help in deciding what kind of growth best suits their needs.

549. Boggs,   J. P.   "Relationships Between Indian Tribes, Science,
      and   Government   in   Preparing   Environmental   Impact
      Statements." *Social Impact Assessment* No. 36 (1979):   3-
      14.

      Discusses reasons why EISs in the United States do not meet
      the needs of Indian tribes.   It is argued that the institu-
      cional arrangements used to produce EISs are inappropriate.
      This argument is illustrated with reference to EISs produced
      for various coal mining developments and power projects in an
      area close to the boundary of the reservation of the Northern
      Cheyenne Tribe in Montana.

  *   Breese,   Gerald, R. J. Klingenmeier, H. P. Cahill, J. E.
      Whelan, A. E. Church, and D. E. Whiteman. *The Impact of
      Large Installations on Nearby Areas: Accelerated Urban
      Growth.* Cited below as item 957.

550. Briscoe,   Maphis, Murray, and Lamont, Inc. and Mountain West
      Research-North, Inc. *Generic Mitigation Program.*   Prepared
      for the Montana Department of State Lands, and U.S. Office
      of Surface Mining and Reclamation.   Billings, Montana:
      Mountain West Research-North, Inc., May 1983. 13 pp.

      Presents a conceptual approach to the development of a
      mitigation management process for the proposed Decker area
      coal mines in Montana.   The mitigation concept is outlined,
      examples of management structures that have worked in other
      interstate environments are offered, and specific guidelines
      and measures are recommended.

551. Brower, David, Candace Carraway, and Thomas Pollard. *Develop-
      ing a Growth Management System for Rural Coastal
      Communities.* Working Paper 81-9.   Chapel Hill, North
      Carolina: University of North Carolina, Center for Urban
      and Regional Studies, December 1981. 178 pp.

      Describes a process for the development of growth management
      systems for North Carolina's rural coastal communities.   The
      process of system design involves (1)   determination of
      community goals, objectives, and policies; (2) analysis of de
      facto growth management systems; (3) inventory of tools and
      techniques to attain goals; (4) adjustment of management
      techniques to the communities; (5) growth management system
      synthesis; and (6) monitoring.   Topics discussed are land
      acquisition, public spending, taxation, and development
      regulation.

552. Centaur Management Consultants, Inc. *Managing the Social and
      Economic Impacts of Energy Developments.* Prepared for the
      U.S. Energy Research and Development Administration. U.S.
      Department of Commerce Publication TID-27184. Washington,
      D.C.: National Technical Information Service, 1976. 171
      pp.

      Is one of the first handbooks designed to provide local,
      regional, state, and federal decision makers with guidance on
      how to assess, plan, and manage the social and economic
      impacts resulting from energy developments. Areas of concern
      include employment, personal income, transportation, housing,
      solid waste collection and disposal, water supply, waste water
      treatment, education, recreation, health care, and safety
      services. For each area of concern, suggested guidelines on
      measurable parameters, required information, and relevant
      methodologies are provided.

553. Cole, Janice Rae, Allison Fargnoli, and Betty Ramage. "Human
      Impacts of Large Scale Development Projects: The Process
      and Legal Basis for Mitigation." *Alaska Symposium on
      Social, Economic, and Cultural Impacts of Natural Resource
      Development.* Edited by Sally Yarie. (Item 593), pp.
      274-89.

      Points out that the central need in any large-scale develop-
      ment situation is the capability to anticipate, plan for, and
      respond to sudden social, cultural, and economic change. This
      includes the need for legal authority to assure that concerns
      of local residents are considered. The authors outline the
      major components of a mitigation program which include (1)
      identification and involvement of all affected parties, (2)
      assessment of impacts and determination of needs, (3) develop-
      ment of a formal agreement or binding plan between industry
      and government authorities, (4) provision for financing needed
      facilities and services, (5) implementation of mitigation
      activities, and (6) monitoring project development and socio-
      economic change.

554. Decision Analysts Hawaii, Inc. *A Proposed Social Impact
      Management System for the City and County of Honolulu.*
      Honolulu, 1983. 88 pp.

      Presents recommendations for a Social Impact Management
      System (SIMS) to be used in making major land use and develop-
      ment decisions. The system was designed to introduce socio-
      economic information early so adjustments to a project could
      be made before starting the formal permit or amendment
      process. Benefits include early, increased opportunity for
      the community to influence the project design, and early
      reading by developers of community reaction to a project.
      Thus, developers should have a more accurate judgment of the

outcome of the permit process, and unexpected opposition
should be reduced.

555. Detomasi, Don D., and J. W. Gartrell, eds. *Resource Commun-
      ities: A Decade of Disruption.*   Boulder, Colorado:
      Westview Press, 1984. 195 pp.

      Consists of eleven original papers that survey the state of
      the art in research and public policy regarding the specific
      problems and opportunities that confront resource communities.
      The papers deal with experiences of resource communities in
      Canada, Norway,   the United Kingdom, and   the United States.
      Specific issues discussed include provision of public services
      and housing, effects of development on community economic
      structure and income distribution, social impacts, impacts on
      indigenous people, project shutdown issues, and impact manage-
      ment alternatives.

556. Devine, Michael D., Steven C. Ballard, Irvin L. White, Michael
      A. Chartock, Allyn R. Brosz, Frank J. Calzonetti, Mark S.
      Eckert, Timothy A. Hall, R. Leon Leonard, Edward J. Malecki,
      Gary D. Miller, Edward B. Rappaport, and Robert W. Rycroft.
      *Energy From the West: A Technology Assessment of Western
      Energy Resource Development.*   Norman, Oklahoma: University
      of Oklahoma Press, 1981. 362 pp.

      Investigates what the consequences of western energy
      development would be and how public and private policymakers
      could deal with the major problems and issues likely to arise.
      The specific objectives were to (1) identify and describe
      energy development alternatives, (2) determine and analyze
      impacts from development, (3) identify and define policy
      problems and issues, and (4) identify, evaluate, and compare
      alternative policy responses.   The study focuses on the
      development of coal, oil shale, uranium, oil, natural gas, and
      geothermal energy in the states of Arizona, Colorado, Montana,
      New Mexico, North Dakota, South Dakota, Utah, and Wyoming.
      Sections of special interest are those dealing with housing,
      growth management, transporting energy, and siting energy
      facilities.

557. Energy Impact Associates, Inc. *Social Impact Assessment,
      Monitoring and Management by the Electric Energy Industry.*
      Washington, D.C.: Atomic Industrial Forum, Inc., 1977. 148
      pp.

      Describes practices of electric energy and related
      industries in performing social impact assessments prior to
      construction and operation of major new facilities, and
      describes industry programs in monitoring and managing
      construction impacts. A random selection of Environmental
      Reports was the principal source of information on industry

practice; included were thirteen nuclear power plants, ten
fossil fuel power plants, and three nuclear fuel cycle and
five fossil fuel cycle facilities.

558. Faas,   Ronald C. *Evaluation of Impact Mitigation Strategies:*
     Case Studies of Four Tax Exempt Facilities. A.E. 82-6.
     Prepared for the Western Rural Development Center. Pullman,
     Washington: Washington State University, Department of
     Agricultural Economics, 1982. 222 pp.

     Reviews   and   evaluates   impact   mitigation   strategies
     associated with several large-scale development projects.
     Specifically, the author describes the nature of mitigation
     activities associated with each of the projects, evaluates
     their effectiveness, and estimates their respective costs.
     The four case studies selected, all in the state of
     Washington, are the Chief Joseph Dam Additional Units (near
     Bridgeport) constructed by the U.S. Army Corps of Engineers;
     the Trident Support Facility (in Kitsap County) constructed by
     the U.S. Navy; Washington Nuclear Power Projects 1, 2, & 4
     (near Richland) constructed by the Washington Public Power
     Supply System (WPPSS); and the Washington Nuclear Power
     Projects (near Satsop) also constructed by WPPSS.   Report
     concludes with a summary of similarities and differences among
     the four case studies and provides recommendations regarding
     mitigation policy to provide more leverage to the local
     communities.

559. Gilmore,   John S.   "Boomtowns May Hinder Energy Resource
     Development." *Science* 191 (1976): 535-40.

     Describes classic boom-town problems in a Rocky Mountain
     town.   It lays out a problem triangle, demonstrating how a
     combination of problems contributes to a degraded quality of
     life.   The boom town is seen as a major source of social
     tension, provoking legislation and litigation and contributing
     to confrontations between state and federal governments.

560. Gilmore,   John S.   "Observations and Comments on the Roles of
     Federal, State, and Local Governments in Socioeconomic
     Impact Mitigation." *Alaska Symposium on Social, Economic,*
     and Cultural Impacts of Natural Resource Development.
     Edited by Sally Yarie. (Item 593), pp. 232-38.

     Discusses the roles and capabilities of federal, state, and
     local governments in the United States with respect to socio-
     economic impact mitigation.   The various levels of government
     are compared in terms of four criteria: (1) responsibilities,
     (2) authority to mitigate or require mitigation, (3) limita-
     tions observed in at least some cases, and (4) examples of
     strengths and weaknesses.

561.   Gilmore,   John S., and Mary K. Duff.   *Boomtown Growth Manage-*
       ment: A Case Study of Rock Springs-Green River, Wyoming.
       Boulder, Colorado: Westview Press, 1975.   177 pp.

       Presents a case study of a community that was in   the middle
       of a boom period due to the construction of a power plant and
       expansion of local mining operations.   Although the major
       construction is complete, the boom is expected to continue for
       a decade or   so due to the increasing need for ancillary
       services.   Three areas of   major impact are identified:
       deterioration in the quality of life, decline in industrial
       productivity (also related to quality of life problems), and
       the inadequate levels of goods and services being provided by
       the   local services sector.   Expected impacts in the future
       (even if the present problems are solved) include recreational
       facility shortages,   traffic problems, and finally continued
       skepticism about the   ability of the town to   adequately plan.
       Planners are hampered by uncertainty and   confusion regarding
       the roles,   responsibilities, and future plans of the major
       corporate interests, and by the memories of experiences of
       cutbacks in the community--all tending to create a sense that
       problems are temporary, while in fact, they continue to
       increase.

562.   Gilmore,   John S., Dona K. Flory, Diane M. Hammond, Keith D.
       Moore, and Dean C. Coddington.   *Socioeconomic Impact Mitiga-*
       tion   Mechanisms   in   Six   States--Generalizations   and
       Unresolved Issues.   Denver: University of Denver Research
       Institute, 1977.   178 pp.

       Comparatively   reviews socioeconomic impact   problems of
       energy development in six states and the mechanisms states
       have established to deal with negative impacts. The following
       tentative   generalizations were made: (1) conflict-type
       negative   socioeconomic   impacts   include   jurisdictional
       conflicts and mismatches, competition for scarce resources,
       and shifts in comparative advantage; and (2) hyperurbanization
       or   boom town impacts are identified   as infrastructure
       shortfalls, housing problems, and social disruption. Conflict
       impacts can be resolved by a broad adoption of new mitigation
       mechanisms by states, by more state-federal decision making,
       and by a federal effort to avoid impacts in energy policy and
       decision making.   Hyperurbanization can be reduced by new
       state and federal mechanisms to deal with risk (politically
       unacceptable to many state and local governments).

563.   Gilmore,   John S., Diane M. Hammond, and J. F. Johnson.
       Assessing and Managing Socioeconomic Impacts of Power
       Plants.   EPRI EA-3660.   Palo Alto, California: Electric
       Power Research Institute (EPRI), 1984.   35 pp.

       Compares the findings of the EPRI report *Socioeconomic*
       Impacts of Power Plants with a report prepared for the Nuclear

Regulatory Commission entitled *Socioeconomic Impacts of Nuclear Generating Stations.* Both studies demonstrate that projections of work force size and associated impacts are often inadequate. The authors point out that this uncertainty should be recognized at the outset of planning for a new project. They also comment that, while computer-based impact assessment models are necessary for conducting detailed socioeconomic impact assessments, the limitations of these models should be recognized, particularly in light of uncertainties associated with model inputs. Given the uncertainties associated with impact projections, the report emphasizes the importance of impact monitoring and a flexible impact management program.

See also items 501, 499.

564. Greene, Marjorie R., and Martha G. Curry. *The Management of Social and Economic Impacts Associated with the Construction of Large-scale Projects: Experiences from the Western Coal Development Communities.* BNWL-RAP-16 UC-11. Richland, Washington: Battelle Pacific Northwest Laboratories, June 1977. 50 pp.

Presents an inventory of management strategies and the capabilities of local governments to implement them as an integral part of social and economic impact assessment. Included are strategies for community cohesion and social structure, education, police and fire services, housing, social and health services, recreation, transportation, utilities, planning and growth management, and financial assistance. Each is documented with a review and analysis of relevant literature.

565. Greene, Marjorie R., and Ted Hunter. *The Management of Social and Economic Impacts Anticipated with a Nuclear Waste Repository: A Preliminary Discussion.* Seattle: Battelle Memorial Institute, 1978. 120 pp.

Written to familiarize federal officials with the difficulties local and state governments will face as they manage socioeconomic impacts associated with a nuclear waste repository. The major problems of financing, coordinating, and involving affected public and private parties, and resolving uncertainty about which government agency or level to approach may be solved by the development of special legislation to provide funds, federal compliance with local and state planning decisions, and formation of a formal communication network between the sponsor and the public. Types of socioeconomic impacts associated with a repository, as well as the range of federal programs useful to state and local governments, are identified.

566.   Halstead,   John M.,   Robert A. Chase, Steve H. Murdock, and F.
       Larry Leistritz.   *Socioeconomic Impact Management: Design
       and   Implementation.*   Boulder,   Colorado: Westview Press,
       1984.   258 pp.

       Attempts   to   be   a   single source reference   on socioeconomic
       impact management which   is applicable   to the   needs   of both
       policymakers and social scientists.   The authors define impact
       management as   the development   of procedures and   programs to
       ensure both the equitable and timely distribution   of benefits
       and   the avoidance   and/or amelioration of   negative socioeco-
       nomic effects of industrial activities or projects.   The book
       attempts to provide a relatively comprehensive overview of the
       pragmatic, conceptual,   and methodological   dimensions   of the
       impact management process   as   they apply   to   large-scale
       resource   development projects   in rural areas.   Chapters are
       devoted to   such topics   as public participation   and negotia-
       tion, facility siting and impact assistance   legislation, work
       force   management measures,   community   facility   planning,
       financing   public and   private sector development,   and coping
       with facility closure.

567.   Halstead,   John M.,   and F. Larry Leistritz.   *Impacts of Energy
       Development on Mercer County, North Dakota.*   Agr. Econ. Rpt.
       No.   170.   Fargo: North   Dakota   Agricultural   Experiment
       Station, 1983.   71 pp.

       Examines   the   economic,   demographic,   public   service,   and
       fiscal impacts of coal resource development in   Mercer County,
       North Dakota.   Special attention   is given   to measuring the
       secondary employment   effects resulting   from development   of
       coal   mines,   power plants,   and a   coal   gasification   plant.
       Efforts of state and local agencies to   mitigate socioeconomic
       impacts are evaluated.

568.   Harthill,   Michalann, ed.   *Hazardous Waste   Management: In
       Whose Backyard?*   Boulder, Colorado: Westview Press, 1984.
       218 pp.

       Reviews U.S. and Canadian strategies for siting and managing
       hazardous waste facilities.   Disposal is still the most common
       means for handling hazardous wastes despite the   potential for
       alternative   methods, such as industrial process   redesign for
       waste reduction, waste detoxification, recycling, or incinera-
       tion.   Issues addressed in   the   book include   methods   for
       assessing health, facility siting,   governmental regulations,
       public participation, cleaning up uncontrolled hazardous waste
       sites, and disposal and management options.

569.   Lee,   Roger D.   "An Analysis of State Energy Impact Mitigation
       Programs in Colorado, Utah, Montana, and Wyoming."   *Journal
       of Energy Law and Policy* 3, No. 2 (1983):   281-328.

Describes the recently enacted legislation in selected western states dealing specifically with rapid growth and with the overall purpose to mitigate problems and prevent negative energy impacts in the future, thereby ensuring the orderly course of growth and development. Lee compares and contrasts the energy impact programs in Colorado, Utah, Montana, and Wyoming and evaluates each state's energy impact program on the criteria of political flexibility, administrative simplicity, flexibility, equity, risk allocation, timely financing, program cost minimization and comprehensiveness.

570. Leistritz, F. Larry, John M. Halstead, Robert A. Chase, and Steve H. Murdock. "Socio-economic Impact Management: Programme Design and Implementation Considerations." *Minerals and the Environment* 4 (1982): 141-50.

Suggests a systems framework to meet the need for an integrated approach to impact management. The usefulness of this approach is demonstrated by (1) reviewing the need for impact management efforts; (2) discussing the objectives of, and considerations in, designing impact management programs; (3) presenting a conceptual framework for, and key components of, such a program; and (4) suggesting an approach for implementing such a system as an integal part of the project development process.

571. Luke, Ronald T. "Managing Community Acceptance of Major Industrial Projects." *Coastal Zone Management Journal* 7, No. 2-3-4 (1980): 271-96.

Describes community acceptance risk, the traditional industrial approach to countering local opposition, and a positive approach to achieving community acceptance. Approach includes (1) careful site selection; (2) affirmative management of the community acceptance problem, including explicit planning of the community acceptance effort, assignment of staff with specific responsibilities to implement plans, and a budget for mitigating impacts of the project; (3) acquisition of sufficient land to buffer unavoidable project impacts; (4) a carefully formed corporate policy on public release of information concerning the project; and (5) constructive participation in state and local governmental policy development. Corporations must recognize that facility siting is as much a political exercise as it is an engineering and economic venture, and communities should seek to channel corporate self-interest to their own benefit.

572. Malamud, Gary. *Boomtown Communities.* Environmental Design Series Vol 5. New York: Van Nostrand Reinhold, 1984. 255 pp.

Discusses the phenomenon of rapid population growth from a historical perspective in a variety of contexts. The author surveys examples of boom town growth, such as tourist towns, railroad towns, government towns, resource development communities, and company towns, and more recent examples of nonenergy and energy boom-and-bust towns. He discusses boom towns created by the new energy rush in Scotland, United States, Canada, and Australia, as well as Latin America, the Persian Gulf, Nigeria, and South Africa, and examines the components to alleviate boom town problems including compensation and siting practices, tax and disbursement systems, and government and industry planning. Malamud discusses recent innovations in boom town growth control and formulates an overall boom town solution.

573. Merrifield, John. "Impact Mitigation in Western Energy Boomtowns." *Growth and Change* 15, No. 2 (April 1984): 23-28.

Critiques the contribution of recent research in impact assessment analysis and impact mitigation as applied to energy resource communities in the western United States. The appropriateness of impact projection models is questioned in their reliance of static algorithms to measure an inherently dynamic adjustment process. Other aspects of computerized models are reviewed, including the indirect effect of growth on local service industries, the commutation of labor force, and the inducement of migration through wage differentials. Prior research on social problems in energy boomtowns is criticized for their overreliance on conjecture and impression. Article concludes with a proposal that research establish the probable effects of particular impact prevention measures and determine cost effectiveness.

574. Metz, William C. "Industry Initiatives in Impact Mitigation." *Alaska Symposium on Social, Economic, and Cultural Impacts of Natural Resource Development.* Edited by Sally Yarie. (Item 593), pp. 239-51.

Provides an overview of recent attempts by development companies to mitigate local impacts of large-scale development projects. Seven types of mitigation efforts are reviewed: (1) transportation; (2) housing; (3) education; (4) public utilities; (5) health, public safety, and recreation; (6) miscellaneous (including planning assistance); and (7) company-community interaction.

575. Metz, William C. "The Mitigation of Socioeconomic Impacts By Electric Utilities." *Public Utilities Fortnightly* 106, No. 1 (September 11, 1980): 34-42.

Reports experiences of electric utility firms in the United States in mitigating impacts associated with facility construction. Utility firms' efforts most frequently fall into the general categories of worker transportation, housing, aid to local school systems, and assistance in upgrading community sewer and water systems. A number of firms have instituted bus or van transportation for their workers, and a few have assisted local governments in improving roads or airports. Company provision of single-status housing for construction workers was found to be prevalent at remote sites, particularly in the western states.

576. Morell, David, and Christopher Magorian. *Siting Hazardous Waste Facilities: Local Opposition and the Myth of Preemption.* Cambridge, Massachusetts: Ballinger Publishing Company, 1982. 266 pp.

Examines the conflicts inherent in the selection of sites for hazardous waste disposal. The authors review the forces leading to a need for more disposal facilities and the sources of local residents' fear of, and opposition to, such facilities. The costs and benefits of siting such facilities are analyzed; the authors find that, while benefits tend to be widely dispersed, costs are concentrated on local residents. Subsequent chapters deal with alternative approaches to public participation and negotiation and with the role of compensation in the site selection process. Recommendations for creating a balanced siting process conclude the work.

* Murdock, Steve H., and F. Larry Leistritz. *Energy Development in the Western United States: Impact on Rural Areas.* Cited above as item 35.

* Murdock, Steve H., F. Larry Leistritz, and Rita R. Hamm, eds. *Nuclear Waste: Socioeconomic Dimensions of Long-Term Storage.* Cited below as item 965.

577. Murray, James A., and William Lamont, Jr. *Action Handbook: Managing Growth in the Small Community.* Part I. *Getting a Picture of What's Ahead.* Part II. *Getting the Community Involved and Organized.* Part III. *Community Action and Growth Management.* Denver, Colorado: U.S. Environmental Protection Agency, 1978. 280 pp.

Is designed to be a detailed how-to-manage manual for small communities undergoing or facing the prospect of rapid population growth. Part I is intended to give an overview of the community management process and to assist the user in estimating how development of a certain type might affect the community's needs for various public services. Part II describes approaches to getting the community involved and

organized   and   suggests   a   working model   for   the   community
organizers.   Part III focuses on community action and   growth
management.

578. Myhra,   David.   *Energy Plant Sites: Community Planning for*
      Large   Projects.   Atlanta,   Georgia: Conway Publications,
      Inc., 1980.   258 pp.

      Designed to   provide information   to local   people,   such as
      city officials,   planners, and   private citizens, so   they can
      play a   major   role in   developing plans   to   minimize adverse
      socioeconomic   impacts.   A well-structured,   open-planning
      approach is presented to assist people in identifying specific
      socioeconomic   changes,   translating change   into   net   fiscal
      costs, developing mitigating measures, carrying out the imple-
      mentation plans, monitoring the program, and   making necessary
      adjustments.   Also included   is information on the nature   of
      socioeconomic   impacts,   energy   facility   site   selection
      procedures,   private   sector   impact   mitigation   involvement,
      impact planning theories, and designing a planning pathway for
      energy impact management.

579. Myler,   Glade   A.   "Mitigating Boom   Town Effects   of Energy
      Development: A Survey."   *Journal of Energy Law and Policy*
      2, No. 2 (1982):   211-35.

      Examines the problems facing boom towns in the West   and the
      various methods   which have   been developed to   mitigate those
      problems.   Problems in three general categories are analyzed:
      socioeconomic (inflation, newcomers, elderly, alcohol and drug
      abuse); government   (education, public works,   and transporta-
      tion);   and   labor   market   problems   (turnover,   absenteeism,
      newcomers).   The following recommendations are made: (1) an
      effective needs assessment program with   public participation;
      (2) changes in the legal   system to   meet the needs   of unique
      situations; and (3) intergovernmental cooperation.

580. National   Research Council.   *Social and   Economic Aspects of*
      Radioactive Waste Disposal: Considerations for Institution-
      al Management.   Washington, D.C.:   National Academy Press,
      1984.   175 pp.

      Reports   results   of   a   study   conducted   by   the   National
      Research   Council Board on Radioactive Waste   Management which
      examined nontechnical criteria for siting   geologic repositor-
      ies for high-level wastes.   Included in the study were public
      concerns, the waste management network (the role   of transpor-
      tation and   repository location),   and   institutional   issues.
      The major   socioeconomic   considerations in   the   location,
      construction,   and operation of a   generic   radioactive waste
      repository were   identified and   assessed; the   extent   of the
      data   base and applicability of what   is known of   the siting

process were assessed; and suggestions were made for an approach for incorporating socioeconomic considerations into the repository selection process.

581. Nelson, J. G., and Sabine Jessen. *The Scottish and Alaskan Offshore Oil and Gas Experience and the Canadian Beaufort Sea.* Copublished by Canadian Arctic Resources, Ottawa, Ontario, and University of Waterloo, Faculty of Environmental Studies, Waterloo, Ontario, 1981. 155 pp.

Presents an analytical framework for assessing the experiences of Alaska and Scotland in managing offshore oil and gas development. The model has four parts: agencies (governmental, industry, other); planning (strategic planning, inventory, classification, and evaluation), implementation (approval, construction, operation, monitoring); and general guides and characteristics (research, coordination, and information access). Similarities, differences, and effectiveness of the management strategies of the two countries are examined. The book closes with a summary and recommendations for the Beaufort Sea area in Canada.

582. Nordlund, Willis J. "Socioeconomic Impacts of Energy Development." *Labor Law Journal* 29, No. 6 (1978): 371-79.

Describes various impacts of energy development including disruption in the labor market, deficiencies in social overhead capital, and imbalances in local political structure. Nordlund comments at length on the inflationary impacts upon indigenous residents, and suggests various solutions to the attendent problems of development, including local autonomy and initiative, private industry cooperation, and state and federal governmental assistance.

583. Pasqualetti, Martin J., and K. David Pijawka, eds. *Nuclear Power: Assessing and Managing Hazardous Technology.* Boulder, Colorado: Westview Press, 1984. 350 pp.

Addresses the major issues surrounding the use of nuclear power--problem recognition, risk estimation, and policy formation and implementation. The authors appraise fundamental policy issues and examine the controversies surrounding specific power plants by examining the acceptability of nuclear risk, spatial aspects of siting and the nuclear fuel cycle, land-use controls and other mitigation options, socioeconomic impacts of power plants, emergency planning, and equity issues.

* Peelle, Elizabeth. "Mitigating Community Impacts of Energy Development: Some Examples for Coal and Nuclear Generating Plants in the U.S." *Nuclear Technology.* Cited below as item 758.

584. Peelle, Elizabeth, Martin Schweitzer, Phillip Scharre, and Bradford Pressman. *A Study of the Cherokee Nuclear Station: Projected Impacts, Monitoring Plan, and Mitigation Options for Cherokee County, South Carolina.* ORNL/TM-6804. Oak Ridge, Tennessee: Oak Ridge National Laboratory, 1979. 182 pp.

Inventories Cherokee County's capabilities and the project characteristics of the Cherokee Nuclear Station, then projects expected impacts from the interaction of the two, defines four options for Cherokee County decision makers, and presents a range of possible mitigation and monitoring plans.

* President's Economic Adjustment Committee. *Boom Town Business Opportunities and Development Management.* Cited above as item 163.

585. President's Economic Adjustment Committee. *Community Impact Assistance Study.* Washington, D.C.: Intergovernmental/ Interagency Task Force on Community Assistance, 1981. 282 pp.

Reports results of a study to identify adverse impacts on communities in areas in which major, new military facilities are constructed and to determine the most effective and practicable means of mitigating such impacts. Five specific tasks and policy issues addressed by the study were to (1) identify those potential Department of Defense actions that are sufficient in scope to warrant impact assistance by the federal government; (2) examine various options and recommend organizational mechanisms to administer the federal community impact assistance to be made available; (3) examine various options and recommend procedures for budgeting community impact assistance funds; (4) recommend such changes in existing programs as may be necessary to provide effective and timely impact assistance to areas adversely affected by the construction of major, new military facilities, and (5) consult with and seek the advice of appropriate state and local leaders and officials regarding the problems and needs of communities that result from the construction of major, new military facilities in or near such communities.

586. Rees, William E. "Planning on Our Arctic Frontier: Setting the Stage." *Plan Canada* 21, No. 4 (1982): 107-16.

Critiques government policy and regulation surrounding energy and mineral resource development in the Yukon and Northwest Territories, Canada. Despite steadily mounting development pressure, the Federal Department of Indian Affairs and Northern Development (DIAND), which is solely responsible for both socioeconomic assessment and environmental protection, has yet to implement a coordinated approach to resources planning or overall development policy. Current regulation of private sector activities is composed of a confusing array of permitting systems and reactive administrative devices. Rees reviews two of the most important administrative regulations, the Territorial Land Use Regulations and the Environmental Assessment Review Process (EARP) and essentially finds them inadequate in advancing the various public interests in northern development.

587. Roberts, Richard, Judy Fisher, Ulise L. Bruchet, and Norm Follett. *A Corporate Response to the Changing Business Environment of the 1980's.* Calgary, Alberta: Praxis, A Social Planning Company, 1982. 21 pp.

Documents a four-year project undertaken by Gulf Canada Resources Inc. to assess the changing environments of political, economic, and public expectations and the impacts these would have on resource policy developments. The objective was to create a statement of socioeconomic principles for the company and to identify a series of company practices to implement these principles.

588. ROMCOE, Center for Environmental Problem Solving. *Rapid Growth Communities Project, Final Report.* 18 volumes. Boulder, Colorado: ROMCOE, Center for Environmental Problem Solving, 1982. 1810 pp.

Summarizes results of in-depth case studies of four communities that had experienced substantial growth resulting from energy resource development. The study team worked with community officials and residents, gathering information about their experiences and advice for others. The information was compiled into four types of publications. *Community Profiles* give a brief historical overview of the experiences of the four communities. *Experiences and Advice* reports describe the ways in which the communities and their residents responded to change and are organized by topic area (such as education, housing, etc.). A *Resource Handbook* provides a "cookbook" of options for solving specific problems or dealing with specific issues. Finally, a *Guidelines for Users* report provides suggestions of how the information base can be used to help a community prepare for change.

589. U.S. Commission on Civil Rights. *Energy Resource Development: Implications for Women and Minorities in the*

Intermountain West. Washington, D.C.:   Government Printing
Office, 1979.   221 pp.

Contains selected papers presented at a consultation
sponsored by the Colorado, Montana, North Dakota, South
Dakota, Utah, and Wyoming Advisory Committees to the U.S.
Commission on Civil Rights. All of the 23 papers deal with
some aspect of the impacts of energy resource development and
associated population growth on women or on such racial and
ethnic minority groups as Blacks, Hispanics, and Indian
people.

590.   Warrack, Alan, and Lynne Dale. "Megaprojects and Small
Communities: Do They Mean Progress?" *Small Town* 12, No. 6
(1982):   9–14.

Discusses the types of impacts incurred by small communities
as a result of megaproject development and questions whether
the resultant growth really constitutes "progress" for the
affected communities. Characteristics of megaprojects (using
examples from Alberta, Canada) and project-community propor-
tionality are described. Level of impact analysis varies
depending on whether accounting is micro (community level) or
macro (regional or national level). The authors challenge the
prevailing public management and planning view by asking
whether each accounting level is expected to be better off as
a result of megaproject construction and operation.

591.   Watson, Keith S. "Measuring and Mitigating Socio-Economic
Environmental Impacts of Constructing Energy Projects: An
Emerging Regulatory Issue." *Natural Resources Lawyer* 10,
No. 2 (1977):   393–403.

Reviews socioeconomic impact mitigation requirements
resulting from licensing actions by the Nuclear Regulatory
Commission (NRC) and the Federal Power Commission (FPC).
Because these were the first power plant licensing proceedings
in which socioeconomic issues had been extensively litigated,
the author believes they merit careful analysis. The NRC
reviewed the socioeconomic mitigation program proposed by the
Tennessee Valley Authority (TVA) for the Hartsville Nuclear
Plant, and TVA committed itself to provide financial and in-
kind assistance to impacted communities. The FPC considered
similar issues in connection with the Bath County Pumped
Storage Project in Virginia and appended conditions to the
project license to require Virginia Electric Power Company to
initiate a mitigation program.

592.   Weber, Bruce A., and Robert E. Howell, eds. *Coping with
Rapid Growth in Rural Communities.* Boulder, Colorado:
Westview Press, 1982.   284 pp.

Contains ten original articles which examine various aspects of impact assessment and management. Many major impact dimensions are discussed, and impact mitigation alternatives are presented.

Contains items 137, 223, 255, 287, 369, 419.

593. Yarie, Sally, ed. *Alaska Symposium on the Social, Economic, and Cultural Impacts of Natural Resource Development.* Fairbanks: University of Alaska, 1983. 297 pp.

Consists of thirty-three papers grouped into four major categories: (1) demographic and economic modeling and analysis; (2) facility siting and public participation; (3) family, social, and cultural concerns; and (4) impact mitigation.

Contains items 553, 560, 574.

Specific Management Measures

COMPENSATION AND INCENTIVES

594. Ackerman, Bruce A. "The Jurisprudence of Just Compensation." *Environmental Law* 7 (1977): 509-18.

Discusses some of the legal and philosophical issues behind "just compensation" and addresses the issue of when a taking of property has occurred and compensation demands arise.

595. Bacow, Lawrence S., and James R. Milkey. "Overcoming Local Opposition to Hazardous Waste Facilities: The Massachusetts Approach." *Harvard Environmental Law Review* 6, No. 2 (1982): 265-305.

Describes the causes of local opposition to siting hazardous waste facilities and analyzes two particular approaches in state siting laws—preemption of local authority and payment of incentives to local communities. The Massachusetts siting statute is held up as an innovative example which requires developers to negotiate compensation agreements with host communities.

596. Bacow, Lawrence, and Judah Rose. *Compensating Diffuse Interest Groups for Social Costs.* Document No. 14, Part B. Energy Impacts Project. Cambridge: Massachusetts Institute

of Technology, Laboratory of Architecture and Planning, 1979. 12 pp.

Discusses the possible sources and motivations for opposition to large-scale energy facilities, such as nuclear power plants and oil refineries. Opponents of these projects may be either local groups or groups with geographically diffuse memberships. Specifically, the authors attempt to identify (1) who should be compensated, (2) what form compensation should take, and (3) possible means of binding parties to compensation agreements.

597. Becker, Jeanne F. "The Use of Incentives and Compensation to Overcome Public Opposition to the Siting of Hazardous Waste Landfills." Masters Thesis. Milwaukee: University of Wisconsin, Department of Urban Planning, 1980. 115 pp.

Discusses the theoretical and practical arguments which exist in support of the offer of compensatory payments and services to help overcome citizen and community resistance to proposed hazardous waste landfills. Although society benefits from the safe and regulated disposal of hazardous substances, small groups of individuals in the vicinity of the landfill site incur large costs in the form of physical, economic, and social impacts, risks, and uncertainties. The offer of economic and noneconomic incentives will improve the benefit-to-cost ratio for these residents and may contribute to an improved siting process. The author recommends the use of negotiation and mediation between representatives of the waste disposal firm and other parties-at-interest in order to formulate a benefit package which meets the unique needs and concerns of the community in question.

598. Bjornstad, David J., and Kim-Elaine Johnson. "Payments-In-Lieu-of-Taxes Between Federal and Local Governments and the Siting of Federally-Owned Waste Isolation Activities." *The Review of Regional Studies* 12, No. 1 (Spring 1982): 19-31.

Presents an analysis of transfer payments between a federally owned nuclear waste isolation facility and local governments affected by the facility siting. Two types of payments-in-lieu-of-taxes to the host community and block grants to other affected communities are examined. Authors conclude that a variety of payment strategies are available, some of which could provide incentives for communities which encourage siting.

599. Brody, Susan E. *Federal Aid to Energy Impacted Communities: A Review of Related Programs and Legislative Proposals.* Prepared for the U.S. Energy Research and Development Administration. Cambridge: Massachusetts Institute of

Technology, Energy Impacts Project, Laboratory of Architecture & Planning, May 1977. 57 pp.

Reviews federal impact assistance programs by analyzing the underlying objectives of federal aid and the administrative strategies of specific programs. The specific federal impact assistance programs reviewed include the Trident Community Impact Assistance Program, Economic Adjustment to Defense Impacted Communities, Relocation Assistance, and Disaster Relief. The author also reviews two types of impact assistance programs peculiar to energy development: grants and loans for planning, facility construction, and impact mitigation (e.g., Coastal Energy Impact Program); and compensation for the loss of expected revenues (e.g., payments-in-lieu-of-taxes).

600. Canadian Resourcecon Limited. *A Renewable Compensation Program for the Northwest Territories: Review of Policy Options.* Yellowknife, Northwest Territories: Government of the Northwest Territories, 1982. 64 pp.

Provides background information for the development of a compensation policy for the Northwest Territories. Topics addressed include the need for a compensation policy, approaches for institutionalizing compensation requirements, and compensation policies in other jurisdictions (Alberta, British Columbia, Manitoba, Yukon Territory, and United Kingdom). A recommended approach to compensation is presented.

601. Carnes, S. A., E. D. Copenhaver, J. H. Reed, E. J. Soderstrom, J. H. Sorensen, E. Peelle, and David J. Bjornstad. *Incentives and the Siting of Radioactive Waste Facilities.* ORNL-5880. Oak Ridge, Tennessee: Oak Ridge National Laboratory, 1982. 83 pp.

Examines the potential usefulness of incentives in increasing local support and decreasing local opposition to hosting nuclear waste facilities. Incentives are classified by functional categories, and the conditions which may be prerequisite to the use of incentives are outlined. Criteria for evaluating the utility of incentives in nuclear waste repository siting are developed.

602. Cole, Ronald J., and Tracy A. Smith. *Compensation for the Adverse Impacts of Nuclear Waste Management Facilities: Application of an Analytical Framework to Consideration of Eleven Potential Impacts.* Seattle: Battelle Human Affairs Research Centers, 1979. 61 pp.

Characterizes eleven socioeconomic impacts created by a nuclear waste repository; provides a framework for analysis of

when compensation for impacts should be considered from the
viewpoints of legal authority, economic efficiency, fairness,
project strategy, and implementation; describes suggested
forms which compensation could take.

603. Cordes, Joseph J. "Compensation Through Relocation
      Assistance." *Land Economics* 55, No. 4 (1979): 486-98.

      Evaluates adequacy of the Uniform Relocation Assistance and
      Real Property Acquisition Policies Act for providing compensa-
      tion to renter households dislocated by urban renewal and
      highway projects. Cordes employs both graphical and mathemat-
      ical analysis to obtain estimates of welfare changes of alter-
      native policies and concludes that relocation assistance
      payments made in 1972 (the study year) provided adequate or
      more than adequate compensation for losses under all alterna-
      tive assumptions.

604. Cordes, Joseph J., and Burton A. Weisbrod. "Governmental
      Behavior in Response to Compensation Requirements." *Journal
      of Public Economics* 11 (1979): 47-58.

      Explores, through the use of models, the response of public
      agencies to requirements that compensation be paid to persons
      harmed by agency activities. These models indicate that
      introduction of compensation requirements restricts the amount
      of budget funds available for direct construction, and also
      alters the relative budgetary costs of competing projects.
      Specific applications of the model to the case of federally
      aided highway construction are examined.

605. Ervin, David E., and James B. Fitch. "Evaluating Alternative
      Compensation and Recapture Techniques for Expanded Public
      Control of Land Use." *Natural Resources Journal* 19 (January
      1979): 21-41.

      Discusses three types of compensation-recapture programs:
      transferable development rights, zoning by eminent domain, and
      zoning auctions in terms of efficiency and equity. These
      techniques may provide potential improvement over existing
      direct regulation procedures if the trend toward expanded
      public control of land use continues. These techniques also
      offer possible improvements in efficiency and equity in the
      compensation-recapture process.

   * Fowler, John M., Jeff M. Witte, and Jerry G. Schickedanz.
      *Oil and Gas Interactions with the Ranching Industry in New
      Mexico.* Bulletin 715. Cited above as item 110.

606. Kasperson, Roger E., ed. *Equity Issues in Radioactive Waste Management.* Cambridge, Massachusetts: Oelgeschlager, Gunn & Hain, Publishers, 1983. 381 pp.

    Examines three major types of equity problems in radioactive waste management: (1) locus or siting issues; (2) legacy issues, such as time dimensions and intergenerational relations; and (3) labor or laity issues relating to radiation protection standards, compensation, temporary workers, and informed consent. The book concludes with a set of proposals for a more equitable approach to the management of radioactive wastes.

607. Leitch, Jay A., and Donald F. Scott. "Improving Wetland Policy Through Amelioration of Adverse Effects on Local Economies." *Water Resources Bulletin* 20, No. 5 (1984): 887-93.

    Uses an input-output model to estimate changes in expenditure and income flows due to restoring drained wetlands in North Dakota. Results indicate a payment in addition to the amount paid to the landowner may be necessary to make local economies as well off after restoration as before.

608. O'Hare, Michael. "Compensation for Development Impacts." *Environmental Comment* (September 1978): 13-15.

    Briefly examines arguments, with respect to efficiency and equity considerations, for compensating those individuals and groups suffering losses due to siting of major facilities.

609. O'Hare, Michael. "Not On My Block You Don't: Facility Siting and the Strategic Importance of Compensation." *Public Policy* 25, No. 4 (Fall 1977): 407-58.

    Contends that an important failing of current practice in siting an ugly or dangerous facility is the strategic problem that results from failure to pay compensation to neighbors who suffer costs (losses in property values or less measurable amenity costs) not found to be a taking under law. Unless such compensation is paid, a socially beneficial project can be stalled or blocked permanently on each possible site. If local sufferers are compensated, choosing the right amount to pay is more important than accurately estimating (uncompensated) social costs for purposes of benefit-cost analysis. Auctioning the facility to the community demanding the least compensation effects correct compensation and overcomes important strategic, efficiency, and equity problems in the siting process; some feasible ways to conduct such auctions are outlined and reviewed.

610. O'Hare, Michael, and Debra R. Sanderson. "Fair Compensation
      and the Boomtown Problem." *Urban Law Annual* 14 (1977):
      101-33.

      Considers the general "boom town problem" and current
      compensation approaches. The appropriateness of subsidy
      schemes is analyzed on theoretical grounds. This analysis
      suggests that the effect of subsidies as usually designed is
      to reward people who are not in fact injured by the develop-
      ment and to miss many of those who deserve aid. The authors
      contend that an appropriate compensation plan requires that
      the affected groups of people be more carefully described.

611. Raimondo, Henry J. "Compensation Policy for Tax Exempt
      Property in Theory and Practice." *Land Economics* 56, No. 1
      (1980): 33-42.

      Describes rationale for tax exemption, discusses current
      policies and obstacles to reform, and examines specific cases
      of Tennessee Valley Authority and national forests.

612. Skiffington, Lucy J. "Constitutionality of State Economic
      Incentives for Energy Development." *Journal of Energy Law
      and Policy* 2, No. 1 (1981) 13-44.

      Critiques the state use of financial incentives to energy
      companies to spur development of energy resources and thus
      stimulate local and state economies. The author discusses the
      possible restrictions on state incentives because of constitu-
      tional debt limits and other legal restrictions which place
      controls on the type and degree of economic aid to private
      enterprise. Skiffington proposes that there is a need to
      identify the limits of state aid to the energy industry and
      explores the legal basis for changing state constitutional
      debt provisions allowing for the broader use of public monies
      in aid to private enterprise.

613. Sorensen, John H., Jon Soderstrom, and Sam A. Carnes. "Sweet
      for the Sour: Incentives in Environmental Mediation."
      Environmental Management 8, No. 4 (1984): 287-94.

      Explores the use of incentive systems as a means of
      achieving equity in environmental mediation over the siting of
      undesirable facilities. Obnoxious and noxious characteristics
      of facilities are discussed as the basis of conflicts. Four
      types of incentives--mitigation, compensation, reward, and
      participation--are discussed. The paper concludes with a
      discussion of the utility and application of incentives for
      solving environmental conflicts.

614. Steeg, Robert M. "Federal Agency Compensation of Intervenors." *Environmental Affairs* 5, No. 4 (1976): 697-719.

Compares different methods of increasing public representation. Techniques discussed include intra-agency public representation, agency cost-shifting, establishing a separate federal public advocacy agency, providing legal services for intervenors, and direct agency compensation of intervenors. Steeg discusses possible legislation for compensation of intervenors and concludes that direct agency compensation of intervenors can achieve widespread, beneficial public participation in administrative proceedings.

615. Susskind, Lawrence, and Michael O'Hare. *Managing the Social and Economic Impacts of Energy Development.* Summary Report. Phase 1 of the MIT Energy Impacts Project. Cambridge: Massachusetts Institute of Technology, 1977. 522 pp.

Summarizes work performed by the MIT Energy Impacts Project. Of primary interest in this document are the authors' treatment of the structure and methods of compensation of impacted individuals and communities, and the so-called "auction" concept. This novel idea involves local governments' competing for (against) a proposed facility by submitting "bids" equal to the amount of compensation the community would require to host the facility. These compensation costs are then factored into the siting process. The study also examines cases of state approaches to impact assistance in Colorado, North Dakota, Texas, and Wyoming.

616. Sutton, Gerry. *Trappers' Rights.* Edmonton, Alberta: Alberta Trappers' Central Association and Native Outreach, 1980. 62 pp.

Examines the rights of trappers with respect to the land on which their traplines are located. The primary thesis of the report is that the trapper does have an interest in the land not only in the matter of compensation but also in the regulation of land use so as to minimize damage to the interest of the trapper.

617. Urban Systems Research and Engineering, Inc. *Using Compensation and Incentives When Siting Hazardous Waste Management Facilities--A Handbook for Developers and States.* Washington, D.C.: U.S. Environmental Protection Agency, 1980. 59 pp.

Informs state government officials, legislators, and developers of hazardous waste facilities about alternative techniques for dealing with many of the issues that stimulate community concern and public opposition. It discusses the concept of compensating people and communities for costs they

bear because of a facility, and the concept of providing
incentives to encourage the siting of hazardous waste management facilities. The handbook explains how to use compensation and incentives and explores some of the major issues and
problems with applying them.

618. Wolpert, Julian. "Regressive Siting of Public Facilities."
     Natural Resources Journal. (Item 687), pp. 103–15.

     Examines recent trends in siting "necessary" but "noxious"
     public facilities, which suggest that such projects have not
     been structured to provide incentives for minimizing costly
     disamenities. The paper focuses on the locational conflicts
     surrounding the siting of urban expressways, airports, and
     urban renewal projects in the United States, Canada, and
     Japan.

FACILITY SITING AND OTHER LEGAL REQUIREMENTS

619. Auger, Camilla S., and Martin E. Zeller. *Siting Major Energy*
     Facilities: A Process in Transition. Boulder, Colorado:
     TOSCO Foundation, 1979. 115 pp.

     Summarizes experience of state energy facility siting
     programs during the 1970s. Reviews federal-state interaction
     in facility-siting decisions and evaluates success of state
     siting legislation in twenty-seven states. Recommendations
     include suggested regulatory reforms to streamline the siting
     process.

620. Begg, Hugh M., and Keith Newton. "Strategic Planning for Oil
     and Gas." *Town Planning Review* 51, No. 1 (1980): 76–85.

     Attempts to develop a conceptual framework within which
     local planning authorities can adopt a positive approach to
     oil- and gas-related development. The framework is applied to
     recent proposals for development of petroleum processing
     facilities in Scotland.

621. Calzonetti, Frank J., and Mark S. Eckert. *Finding a Place*
     for Energy: Siting Coal Conversion Facilities. Resource
     Publication in Geography No. 2. Washington, D.C.: Associa-
     tion of American Geographers, 1981. 70 pp.

     Broadly addresses the energy facility siting problem,
     focusing on some critical locational issues. Of particular
     concern is the process of identifying, licensing, and develop-
     ing energy facility sites. Throughout the discussion, the
     decision-making environment surrounding facility siting is

emphasized. Discussed are the permiting process, utility firm's organizational behavior, least-cost siting approaches, strategies for resolving locational conflict, and impact mitigation options.

622. Calzonetti, Frank J., Mark S. Eckert, and Edward J. Malecki. "Siting Energy Facilities in the U.S.A.: Policies For the Western States." *Energy Policy* 8 (1980): 138-52.

Reports that the current system for siting energy facilities in the western United States is based on a piecemeal approach to planning and leads to conflict and delay. The authors suggest that many of the problems associated with siting energy conversion plants can be substantially reduced by an anticipatory system of siting and that such a system could reduce the effects of the plant on the local area. Three general policy options are examined: (1) administrative site screening, (2) impact mitigation, and (3) one-stop siting.

623. Canter, Bram D. E. "Hazardous Waste Disposal and the New State Siting Programs." *Natural Resources Lawyer* 14, No. 3 (1982): 421-36.

Briefly outlines the dimensions of the hazardous waste dilemma and reviews regulatory frameworks of Resource Conservation and Recovery Act (RCRA) and typical state hazardous waste management programs. Canter then compares twelve state siting programs. Three common elements were found: special siting boards, exercise of override authority over local government vetoes, and measures of enhancing public participation. The author offers suggestions for optimum state siting programs and includes an appendix of siting criteria.

624. Dames & Moore. *Methodology for the Analysis of Cumulative Impacts of Permit Activities Regulated by the U.S. Army Corps of Engineers--Final Handbook.* Prepared for the U.S. Army Corps of Engineers, Institute for Water Resources, Fort Belvoir, Virginia. Contract DACW72-80-C-0012. Bethesda, Maryland: National Technical Information Service, 1981.

Was prepared to guide Corps' regulatory personnel in performing analyses of the cumulative environmental impacts of activities requiring permit applications. The methodology is generalized yet flexible for accomplishing cumulative impact assessment for any of a range of engineering activities. The approach is oriented around a system for "tiering" the analysis to fit the activity and its range of anticipated impacts. One basic approach, the "top-down" method tracks exogenous, growth-inducing, and growth-induced activity for the purpose of analyzing regional social and economic effects in rapidly urbanizing areas. The other basic approach, the "bottom-up" method, handles social and economic impacts by tracing biological effects through a causal network and establishing their secondary and higher order impacts on social and economic systems.

625. Fletcher, W. Wendell. *Energy Facility Siting.* Washington, D.C.: Congressional Research Service, Library of Congress, 1975. 49 pp.

Provides overview analysis of state and federal involvement in electric utility facility siting with treatment of various projections of future siting needs, secondary impacts of energy facility siting, and efficiency of the electric power industry, including an interesting section on special issues pertaining to siting.

626. Hamilton, Michael S. "Developing an Energy Policy on Power Plant Siting: The Utah Experiment." *Journal of Energy Law and Policy* 3, No. 1 (1983): 169–88.

Surveys the site selection process of the Kaiparowits Project and the Intermountain Power Project in Utah and traces the development of an energy policy for the state of Utah and the establishment of a unique intergovernmental coordination mechanism—the Utah Interagency Task Force on power plant siting. Hamilton argues that the Utah experience affords an interesting and significant case study in policy adaptation designed to minimize the unproductive political confrontation in regulatory forums, and proposes that the Utah example could serve as a model of conflict resolution over energy facility site selection in other states.

627. Lapsley, H. A. Graeme. "The Community Impact of North Sea Oil." *Onshore Impact of Offshore Oil.* Edited by W. J. Cairnes and P. M. Rogers. Englewood, New Jersey: Applied Science Publishers, 1981. pp. 173–83.

Discusses the effect of oil-related development on the Orkney community. Private legislation achieved wider control of oil-related development than that provided by the existing statute. Development was controlled by planning conditions, contractual agreements and licensing, with minimal local authority participation in management and finance. Social impacts include crime, local employment prospects, and effects on indigenous industry. Financial impacts include an anomalous rating situation and the effects of additional revenues accruing to the local authority.

628. MacDonnell, Lawrence J. "Regulating Socioeconomic Impacts: Comparing the Colorado and Wyoming Approaches." *Land and Water Law Review* 20, No. 1 (1985): 193–206.

Presents a descriptive analysis of two western states in their approaches to mitigate socioeconomic impacts associated with recently developed large-scale energy projects. Differences between Colorado and Wyoming in regulatory bodies, control of impact areas, and mitigation responsibilities are compared.

629. Morell, David, and Grace Singer. *Refining the Waterfront: Alternative Energy Facility Siting Policies for Urban Coastal Areas.* Cambridge, Massachusetts: Oelgeschlager, Gunn, and Hain, Publishers, Inc., 1980. 343 pp.

Comprised of thirteen articles which examine various aspects of energy facility siting. Attention is focussed on petrochemical facilities located in the East Coast and Gulf Coast regions. The trade-offs associated with coastal vs. inland and urban vs. rural siting are examined.

⋆ Murdock, Steve H., F. Larry Leistritz, and Rita R. Hamm, eds. *Nuclear Waste: Socioeconomic Dimensions of Long-Term Storage.* Cited below as item 965.

630. Murray, William G., and Carl J. Seneker. "Implementation of an Industrial Siting Plan." *The Hastings Law Journal* 31 (1980): 1073-89.

Discusses ways in which the decisionmaking process for major industrial facilities can be improved. The first section discusses the need for a master siting agency and a one-stop siting process. The second section discusses who should make industrial siting decisions and focuses on the need to have the decision made by those who will best represent public opinion. The third section considers the problems inherent in the conflict between state and local control. Fourth, the authors review and reject the concept of a master industrial siting plan. Finally, they propose specific procedures that should govern an industrial siting commission.

631. Murray, William G., and Carl J. Seneker. "Industrial Siting: Allocating the Burden of Pollution." *The Hastings Law Journal* 30 (1978): 301-36.

Addresses the problems of major-facility industrial growth as they apply to environmental concerns. It is based on two premises: first, the pressure for industrial expansion, including public pressure from those who would directly benefit from such expansion, will continue; second, such additional industrial facilities will pollute. Accepting these premises, the authors feel industrial siting becomes a problem of finding the best way of using available resources to maximize the quality of life.

632. O'Hare,   Michael,   Lawrence   Bacow,   and   Debra   Sanderson.
      Facility Siting and Public Opposition.   New   York: Van
      Nostrand Reinhold Company, 1983.   223 pp.

      Proposes   a fundamentally new approach to   facility siting--
      based on negotiated compensation for the local disamenity--and
      provides theoretical   analysis of   the use of   information and
      compensation in the major public decision of   facility siting.
      Focus is   on the relationship between facility developers and
      the near neighbors of new facilities.   The siting process
      recommended is based on a critical review of   current practice
      and   proposed reforms with particular consideration   placed on
      information and   its   use   in public decision making.   The
      theoretical analysis is supported by a series of   case studies
      of facility siting disputes in proposed nuclear   power facili-
      ties in Searsport, Maine,   and Seabrook, New Hampshire;   a
      hazardous waste   facility in Wilsonville,   Illinois; Grayrocks
      Dam in Wyoming; proposed nuclear power plants   near Montague,
      Massachusetts, and Skagit, Washington;   a   resource recovery
      facility in Haverhill, Massachusetts;   and   Wes-Con hazardous
      waste facility in Idaho.

633. Openshaw,   S.   "The Siting of Nuclear Power Stations and
      Public Safety in the UK."   *Regional Studies* 16, No. 3 (June
      1982):   183-98.

      Considers current   siting procedures of   nuclear power
      stations and the tendency to neglect the importance of siting
      as an   additional safety measure.   Past and present siting
      policies   are examined,   and   a   number   of deficiencies
      identified.   Methods are   demonstrated that   can be   utilized
      both to search for optimal safe sites and to measure the
      suboptimality of current sites.

634. Organization   for Economic   Co-operation and Development
      (OECD).   *The Siting of Major Energy Facilities.*   Paris:
      OECD, 1979.   124 pp.

      Is   primarily addressed to those who formulate national
      environmental or energy policies.   It concentrates on siting
      policies and procedures and the division of responsibility
      between national, regional, and local authorities. Comprehen-
      sive information on socioeconomic impacts resulting from the
      siting of major energy facilities also is provided.   Electric
      generating plants are often used as an example for describing
      the   different phenomena, but the conclusions and recommenda-
      tions are considered to be generally applicable to such energy
      facilities   as oil refineries, liquified natural gas plants,
      oil terminals, and coal synthetic fuel plants.

635. Organization for Economic Cooperation and Development (OECD).
      *Siting Procedures for Major Energy Facilities: Some
      National Cases.* Paris: OECD, 1980. 142 pp.

      Is a companion volume of an earlier OECD report (item 634)
      which concentrated on siting policy and the division of
      responsibility between national, regional, and local
      authorities in various OECD member countries. The present
      monograph is concerned with the siting procedures for nuclear
      power plants in the United States, France, and the Federal
      Republic of Germany. The American experience with EISs and
      the role of environmental groups in the siting of nuclear
      power plants are described along with the developments in the
      procedures for siting thermal power plants in France and
      Germany. A concluding discussion concentrates on the social
      and economic impacts of siting on local communities, using
      statistics of nuclear power plants from France, Belgium,
      Switzerland, United States, Japan, and Italy

636. Paget, G. E., and M. G. Lloyd. "Resource Management and Land
      Use Planning: Natural Gas in Scotland." *Journal of
      Environmental Management* 15 (1982): 15–23.

      Reports that successive governments have attempted to manage
      the development of North Sea oil and gas in order to serve the
      wider social interest, and to maximize the associated economic
      and strategic benefits. The responsibility, however, for
      managing the necessary onshore investments in the social
      interest lies with the statutory land use planning system.
      There is evidence to suggest, however, that the innovations in
      the planning system, at national and local levels, will be
      marginal in effect.

637. Peelle, Elizabeth. "Socioeconomic Impact Assessment and
      Nuclear Power Plant Licensing: Greene County, New York."
      *Improving Impact Assessment: Increasing the Relevance and
      Utilization of Scientific and Technical Information.* Edited
      by Stuart L. Hart, Gordon A. Enk, and William F. Hornick.
      Boulder, Colorado: Westview Press, 1984. pp. 93–117.

      Points out that the Final Environmental Statement (FES) for
      the proposed Greene County Nuclear Power Plant (on the Hudson
      River below Albany, New York) is unique among Nuclear Regula-
      tory Commission impact statements because (1) it contains an
      extensive socioeconomic analysis and an unprecedented
      aesthetic analysis and (2) it is the first Nuclear Regulatory
      Commission FES ever to recommend denial of a construction
      permit on aesthetic and socioeconomic grounds.

638. Pring, George W. "'Power to Spare': Conditioning Federal
      Resource Leases to Protect Social, Economic, and

Environmental Values."   *Natural Resources   Lawyer* 14, No. 2
(1981):   305-38.

Analyzes the federal government's constitutional, statutory,
judicial, and departmental authority to condition federal
resource leasing. Next, it examines conditioning authority in
five specific areas: off-site, wildlife, transportation,
socioeconomic, and application of state-local laws. The
federal government's actual track record in 1980-81 is
examined, and the argument is addressed that the federal
government has not only the power but the legal duty to
regulate these impacts through specific lease conditions.

639. Randle,   Russell V.   "Coastal Energy Siting Dilemmas."
      Natural Resources Journal 21 (1981):   125-59.

Examines disputes over the siting of a liquid propane gas
terminal and an oil refinery in coastal North Carolina in
order to understand the obstacles to using a trade-off
approach to facility siting. The author feels that there are
three major obstacles to a successful trade-off policy for
siting: preemption of important regulatory matters by the
federal government, fragmentation of permit processes and
appeals, and failure of state and federal regulatory programs
to adequately address liability and insurance aspects of
energy facilities. Finally, the author suggests the nature of
institutional arrangements he believes are necessary to enable
siting of facilities at an acceptable speed and in an acceptable manner.

*   Skiffington,   Lucy J.   "Constitutionality of State Economic
     Incentives for Energy Development."   *Journal of Energy Law
     and Policy.* Cited above as item 612.

640. Stenehjem,   E., and E. J. Allen.   "Constraints to Energy
      Development."   *American Behavioral Scientist* 22, No. 2
      (November/December 1978):   191-213.

Discusses the problems associated with siting energy facilities in areas having a limited capacity to assimilate social
and economic impacts. It emphasizes the importance of finding
solutions at the state and local levels of government with the
federal government playing a facilitative role. Experience
with western energy development, and resultant concern over
environmental and socioeconomic impacts, has resulted in
significant "impact legislation" in the decade of the 1970s
that is aimed at implementing state control over the quantity
and quality of investment in the energy industry on the one
hand and insuring substantial benefit flows into the producing
states on the other. This paper concludes that a major
problem with energy development is due to underinvestment in
the infrastructure required to support development and that

underlying the problem is an apparent inability of the process to consider public interests and needs, both within and without the local impact area.

641. White, Irvin L., and John P. Spath. "How are States Setting Their Sites?" *Environment* 26, No. 8 (1984): 17-20, 36-42.

Provides a history of low-level radioactive waste disposal practices and discusses the problems and logistics that states now face in contending with this issue.

PUBLIC PARTICIPATION, NEGOTIATION, AND MEDIATION

642. Albrecht, Stan L. "Community Response to Large-Scale Federal Projects: The Case of the MX." *Nuclear Waste: Socioeconomic Dimensions of Long-Term Storage.* Edited by Steve H. Murdock, F. Larry Leistritz, and Rita R. Hamm. (Item 965), pp. 233-50.

Provides (1) a brief overview of the MX missile system's characteristics and the potential impacts it would have had on the rural areas of Utah and Nevada where it was to be located, (2) a description of the patterns of community mobilization that occurred in Utah and Nevada in response to the MX system, and (3) a discussion of the parallels between patterns of community response to the MX and those likely to be important in nuclear waste repository siting.

643. Amy, Douglas James. "Environmental Mediation: An Alternative Approach to Policy Stalemates." *Policy Sciences* 15 (1983): 345-65.

Discusses an alternative process for resolving environmental conflicts. The approach called environmental mediation has advantages over other approaches in its emphasis on direct dialogue between competing interests, the unique role of the mediator in facilitating an agreement, and the delicate balance of power it engenders between the opposing parties. Using a case study of mediation between Indian tribal authorities and local planning officials in Portage Island, Washington, the author illustrates that mediation can provide more direct and meaningful participation by interested parties in the decision-making process, can prove more efficient than administrative and judicial policymaking, and can result in longer lasting and more satisfying solutions to difficult policy disputes. A concluding statement recommends environmental mediation as a significant development in resolving political conflict.

644. Armour,   Audrey,   ed.   *The Not-In-My-Backyard Syndrome,*
      Symposium Proceedings. Downsview, Ontario: York Univer-
      sity, Faculty of Environmental Studies, 1984.   296 pp.

      Summarizes results of a symposium that attempted to provide
      a neutral forum where the various parties involved in or
      affected by waste management disputes could examine the nature
      of public opposition, consider its causes and implications,
      and explore ways of dealing with the problem of siting waste
      management facilities.

645. Arnstein,   Sherry R.   "A Ladder of Citizen Participation."
      Journal of the American Institute of Planners (July 1969):
      216-24.

      Offers a typology of citizen participation using examples
      from federal urban renewal, anti-poverty, and model cities
      programs. The central feature of the piece is the division of
      citizen participation into levels of power, tokenism, and
      nonparticipation.   This is done under the framework of an
      eight-rung "ladder" whose rungs correspond to (1) manipulation
      and (2) therapy, as levels of nonparticipation; (3) informing,
      (4) consultation, and (5) placation, as degrees of tokenism;
      and (6) partnership, (7) delegated power, and (8) citizen
      control, as degrees of citizen power.

646. Bishop,   A. Bruce, Mac McKee, and Roger D. Hansen.   *Public*
      Consultation in Public Policy Administration: A State-of-
      the-Art Report. Washington, D.C.:   U.S. Energy Research and
      Development Administration, 1977.   155 pp.

      Examines the concept and state-of-the-art of public involve-
      ment in public policy decision.   Questions addressed include
      (1) What are the basic objectives of public participation in
      policy formation and program decisions?, (2) Who are the
      "publics" that should be involved and how can they be
      identified?, (3) What information should be communicated
      between the agency and the publics?, and (4) What techniques
      are available to elicit public participation and involvement
      and what are their capabilities?

647. Burch,   William R.,   Jr.   "Who Participates--A Sociological
      Interpretation of Natural Resource Decisions."   *Natural*
      Resource Journal. (Item 687), pp. 23-54.

      Explores both the social factors that make participation
      claims possible and the nature of natural resources decisions
      which are not readily susceptible to increased participation.

648. Burgess,   Anne Heidi Greenwald. "Public Participation in
      Energy Facility Siting Decision Making."   Unpub. Ph.D.

dissertation. Boulder: University of Colorado, Department of Sociology, 1979. 235 pp.

Evaluates the effects of several forms of public participation on governmental processes for locating major new energy facilities. A theory was developed from sociological literature on decision making and from the extensive descriptive and normative literature on public participation from public administration, energy, and environmental journals. The theory was tested with data collected in lengthy semistructured interviews with about ten respondents in each of four primary sample states (Minnesota, Wyoming, Washington, and Kentucky) which illustrated a wide variety of approaches to public participation in their energy facility siting process.

649. Burt, R. S. *Resolving Community Conflict in the Nuclear Power Issue: A Report and Annotated Bibliography.* Oak Ridge, Tennessee: Office of Waste Isolation, 1978. 184 pp.

Is an initial discussion of conflict resolution intended to aid in the development and presentation of information to help assure that conflicts concerning siting of nuclear facilities will turn on a clear understanding of the issues involved. The author describes the nature of community conflict escalation in the nuclear power siting process, outlines the community level determinants of conflict escalation, discusses alternative methods of containing and resolving conflicts, and develops a list of principles for dealing with community conflict. The final section of the report is a partially annotated bibliography of the literature reviewed in the report; it contains 840 entries.

* Campbell, Kimberly A. *NACo Case Studies on Energy Impacts. No. 2, Controlling Boomtown Development, Sweetwater and Uinta Counties, Wyoming.* Cited below as item 884.

650. Casper, Barry M., and Paul David Wellstone. *Powerline: The First Battle of America's Energy War.* Amherst, Massachusetts: The University of Massachusetts Press, 1981. 314 pp.

Describes community reaction to construction of a high voltage power line in Minnesota. The protest by farmers whose land was crossed began during the siting process, but continued into the construction phase with farmers actively interfering with survey crews. Even after the line was completed, acts of vandalism were common. Reasons for this continuing protest are explored.

651. Centaur   Associates, Inc.   *Siting of Hazardous Waste Manage-*
      ment Facilities and Public Opposition.   Washington, D.C.:
      U.S. Environmental Protection Agency, 1979.   388 pp.

      Provides insights into those factors which give rise to
      public opposition to the siting and operation of hazardous
      waste management facilities and identifies actions taken to
      try to reduce or to overcome that opposition.   Case studies
      were prepared for twenty-one sites, including cases where no
      opposition occurred, where opposition was overcome, and where
      opposition led to either an abandoned siting attempt or the
      closing of a facility.   The authors conclude that public
      opposition to the siting of hazardous waste management
      facilities, particularly landfills, is a critical problem. It
      is the most critical problem in developing new facilities, in
      the   opinion of most government and industry officials
      interviewed.   Once a facility is sited, problems with public
      opposition are not over.   Local communities can and have
      forced operating facilities to close.

652. Charter,   Richard.   "Negotiating for the Nonnegotiable on the
      California Coast."   *Environmental Impact Assessment Review*
      4, Nos. 3-4 (1983):   577-96.

      Offers a history of the conflict over California offshore
      drilling, a perspective on the major issues, and an overview
      of the efforts toward a negotiated settlement concerning a
      recent central California OCS leasing action known as Lease
      Sale #73.   Spokesmen for both the State of California and the
      U.S. Department of the Interior have described the agreement
      as one that heralds a new era of consultation.

653. Clark,   Roger N., and George H. Stankey.   "Analyzing Public
      Input to Resource Decisions: Criteria, Principles and Case
      Examples of the Codinvolve System."   *Natural Resources
      Journal.*   (Item 687), pp. 213-36.

      Describes   the development,   application,   and problems
      associated with an objective and reliable system that could be
      uniformly applied for analyzing public input.

654. Coppock, Rob. "Decision-Making When Public Opinion Matters."
      Policy Sciences 8 (1977):   135-46.

      Applies topological concepts to the description of decision
      making when support for the resulting policy is an important
      criterion. Coppock uses the example of governmental decisions
      concerning construction of a nuclear energy plant in West
      Germany to develop a model that describes how certain input or
      control factors (need for energy and danger of nuclear
      technology) can combine to produce discontinuous or divergent
      policy decisions.

655. Creighton, James, Jerry Delli Priscoli, and C. Mark Dunning. *Public Involvement Techniques: A Reader of Ten Years Experience at the Institute for Water Resources.* IWR Research Rpt. 82-R1. Ft. Belvoir, Virginia: U.S. Army Corps of Engineers, Institute for Water Resources, 1982. 493 pp. plus appendix.

Contains forty-five articles organized into nine major sections. Drawing primarily from the experience of the Corps of Engineers in structuring public involvement programs, the authors examine (1) the rationale and need for public involvement, (2) principles for structuring public involvement programs, (3) institutional implications and constraints, (4) identifying public interest groups, (5) planning public meetings, (6) other (non-meeting) public involvement techniques, (7) public involvement in general permitting, (8) evaluation of public involvement programs, and (9) future issues in public involvement.

656. Crompton, John L., Charles W. Lamb, and Patrick Schul. "The Attitude of Public Agencies Toward Public Participation as Perceived by Their Senior Administrators." *Journal of the Community Development Society* 12, No. 1 (1981): 21-31.

Examines attitudes toward public participation via a survey of Texas public recreation and park agency officials. Three major findings resulted from the survey. First, public agencies contacted in the survey appeared to favor public involvement in decision making. Second, larger agencies tended to be more positively disposed toward implementing public involvement procedures than were smaller agencies. Third, attitudes regarding public involvement did not vary significantly with respect to age, sex, or educational levels.

657. Daneke, Gregory A. "Public Involvement in Natural Resource Development: A Review of Water Resource Planning." *Environmental Affairs* 6 (1977): 11-31.

Offers several alternatives to increase public participation in environmental decision making: (1) alerting affected publics as to the indirect and broadly distributed benefits and burdens which may accrue to them; (2) underwriting a substantial portion of the informational investment required for effective participation; (3) conducting workshops designed to provide the organizational skills necessary for effective participation; and (4) providing, in some instances, actual financial inducements to invoke involvement.

658. Deal, D. "Durham Controversy: Energy Facility Siting and Land Use Planning and Control Process." *Natural Resources Lawyer* 8, No. 3 (1975): 437-53.

Discusses the public controversy associated with the proposed siting of an off-shore oil refinery terminal in the rural town of Durham, New Hampshire. Though there was support for the proposal among businessmen and blue-collar workers in the town, the proposal was withdrawn even before formally requesting the necessary rezoning because public sentiment had become so unfavorable.

659.   Delli   Priscoli,   Jerry.   "Implementing   Public   Involvement
       Programs   in Federal   Agencies."   *Citizen Participation   in
       America*.   Edited   by   Stuart   Langton.   Lexington,
       Massachusetts: Lexington Books, 1979. pp. 97-108.

Examines three topics related to implementation of citizen-involvement programs by federal agencies: (1) the inherent problems that are common in all attempts to implement citizen involvement; (2) the most common pitfalls of agencies in the implementation process and how they can be avoided or managed; and (3) practical guidelines to simplify the planning and implementation of citizen involvement.

660.   Dotson,   A. Bruce.   "Who and How?   Participation in Environ-
       mental Negotiation." *Environmental Impact Assessment Review*
       4, No. 2 (1983): 203-17.

Contends that how negotiations are structured has signifi-cant consequences for the eventual outcome of a dispute resolution effort. Who participates and in what ways are among the key elements of this structure. Three negotiations over local land use are described here to illustrate how the element of participation was critical in each instance to the results achieved.

   *   Draper,   Dianne.   *Public   Participation   in   Environmental
       Decision-making*. No. 396. Cited below as item 983.

661.   Duberg,   John A.,   Michael L.   Frankel,   and   Christopher   M.
       Niemczewski.   "Siting   of   Hazardous   Waste   Management
       Facilities and Public Opposition." *Environmental Impact
       Assessment Review* 1 (1980): 84-88.

Reports results of a project, sponsored by the U.S. Environ-mental Protection Agency, which was intended to provide insights into those factors which give rise to public opposi-tion to the siting and operation of hazardous waste management facilities, and to identify the actions taken to try to reduce or overcome that opposition. The project addressed cases where no opposition occurred, where opposition was overcome, or where opposition led to either an abandoned siting attempt or the closing of a facility.

662. Ducsik, Dennis W. "Citizen Participation in Power Plant Siting: Aladdin's Lamp or Pandora's Box?" *Journal of the American Planning Association* 47, No. 2 (April 1981): 154-66.

Presents a discussion on the relative merits of citizen participation and a response in particular to some basic concerns utility companies often voice about the practical implications of collaboration with environmentalists and other affected persons. Author concludes that the participatory process has much more to commend it than the electricity industry has heretofore acknowledged, although a great deal has yet to be learned through empirical work as to the design of a constructive interaction process.

663. Farkas, Alan L. "Overcoming Public Opposition to the Establishment of New Hazardous Waste Disposal Sites. *Capital University Law Review* 9, No. 451 (1980): 451-65.

Discusses the need for state action in hazardous waste facility siting. Limiting local zoning powers and possible means for mediating disputes are examined. The author also stresses the need for assurances of sound operating and post-closure management of these sites. The issues of compensation and incentive payments for locally affected areas are also discussed.

664. Fisher, Roger, and William Ury. *Getting to Yes.* Boston: Houghton Mifflin Company, 1981. 163 pp.

Describes the method of principled negotiation developed at the Harvard Negotiation Project. The principled negotiation method is to decide issues on their merits rather than through a haggling process. Mutual gains should be sought whenever possible; when interests conflict, the result should be based on some fair standards independent of the will of either side. The authors suggest the method can be used for any negotiation, from international arms control talks to divorce settlements to hijackings.

665. Freudenburg, William R., and Darryll Olsen. "Public Interest and Political Abuse: Public Participation in Social Impact Assessment." *Journal of the Community Development Society* 14, No. 2 (1983): 67-82.

Discusses potential benefits, costs, and misuses of public participation programs in SIA. Potential advantages might include: (1) democracy and locality development--increased public access to decision making, (2) communication, (3) enhanced project legitimacy leading to greater faith in the final outcome, and (4) equity and mitigation--identification of potential mitigation strategies, options, and alternatives.

Possible risks of implementing public participation programs
are (1) tokenism, (2) creation of barriers to communication,
(3) loss of legitimacy, and (4) fostering of adversarial
decision making.

666. Friedman, Ben, Karen M. Higgs, Anthony Messina, and Debra R.
      Sanderson. *Energy Facilities and Public Conflict: Four
      Case Studies.* Energy Impacts Project Document No. 13.
      Cambridge: Massachusetts Institute of Technology, 1979.
      138 pp.

      Contains four case studies of efforts to site various types
      of energy facilities. The studies do not provide detailed
      descriptions of the siting procedures followed, but instead
      highlight evidence that helped design and recommend improve-
      ments in siting procedures. Especially important are the
      sources of opposition, factors motivating participants in each
      process, efforts to negotiate either before or after conflicts
      developed, efforts to use compensation or mitigation
      techniques, and the role of information in decision making.
      The case study locations and facility types were as follows:
      Eastport, Maine--oil refinery; Searsport, Maine--oil refinery,
      nuclear power plant, and coal-fired power plant; Haverhill,
      Massachusetts--resource recovery facility; and Boston,
      Massachusetts--cogeneration facility.

667. Garcia-Zamor, Jean-Claude, ed. *Public Participation in
      Development Planning and Management: Cases from Africa and
      Asia.* Boulder, Colorado: Westview Press, 1985. 240 pp.

      Examines the position held by most development administra-
      tors that citizen participation in the planning and management
      of development projects is crucial to their lasting success.
      The contributors view inadequate participation as part of the
      larger problem of ineffective management, policies, and
      planning performance. They show that development objectives
      have been hampered by failures in program implementation.
      Assistance agencies often falter in delivering projects, while
      their clients often fail to sustain them. Case studies from
      African and Asian countries are used to analyze successes and
      failures in efforts to create a participatory process of
      project planning and management.

668. Gibson, Lay James, and Marshall A. Worden. "A Citizen's
      Handbook for Evaluating Community Impacts: An Experiment in
      Community Education." *Journal of the Community Development
      Society* 15, No. 1 (1984): 27-43.

      Reports that four nonmetropolitan communities were selected
      for an experimental community education program designed to
      train local citizens in the general procedures of economic
      impact research. It is argued that citizen participation is

enhanced by a fuller understanding of the technical content of the planning problem at hand and that this understanding is best developed through involvement in a citizen research process prior to policy formulation.

669. Gold, Raymond L. "On Local Control of Western Energy Development." *The Social Science Journal* 16 (April, 1979): 121-27.

Discusses attempts by ranchers and small town residents in coal development areas of the West to retain and regain control of the social structures and practices they believe the energy companies are apt to destroy in the course of extracting and processing western energy resources. The author writes that some locals experience industrial invasion as "people pollution." A big problem for these rural areas is that of trying to find out if development is actually going to happen, on what scale, at what speed, and with what consequences.

 * Gundry, Kathleen. *Public Participation in Planning and Resource Management: An Annotated Bibliography.* No. 1551. Cited below as item 992.

670. Gusman, Sam. "Selecting Participants for a Regulatory Negotiation." *Environmental Impact Assessment Review* 1, No. 2 (1983): 195-202.

Focuses on one aspect of regulatory negotiation—the selection of negotiators to represent parties with an interest in the regulatory issue. Selection of negotiators is felt to be a difficult and important problem from both practical and theoretical points of view.

671. Hadden, Susan G., James R. Chiles, Paul Anaejionu. *High Level Nuclear Waste Disposal: Information Exchange and Conflict Resolution.* DOE/ET/46608-1. Washington, D.C.: Texas Energy and Natural Resources Advisory Council and U.S. Department of Energy, 1981. 205 pp.

Examines public participation and intergovernmental relations issues associated with the siting of a controversial facility, a high-level nuclear waste repository. The authors present both theoretical perspectives and practical considerations. The latter include discussions of experiences and case studies of issues similar to the high-level waste disposal issue and suggestions for avoiding some of the pitfalls identified by those past experiences.

672. Harter,   Philip J.   "Negotiating Regulations: A Cure for the
      Malaise?" *EIA Review* 3, No. 1 (1982): 75–91.

      Excerpts from a report published in the *Georgetown Law
      Journal* (October 1982).   Harter presents two sides of the
      debate over the political and procedural processes of rule-
      making and the nature of government regulation as a whole. He
      argues that a form of negotiation among affected parties would
      be an alternative.

673. Havelock,   Ronald G.   *Planning for Innovation Through
      Dissemination and Utilization of Knowledge.* Ann Arbor,
      Michigan: Center for Utilization of Scientific Knowledge
      and Institute for Social Research, 1975. 532 pp.

      Provides a framework for understanding the processes of
      innovation, dissemination, and knowledge utilization.   The
      modes of dissemination and understanding are grouped into
      three perspectives: (1) research development and diffusion,
      (2) social interaction, and (3) problem solving.   The seven
      factors identified as being highly related to successful
      dissemination and utilization are (1) linkage to internal and
      external resources; (2) degree of structure in resource
      system, user, message and medium; (3) openness of user and
      resource systems; (4) capacity to marshall diverse resources;
      (5) reward; (6) proximity to resources and other users; and
      (7) synergy.   The book thus provides a theoretical basis for
      designing   public–participation   and   information–exchange
      programs.

674. Heberlein,   Thomas A.   "Some Observations on Alternative
      Mechanisms for Public Involvement: The Hearing, Public
      Opinion Poll, the Workshop and   the Quasi–Experiment."
      Natural Resources Journal. (Item 687), pp. 197–212.

      Qualitatively reviews several alternative mechanisms for
      public involvement and discusses their strengths and
      weaknesses.

675. Howell,   Robert E. , and Darryll Olsen.   *Citizen Participation
      in Nuclear Waste Repository Siting.* ONWI–267. Columbus,
      Ohio: Office of Nuclear Waste Isolation, 1982. 71 pp.

      Presents a proposed strategy for citizen participation
      during the planning stages of nuclear waste repository siting.
      It discusses the issue from the general perspective of citizen
      participation in   controversial issues and   in community
      development.   Second, rural institutions and attitudes toward
      energy development as the context for developing a citizen
      participation program are examined.   Third, major citizen
      participation techniques and the advantages and disadvantages
      of each approach for resolving public policy issues are

evaluated. Fourth, principles of successful citizen participation are presented. Finally, a proposal for stimulating and
sustaining effective, responsible citizen participation in
nuclear waste repository siting and management is developed.

676. Howell, Robert E., Marvin E. Olsen, Darryll Olsen, and
Georgia Yuan. "Citizen Participation in Nuclear Waste
Repository Siting." *Nuclear Waste: Socioeconomic Dimen-
sions of Long-Term Storage.* Edited by Steve H. Murdock, F.
Larry Leistritz, and Rita R. Hamm. (Item 965), pp. 267-88.

Describes the general dimensions essential for establishing
an effective citizen participation model for use in siting
controversial facilities. In the first section, the authors
briefly review public involvement efforts at selected large-
scale projects throughout the United States and suggest basic
considerations for designing a citizen participation program
that can be drawn from these efforts. In the second section,
they describe a theoretical basis for designing an effective
public participation program. In the third section, they draw
on both the experiences of past public involvement efforts and
on social theory to describe the dimensions and forms of a
public participation program that they believe could be
effectively applied to nuclear repository siting.

677. Institute for Participatory Planning (IPP). *Citizen Participation Handbook for Public Officials and Other Professionals
Serving the Public.* 3d ed. Laramie, Wyoming: IPP, 1978.
124 pp.

Designed primarily as a text for several short courses on
public participation. Presents principles, objectives,
techniques, and management of public participation. Some case
studies and an extensive bibliography are included.

678. Kent, George. "Community-Based Development Planning." *Third
World Planning Review* 3, No. 3 (1981): 313-26.

Explores the potentials and methods of community-based
development planning. *Community-based* means face-to-face
groups within communities working essentially at their own
initiative. *Planning* is defined as deliberate analytic
efforts designed to guide future decisions and action.

679. Krawetz, Natalia M. *Hazardous Waste Management: A Review of
Social Concerns and Aspects of Public Involvement.* Staff
Report 4. Edmonton, Alberta: Alberta Environment, 1979.
33 pp.

Reviews literature on hazardous waste management in terms of
the social concerns which arise and the design of public

participation programs. Major concerns were effects on human
health and environment, risk and safety, policy considerations, site planning factors, and quality of life. Elements
of public involvement examined were rationale, objectives,
identifying publics, selecting techniques, preparing information, relationships with the media, selecting personnel, and
monitoring and evaluation.

680. Langton, Stuart, ed. *Citizen Participation in America:
      Essays on the State of the Art.* Lexington, Massachusetts:
      Lexington Books, 1978. 125 pp.

      Approaches the subject of citizen participation from an
      integrative perspective that seeks to consider and draw upon
      various approaches and to identify common issues. These
      approaches vary from democratic theory to studies of political
      behavior, community development, and citizen action.

681. Lucas, Alastair R. "Legal Foundations for Public Participa-
      tion in Environmental Decisionmaking." *Natural Resources
      Journal.* (Item 687), pp. 73-102.

      Examines the legal case for public participation in the
      Canadian context. A review of legislation and case law
      suggests that citizens' rights to participate in decisions by
      resource and environmental management agencies are not
      extensive; however, private prosecutions appear to offer
      potential for participation in enforcement through the courts.
      Participation has been extremely limited at the issue-
      formulation stage and in implementing and enforcing agency
      decisons.

682. MacNair, Ray H. "Citizen Participation as a Balanced
      Exchange: An Analysis and Strategy." *Journal of the
      Community Development Society* 12, No. 1 (1981): 1-19.

      Reviews the structure of citizen participation as it applies
      to social exchange theory. The role of reciprocity is viewed
      as playing a central role in the participation process. In
      particular, the four features of reciprocity examined in the
      citizen participation process are (1) the benefits and rewards
      of citizen participation; (2) empathy--that is, mutual under-
      standing of the circumstances and motives of the other party;
      (3) power, as it affects the exchange relationship; and (4)
      the nature of formal and informal rules of the relationship.

683. Meier, Peter M., David Morell, and Phillip F. Palmedo.
      "Political Implications of Clustered Nuclear Siting."
      Energy Systems and Policy Vol 3, No. 1 (1979): 17-36.

Examines the sociopolitical ramifications of nuclear energy centers, as emerging from a case study in Ocean County, New Jersey, from the standpoint of identifying key issues of public controversy, and with emphasis on implications for national energy planning and the course of nuclear debate. Various dimensions of institutional tension are analyzed, including interstate issues and federal preemption, and the ability of the institutional and political framework to address the many equity issues that are exacerbated by clustered siting.

684. Metzger, John M., and David C. Colony. "Citizens and Project Design: Management Team." *Journal of the Urban Planning and Development Division* 106, No. UP1 (1980): 59-69.

Examines the development of a citizen participation program in transportation planning decisions. The authors study the case of the Buckeye Basin Greenbelt Parkway in Toledo, Ohio. The so-called management team, or MT approach, is considered a unique means of involving area citizens in decision making. The MT was composed of ten citizens and five public officials, and was granted a role as a participant in the decision-making process.

685. Ministry of Works and Development. *Public Participation in Planning.* Wellington, New Zealand: Ministry of Works and Development, Town and Country Planning Division, 1978. 79 pp.

Examines methods for increasing public involvement in the planning process. Five case studies highlight experiences of New Zealand agencies in increasing public involvement. Then a wide variety of potential techniques for public participation are reviewed and evaluated.

686. Mumphrey, Anthony J., and Julian Wolpert. "Equity Considerations and Concessions in the Siting of Public Facilities." *Economic Geography* 49 (1973): 109-21.

Examines issues in public facility siting through a case study of a bridge-siting controversy in New Orleans. The case study is then abstracted into a simpler framework for analysis by means of a proposed referendum model.

* Murdock, Steve H., F. Larry Leistritz, and Rita R. Hamm, eds. *Nuclear Waste: Socioeconomic Dimensions of Long-Term Storage.* Cited below as item 965.

* Myhra, David. *Energy Plant Sites: Community Planning for Large Projects.* Cited above as item 578.

687. *Natural   Resources   Journal.*   Special   Issue: *Symposium on*
      Public Participation in Resource Decisionmaking.   Vol. 16,
      No. 1 (1976):   241 pp.

      Discusses public participation in the context of theory, who
      participates, environmental decision making, legal founda-
      tions, facility siting, and case studies of water management
      in France and of the Goldstream River and the Okanagan Basin
      in British Columbia, Canada.

      Contains items 618, 647, 653, 674, 681, 691,
                      702, 705, 709, 710, 711.

688. Nelkin,   Dorothy.   *Technological Decisions and Democracy:*
      European Experiments in Public Participation.   Beverly
      Hills, California: Sage Publications, 1977. 110 pp.

      Originated with the idea that understanding of participatory
      procedures might be enhanced by examining the experiences of
      several small European countries with more centralized and
      often more manageable programs, all in an attempt to better
      understand the relationship between participatory mechanisms
      and the political and social context in which they develop.

689. Nichols,   K. Guild.   *Technology on Trial: Public Participa-*
      tion in Decision-Making Related to Science and Technology.
      Paris: Organisation for Economic Co-Operation and Develop-
      ment (OECD), 1979. 122 pp.

      Summarizes findings based on an examination of different
      national participatory mechanisms and experiences. The author
      suggests that public participation is a concept in search of a
      definition. Public participation in government decision-
      making takes many different direct and indirect forms.
      However, citizens of many countries appear no longer to be
      content to rely solely on traditional, indirect democratic
      procedures but rather are demanding more direct forms of
      representation and participation in decision-making.   The
      report presents an overview of the diverse approaches and
      mechanisms which some OECD member countries have devised to
      respond to these new demands and needs.

690. Olsen,   Marvin E.   *Participatory Pluralism.*   Chicago,
      Illinois: Nelson-Hall, 1982. 318 pp.

      Focuses on political participation and influence in the
      United States and Sweden.   To that end, the author has three
      concerns: (1) a theoretical concern with the sociopolitical
      processes and structures necessary to promote political parti-
      cipation and exertion of influence; (2) an empirical concern
      with the ways in which individuals participate in political
      activities and the factors that encourage such activity; and

(3) an empirical concern with the role of private-interest organizations as influence mediators between the public and the government.

691. O'Riordan, Jon. "The Public Involvement Program in the Okanagan Basin Study." *Natural Resources Journal.* (Item 687), pp. 177–96.

Discusses the main approaches and methods selected to involve the public in developing a comprehensive framework plan for water and related resource management in the Okanagan valley in British Columbia.

692. Paul, Benjamin D., and William J. Demarest. "Citizen Participation Overplanned; The Case of a Health Project in the Guatemalan Community of San Pedro La Laguna." *Social Science and Medicine* 19, No. 3 (1984): 185–92.

Relates the case of San Pedro's mayor, who attracted funds to build a clinic and hire a doctor and project director. The director's insistence on creating a representative community committee discouraged rather than increased participation. The case chronicles the interplay of interests and strategies and points toward potentially more productive approaches to issues of leadership, factionalism, and public participation.

693. Plesuk, Brian, ed. *The Only Game in Town: Public Involvement in Cold Lake.* Edmonton, Alberta: Alberta Environment, 1982. 114 pp.

Describes the process of public involvement in siting a large-scale heavy oil recovery plant in the Cold Lake region of Alberta. The document contains twenty-three chapters organized in six sections which provide observations from the viewpoints of the project's proponent, local business leaders, local officials, citizen groups, and native peoples.

694. Robbins, Lynn A. "Social Impact Assessment and the Proposed Skagit Nuclear Power Plant." *Social Impact Assessment* 49/50 (January–February 1980): 4–6.

Explores the background surrounding the citizen concern over nuclear power and the importance of social impact assessment as an analytical tool in the siting of a proposed nuclear power plant in Skagit, Washington.

695. Roddewig, Richard J. *Green Bans, The Birth of Australian Environmental Politics: A Study in Public Opinion and Participation.* Sydney, Australia: Hale and Iremonger, 1978. 180 pp.

Relates the findings of a study of Australia's environmental policies and planning procedures, and in particular of the problems of urban growth, ensuring environmental quality in major developments, and protecting environmental resources. Central to this discussion is the environmental and land-use controversy that manifested itself in a series of green bans-- environmental strikes in which leftist building unionists joined environmental activists to shut down billions of dollars worth of construction they found objectionable.

696. Sachs, Andy. "Nationwide Study Identifies Barriers to Environmental Negotiation." *EIA Review* 3, No. 1 (1982): 95-100.

Summarizes results of a five-year, nationwide experiment in which nine disputes were selected for testing new dispute resolution procedures.

697. Sager, T. "The Family of Goals-Achievement Matrix Methods: Respectable Enough for Citizen Participation in Planning?" *Environment and Planning A* 13 (1981): 1151-61.

Discusses three purposes of goals-achievement matrix (GAM, the predominant method for evaluation of British structure planning): to show that economists' critique of GAM is too general, to clarify the connections between GAM and other well-known evaluation methods, and to discuss how GAM could best be structured for use in local participatory planning.

698. Schaller, David A. "An Energy Policy for Indian Lands: Problems of Issue and Perception." *Policy Studies Journal* 7 (Fall 1978): 40-49.

Discusses five major issues which should be considered in planning energy policy for tribal lands: (1) availability and cost of development of resources; (2) tribal jurisdiction and sovereignty; (3) economic development of the reservations; (4) Indian culture and tradition, and (5) the role of Indian tribes in intergovernmental relations within the federal system.

699. Schilling, A. Henry, and Stanley M. Nealey. *Public Partici- pation in Nuclear Waste Management.* B-HARC-411-021. Seattle, Washington: Battelle Human Affairs Research Centers, 1979. 20 pp.

Discusses major issues which must be considered before attempting to design and implement a program to encourage public participation in the complex and sensitive area of nuclear waste management. For example, should the Department of Energy (DOE) be strongly proactive in stimulating public participation or should it pursue its technical mission and limit its involvement in public participation to legally mandated actions and reactions to efforts initiated by others? What should be the balance between attempts to win acceptance of existing DOE programs versus stimulating input to help change existing plans? In structuring DOE's public participation efforts, what relative emphasis should be given to state officials, standing interest groups, or the general public?

700. Schroth, Peter W. "Public Participation in Environmental Decisionmaking: A Comparative Perspective." *The Forum* 14, No. 2 (1978): 352-68.

Divides public participation into economic and political aspects. Limitations on political participation may harm the environment, while limitations on economic participation may or may not. Schroth addresses the issue of who the public is, with four classifications: (1) neighbors directly affected by a project, (2) interest groups, (3) outside experts, and (4) the "undigested citizenry in general." Schroth also discusses some experiences of foreign countries with public participation, especially in environmental issues.

701. Sewell, W. R. Derrick, and J. T. Coppock, eds. *Public Participation in Planning.* London, England: John Wiley and Sons, 1977. 217 pp.

Presents a variety of papers on public participation in North America and the United Kingdom. Topics include political trust, influence of the public, the politician's viewpoint, participation in practice, the Turnhouse expansion (Edinburgh, Scotland, Airport), London Motorway Plan, the Goldstream Case (Victoria, British Columbia), the U.S. Forest Area, and the International Joint Commission of the United States and Canada.

702. Sewell, W. R. Derrick, and Timothy O'Riordan. "The Culture of Participation in Environmental Decisionmaking." *Natural Resources Journal.* (Item 687), pp. 1-22.

Examines experiences in the United States, the United Kingdom, and Canada of the demand for more direct involvement of the public in environmental policymaking. The political culture is examined and criteria for evaluating participation are presented.

703. Spangler, Don, Lynda Given, and Sue Guenther. *Coping with Growth: Energy Impacts in Five Appalachian Counties.* Washington, D.C.: National Association of Counties, 1979. 37 pp.

Examines the experiences of five Appalachian counties in
which rapid population growth due to energy development
occurred in the 1970s. These counties were chosen to demonstrate several different approaches to solving problems
associated with rapid growth.

* Steeg, Robert M. "Federal Agency Compensation of Intervenors." *Environmental Affairs.* Cited above as item 614.

704. Taylor, J. F. "Mossmorran: Planning Considerations."
     Onshore Impact of Offshore Oil. Edited by W. J. Cairnes and
     P. M. Rogers. Englewood, New Jersey: Applied Science
     Publishers, 1981. pp. 67-74.

     Discusses planning for the Mossmorran natural gas liquids
     (NGL) fractionation plant and Braefoot Bay marine terminal
     which will be the last parts to be completed of an extensive
     system to make gas and gas liquids from the Brent field in the
     North Sea available for commercial use. Stringent standards
     have been set by local authorities and by the company to
     virtually eliminate the environmental impact on nearby
     communities. Acceptance by the entire community is another
     kind of planning consideration.

705. Teniere-Buchot, P. F. "The Role of the Public in Water
     Management Decisions in France." *Natural Resources Journal.*
     (Item 687), pp. 159-76.

     Discusses active and passive public involvement in water
     resource development in France. The discussion distinguishes
     between the public at large, the paying public, and the
     deciding public.

706. Utton, Albert E., W. R. Derrick Sewell, and Timothy
     O'Riordan, eds. *Natural Resources for a Democratic Society:
     Public Participation in Decision-Making.* Boulder, Colorado:
     Westview Press, 1976. 236 pp.

     Attempts to address the questions of who should participate,
     who is likely to participate, at what stages are inputs from
     the public most necessary and useful, what weights should be
     attached to opinions of different groups, and how can meaning-
     ful views on national or regional issues be obtained? Experts
     from Europe and North America address these questions and
     offer viewpoints on the shape of future public participation.

707. Vander Muelen, Allen Jr., and Orman H. Paananen. "Selected
     Welfare Implications of Rapid Energy-Related Development
     Impact." *Natural Resources Journal* 17 (1977): 301-23.

Examines problems of economic efficiency and equity posed by rapid development of energy resources in the Rocky Mountain region and suggests negotiation of impact agreements between developers and affected communities as a means of resolving most problems.

708. Walsh, Edward J. *Resource Mobilization, Three Mile Island Protest, and Nuclear Waste Repository Siting.* University Park, Pennsylvania: Pennsylvania State University, Department of Sociology, 1982. 312 pp.

Provides a focused review of "resource mobilization" literature with particular emphasis on the processes of citizen mobilization in the wake of the Three Mile Island (TMI) accident. The nuclear waste repository issue is also addressed, but only in a limited manner and in light of the TMI data.

709. Wengert, Norman. "Citizen Participation: Practice in Search of a Theory." *Natural Resources Journal.* (Item 687), pp. 23-40.

Reviews some of the conceptual problems, both implicit and explicit, in the current emphasis on public participation, examines some of the previous thought on the subject, and indicates points at which both normative and empirical social theory may contribute toward putting citizen involvement and public participation into a philosophic perspective, thereby suggesting lines for subsequent philosophic inquiry and empirical research.

710. Wilkinson, Paul. "Public Participation in Environmental Management: A Case Study." *Natural Resources Journal.* (Item 687), pp. 117-35.

Examines two cases: Toronto's Spadina Expressway which was finally halted midway through construction by public opposition, and a campground on Lake Lulu in Ontario. Both point to the lack of mechanisms for public involvement in the planning process.

   * Wolpert, Julian. "Regressive Siting of Public Facilities." *Natural Resources Journal.* Cited above as item 618.

711. Wood, Colin J. B. "Conflict in Resource Management and the Use of Threat: The Goldstream Controversy." *Natural Resources Journal.* (Item 687), pp. 137-58.

Attempts to unravel the conflict that arose over the allocation of water between urban needs and requirements of a salmon

spawning stream in British Columbia. After refusing to
provide water to maintain fish populations, the commissioner
changed his position as a result of indirect public pressure.

712. Zinberg, Dorothy S. "Public Participation In Nuclear Waste
      Management Policy: A Brief Historical Overview." *Public
      Reactions to Nuclear Power: Are There Critical Masses?*
      Edited by William R. Freudenburg and Eugene A. Rosa. (Item
      794), pp. 233-53.

      Examines the history of nuclear waste management as a
      perspective from which to view current attitudes and
      practices. The issue is conceptualized in a triangular form,
      in which the three points of the triangle consist of
      scientific and technical information, government policies, and
      public attitudes, each influencing and being influenced by the
      other two in varying degrees.

                        WORK FORCE RELATED MEASURES

713. Amok/Cluff Mining Ltd.. *New Dimensions in Northern Participa-
      tion.* Saskatoon, Saskatchewan: Amok/Cluff Mining Ltd.,
      1981. 20 pp.

      Reports results of efforts to achieve high levels of employ-
      ment of local workers and purchasing from local businesses in
      connection with development of a uranium mine and mill at a
      remote location in northern Canada. A comprehensive program
      for recruiting, hiring, training, orienting, and counseling
      area workers has been successful in achieving the employment
      goal.

714. Baker, Joe G. *Labor Allocation in Western Energy Develop-
      ment.* Monograph No. 5. Salt Lake City: University of
      Utah, College of Business, Human Resources Institute, 1977.
      113 pp.

      Examines whether existing labor market information systems
      are adequate to provide needed workers to an expanding energy
      industry. Case studies were conducted in three energy
      development areas in the western United States. The
      mechanisms by which promotion, wage rates, occupational
      mobility, and filling of vacant positions are determined in
      the energy industry are discussed in detail. Labor allocation
      systems for both construction and permanent positions are
      described, and the potential of training programs in
      increasing the supply of qualified workers is examined.

715. Braid, Robert B., Jr., and Stephen D. Kyles. *The Clinch River Breeder Reactor Plant: Suggested Procedures for Monitoring and Mitigating Adverse Construction-Period Impacts on Local Public Services.* Knoxville, Tennessee: East Tennessee Energy Projects Coordinating Committee, 1977. 98 pp.

Suggests various procedures which could be used to monitor and mitigate the impacts on local public services which are projected to occur during the construction of the Clinch River Breeder Reactor Plant. Major classes of mitigation measures considered include reducing the number of inmigrating (relocating) workers, developing housing for inmigrants, financing capital expenditures, and payments from the developer to compensate for cost-revenue deficits of local governments. Measures to reduce inmigration include local-hiring provisions and job-training programs to increase hiring of local workers, and a transportation program (van pooling) to encourage commuting as an alternative to relocation. The advantages and limitations of each of these alternatives are discussed.

716. Brealey, T. B., and P. W. Newton. "Commuter Mining--An Alternative Way." *Proceedings, Australian Mining Industry Council Environmental Workshop.* Canberra, Australia: Australian Mining Industry Council, 1981. pp. 201-27.

Argues that daily commuting to Australian mine sites from strategically placed regional centers could eliminate many problems associated with small single-company towns located at the mine sites. Disadvantages of the single-company town are discussed.

717. Brealey, T. B., and P. W. Newton. "Migration and New Mining Towns." *Mobility and Social Change in Australia.* Edited by Ian H. Burnley, Robin J. Pryor, and Don T. Rowland. Brisbane, Australia: Queensland University Press, 1978. pp. 49-66.

Aims to provide answers to the following questions: Who goes to the new mining towns?, Why do they go there?, What happens to them when they get there?, and Why do they leave? Most new workers, and hence most migrants to the mining towns, were found to come from urban areas. About 70% of the new mining town residents were male, and only 46% were married. Almost half of the residents were in the 20- to 34-year age group. Turnover rates in these towns are high, often exceeding 100% per year and rarely falling below 40%.

718. Browne, Bortz, and Coddington. *A Retrospective Analysis of the Jim Bridger Complex Socioeconomic Effects.* Denver, Colorado: Browne, Bortz, and Coddington, 1981. 78 pp.

Examines the socioeconomic impacts of the permanent work force of a large (2,000 megawatt) power plant and coal mine located in southwestern Wyoming. At the time of the study, the complex employed about 1,250 workers. A survey of the work force (76% response rate) provided information regarding worker origins, demographic characteristics, and housing.

719. Chalmers, J. A. *Bureau of Reclamation Construction Worker Survey.* Tempe, Arizona: Mountain West Research, Inc., 1977. 70 pp.

Focuses on problems associated with estimating economic-demographic impacts of a project's construction activities. Data were collected from 688 workers (52% response rate) at twelve water resource development projects in seven western states in an attempt to expand the primary data base on construction workers and evaluate the transferability of data previously collected from energy projects (item 740) to construction workers on water projects. Demographic, housing, and employment characteristics were examined.

720. Chase, Robert A., and F. Larry Leistritz. *Profile of North Dakota's Petroleum Work Force, 1981-82.* Agricultural Economics Rpt. No. 174. Fargo: North Dakota Agricultural Experiment Station, North Dakota State University, 1983. 67 pp.

Reports results of a survey of 1,377 oil and gas workers in North Dakota's Williston Basin. Worker characteristics emphasized include locational origin, housing type, commuting patterns, marital status, and family characteristics.

721. Deines, Anne, Catherine Littlejohn, and Terence Hunt. *Native Employment Patterns in Alberta's Athabasca Oil Sands Region.* AOSERP Rpt. 69. Edmonton, Alberta: Alberta Oil Sands Environmental Research Program, 1979. 216 pp.

Reports findings of a study designed to generate research problems and questions pertinent to a study of native employment patterns in the Athabasca Oil Sands region. Primary information sources were existing literature on native employment and training programs across Canada and in the local area, interviews with key persons in industry, government, and training institutions, and file data of employers, training institutions, and employment-related institutions in the area.

722. DePape, Denis. "Alternatives to Single Project Mining Communities: A Critical Assessment." *Mining Communities: Hard Lessons for the Future.* Kingston, Ontario: Queen's University, Centre for Resource Studies, pp. 83-95.

Argues that several alternatives to the remote community dependent on a single mining project should be examined. Some problems associated with such communities include long-term instability (community exists only for life of a depletable ore body), short-term instability (vulnerability to market forces and strikes), and limited choices of private and public services, employment opportunities, and social interaction. As a result, remote mining communities often experience high employee and population turnover. Alternatives advanced include commuter-rotation, relocatable communities, and diversification to broaden the community's economic base. Commuter-rotation is viewed as being by far the best alternative.

723. Dobbs, Thomas L., and Phil E. Kiner. *Profile of a Rural Area Work Force: The Wyoming Uranium Industry.* Res. Journal 79. Laramie, Wyoming: Wyoming Agricultural Experiment Station, University of Wyoming, 1974. 29 pp.

Reports job category, earnings, job tenure, and personal characteristics of Wyoming uranium workers. Data were drawn from personnel files of six of the eight firms with uranium facilities in the state and covered about 1,050 workers. Demographic and employment characteristics were examined.

724. Dobbs, Thomas L., and Phil E. Kiner. "Two Manpower Location Aspects of Energy Resource Development: Case of the Wyoming Uranium Industry." *The Annals of Regional Science* 8 (1974): 118-30.

Examines the work force of Wyoming's uranium industry with respect to both locational origins of employees and workers' commuting patterns. Data for the study came from the personnel files of six of the eight firms with uranium mining and milling operations in the state. Information was obtained for 989 workers.

725. Dunning, C. Mark. *Report of Survey of Corps of Engineers Construction Work Force.* Res. Rpt. 81-R05. Fort Belvoir, Virginia: U.S. Army Corps of Engineers, Institute for Water Resources, 1981. 119 pp.

Summarizes results of a survey of workers at fifty-one Corps of Engineers construction projects in 1979. Complete responses were obtained from 4,089 workers, representing a 65% response rate. Employment and demographic characteristics were examined.

726. Fookes, T. W. *Huntly Power Project: A Description.* Final Rpt. Paper No. 2. (Item 524), 47 pp.

Describes development of a large coal-fueled power plant in
rural New Zealand. Extensive commuting at this site reduced
worker relocation and associated needs for housing and public
service provision. Of special interest is the travel
allowance program used to encourage commuting. Although the
cost of travel allowances was substantial (about $1,400 per
worker per year in 1977), this cost was estimated to be only
about one-fourth that required to provide housing and basic
services for relocating workers.

727. Fuchs, Richard P. "Rural Residents in the Exploration Phase
of Newfoundland's Offshore Oil Industry, 1981."
*Proceedings, International Conference on Oil and the
Environment, 1982.* Part B. Halifax, Nova Scotia:
Technical University of Nova Scotia, 1983. pp. 221-28.

Attempts to provide an initial "snapshot" of residents'
adaptations to oil industry employment. Data came from
surveys of workers on oil rigs and supply vessels. The
previous occupations reported most frequently were in water
transportation and construction. A substantial group of
residents indicated the petroleum industry as their previous
occupation. This may indicate that return migration from oil
industry employment in western Canada is occurring.

728. Gale, Maradel, Kristi Branch, and Michael MacFadyen. *Trans-
mission Line Construction Worker Profile and Community/
Corridor Resident Impact Study.* Prepared for Bonneville
Power Administration, Portland, Oregon. Billings, Montana:
Mountain West Research, Inc., 1982. 94 pp.

Presents the results of two worker surveys of transmission
line construction in the Pacific Northwest during 1981. The
short-term nature of the construction activity coupled with
the division of the work force into separate crews which pass
through a community sequentially were found to significantly
reduce the project's impacts on communities along the right-
of-way. Only 13 of the 175 respondents in the construction
worker survey were local workers. Results of the survey
indicated that the population influx associated with nonlocal
transmission line workers is substantially lower than that
generally associated with fixed-site construction activity.

* Gilmore, John S., D. M. Hammond, Keith D. Moore, J. Johnson,
and Dean C. Coddington. *Socioeconomic Impacts of Power
Plants.* EPRI EA-2228. Prepared for Electric Power Research
Institute, Palo Alto, California by Denver Research
Institute and Browne, Bortz, and Coddington. Cited above as
item 501.

729. Halstead, John M., and F. Larry Leistritz. "Energy Development and Labor Market Dynamics: A Study of Seven Western Counties." *Western Journal of Agricultural Economics* 9, No. 2 (1984): 357-69.

     Reports the results of a survey of secondary businesses in six western counties affected by rapid growth due to energy development, and compares these results to a seventh county which had experienced a stable population over the same period. The survey addressed both business owners and employees. Principal findings of the study were that (1) most businesses in the energy-impacted counties had expanded to meet growing community demands; (2) many businesses had been established since the onset of the energy development; and (3) turnover and difficulty attracting quality workers were not viewed as serious problems by area businessmen.

730. Halstead, John M., and F. Larry Leistritz. *Impacts of Energy Development on Secondary Labor Markets: A Study of Seven Western Counties.* Agr. Econ. Rpt. 178. Fargo: North Dakota Agricultural Experiment Station, North Dakota State University, 1983. 46 pp.

     Documents the results of a four-state survey conducted to identify the characteristics of secondary businesses and their employees. States included were North Dakota, Texas, Utah, and Wyoming.

731. Herzog, Henry W., Jr., Alan M. Schlottmann, and William R. Schriver. "Regional Planning and Interstate Construction Worker Migration." *Growth and Change* 14, No. 2 (April 1983): 50-54.

     Reviews one of the major issues in assessing impacts on local communities from large-scale developments, that is, the extent to which the construction labor force consists of inmigrants. The authors analyzed the socioeconomic characteristics of both migrant and nonmigrant construction workers and compared such characteristics with other labor-force migrants.

  * Hobart, Charles W. "Impact of Resource Development Projects on Indigenous People." *Resource Communities: A Decade of Disruption.* Edited by Don D. Detomasi and John W. Gartrell. Cited above as item 272.

732. Hobart, Charles W. "Industrial Employment of Rural Indigenes: The Case of Canada." *Human Organization* 41, No. 1 (1982): 54-63.

Analyzes the consequences of industrial employment experiences of Indian and Inuit (Eskimo) people in Canada during the
1960s and 1970s, with special emphasis given to relocation and
rotation or commuting employment experiences. Included are
brief discussions of the native workers' mastery of industrial
skills; of the stressful effects of industrial employment; of
the worker and his/her family with particular reference to
support, child rearing, and conflict; of the community with
emphasis on maintenance of cultural traditions and community
viability; of the harvesting of traditional resources; and of
the maintenance of traditional cultural patterns.

733. Hooper, Janet E., and Kristi M. Branch. *Big Horn and Decker
      Mine Worker Survey Report.* Billings Montana: Mountain West
      Research-North, Inc., 1983. 70 pp.

      Discusses results of surveying 438 workers (86.2% response
      rate) at three mine sites in Wyoming and Montana. Worker
      characteristics, such as age, education, occupation, housing
      preference, marital status, and place of residence are
      discussed. Differences in geographic mobility among the
      different sites (and between miners and support staff) arose
      primarily from the young, former students, who had recently
      moved into the area to fill technical, managerial, or
      professional positions.

   * Intermountain Power Project. *IPP Socioeconomic Monitoring
      Report No. 9, 1983 Annual Report.* Cited above as item 532.

734. Krahn, Harvey J. "Labour Market Segmentation in Fort
      McMurray, Alberta." Ph.D. dissertation. Edmonton, Alberta:
      University of Alberta, Department of Sociology, 1983. 329
      pp.

      Discusses secondary sources showing changing local
      industrial and occupational structures of Fort McMurray,
      Alberta as a result of large-scale development of the
      Athabasca oil sands deposits. Four hundred thirty residents
      of Fort McMurray were surveyed in 1979 to examine experiences
      and rewards of work in the community, the attitudinal
      responses to participation in the local labor market, and the
      nature of the community's stratification system. Study
      concludes that development has provided improved employment
      opportunities in terms of income and occupational status for
      many inmigrants; however, Native peoples (e.g., Indian,
      Eskimo) were only marginal participants. Analysis revealed a
      very pronounced pattern of gender-based inequality in the
      workplace, possibly more widespread work values, and a
      distinct absence of working-class consciousness. A labor
      market segmentation model is used to organize the study and to
      suggest hypotheses and explanations of findings.

735. Leholm,   Arlen G. , F. Larry Leistritz, and James S. Wieland.
      Profile of North Dakota's Electric Power Plant Construction
      Work Force. Agricultural Economics Stat. Rpt. 22.   Fargo:
      North Dakota Agricultural Experiment Station, North Dakota
      State University, 1976. 53 pp.

      Examines socioeconomic characteristics of construction work
      forces in western North Dakota in 1975.   Two hundred sixty-
      four workers responded (24% of the work force at two sites).
      Demographic characteristics, such as age, marital status, size
      of household, education, occupation, and wage were examined.

736. Lovejoy, Stephen B. "Employment Predictions in Social Impact
      Assessment: An Analysis of Some Unexplored Variables."
      Socio-Economic Planning Sciences 17, No. 2 (1983): 87-93.

      Contends that some recent investigations and predictive
      models are based on analytical and methodological faults,
      including improper assumptions about local labor supply and
      local preferences. Lovejoy suggests that some analysis of the
      following factors seems imperative: (1) the desire of rural
      residents for positions with new industry locating in their
      community, (2) whether rural residents possess industrial
      skills necessary for employment, (3) whether rural residents
      are willing to undergo training to obtain such skills, and (4)
      whether local potential applicants meet industry's desired
      social and demographic characteristics. Discriminant analysis
      of residents employed and not employed at the Navajo
      Generating Station yielded three significant independent
      variables: union affiliation, occupation, and years of formal
      education.   Although the results are site- and project-
      specific, they do indicate the potential importance of these
      personal characteristics in predicting the number of local
      workers and therefore the population impacts of a large-scale
      project.

737. MacMillan, J. A. , J. R. Tulloch, D. O'Brien, and M. A. Ahmad.
      Determinants of Labor Turnover in Canadian Mining
      Communities. Winnipeg, Manitoba: University of Manitoba,
      Center for Settlement Studies, 1974. 139 pp.

      Has as its objectives to determine the levels of labor turn-
      over in the Canadian mining industry, to determine factors
      associated with variations in turnover (e.g., isolation,
      fringe benefits, housing and community services), and to
      determine company estimates of turnover costs.

738. Malhotra, Suresh, and Diane Manninen. *Migration and*
      Residential Location of Workers at Nuclear Power Plant
      Construction Sites. Vol. 1, *Forecasting Methodology.*   Vol
      2, *Profile Analysis of Worker Surveys.* Seattle: Battelle
      Human Affairs Research Centers, September 1980. 469 pp.

Provides a methodology for predicting the number of inmigrating workers and their residential location patterns at future nuclear power plant construction projects. Procedures were also developed to estimate relocation of dependents, intention to remain in the area, type of housing selected, marital status, and family size. Analysis was based on secondary data on site-specific regional and project characteristics and on surveys of workers at 13 nuclear power plant sites. The study emphasizes the need for multivariate analysis across sites using craft-specific worker groups as the unit of analysis, and suggests that separate models be developed for construction and nonconstruction workers. The authors suggest that models also include variables which reflect various regional and project characteristics, as well as variables which reflect availability of labor in the area and the relative attractiveness of employment opportunities.

739. Metz, William C. "Energy Industry Involvement in Worker Transportation." *Transportation Quarterly*, 36 (October 1982): 563-84.

Discusses the expanding involvement by energy companies in worker transportation by presenting a checklist of influential factors and describing these factors in relation to company-sponsored transportation programs. Benefits of transportation programs include reduced socioeconomic impacts to the area community, an expanded labor market (increased number of low income, minority, and nonmobile workers are employed), and increased worker productivity through improved morale, less travel strain, and a reduction in turnover and absenteeism.

740. Mountain West Research, Inc. *Construction Worker Profile.* Washington, D.C.: Old West Regional Commission, 1975. 129 pp.

Reports results of a survey of construction workers at fourteen energy-related construction sites in seven states in the Rocky Mountains-Great Plains region. Information was obtained from about 3,150 workers and included worker origin (local vs. nonlocal), occupation, and demographic characteristics.

741. Mountain West Research, Inc. *Pipeline Construction Worker and Community Impact Surveys.* Final Rpt. Billings, Montana, 1979. 228 pp.

Presents results of surveys of pipeline construction workers on four projects and of interviews with personnel from pipeline construction companies and from impacted communities. Community personnel were also surveyed regarding community facilities and services, the nature of the impact, and the perception of residents concerning the pipeline project.

Results indicate that workers' demographic profiles are quite different from those of workers on other major construction projects and that communities experience much less intense and short-lived impacts.

742. Murdock, Steven H., Pamela Hopkins, John de Montel, Rita R. Hamm, Tom Brown, Margaret Bauer, and Richard Bullock. *Employment, Population and Community Service Impacts of Uranium Development in South Texas.* Tech. Rpt. 81-1. College Station, Texas: Texas Agricultural Experiment Station, Texas A&M University, 1981. 73 pp.

Presents both survey results of four uranium firms and projections of impacts for each of forty-one communities, seventeen counties and the total study area regarding direct and indirect employment, total population, housing, school enrollments, police and emergency services, water treatment and storage, solid waste disposal, and medical and social services. Results suggest that the impacts of uranium development have been less concentrated in rural areas. Nonetheless, because the rural areas have poorly developed baseline service structures, the impacts may require local governments to increase services beyond levels they are capable of supporting. Results also suggest that employment advantages are more likely to go to local residents than has been true for other parts of the United States.

743. Paik, Soon, and Gary A. Hall. "Craft Requirements for Construction of Electric Power Plants." *Growth and Change* 12, No. 4 (October 1981): 16-21.

Presents a manpower forecasting model which could provide state and local planners with timely and accurate project-related forecasts of construction labor requirements for twenty-nine different crafts at several levels of disaggregation. Combining forecasts of labor requirements with local and regional knowledge of craft availability could possibly allow local officials to avert serious impediments to labor supply in rural areas associated with the construction of large-scale developments.

744. Rapp, Donald A. *Uranium Mining and Milling Work Force Characteristics in the Western U.S.* LA-8656-MS. Los Alamos, New Mexico: Los Alamos Scientific Laboratory, 1980. 41 pp.

Presents results of a survey of socioeconomic characteristics of work forces at eleven uranium mine and mill operations in Colorado, New Mexico, South Dakota, Utah, and Wyoming. Comparisons were made with characteristics of similarly skilled work forces at coal mines and utility plants at comparable locations in eight western states. Results

indicate there were no significant differences in socioeconomic characteristics of the construction and operating work
forces and the secondary employment impacts when the two types
of facilities were compared. High employee turnover and
various social problems among uranium workers (noted by some
state officials) are a function of mine site locations in
remote areas and/or are directly related to front-end investments by industry affecting the quality of housing and service
facilities for both single and married workers.

745.   Sewel, J.   *Social Consequences of Oil Developments.*
       Edinburgh, Scotland: Scottish Development Department, 1983.
       18 pp.

       Attempts to provide a framework to help local authorities
       consider the potential social effects of oil and gas develop-
       ments rather than provide policy prescriptions. Case studies
       were carried out in oil development areas of northern
       Scotland, and the literature on social and economic aspects of
       industrial change was reviewed. The report highlights four
       factors which are central to determining the ultimate social
       consequences of development--characteristics of the develop-
       ment activities, the socioeconomic character of the receiving
       area, the local authority's development strategy, and the
       public response to both the activity and the local authority
       action. An item of special interest is the use of special
       controls to minimize the hiring of local workers at several
       large projects. The reason for implementing such policies
       apparently was to minimize the competition of the oil projects
       with other local employers. These policies have been diffi-
       cult to maintain, however, in the face of pressures by area
       residents for access to the highly paid jobs.

746.   Storey, Keith.   "Impacts and Implications of Regional Labor
       Preference Policies." *Proceedings, International Conference
       on Oil and the Environment, 1982.* Part B. Halifax, Nova
       Scotia: Technical University of Nova Scotia, 1983. pp.
       193-203.

       Reviews some of the outcomes and implications of preferen-
       tial hiring policies as they apply to offshore petroleum
       development in Newfoundland. Provincial hiring regulations
       have been in effect since 1977 and appear to have significant-
       ly accelerated the rate at which Newfoundlanders have been
       hired to work offshore.

747.   Wieland, James S., F. Larry Leistritz, and Steven H. Murdock.
       *Characteristics and Settlement Patterns of Energy Related
       Operating Workers in the Northern Great Plains.* Agricul-
       tural Economics Rpt. No. 123. Fargo: North Dakota Agricul-
       tural Experiment Station, North Dakota State University,
       1977. 72 pp.

Presents results of surveys conducted in 1974 and 1976 to
determine socioeconomic characteristics, such as age, length
of employment, and commuting patterns, of workers at seven
coal mines and six electric generating plants in North Dakota,
Montana, and Wyoming, in addition to describing the development of models to predict local hiring rates and settlement
patterns. A total of 753 employees responded (55% response
rate). A model was developed to predict the local hiring
rate, and another model was developed to predict settlement
patterns of nonlocal workers.

PLANNING COMMUNITY INFRASTRUCTURE

748. Bradshaw, Ted K., and Edward J. Blakely. *Rural Communities
     in Advanced Industrial Society; Development and Developers,*
     New York: Praeger Publishers, 1979. 188 pp.

     Focuses on California as a special setting where advanced
     industrialism, rural policy, and community development
     practice lead to new solutions for old problems, as well as to
     new issues needing the attention of policymakers. Specific
     chapters discuss rural economic development in a high techno-
     logy society, new knowledge institutions in rural communities,
     rural government, poverty and welfare, and new roles for the
     rural community development professional.

749. Branch, Kristi M., Douglas A. Hooper, and James R. Moore.
     "Decision-Making Under Uncertainty: Public Facilities and
     Services Provision in Energy Resource Communities."
     Resource Communities: A Decade of Disruption. Edited by
     Don D. Detomasi and John W. Gartrell. Boulder, Colorado:
     Westview Press, 1984. pp. 23-39.

     Examines service provision as a complex decision-making
     process and considers how it is affected by the changes in
     demand, resources, and the uncertainty associated with energy
     resource development. Initially, the analysis focuses on
     small, rural communities in the western U.S. where the
     pregrowth service provision process is well established, if
     limited. A framework is then developed to examine the effects
     of energy development on the service provision process in
     company towns and in other countries--e.g., Norway and Canada
     --where the roles of governments and companies are quite
     different.

750. Butler, Lorna Michael, and Robert E. Howell. *Coping with
     Growth: Community Needs Assessment Techniques.* WREP 44.
     Corvallis, Oregon: Western Rural Development Center, 1980.
     22 pp.

Provides background information on the purposes for conducting a community needs assessment; guidelines for determining
which techniques are most appropriate; and a brief description
of thirteen different needs assessment techniques, including
the advantages of each method and a list of references to
which the reader can go for further information.

751.   Christenson,   James A.,   and Jerry W. Robinson,   Jr.,   eds.
       Community Development in America.   Ames, Iowa: Iowa State
       University Press, 1980.   245 pp.

       Published in celebration of the tenth anniversary of the
       Community Development Society.   The book begins with a
       discussion of major concepts that surround community develop-
       ment (CD), then provides a thorough history of CD in American
       society.   Three specific development approaches (technical
       assistance, self-help, and conflict) are critiqued,   and the
       various roles of the CD professional are discussed.   A frame-
       work for teaching CD is presented, and several major research
       efforts are reviewed.   The final chapters concern the integra-
       tion of theory and practice, and the future trends in
       community development.

752.   Egeland,   K. E.   "The Impact of North Sea Oil on Stavanger."
       Onshore Impact of Offshore Oil.   Edited by W. J. Cairnes and
       P. M. Rogers.   Englewood, New Jersey: Applied Science
       Publishers, 1981.   pp. 185-93.

       During the 1970s oil-related activities in the Stavanger
       area increased rapidly; employment rose from 500 to over
       14,000.   This development was in an area having about 140,000
       inhabitants and fairly modern export-oriented industry.   Until
       1981 interest has largely been concentrated on ways of coping
       with the rapid increase in employment and on methods of
       channelling some of the expansion to other areas.   The long-
       term implications of oil-related activities on the local
       community and industry should now receive greater emphasis.

753.   Fletcher   Environmental Planning Associates, and Maksymec &
       Associates Limited.   *Alternative Approaches to the Planning
       and Development of Canadian Resource Communities.*   Prepared
       for the Urban Policy Analysis Branch, Non Metropolitan
       Community Development Directorate, Ministry of State for
       Urban Affairs.   Ottawa, Ontario, October 1977.   138 pp.

       Examines and compares three possible approaches to the
       planning and development of Canadian resource communities:
       private, public, and a private-public mix.   The objectives are
       as follows: (1) a description of the major characteristics of
       each of the approaches as they relate to economic considera-
       tions and their impacts, (2) formulation of criteria for
       assessing the characteristics of each approach for achieving a

balanced community, and (3) the application of the criteria to
demonstrate the merits and limitations of each approach in
achieving balanced communities.

754. Galantay, Ervin Y. "The Planning of Owerri: A New Capital
      for Imo State, Nigeria." *Town Planning Review* 49 (1978):
      371-86.

      Discusses the role of state capitals as growth centers,
      examines the demographic structure of Owerri and the problems
      faced by the newly formed state government, argues that a
      flexible master plan identifying investment thresholds for
      phased implementation is an appropriate operational tool in
      the rather unpredictable conditions in Owerri's development,
      and discusses problems posed by the need for immediate imple-
      mentation, new institutional requirements, and the likely
      investment outlays involved.

*   Honadle, Beth Walter. *Capacity-Building (Management Improve-
      ment) For Local Governments: An Annotated Bibliography.*
      Rural Development Research Report No. 28. Cited below as
      item 996.

755. Honadle, Beth Walter. *Public Administration in Rural Areas
      and Small Jurisdictions: A Guide to the Literature.* New
      York: Garland Publishing, Inc., 1983. 146 pp.

      Is significant because it closes a gap in the public admini-
      stration literature by assembling the available books and
      articles on the administration of human and fiscal services,
      on development, and on governmental management, administra-
      tion, organization, and service delivery in small communities
      and rural areas. It is a product of a systematic search of
      relevant journals and computerized data bases. It contains
      426 listings and also provides three indexes (author, subject,
      and place) and a directory of addresses and telephone numbers
      for sixteen national organizations that have either a public
      administration perspective, a rural perspective, or some rele-
      vance to the subject.

756. Howes, Helen Claire. "Brasilia: Not Yet a Home for Its
      People." *Canadian Geographical Journal* 90 (1975): 30-35.

      Reviews the history of the planning and architecture of
      Brasilia, Brazil's planned new capital.

757. Lajzerowicz, J., S. Derrick, and R. Santi. *Mining Communi-
      ties.* MR 154. Ottawa, Ontario: Department of Energy,
      Mines, and Resources, 1976. 49 pp.

Stresses the need for comprehensive social planning of resource communities to achieve an adequate quality of life and to stimulate discussion among government, industry, union, workers, and residents on the alternatives available. The physical and social settings of mining settlements, the work environment, and community services and facilities are examined in light of residents' perceptions of the quality of life. Finally, options for future community developments are explored.

*   Little, Ronald L., and Richard S. Krannich. "Organizing for Local Control in Rapid Growth Communities." *Coping with Rapid Growth in Rural Communities.* Edited by Bruce A. Weber and Robert E. Howell. Cited above as item 287.

758. Peelle, Elizabeth. "Mitigating Community Impacts of Energy Development: Some Examples for Coal and Nuclear Generating Plants in the U.S." *Nuclear Technology* 44 (June 1979): 132-40.

Examines three mitigation plans aimed at internalizing community-level social costs at the following plants: the Tennessee Valley Authority four-unit nuclear plant near Hartsville, Tennesse; the Puget Sound Power and Light two-unit nuclear plant in Skagit County, Washington; and the Missouri Basin Power Project three-unit coal plant near Wheatland, Wyoming. Viewed as new institutional responses to social impact mitigation planning, these plans are analyzed in terms of their origins, scope, goals, local participation, financing, and costs.

759. Rose, Adam. "Geothermal Energy in California: Policies to Improve the Economic Impact of Energy Resource Development." *Growth and Change* 11, No. 1 (1980): 41-47.

Examines the regional benefits and costs of geothermal energy development in California's Imperial Valley. Policies to increase the local economic benefits of the project are evaluated.

760. Sprott, T. F. "The Impact of North Sea Oil on the Grampian Region and Aberdeen." *Onshore Impact of Offshore Oil.* Edited by W. J. Cairnes and P. M. Rogers. Englewood, New Jersey: Applied Science Publishers, 1981. pp. 195-204.

Outlines the economic and environmental character of the Grampian Region, its settlement pattern, and the role of Aberdeen City as the offshore oil and gas "capital" of Europe. During the 1970s exploitation of North Sea oil and gas had significant social and economic effects; extensive development of infrastructure was required. Authorities were presented with problems and opportunities for economic forecasting and forward planning. In the 1980s North Sea exploitation may be at different scales and involve a new economic and social change. Oil and nonoil industries have diverging prospects; oil-related employment will increase, affecting the rural economy, and the need to expand infrastructure in certain areas will continue. There will be opportunity for science-based industries, for greater community support by the oil-majors, and continued need for financial support from central government. Thus the 1980s will see new planning opportunities and continued need for coordinated central and local government policies.

HOUSING

761. Allen, James B. *The Company Town in the American West.* Norman, Oklahoma: University of Oklahoma Press, 1966. 205 pp.

Describes the development of company towns in eleven western states (Washington, Oregon, California, Nevada, Idaho, Montana, Utah, Wyoming, Colorado, Arizona, and New Mexico). Questions addressed include the following: How and why did the company towns develop? How extensive has been the existence of such towns, and how many are still functioning? What special advantages and problems for companies were associated with company-town ownership? What effect have changing economic conditions had upon the company town as an institution?

762. Bowers, James M., and D. Blake Chambliss. *Energy Impacted Housing: A Shared Responsibility.* 2 volumes. Cheyenne, Wyoming: Wyoming Department of Economic Planning and Development, 1978. 122 pp.

Examines alternatives for meeting the housing needs of energy-impacted communities in Lincoln and Uinta counties, Wyoming. The study focuses on factors that contribute to the unavailability or excessive cost of desirable housing in energy communities and on alternative approaches to overcoming such problems.

763. Bradbury, John H. "Towards an Alternative Theory of Resource-Based Town Development in Canada." *Economic Geography* 55, No. 2 (April 1979): 147-66.

Discusses some of the gaps in the literature of Canadian resource-based settlements and presents a framework of analysis. Resource-based towns are discussed in the context of capital accumulation, the internationalization of capital, and the law of uneven development. It is concluded that Canadian resource towns and their socioeconomic problems can only be understood when they are viewed as integral and dependent parts of what has become a global system of resource extraction.

764. Brealey, T. B., and P. W. Newton. *Living in Remote Communities in Tropical Australia: The Hedland Story.* Melbourne, Australia: Commonwealth Scientific and Industrial Research Organization, 1978. 100 pp.

Analyzes residents' satisfaction with town planning and housing design and quality in a remote mining town in northwestern Australia. One fact that leads to dissatisfaction with Hedland as a long-term or permanent residence is the substantial disparities in remuneration and housing quality between mine employees and other (secondary) workers.

765. Brotchie, John, Peter Newton, Peter Hall, and Peter Nijkamp, eds. *Technological Change and Urban Form.* London: Croom Helm, 1984. 367 pp.

Examines the latest major societal transition—the computer-based information revolution—and the accompanying move by industry to newer, non-industrial locations. Among the topics addressed are the interactions of technologies, biotechnology, deskilling and job loss, suspicion of detrimental physical (e.g., atomic energy) and privacy effects, and the overall dispersal of information-processing activities to residential areas in suburbs and beyond and of activities involving trust (e.g., banking) to the central city. The book focuses on the problems of metropolitan planning authorities and private organizations to direct and accommodate these changes through their location and built form.

766. Campbell, W. J. *Hydrotown.* Dunedin, New Zealand: University of Otago, 1957. 122 pp.

Tells the story of life in the industrial boom town that sprang up around the construction of New Zealand's first major hydroelectric project. The main purpose of the study was to analyze social interaction within a transient settlement and to attempt to discern the lessons to be learned from the experience.

767. Clement, Wallace. *Hardrock Mining: Industrial Relations and Technological Changes at INCO.* Toronto, Ontario: McClelland and Stewart Limited, 1981. 392 pp.

Portrays work experiences in the mining industry, particularly from the perspective of those actually engaged in the work, and examines class struggle within this industry in the context of a larger class relationship between capital and labor. This is accomplished through an intensive examination of INCO Limited of Canada and relating it to hardrock mining industry in general. The book also attempts to analyze and explain the class transformations in Canada since World War II.

768. *Contact, Journal of Urban & Environmental Affairs.* Special Issue: *New Communities in Canada: Exploring Planned Environments.* Edited by Norman E. P. Pressman. Faculty of Environmental Studies, University of Waterloo, Waterloo, Ontario. Vol. 8, No. 3 (August 1976). 369 pp.

Is a collection of thirty-five papers that examine planned new towns and communities from the multidisciplinary perspective of some of Canada's leading authorities in the field. Both urban-centered and more or less remote resource-based towns (particularly in northern Canada) are included. Topics include national urban land strategy, problems of local government, environmental planning and management, and public policy to economic aspects, transportation, housing, and residents' attitudes to quality of life. A selected bibliography of about 225 references is included.

769. Detomasi, Don D. "The Delivery and Financing of Housing." *Resource Communities: A Decade of Disruption.* Edited by Don D. Detomasi and John W. Gartrell. Boulder, Colorado: Westview Press, 1984. pp. 41-54.

Surveys the more important and common approaches to providing housing and creating satisfactory residential environments in remote resource communities and attempts to identify alternatives which might deserve further exploration. Experiences in Canadian resource communities are emphasized.

770. Duvernoy, Eugene, Craig Aronson, Mary McGuire, and C. Richard Schuller. *Energy Development in Rural Areas: Corporate Provision of Housing and Community Infrastructure.* BHARC-320/81/003. Seattle, Washington: Battelle Human Affairs Research Centers, 1981. 138 pp.

Describes the current role of energy development companies in the provision of housing and infrastructure to regions that are experiencing intensive energy development. Provision of housing and infrastructure by private companies ranges from participation in the planning for the necessary development, through intermediate stages involving front-end financing for facilities, to the ultimate step of actually building a complete company-sponsored town.

771. Holmes   and Narver, Inc.   *Life Support Facility Planning and
      Evaluation Concept Study for Construction and Deployment
      Personnel, M-X Weapons System.*   San Francisco, California:
      U.S. Army Corps of Engineers, 1980. 510 pp.

      Analyzes   alternative   approaches   for   providing   temporary
      housing for workers involved in developing strategic missile
      system facilities in the western United States.   Previous
      experience in providing such housing for workers at projects
      in   remote   areas   is   reviewed with special   emphasis on
      estimating costs of providing facilities of various types and
      designs.   Approaches which have been employed to prevent
      workers' dependents from relocating into the site area also
      are reviewed.   Finally, specific facility designs appropriate
      to support M-X construction in desert areas of Utah and Nevada
      are described.

772. Krahn, Harvey, John Gartrell, and Lyle Larson.   "The Quality
      of Family Life in a Resource Community."   *Canadian Journal
      of Sociology* 6 (1981): 307-24.

      Examines family adjustment and satisfaction in a rapidly
      developing Canadian resource community.   Analysis of survey
      data from 430 residents of a "new" town in northern Alberta
      showed that satisfaction with family life was very high and
      unrelated to community satisfaction which was moderately high.
      Migration to the community appeared to positively affect
      parent-child interaction, a positive correlate of family
      satisfaction.   Although the hypotheses linking family role
      flexibility and family satisfaction were not supported, there
      is evidence that strong interpersonal relationships within the
      family are associated with a higher level of satisfaction with
      family life among residents of the community.

 *   Levenson,   Rosaline.   *Company Towns: A Bibliography of
      American and Foreign Sources.*   Exchange Bibliography No.
      1428. Cited below as item 1004.

773. Lucas,   Rex A.   *Minetown, Milltown, Railtown: Life in
      Canadian Communities of Single Industry.*   Toronto, Ontario:
      University of Toronto Press, 1971. 433 pp.

      Examines the way of life in Canadian communities with
      populations of 30,000 or less which are economically dependent
      on a single industry.   Topics examined include (1) construc-
      tion of the community, (2) recruitment of citizens, (3) the
      organization of work, (4) occupation, stratification, and
      association, (5) recreation, (6) goods and services, (7)
      schools, (8) social conflict and social control, and (9)
      marriage and migration of youth.

774. McCann, L. D. "The Changing Internal Structure of Canadian Resource Towns." *Plan Canada* 18, No. 1 (March 1978): 46-59.

Examines Canadian communities that have been built to house and service workers engaged in extraction, developent, or primary processing of a forest, mineral, fishery, or power resource. There are at least ninety-five of these settlements with a 1971 population of at least 1,000. Nearly half of these towns were built since World War II as comprehensively planned communities. These newer towns display remarkable uniformity in physical and social character, and all contrast sharply in form and pattern with the resource town of the nineteenth century.

775. Massey, Garth, and D. Lewis. "Energy Development and Mobile Home Living: The Myth of Suburbia Revisted." *The Social Science Journal* 16, No. 2 (1979): 81-91.

Examines mobile home living in impacted communities and asks one basic question: To what degree does this type of housing contribute to associational behavior among newcomers living in mobile homes? Data were drawn from personal interviews with mobile home residents in several energy communities in Wyoming.

776. Metz, William C. "American Energy and Mineral Industry Involvement in Housing." *Minerals and the Environment* 4 (1982): 131-40.

Examines recent efforts by United States firms to assure adequate housing for their work forces. Such involvement differs from the heavy reliance on company towns that was common during the nineteenth and early twentieth centuries. Substantial reliance is now placed on stimulation, as well as on direct supply, of the housing market.

* Newton, P. W. "The Problems and Prospects of Remote Mining Towns: National and Regional Issues." *Urban Australia: Living in the Next Decade.* Papers presented at symposium on Macro-Economic and Social Trends in Australia. Cited above as item 56.

777. Parkinson, A., S. W. Montgomery, and R. D. Humphreys. *A Study of the Impact of Construction Camps on the People of Northeast Alberta.* Edmonton, Alberta: Alberta Oil Sands Environmental Research Program, 1980. 116 pp.

Discusses the effect of camp organization and management on the construction workers living in the camp and on their

families who live elsewhere, and examines how camp organization, location, and management affect the impacts experienced
by nearby communities. After outlining the methodology and
terms of reference, the regional contexts, historical background, and regulatory environment are briefly reviewed. The
design, organization, and functioning of camps are described,
followed by a descriptive profile of camp personnel. An
analysis follows of the way in which the functioning of the
camp and the camp personnel impact the local communities. The
way in which camp employment, camp organization, and camp
location relate to the impact on the construction worker and
the family is discussed, and finally some observations,
conclusions, and suggestions for future research are presented
with regard to future camps.

778. Pinfield, Lawrence T., and Lois D. Etherington. *Housing
      Strategies of Resource Firms in Western Canada.* Burnaby,
      British Columbia: Simon Fraser University, Department of
      Business Administration, 1982. 148 pp.

      Presents a framework for considering the wide variety of
      housing policies in current use by resource firms in western
      Canada, describes the policies being used by a number of firms
      in 1981, presents a detailed analysis of the affordability of
      housing together with a case study of housing affordability in
      the East Kootenay region of British Columbia, and provides a
      discussion of the implications of proposed changes to the tax
      legislation which will impact on housing benefits.

779. Riffel, J. A. *Quality of Life in Resource Towns.* Ottawa,
      Ontario: Ministry of State for Urban Affairs, 1975. 107
      pp.

      Provides an overview of current thought and research related
      to quality of life issues in resource towns. It focuses
      primarily, though not exclusively, on the Canadian experience.
      The emphasis is on compiling basic information on quality-of-
      living conditions in both "objective" and "subjective" terms.

780. Roberts, Richard, and Judith Fisher. *Debunking the Myths of
      Canadian Resource Communities.* Calgary, Alberta: Praxis, A
      Social Planning Company, 1983. 20 pp.

      Summarizes results of interviews with residents of five
      Canadian resource towns to determine residents' perceptions of
      their quality of life, their future needs and preferences, and
      their priorities for housing and for recreational and cultural
      programs and facilities. The study also sought to establish a
      sociodemographic profile of resource town residents, and
      ultimately to provide input to new town planning. The
      findings run counter to some commonly held beliefs concerning
      isolated resource towns. For example, the ratings for quality

of life indicators were very high except for education, shopping, and the community as a place to retire. More than 50% of the residents had lived in the community for more than five years.

781. Robinson, Ira M. "New Resource Towns on Canada's Frontier: Selected Contemporary Issues." *Resource Communities: A Decade of Disruption.* Edited by Don D. Detomasi and John W. Gartrell. Boulder, Colorado: Westview Press, 1984. pp. 1-21.

Examines special problems faced by remote, single-industry towns in Canada. Special attention is given to economic instability (often manifested through a boom-bust cycle of growth), unbalanced demographic structure (male-dominated), and difficulties in provision and financing of affordable housing and an adequate range of physical and social infra structures. An underlying premise of the paper is that, despite the many improvements made over the years in planning, design, development, and governance of these towns, the basic problems, especially instability and impermanence, remain.

782. Siemens, L. B. *Single-Enterprise Community Studies in Northern Canada.* Prepared for Seminar on Man and the Environment: New Towns in Isolated Settings, held in Kambalda, Western Australia, August 1973. Winnipeg, Manitoba: The University of Manitoba, Center for Settlement Studies, December 1973. 54 pp.

Examines both the theory and practice of living in remote communities. The author presents an overview of some Canadian studies and deals with the planning and quality of life in single-enterprise communities along the Canadian resource frontier. Five central concerns facing planners of new towns in the North are discussed: environment and ecology; social and psychological problems; values in planning; converting residents into citizens; and regional, permanent, or nonper- manent communities.

MANAGING SOCIAL AND PSYCHOLOGICAL IMPACTS

783. Bates, V. Edward. "The Impact of Energy Boom-Town Growth on Rural Areas." *Social Casework* 59, No. 2 (February 1978): 73-82.

Explores the implications of rapid growth on social work needs of rural areas. The aim is first to define and inte- grate the wide range of social work concerns involved in rural development and then to develop an identified practice model for social workers which permits a flexibility of approach to community problems.

784. Bealer, Robert C., Kenneth E. Martin, and Donald M. Crider. *Sociological Aspects of Siting Facilities For Solid Wastes Disposal.* A. E. & R. S. 158. University Park, Pennsylvania: Pennsylvania State University, Department of Agricultural Economics and Rural Sociology, 1982. 88 pp.

Considers some of the sociological and/or social psychological aspects of solid waste disposal in the United States, with particular emphasis on what we might know presently from empirical research studies. An extensive bibliography, partially annotated, is included.

785. Buxton, Edward B. "Delivering Social Services in Rural Areas." *Public Welfare* 31, No. 1 (1973): 15-20.

Outlines the limitations which apply to the development of social service programs in rural areas and suggests procedures to effectively handle a community's social problems. Some limitations include the erroneous assumption that rural situations are simple, the visible separation (clothes, new car, etc.) of social workers from the people around them, and an approach to problem solving different from that of others in the community. Public welfare agencies are often viewed as an affront to all that is held to be of value to many communities: self-sufficiency, independence, thrift, and family loyalty.

786. Covello, Vincent T., W. Gary Flamm, Joseph V. Rodricks, and Robert G. Tardiff, eds. *The Analysis of Actual Versus Perceived Risks.* New York: Plenum Press, 1983. 377 pp.

Is the proceedings of the first annual meeting of the Society for Risk Analysis that was formed in 1981 to address the complex problems of assessing the risks inherent in modern society. The workshop theme, actual versus perceived risks, was stimulated by the research finding that technical experts and nonexperts differ substantially in their risk estimates. Topics covered were automobile accidents, nuclear power plants, cancer chemotherapy, cigarette smoking, toxic wastes, and depletion of stratospheric ozone.

787. Davenport, Joseph, III, and Judith Ann Davenport, eds. *The Boom Town: Problems and Promises in the Energy Vortex.* Laramie: University of Wyoming, 1980. 212 pp.

Contains fifteen articles about human service needs and social problems in rapidly growing resource communities in the western United States. Individual articles focus on such topics as mental health problems, alcohol-related problems, child abuse, needs of the elderly, and experiences of Native Americans in energy development areas. Other articles address preventative and mitigative measures.

788. Davenport, Joseph III, and Judith Ann Davenport. "Boom Town Victims: Social Work's Latest Clients." *Journal of Sociology and Social Welfare* 8 (1981): 150-63.

Examines the magnitude of energy development in the western United States, discusses the social consequences and human costs of such development, and suggests possible responses by the profession of social work. Boom town victims may include individuals, groups, entire communities, or even a geographical region. Authors contend that while social work has not played an active role in energy-impacted boom towns, the profession is uniquely equipped to deal with the concomitant social and human problems.

789. El Sendiony, M. F. M., M. G. M. Abou-El Azaem, and F. Luza. "Culture Change and Mental Illness." *International Journal of Social Psychiatry* 23, No. 1 (1977): 20-25.

Studies the relationship of culture change to the frequency of mental illness in the outpatient clinic in Cairo, Egypt. Rapid industrialization tends to produce significantly higher rates of patients who were judged to have serious symptoms of depression, especially among migrants who moved from their villages to work in the city's factories. The authors suggest that the higher rates may be a factor of social disorganization associated with relocating.

790. England, J. Lynn, and Stan L. Albrecht. "Boomtowns and Social Disruption." *Rural Sociology* 49, No. 2 (1984): 230-46.

Evaluates the social disruption hypothesis that states that boom towns enter a period of generalized crisis and loss of traditional routines and attitudes. The hypothesis is evaluated with respect to the impact of energy development on residents' involvement in their community, their attachment to it, and the perceived quality of community services. Two models are examined: (1) a linear model based on the assumption that boom towns result in weakened ties to the community, a decline in the importance of the community, and a rise in formal ties; and (2) a systemic model assuming that boom communities have mechanisms to re-establish ties to the community and to others. Data from three boom towns indicate that the social ties are not disrupted nor do they give way to formal ties; informal ties increase. In addition, boom towns do experience a decline in the quality of virtually all aspects of community services. In sum, both models are operative, but on differing dimensions.

791. Fischhoff, Baruch, Sarah Lichtenstein, Paul Slovic, Stephen L. Derby, and Ralph L. Keeney. *Acceptable Risk*. Cambridge, Massachusetts: Cambridge University Press, 1981. 185 pp.

Presents a critical analysis of possible approaches to making acceptable-risk decisions which not only arise in everyday life and in such large-scale interventions as social reforms and new technologies but also are a weak or missing link in the management of technological hazards. Three major approaches are evaluated: (1) professional judgment--allowing technical experts to devise solutions; (2) bootstrapping--searching for historical precedents to guide future decisions; and (3) formal analysis--using theory-based procedures for modeling problems and calculating the best decision. A conceptual guide, the book focuses on what these approaches try to do and how likely they are to achieve the goals they set for themselves. The approaches are evaluated relative to one another and are contrasted with the absolute standard of the expectations of an ideal method. Recommendations aimed at improving society's ability to make acceptable-risk decisions are offered in the areas of policy, practice, and research.

792. Fischhoff, Baruch, Paul Slovic, and Sarah Lichtenstein. "Weighing the Risks." *Environment* 21, No. 4 (1979): 17-20, 32-38.

Explores the pros, cons, uses, and limitations of four approaches to determining whether a given technology is sufficiently safe. The approaches are cost-benefit analysis, revealed preferences, expressed preferences, and natural standards.

793. Freudenburg, William R. "Women and Men in an Energy Boomtown: Adjustment, Alienation, and Adaptation." *Rural Sociology* 46, No. 2 (1981): 220-44.

Finds little support for the proposition that women in rapid-growth areas perceive themselves as being more negatively affected than men. Data on social integration, alienation, and overall social-psychological adjustment were examined from a sample of four western Colorado energy communities. Nevertheless, no net personal benefit for women was found; the boomtown women were highly unlikely to receive a direct economic benefit from development. The data suggest that long-time women residents may actually be adapting more successfully than men.

794. Freudenburg, William R., and Eugene A. Rosa, eds. *Public
      Reactions to Nuclear Power.* Boulder, Colorado: Westview
      Press, 1984. 300 pp.

      Presents a state-of-the-art overview of public attitudes
      toward nuclear power, of the ways in which the attitudes are
      interpreted by major actors in the ongoing debate, and of the
      implications that public reactions will have for the future of
      the nuclear option in the United States. The following facets
      of public attitudes are examined: longitudinal analysis,
      degree of polarization, media influences, perceptions of risk,
      public participation in waste management policy, and regula-
      tions of the industry.

      Contains items 248, 712.

795. Lindell,   Michael K.,   and Timothy C. Earle.   "How Close is
      Close Enough: Public Perceptions of the Risks of Industrial
      Facilities." *Risk Analysis* 3, No. 4 (1983): 245-54.

      Used a purposive or judgmental sampling strategy for two
      surveys that examined the public's response to perceived risks
      and benefits of industrial facilities. The proportion of
      respondants who are willing to have a nuclear power plant in
      their own community is smaller than the proportion who agree
      that more nuclear plants should be built in this country.
      Respondants' judgments of the minimum safe distance from each
      of eight hazardous facilities confirmed that this finding
      results from perceived risk gradients that differ by facility
      (e.g. nuclear vs. natural gas power plants) and social group
      (e.g., chemical engineers vs. environmentalists) but are
      relatively stable over time. The data also suggest that a
      perceived lack of personal control over risk exposure may be
      an important factor in stimulating public opposition to
      facility siting.

  *   Lindell, M. K., T. C. Earle, J. A. Hebert, and R. W. Perry.
      *Radioactive Wastes: Public Attitudes Toward Disposal
      Facilities.* B-HARC-411-004. Cited below as item 963.

796. Rosen, David H., and Deborah Voorhees-Rosen. "The Shetland
      Islands: The Effects of Social and Economic Change on
      Mental Health." *Culture, Medicine and Psychiatry* 2 (1978):
      41-67.

      Describes a long-term study of the effects of rapid social
      and ecological change (from North Sea oil developments) on
      Shetland islanders. Preliminary results are presented both
      from a general survey that monitored reported data on
      ecological, epidemiological, and sociological change including
      psychiatric morbidity, crime, divorce, and suicide, and from
      an individual survey designed to examine individuals'

reactions to change and variables associated with those
reactions, including the prevalence of medical and psychiatric
symptoms and illnesses.

797.   Slovic, Paul, Baruch Fischhoff, and Sarah Lichtenstein.
       "Perception and Acceptability of Risk from Energy Systems."
       Advances in Environmental Psychology. Vol. 3, *Energy:
       Psychological Perspectives.* Edited by A. Baum and J. E.
       Singer. Hillsdale, New Jersey: Erlbaum, 1981. pp. 155-
       69.

       Points out that public opposition and fear of nuclear power
       stem from recognition of the unresolved technical issues in
       the risk assessment process and from the fundamental thought
       processes that determine perceptions of risk. The special
       qualities of nuclear hazards blur the distinction between the
       possible and the probable, and produce an immense gap between
       the views of most technical experts and a significant portion
       of the public--a gap that must be recognized by planners and
       policymakers.

798.   Slovic, Paul, Sarah Lichtenstein, and Baruch Fischhoff.
       "Images of Disaster: Perception and Acceptance of Risks
       from Nuclear Power." *Energy Risk Management.* Edited by G.
       Goodman and W. Rowe. London: Academic Press, 1979. pp.
       223-45.

       Describes the images that have formed in the public's mind
       regarding potential nuclear disasters. The authors speculate
       on their origins, permanence, and their implications.

799.   Slovic, Paul, Sarah Lichtenstein, and Baruch Fischhoff.
       "Modeling the Societal Impact of Fatal Accidents." *Manage-
       ment Science* 30, No. 4 (1984): 464-74.

       Proposes that models based solely on utility functions of N
       lives lost in a single accident be abandoned in favor of
       models that elaborate in detail the significant events and
       consequences likely to result from an accident, the conse-
       quences of these consequences, the probabilities of all these
       direct and higher order effects, and some measures of their
       costs.

800.   Willard, Daniel E., and Melinda M. Swenson. "Why Not in Your
       Backyard? Scientific Data and Nonrational Decisions About
       Risk." *Environmental Management* 8, No. 2 (1984): 93-100.

       Illustrates and analyzes several examples that combine
       features common to many "no win" environmental decisions, and
       suggests methods which would lead toward a scientific and
       politically useful resolution. The common features are (1) we

must decide something, (2) the decision affects some people more than others, (3) as scientists we are not 100% confident of our results, (4) elements of the decision remain unquantifiable, and (5) decisions combine both scientific and politically useful resolution.

FINANCING

801. Allen, Debra L., and Jack R. Huddleston. *Tax Incremental Financing*. No. 9. Chicago, Illinois: Council of Planning Librarians, June 1979. 13 pp.

Annotates articles, reports, journal notes, and state laws and reports that relate to tax incremental financing (TIF), a method of financing local governmental public expenditures. TIF is a potential alternative to state and federal urban renewal assistance and has been popularized as a means for encouraging local public-private partnerships in redevelopment.

802. Bender, Bruce, and Steven Schwiff. "The Appropriation of Rents by Boomtown Governments." *Economic Inquiry* 20, No. 1 (1982): 84-103.

Explores the issue of the appropriation by boom towns of economic rents accruing to private capital investments as the means of financing capital investments induced by the boom. The authors present a qualitative analysis of generation of rents and discuss the incentives of boom town governments to appropriate part of those rents in light of a current home-owner model of local government behavior. Specific mechanisms are described which local governments can employ to capture those rents. The behavior of six Wyoming boom towns and another control group of six Wyoming towns are empirically analyzed. Results indicate that the evidence is consistent with a policy of rent appropriation by boom towns and suggests a method of financing local government capital expenditures consistent with the current homeowner model of local government behavior. The article concludes questioning both the efficiency and equity of the substantial subsidization by the U.S. Environmental Protection Agency of capital expenditures by boom towns.

803. Bender, Lloyd D., and Thomas F. Stinson. "Mitigating Impacts of Rapid Growth on Local Government." *Journal of the Community Development Society* 15, No. 1 (1984): 59-73.

Suggests a diagnostic approach to enable local officials to anticipate fiscal imbalances resulting from new development. Four separate types of public sector fiscal impacts are identified--spillovers, front-end deficits, boomtown effects, and uncertainties. This fiscal impact taxonomy is later matched to the characteristics of large-scale developments to provide local officials a framework by which to gauge future problems. Alternative mitigation measures, either currently in use or proposed, are then categorized by their effectiveness against each type of anticipated impact. Results indicate that all impact mitigation measures are not equally effective against all types of impacts.

804.   Bronder, Leonard D., Nancy Carlisle, and Michael D. Savage, Jr. *Financial Strategies for Alleviation of Socioeconomic Impacts in Seven Western States.* Denver, Colorado: Western Governors' Regional Energy Policy Office, 1977. 575 pp.

Addresses the problems of small communities in seven western states which have been or in the future may be impacted by large and rapid population increases. Each of the states (Arizona, Colorado, Montana, New Mexico, North Dakota, Utah, and Wyoming) is treated separately; state, county, municipal, and school district sources of revenue and patterns of spending are analyzed for each state, and strategies for alleviation of impacts are recommended. Finally, an overview of financial strategies is presented.

805.   Combs, Robert P., Glen C. Pulver, and Ron E. Shaffer. *Financing New Small Business Enterprise in Wisconsin.* R3198. Madison, Wisconsin: University of Wisconsin, College of Agricultural and Life Sciences, 1983. 24 pp.

Reviews information derived from a survey of 134 new small businesses which were started in Wisconsin during 1976 and 1977. These firms represent nine types of business activity including construction, manufacturing, wholesaling, and retailing. Owners were asked how they acquired the equity and debt capital to get started, how sources changed during their first years of operation, and what problems, if any, they had encountered.

806.   Conrad, Robert F., and R. Bryce Hool. *Taxation of Mineral Resources.* Lexington, Massachusetts: Lexington Books, 1980. 109 pp.

Provides a comprehensive economic analysis of the effects of mining taxation on the extraction of mineral resources. Specific topics include mining taxes, mining decisions (the effects of uncertainty and risk), effects of mineral taxation, and policy implications. The book closes with an appendix of state tax collections by source from 1971 to 1978.

807. Davis, A. John. "Western Boom Town Financing Problems: Selected State Legislative Responses." *Journal of Contemporary Law* 5, No. 2 (1979): 319-38.

Describes the adverse impacts associated with energy development in the western United States. Even though problems are not financial in nature, the author contends that many problems would be solved by the timely acquisition of adequate funds, and he argues that since the growth-generated problems of boom towns are unconventional, the conventional money sources available to local governments are generally inadequate. Local governments' financing problems are illustrated by surveying the state responses in Utah, Montana, and Wyoming.

808. Fisher, Peter S. "The Role of the Public Sector in Local Development Finance: Evaluating Alternative Institutional Arrangements." *Journal of Economic Issues* 17, No. 1 (1983): 133-53.

Develops a framework for evaluating alternative economic institutions and applies that framework to various arrangements for financing housing and local economic development. An *institution* is defined here as a set of property rights or rules for decision making. The framework for analyzing institutions is based on the notion that alternative specifications of property rights or decision rules will affect the nature of the outcomes produced by economic entities. Choice among alternative institutions then requires an evaluation of these outcomes and of the institutional processes themselves against some set of social value criteria. The framework is applied to the evaluation of two alternative institutional arrangements for the provision of debt and equity capital for investment in housing and in commercial and industrial enterprises: government regulation of private banks and creation of publicly owned banks.

809. Floyd, Kennedy, and Associates, Inc. *Alternate Sources of Municipal Development Capital: Tax Increment and Industrial Revenue Bond Financing for Cities.* Vol. 1: *Description of Financing Tools.* Vol. 2: *State-by-State Analysis.* Washington, D.C.: National League of Cities, 1979. 23 pp. and 84 pp.

Provides, in volume one, a general understanding of how development financing mechanisms were developed and how they may be used to further locally defined economic development objectives. Volume two is an appendix that provides a state-by-state description of cities' authority to use tax increment and industrial revenue bond financing.

810.   Gillis, Malcolm. "Severance Taxes on Energy Resources in the
       United States: A Tale of Two Minerals." *Growth and Change*
       10, No. 1 (1979): 54-71.

       Compares and contrasts the severance taxes on coal and
       uranium in the western United States. Gillis analyzes their
       similarities (e.g., rising rents and rent capture, derived
       demand, environmental concerns) and differences (e.g.,
       reserves and exploration), discusses the recent changes in
       severance taxes on coal and uranium, and evaluates the theory
       of tax exporting.

811.   Gilmore, John S., Keith D. Moore, Diane Hammond, and Dean
       Coddington. *Analysis of Financing Problems in Coal and Oil
       Shale Boom Towns.* Washington, D.C.: Federal Energy
       Administration, 1976. 253 pp.

       Uses a case study approach to analyze impacts resulting from
       energy development in four communities located in Colorado,
       Utah, and Wyoming. For each community the adequacy of
       facilities, the tax revenues, and capital needs for facility
       construction are examined. A variety of financing options are
       evaluated for their effectiveness based on eight criteria.

812.   Gray, Mary, and Stephen Hoffman. *Mitigating the Socioeco-
       nomic Impacts of Coal-to-Methanol Plants in Wyoming.* Report
       prepared for the U.S. Department of Energy, Office of Oil,
       Gas, and Oil Shale Technology. Bethesda, Maryland: Booz-
       Allen & Hamilton, Inc., Energy and Environment Division,
       1981. 106 pp.

       Investigates fiscal methods for mitigating the major public
       service costs from a hypothetical 24,000 bbl per day coal-
       to-methanol plant in Wyoming. The revenues investigated
       include both available and potential sources. The potential
       funding sources require either enabling legislation or local
       action. Rawlins, Wyoming, was selected as the study location
       because it typifies the small urban areas where a coal-
       to-methanol plant could be located.

813.   Kieffer, David, and Jon Miller. "Public Budgets and Public
       Capital in Boom Towns." *Policy Sciences* 16 (1984): 349-69.

       Explores the proposition that local governments, being
       inflexible bureaucratic institutions, are subject to severe
       fiscal stress in periods of rapid change, such as boom town
       growth, and attempts to quantify this stress by measuring the
       inadequacy of public facilities and budget deficits in these
       situations. The authors evaluate the efficacy of existing
       intergovernmental aid programs and other policies in
       mitigation. Towards this end, a dynamic econometric model of

local public finance and capital accumulation is presented and
applied to a case study of Utah cities during 1970-1979.

814. Lamont, William, George Beardsley, Andy Briscoe, John Carver,
Dan Harrington, John Lansdowne, and James Murray. *Tax Lead
Time Study: The Colorado Oil Shale Region.* Denver:
Colorado Geological Survey, 1974. 245 pp.

Reviews alternative revenue sources for local governments
and potential techniques for handling revenue timing and
distribution problems created by rapid population growth.
Although the study focuses on Colorado and, more specifically,
on the oil shale region, much of the analysis is generally
applicable to communities facing rapid growth.

815. Leistritz, F. Larry, Steve H. Murdock, Norman E. Toman, and
Donald M. Senechal. "Local Fiscal Impacts of Energy
Resource Development: Applications of an Assessment Model
in Policy Making." *North Central Journal of Agricultural
Economics* 4, No. 1 (January 1982): 47-57.

Describes the use of a fiscal impact simulation model as a
tool for the development of state taxation policies, as a
guide for administration of an impact assistance program, and
as an aid to local governments in public facility planning.
Insight is thus provided into often neglected aspects of the
use of policy-oriented analytical techniques.

816. Lillydahl, Jane H., and Elizabeth W. Moen. "Planning,
Managing, and Financing Growth and Decline in Energy
Resource Communities: A Case Study of Western Colorado."
Journal of Energy and Development 8, No. 2 (Spring 1983):
211-30.

Retrospectively views recent experiences in western Colorado
and the continued uncertainty of energy development in the
region. Authors describe the "boom-bust" cycle and proffer
the opinion that more coordination between industry and local
government is needed. Such planning could involve a joint
effort of local government and industry to negotiate and
manage future growth in the area and may require industry to
pay the costs of busts as well as booms. Contingency plans
for sudden, premature shutdowns of projects should be included
in government permits, agreements, and impact statements.

817. Lowe, John S. "Severance Taxes as an Issue of Energy
Sectionalism." *Energy Law Journal* 5, No. 2 (1984): 357-81.

Recounts the past and current tension between the producing
and consuming states over energy matters, noteably the issue
of severance taxes. Such tension worsened by the rapid

escalation of energy prices in the 1970s and early 1980s as prices and production soared resulting in the economies of major producing states booming while the consuming states experienced the deep throes of an economic recession. Lowe compares the fiscal disparities among states and the distribution of economic rents due to energy production and taxation. He reviews and assesses the debate on severance taxes, which is the focal point of the sectionalist argument, and illustrates the conflict over severance taxes with the recent court cases involving Montana and the Jicarilla Apache Indian severance tax laws.

818. Lubov, Andrea. *Issuing Municipal Bonds: A Primer for Local Officials.* Agr. Info. Bull. No. 429. Washington, D.C.: U.S. Department of Agriculture, 1979. 20 pp.

Gives an overview of how bonds of small local governments are issued, underwritten, marketed, and serviced. The manual distinguishes the different types of bonds, discusses the appropriateness of each type for different purposes, and illustrates the effect of different repayment structures on interest costs. The types of documents that a community must prepare in connection with a bond offering are also discussed.

819. MacDonnell, Lawrence, Keith Moore, Mark Lawson, Belden Daniels, Steven Klein, Bruce Posner, and Ted Browne. *Facilitating Private Sector Capital Availability in Rapid Growth Communities.* Denver, Colorado: Denver Research Institute, 1982. 96 pp.

Considers the effect of oil shale development on the availability of capital required for private development in the three counties of western Colorado that were expected to be most affected by that development—Garfield, Mesa, and Rio Blanco counties. The study found that the primary private sector capital requirements were for housing but that expansion of the commercial business sector would also require substantial investments. The primary local sources of capital—commercial banks and savings and loan associations—were expected to be able to meet only a fraction of these needs. Means of drawing additional capital into the region are then explored.

820. McGill, Stuart. "Project Financing Applied to the OK Tedi Mine—A Government Perspective." *Natural Resources Forum* (published for the United Nations) 7, No. 2 (April 1983): 115-30.

Presents a case study of the financing of the OK Tedi gold-copper mine in Papau, New Guinea, that illustrates the nature of project financing and outlines the arrangements made in the project. The author contends that the limitation of financial exposure is an important goal for governments involved in developing their resources sector.

821. Markusan, Ann R. "Federal Budget Simplification: Preventative Programs vs. Palliatives for Local Governments with Booming, Stable, and Declining Economies." *National Tax Journal* 30, No. 3 (1977): 249-58.

Comments on contemporary budget problems of local governments which stem in large part from unhealthy rates of economic growth or decline rather than primarily from institutional constraints on budgets. Markusan contends that intergovernmental policy plays a large but not deliberate role in fostering differential growth rates. A policy change from further proliferation of categorical grants and general revenue sharing towards regional growth and development strategies as the primary basis for intergovernmental transfers (i.e., from palliatives to preventative fiscal programs) is suggested.

822. Minnesota State Planning Agency. *Community Capital Improvements: Needs and Financing: Case Studies of Four Minnesota Cities.* St. Paul, Minnesota: Minnesota State Planning Agency, Office of Local and Urban Affairs, 1981. 150 pp.

Includes a background section on each city's financial situation, its capital improvement needs, its financing, and its planning and decision-making process. The four cities are Woodbury and Robbinsdale in the metropolitan Twin Cities area, Aitkin, and Owatonna.

823. Muller, Thomas, and Carol E. Soble. *Financing Rapid Growth.* President's Economic Adjustment Committee, Office of Economic Adjustment. U.S. Department of Defense. Community Guidance Manual VIII. Washington, D.C.: The Pentagon, December 1982. 48 pp.

Presents the fundamentals for financing municipal facilities and services in rapid growth situations. The authors emphasize that the community's primary tasks in the face of rapid growth are to expand its revenue base and, whenever possible, to shift the added costs of public services to commuters and temporary residents. They suggest that local governments have several financing strategies at their disposal including tax mechanisms (e.g., local property taxes, taxes on lodging, meals, and earnings), user fees and charges (e.g., one-time development fees, utility tap fees), and other methods of financing or providing public services (e.g., public contracting with private firms, tax prepayment, tax incremental financing, and local development corporations). The report concludes with a brief statement that the success of a community's endeavors in the face of rapid growth is largely determined by the management strategy selected.

824.   National Association of Towns and Townships. *Financing Public Services and Facilities in Rural Communities: Who Will Pay and How?* Washington, D.C.: National Association of Towns and Townships, 1982. 14 pp.

Highlights the comments of a four-member panel of public finance experts at a seminar to examine the current financial condition of rural governments, rural public works needs, and innovative revenue-raising methods.

825.   Olson, Dean F. "The Alaska Renewable Resources Corporation: Toward Economic Permanence Through Venture Capital." *Expanding the Opportunity to Produce: Revitalizing the American Economy Through New Enterprise Development: A Policy Reader.* Edited by Robert Friedman and William Schweke. Washington, D.C.: The Corporation for Enterprise Development, 1981. pp. 387-98.

Describes the Alaska Renewable Resources Corporation (ARRC) state-supported venture capital firm, financed from the state's oil and gas royalty receipts, with the goal to create a more diversified, sustainable economy. Expansion of economic activity and creation of jobs in Alaskan-owned businesses, largely in the renewable resources of agriculture, forestry, and fishing were specific objectives of the ARRC. Also traces the development of the ARRC with particular discussion of its investment portfolio.

*   Skiffington, Lucy J. "Constitutionality of State Economic Incentives for Energy Development." *Journal of Energy Law and Policy.* Cited above as item 612.

826.   Sullivan, Patrick J. *Examining the Rural Municipal Bond Market.* RDRR-4. Washington, D.C.: U.S. Department of Agriculture, Economic Research Service, 1983. 40 pp.

Suggests that the municipal bond market may become even more important for rural governments in financing the construction of public facilities as federal assistance to local governments becomes more scarce. Changes in borrowing techniques which could help to reduce the cost of borrowing are discussed.

Closure and Cancellation of Projects

827. Amos, John M., and W. S. Rumburg. *Effects of the Loss of St. Joseph Minerals Corporation as a Major Employer on St. Francois County, Missouri.* Rolla, Missouri: University of Missouri, Center for Applied Engineering Management, 1978. 79 pp.

Reviews the chain of events resulting from the cessation of operations by St. Joseph Minerals Corporation on the cities of Bonne Terre and Flat River and the surrounding St. Francis County, Missouri, during the period 1958 to 1977. The authors examine the actions taken by the company itself and by municipalities and other government agencies in the area. Economic indicators analyzed include property valuation, population, employment, utility and telephone connections, sales tax collections, number of retail outlets, and income taxes paid.

828. Aronson, Robert L., and Robert B. McKersie. *Economic Consequences of Plant Shutdowns in New York State.* Ithaca, New York: Cornell University, 1980. 171 pp.

Provides an overview of the problems involved in a shutdown and points out the need for further development of human resources policy. Three communities in New York were studied as the basis for this report. The primary focus is on the community level or macro-effects and adjustments to the economic trauma. It also reviews worker adjustment and behavior.

829. Arrowhead Regional Development Commission. *Economic Adjustment Strategies: In the Event of the Loss of a Major Regional Employer.* Duluth, Minnesota: Arrowhead Regional Development Commission, 1977. 289 pp.

Prepared in response to the potential court-ordered closure of the Reserve Mining Company of Silver Bay, Minnesota. The firm employed 2,870 persons in 1977. The threatened closure would bring about economic and social disaster for seven communities and nine townships, as well as have lesser effects on all of northeastern Minnesota. Topics covered in the report include methodology; regional setting; state and federal responses; job placement, retraining, and income maintenance; housing investment protection; local governmental services maintenance; business and commercial strategies; and growth impacts and related economic adjustments.

830. Bagshaw, Michael L., and Robert H. Schnorbus. "The Local Labor-Market Response to a Plant Shutdown." *Economic Review*

(Federal Reserve Bank of Cleveland), (January 1980):   16–
24.

Attempts to identify and differentiate between the direct
and indirect effects of postshutdown labor–market adjustments
in the Youngstown–Warren (Ohio) SMSA.   The analysis is
focussed on the 1977 shutdown of the Campbell Works of the
Youngstown Sheet and Tube Co., an action that idled about
4,200 workers.

831.   Bale, Malcolm D., and Diane P. Miller. *The Effects of Adjust-*
       ment Assistance on Trade-Displaced Workers: A Case Study.
       Bozeman, Montana: Montana State University, 1976. 75 pp.

       Attempts to determine the effects of the timing of receipt
       of trade assistance upon worker adjustment.   Chosen as the
       experimental group were workers who   received adjustment
       assistance within one month of layoff. The control group were
       workers who received assistance more than one year after the
       layoff.   The study used two multiple regression models to
       compare worker adjustment.   The research showed that receipt
       of trade adjustment assistance shortly after layoff resulted
       in a   higher wage upon re-employment, that   receipt of
       assistance shortly after layoff did not decrease the length of
       unemployment but rather increased it, and the receipt of
       assistance clearly altered the opportunity cost of employment
       and the acceptance wage of workers resulting in a longer
       duration of transitory unemployment.

832.   Barkley, David L., and Arnold Paulsen. *Patterns in the*
       Openings and Closings of Manufacturing Plants in Rural Areas
       of Iowa. Ames, Iowa: Iowa State University, North Central
       Regional Center for Rural Development, 1979. 71 pp.

       Compares industrial migration and rates of openings and
       closings, first among groups of industries in Iowa for an
       entire decade and second by phases of the business cycle.   It
       was found that (1) the rate of openings and closings of branch
       plants exceeded that of locally owned firms and (2) branch
       plants exhibited a   greater propensity to   open during
       prosperity and to close during a recession.

833.   Behn, Robert D. "Closing a Government Facility." *Public*
       Administration Review 38, No. 4 (1978): 332–38.

       Examines approaches to closing government facilities that
       can help to minimize the political conflict and personal
       trauma often associated with such closures.

834.   Bluestone, Barry, and Bennett Harrison. *The Deindustrializa-*
       tion of America: Plant Closings, Community Abandonment, and

the Dismantling of Basic Industry. New York: Basic Books, 1982. 323 pp.

Documents the widespread closure of manufacturing plants in the United States, analyzes the reasons for and consequences of plant closings, and proposes a new industrial strategy which the authors call "reindustrialization with a human face." The authors point out that plant shutdowns wiped out a total of 22 million jobs in the U.S. during the period 1969 through 1976. They argue that the commonly proposed solutions of supply-side income distribution, tax reform, corporate emulation of Japanese planning, promotion of small-business entrepreneurship, and creation of urban enterprise zones all are inadequate. They contend that what is needed is nothing less than a fundamental restructuring of the American economy. In the short term, their agenda includes rebuilding the social safety net and the passage of plant-closing legislation. For the long run, they propose a comprehensive policy of "reindustrialization with a human face" with such objectives as the equitable sharing of economic growth, production of useful goods and services, a humane work environment, and economic democracy.

835. Bowen, Richard L., and David L. Foster. *A Profile of Displaced Pineapple Workers on Moloka'i.* Research Extension Series 031. Honolulu: University of Hawaii, College of Tropical Agriculture and Human Resources, 1983. 24 pp.

Summarizes a survey of workers being terminated as Del Monte Corporation shut down its pineapple operations on the island of Moloka'i. About 64% of the 220 affected workers responded. Information obtained included demographics (place of residence, age, gender, arrival in Hawaii, nationality-ethnicity, language skills, education, and family status), assets, sources of income, plans for relocation or retirement, present occupation, skill areas, future employment interests, and perceived needs for support services.

836. Brownrigg, Mark. "Industrial Contraction and the Regional Multiplier Effect: An Application in Scotland." *Town Planning Review* 51, No. 2 (1980): 195-210.

Analyzes a very typical situation of threatened economic contraction in western Scotland, in the form of the impending closure or severe rationalization of a manufacturing plant in Kilmarnock. The author's objectives are (1) to provide quantitative estimates of the possible repercussions of the plant contraction (the *direct* effect) on employment in other linked industries (the *indirect* effect), and in the local services sector generally, as a result of falling income and expenditure levels locally (the *induced* effect), and (2) to evaluate the unique circumstances associated with industrial decline and determine the extent to which these must be incorporated by modifications into the employment multiplier model.

837. Bubolz, Margaret J. "Family Adjustment Under Community Decline." *Communities Left Behind: Alternatives for Development.* Edited by Larry R. Whiting. (Item 876), pp. 54-66.

Draws upon previous research related to families and family response to crises and social change to suggest a model for analyzing family response to community decline. The author indicates areas where change and adaptation in families in declining communities might be anticipated.

838. California Employment Development Department. *Planning Guidebook for Communities Facing a Plant Closure or Mass Layoff.* Sacramento: State of California, 1983. 176 pp.

Designed to provide communities with a framework for organizing a community response program to deal with closure of a major business. The first section introduces the reader to the problem of plant closures and outlines the recent history of California's efforts to understand and mitigate the worst effects of closures. The second section presents a detailed description of the organization of a community response program and provides guidelines for the development of a community committee and a re-employment center. The third section focuses on the state's experience in the development of retraining programs and highlights successful components of programs developed throughout the state. The fourth section of the guidebook consists of appendices containing resource materials, specific programatic descriptions and guidelines, as well as detailed descriptions of local plant closures.

839. Casner-Lott, Jill. "Plant Closings, Relocations Increase: Federal Regulation Proposed to Reduce Disruption to Communities, Employees." *World of Work Report* 4, No. 12 (December 1979): 89, 93.

Discusses the reasons for plant closings and addresses the pros and cons of government intervention and legislation dealing with the shutdown issue. Also, alternatives to legislation are discussed. Tax and financial incentives for companies, reducing the work force gradually, and advance notice to alert workers and the community are some of the current ideas under consideration.

840. Centre for Resource Studies. *Mining Communities: Hard Lessons for the Future.* Kingston, Ontario: Queen's University, 1984. 205 pp.

Contains the proceedings of a policy discussion seminar on the problems posed by mine closures and shutdowns in Canada. Emphasis was placed on new planning approaches that are being designed to avoid single-industry dependence and to share financial risks. Contains nine papers and a digest of discussions.

841. Congressional Budget Office. *Dislocated Workers: Issues and Federal Options.* Washington, D.C.: Congress of the United States, 1982. 56 pp.

Examines problems facing workers displaced by structural changes in the economy, who often face particular difficulty adjusting to changed employment demands and thus often experience longer-than-usual periods of unemployment. Whether the federal government should provide special assistance to such workers and what form any aid might take are issues examined in this study.

* Cottrell, William F. "Caliente." *Technology, Man, and Progress.* Authored by William F. Cottrell. Cited above as item 226.

* Cottrell, William F. "Death by Dieselization: A Case Study in the Reaction to Technology Change." *American Sociological Review.* Cited above as item 227.

842. Doeksen, Gerald A., John Kuehn, and Joseph Schmidt. "Consequences of Decline and Community Economic Adjustment To It." *Communities Left Behind: Alternatives for Development.* Edited by Larry R. Whiting. (Item 876), pp. 28-42.

Attempts to (1) delineate the economic dynamics of rural communities, (2) rationalize the reactions of economic institutions given the historical setting, and (3) consider the economic outlook for rural communities.

843. Energy Information Administration. *Nuclear Plant Cancellations: Causes, Costs, and Consequences.* DOE/EIA-0392. Washington, D.C.: U.S. Government Printing Office, 1983. 122 pp.

Presents a historical overview of nuclear plant cancellations through 1982, the costs associated with those cancellations, and the reasons that the projects were terminated. A survey is presented of the precedents for regulatory treatment of the costs, the specific methods of cost recovery that were adopted, and the impacts of these decisions upon ratepayers, utility stockholders, and taxpayers. Finally, the report identifies a series of other nuclear plants that remain at

risk of cancellation in the future, principally as a result of
similar demand, finance, or regulatory problems cited as
causes of cancellation in the past. The costs associated with
these potential cancellations are estimated, along with their
regional distributions, and likely methods of cost recovery
are suggested.

844. Gordus, Jeanne P., Paul Jarley, and Louis A. Ferman. *Plant
      Closing and Economic Dislocation*. Kalamazoo, Michigan: W.
      E. Upjohn Institute for Employment Research, 1981. 173 pp.

      Provides a comprehensive review of the plant-closing
      research undertaken over the past two decades. The authors
      attempt to identify conceptual and methodological limitations
      of past research, areas where policy needs to be developed,
      and directions in which programming efforts should move. The
      book is intended as a compendium of information which could
      promote the formulation of a new research agenda and assist
      policymakers and planners who might wish to review past
      efforts in order to find directions for the present and
      future.

845. Gulliford, Andrew. "From Boom to Bust: Small Towns and
      Energy Development on Colorado's Western Slope." *Small Town*
      13, No. 5 (1983): 15-22.

      Describes the rapid economic growth, and equally rapid
      decline, associated with oil shale development in western
      Colorado. Discussion centers on the abandonment of the Colony
      Oil Shale project and the effects of this shutdown on small
      towns in Garfield County.

846. Hansen, Gary B., and Marion T. Bentley. *Mobilizing Community
      Resources to Cope With Plant Shutdowns: Final Report of A
      Demonstration Project*. Logan, Utah: Utah State University,
      Center for Productivity and Quality of Working Life, 1981.
      185 pp.

      Describes the results of a demonstration project carried out
      over a period of three years, which was designed to help the
      workers in four communities, displaced when a major U.S. sugar
      producer closed its sugar refining business in 1979. The
      objectives of the project were to (1) develop a systematic
      approach that could be used by communities to plan for and
      mobilize their resources to more effectively deal with
      shutdowns, (2) prepare a set of materials which could be used
      by communities which are desirous of organizing to cope with
      shutdowns, and (3) document the effectiveness of the responses
      of the communities in meeting the problems presented by the
      shutdowns.

847. Hansen, Gary B., and Marion T. Bentley. *Problems and Solutions in a Plant Shutdown: A Handbook for Community Involvement.* Logan, Utah: Utah State University, Center for Productivity and Quality of Working Life, 1981. 388 pp.

Is a "how to" manual which briefly discusses the phenomenon of plant shutdowns, their nature, extent, and impact and then discusses and evaluates the various ways that a community can respond. If a community approach is contemplated, the handbook outlines how this can be accomplished and what may be some of the major problems that will be encountered. Various techniques and approaches for helping the displaced workers are outlined, along with strategies for replacing economic activities. Successful examples and case studies are included to illustrate what might be done. Finally, the steps necessary to get started are outlined, and a listing of printed, audio-visual, and other resources available to help communities, employees, and unions in organizing to cope with the effects of a plant shutdown is included.

848. Hansen, Gary B., Marion T. Bentley, and Richard A. Davidson. *Hardrock Miners in a Shutdown: A Case Study of the Post-Layoff Experiences of Displaced Lead-Zinc-Silver Miners.* Monograph No. 1. Logan, Utah: Utah State University, Center for Productivity and Quality of Working Life, 1980. 98 pp.

Attempts to (1) document the unemployment and re-employment problems of the displaced workers from two mine shutdowns, (2) determine the effectiveness of various job search methods employed by the workers, and (3) make appropriate comparisons between the displacement experiences of the miners and those experiences reported in previous research studies. The study deals with closures of two hardrock mines in Utah which displaced about 500 workers.

849. Hansen, Gary B., Marion T. Bentley, Jeannie Hepworth Gould, and Mark H. Skidmore. *Life After Layoff: A Handbook for Workers in a Plant Shutdown.* Logan, Utah: Utah State University, Center for Productivity and Quality of Working Life, 1981. 166 pp.

Is a practical handbook written for laid-off workers and those facing a plant shutdown. It is much more than just a job-hunting guide; it deals with many of the crucial aspects of a plant shutdown that concern the employees, including financial resources, transfers, family adjustment, and retraining. The job search chapter in the book explains the job-hunting process and tells how to do it. The importance of self-assessment and job targeting is stressed.

*   Hansen, Gary B., Marion T. Bentley, Rexanne Pond, and Mark H.
      Skidmore. *A Selective Annotated Bibliography on Plant Shut-
      downs and Related Topics.* Cited below as item 994.

850. Hansen, Gary B., Marion T. Bentley, and Mark H. Skidmore.
      *Plant Shutdowns, People and Communities: A Selected
      Bibliography.* Logan, Utah: Utah State University, Utah
      Center for Productivity and Quality of Working Life, 1981.
      81 pp.

      Cites primarily case studies dealing with plant shutdowns.
      Topics covered are case studies, alternatives to shutdowns and
      new approaches to work, job search and job finding activities,
      organized community programs and other forms of assistance,
      training and retraining, and employment problems of older
      workers.

851. Hardin, Einar, and Michael E. Borus.   *The Economic Benefits
      and Costs of Retraining.* Lexington, Massachusetts: D.C.
      Heath and Company, 1979. 235 pp.

      Contains an in-depth study of the economic benefits and
      costs of retraining. The book contains statistical informa-
      tion, charts, graphs, and equations that represent some of the
      research findings. The design and statistical methods used in
      the benefit-cost analysis are included.

852. Hegadoren, D. B., and J. C. Day. "Socioeconomic Mine Termin-
      ation Policies: A Case Study of Mine Closure in Ontario."
      Resources Policy 7, No. 4 (December 1981): 265-72.

      Discusses the inevitable socioeconomic changes induced by
      mine closure. The article documents and evaluates the public
      and private sector's arrangements to ameliorate closure
      impacts at the Marmoraton mining facility in Ontario during
      1978. Measures used to reduce detrimental hardships of mine
      terminations on Canadian communities are presented. Such
      recommended measures include an ex ante economic impact
      analysis of mine termination, local hiring policy, termination
      benefits for workers, and government-financed economic feasi-
      bility studies.

853. Hodge, Ian. *Employment Adjustments and the Economic Costs of
      Decline in a Small Rural Community: A Case Study in
      Kellogg, Idaho.* Bulletin No. 629. Moscow, Idaho: Idaho
      Agricultural Experiment Station, 1984. 18 pp.

      Seeks to identify and measure some of the costs that are
      borne by the employees and by the community when a major
      employer closes its operation. Such costs or losses are

grouped into four categories: (1) loss of productive employment, (2) costs of seeking alternatives, (3) financial and psychic costs of making the adjustment to the change, and (4) costs of providing services to the redistributed population. These costs are estimated for the community of Kellogg, Idaho, in connection with the closure of the Bunker Hill metal mine and associated smelting and refining facilities.

854. Keyes, Robert J., Edward Tunis, J. E. Reeves, R. D. Hutchinson, Andre Lemieux, Nancy Porter, and Mark Kennedy. *Report of the Task Force on Mining Communities.* Ottawa, Ontario: Energy, Mines, and Resources Canada, 1982. 130 pp.

Focuses on mining communities and the impacts of mine closure upon them. It suggests possible steps that could be taken to alleviate distress both in recessionary periods and in permanent closures. Shared risk is a basic tenet of this study. The Task Force firmly believes that the burden of responsibility for mining communities in Canada must be shared by all involved--industry, labor, governments, and the mining communities themselves.

855. Langerman, Philip D., Richard L. Byerly, and Kenneth A. Root. *Plant Closings and Layoffs: Problems Facing Urban and Rural Communities.* Des Moines, Iowa: Drake University, 1982. 143 pp.

Summarizes findings of a review of displaced worker and community experiences following closure of two major industrial plants in Des Moines. A total of sixty-seven displaced workers and spouses were interviewed. The aim of the study was to identify the traumatic areas of concern and to propose strategies for other communities to follow should they face similar crises.

856. McCarthy, James E. *Trade Adjustment Assistance: A Case Study of the Shoe Industry in Massachusetts.* Research Report 58. Boston: Federal Reserve Bank of Boston, 1975. 235 pp.

Presents information on worker and firm recipients of assistance under the Trade Expansion Act of 1962. (The act allows assistance to workers who have suffered effects from increased imports.) To study the worker program, a systematic sample consisting of 200 workers was chosen. Each worker was interviewed, and the shoe firms were visited to obtain information. The results showed that the adjustment assistance program was ineffective for a variety of reasons.

857.   McCraken, Colleen L. "The Socio-Economic Impacts of the Rise
       and Fall of Esso Resources Canada Limited's Cold Lake
       Project."   Master's Thesis.   Calgary, Alberta: University
       of Calgary, School of Environmental Design, February 1984.
       244 pp.

       Is a case study of the socioeconomic impacts of the annouce-
       ment, planning, preparation, and cancellation of the Cold Lake
       project in northern Alberta, Canada.   Public perception forms
       the data base of the study and is utilized as the indicator of
       relevant socioeconomic impacts in the Cold Lake region.
       Overall opinions of the rise and fall of the large-scale heavy
       oil project were negative especially among the business
       community; although less significant, other impacts were
       described including environmental, psychological, and social
       change.

858.   McKenzie, Richard B., ed.   *Plant Closings: Public or Private
       Choices?* Washington, D.C.:   Cato Institute, 1982.   164 pp.

       Presents a case against plant-closing legislation and
       similar restrictions on the free movement of capital.   The
       authors question the need for such restrictions by first
       presenting empirical evidence concerning plant closings and
       relocations, and second by arguing that restrictions are
       generally counterproductive and lead to a loss in societal
       welfare.   According to their analysis, restrictions on
       business mobility will increase production costs by reducing
       efficiency in the allocation of resources.   Resources will
       tend to be tied up in comparatively inefficient sectors
       resulting in retardation of development across all regions.
       On balance, the nation will be poorer because of such reloca-
       tion laws.

859.   McKersie, Robert B., and Werner Sengenberger.   *Job Losses in
       Major Industries.*   Paris: Organization for Economic
       Cooperation and Development (OECD), 1983.   125 pp.

       Deals with large-scale dislocations of industrial employment
       in a number of OECD countries, and describes their signifi-
       cance and the consequences (economic and other) for the
       workers, communities, and regions affected.   It also discusses
       the structural changes which have led up to these situations,
       and the range of national and industrial strategies applied to
       respond to them.   The bulk of the report is devoted to a
       detailed analysis of integrative strategies and conversion
       programs that seek to reconcile capital mobility with labor
       protection.   Based on examples of such approaches--in
       particular in the Federal Republic of Germany and Japan--the
       report describes internal and external restructuring programs.
       Apart from the role of central and local governmental
       authorities, the report discusses the extent of worker

participation in these restructuring programs, and the
problems that it poses for employers and trade unions.

860. MacKinnon, David A. "Military Base Closures: Long Range
      Economic Effects and the Implications for Industrial
      Development." *American Industrial Development Council
      Journal* 13, No. 3 (1978): 7-41.

      Explores the economic climate of seven communities, each of
      which had an Air Force base that closed in the mid-1960s, to
      determine what the actual long-term economic impact has been.
      A topic of special interest was to determine what implications
      these base closures have had for local industrial
      development.

861. Mazza, Jacqueline, Virginia Mayer, Mary Chione, Leslie
      Cutler, Timothy Hauser, and Amy Spear. *Shutdown: A Guide
      for Communities Facing Plant Closings.* Washington, D.C.:
      Northeast-Midwest Institute, January 1982. 65 pp.

      Designed as a practical reference guide for local decision-
      makers concerned with the closing of a major local public or
      private facility. Presents a host of available ideas and
      strategies for use by communities involved in various stages
      of economic dislocation. Such strategies are subdivided by
      temporal stages: preliminary indications of plant closings,
      immediate actions, designing and implementing economic
      recovery, and achieving full recovery.

862. Mick, Stephen S. "Social and Personal Costs of Plant
      Shutdowns." *Industrial Relations* 14, No. 2 (May 1975):
      203-8.

      Introduces the reader to the subject of plant shutdowns and
      the problems arising from them. Three areas are discussed: a
      definition of a plant shutdown, a review of literature about
      the effects of shutdowns on employees, and an analysis of a
      plant shutdown in one industry over a sixteen-year period.

863. National Alliance of Business. *Worker Adjustment to Plant
      Shutdowns and Mass Layoffs: An Analysis of Program
      Experience and Options.* Washington, D.C.: National
      Alliance of Business, 1983. 154 pp.

      Attempts to develop a thorough understanding of worker
      adjustment programs that have assisted, or might assist,
      persons affected by plant closings and mass layoffs. Major
      topics addressed include: (1) the nature and extent of the
      problem of worker dislocation; (2) current and historical
      employment and adjustment programs; (3) a case study of an
      interesting and applicable Canadian program, the Manpower

Consultative Service; and (4) a distillation of potential programmatic options, including a very brief sketch of the key elements of a program concept that might be developed in the United States by the public and private sectors to deal on a local basis with worker dislocation problems.

864. President's Economic Adjustment Committee. *Summary of Completed Military Base Economic Adjustment Projects: 1961-1981, 20 Years of Civilian Reuse.* Washington, D.C.: U.S. Department of Defense, Office of Economic Adjustment, 1981. 25 pp.

Reports on the results of economic adjustment assistance which has been provided to alleviate local impacts of defense program changes. This summary of 94 military base economic adjustment projects identifies the military and civilian job losses; the replacement of civilian jobs; the principal industrial, commercial, and public reuse activities; and the individual community contacts who can provide additional information.

865. Redburn, F. Stevens, and Terry F. Buss, eds. *Public Policies for Distressed Communities.* Lexington, Massachusetts: Lexington Books, 1982. 287 pp.

Contains eighteen original articles that discuss the economic crisis that communities often face as a result of the restructuring of the national and world economies. Discussion of the wisdom of aid to distressed areas and communities and the most appropriate forms of such aid is now highly polarized. The papers in this book examine these issues from a variety of perspectives.

*   Root, Kenneth. *Companies, Mines and Factories--Shutdowns, Closures and Moves: A Bibliography.* Cited below as item 1013.

866. Root, Kenneth A. *Perspectives for Communities and Organizations on Plant Closings and Job Dislocations.* Ames, Iowa: North Central Regional Center for Rural Development, 1979. 32 pp.

Provides an overview of the impacts affecting displaced workers, their families, and the communities in which they were employed. The aim is to identify problems that can be anticipated from such shutdowns and to suggest viable solutions and alternatives.

867. Rowthorn, Bob, and Terry Ward. "How to Run a Company and Run Down an Economy: The Effects of Closing Down Steel-Making

in Corby." *Cambridge Journal of Economics* 3 (1979): 327-40.

Attempts to quantify the overall economic implications of the British Steel Corporation's plan to close down an iron- and steel-making plant at Corby in Northamptonshire. The more general purpose is to argue that projects should not be evaluated solely on the narrow commercial criterion of profit and loss to the firm in question but rather that, in comparing various alternatives, their macroeconomic implications should be taken explicitly into account.

868. Schriver, William R., Roger L. Bowlby, and Donald E. Pursell. "Evaluation of Trade Readjustment Assistance To Workers: A Case Study." *Social Science Quarterly* 57, No. 3 (1976): 347-56.

Evaluates the effectiveness of trade readjustment assistance (TRA) in aiding workers affected by a plant shutdown. Workers at an electronics assembly plant in a large mid-southern city constituted the study population. The authors found that workers who were eligible for TRA benefits were unemployed for a longer period prior to accepting a new job compared to those who were not eligible. However, workers who received TRA benefits also received somewhat lower wage rates in their new positions than did those not receiving benefits.

869. Smith, I. J., and M. J. Taylor. "Takeover, Closures, and the Restructuring of the Ironfoundry Industry." *Environment and Planning A* 15 (1983): 639-61.

Explores the regional dimension of plant and firm closure in the United Kingdom using data for the ironfoundry industry over the whole of the post-war period but with particular emphasis on the 1967-1980 period. Impact of ownership on plant closure is stressed and patterns of ownership change are shown to seriously prejudice the survival of plants in the United Kingdom's peripheral regions.

870. Stern, James L. "Consequences of Plant Closure." *The Journal of Human Resources* 7, No. 1 (1972): 3-25.

Uses pre- and postshutdown annual earnings reported to the Social Security Administration to measure the economic impact of plant closure on the income of workers exercising different vocational choices. Workers who sought new jobs in the local labor market suffered substantial reductions in postshutdown annual earnings. With the influence of age, skill, sex, seniority, education, race, and preshutdown earnings held constant, short-term training did not improve the situation significantly. Workers who elected the interplant transfer option increased their annual earnings by more than $2,000, suggesting that government support of measures to increase the use of interplant transfers should be considered.

871. Stern,   Robert N.,   K. Haydn Wood, and Tove   Helland Hammer.
      *Employee Ownership in Plant Shutdowns: Prospects for
      Employment Stability.*   Kalamazoo, Michigan: The W.   E.
      Upjohn Institute for Employment Research, 1979.   219 pp.

      Examines one   alternative to   a plant shutdown: community-
      employee purchase.   Three major parts are presented: Part I
      considers the nature of the plant location problem in terms of
      community-industry relationships and the effects of closing;
      Part   II evaluates the   strategy involved in the investment
      through a cost-benefit approach; and Part III re-examines the
      community-employee firm in terms of its   control and worker
      participation.   Case studies are used to illustrate the ideas
      presented.

872. Stucker,   James P., Charles L. Batten, Kenneth A. Solomon, and
      Werner Z. Hirsch.   *Costs of Closing The Indian Point Nuclear
      Power Plant.*   R-2857-NYO.   Santa Monica, California: RAND
      Corporation, 1981.   85 pp.

      Estimates the monetary costs that would result from closing
      the nuclear power generating facilities at Indian Point, New
      York.   The report estimates the total magnitude of the costs,
      the major components of cost, and the sensitivity of those
      components to major underlying assumptions.

873. Taber,   Thomas D.,   Jeffrey T. Walsh, and Robert A. Cooke.
      "Developing a Community-Based Program for Reducing the
      Social Impact of a Plant Closing."   *The Journal of Applied
      Behavioral Science* 15, No. 2 (1979):   133-55.

      Reports results of an innovative approach to coping with the
      impact of a shutdown.   The experiment organized management,
      union, university, and community representatives in Great
      River, Michigan, into a temporary coalition.   This group
      assumed responsibility for organizing available human services
      into a coordinated attack on the complex and intense problems
      expected to result from sudden widespread unemployment.

874. Tweeten, Luther. "Enhancing Economic Opportunity." *Communi-
      ties Left Behind: Alternatives for Development.*   Edited by
      Larry R. Whiting.   (Item 876), pp. 91-107.

      Sets   forth a comprehensive program for enhancing economic
      opportunity in communities and areas characterized by either
      population decline or stability.   Several important issues are
      discussed: (1) increasing the quantity of local resources
      versus using existing resources more   efficiently, (2)

resolving local problems by action of the community itself versus action at the multicounty or national level, (3) the perennial dilemma of equity versus efficiency in development programs, and (4) whether to emphasize place or people prosperity in development programs.

875. Wendling, Wayne R. *The Plant Closure Policy Dilemma: Labor, Law and Bargaining.* Kalamazoo, Michigan: W. E. Upjohn Institute for Employment Research, 1984. 166 pp.

Has as its objective to answer the following questions: What is the potential for collective bargaining to alter the decision to close when continued operation is a reasonable alternative, Can bargaining over the effects of closure provide a reasonable opportunity for workers to mitigate some of the consequences, and Have management and labor used formal contract negotiations to obtain protections and to develop solutions for workers and firms at risk of closure"?

876. Whiting, Larry R., ed. *Communities Left Behind: Alternatives for Development.* Ames, Iowa: The Iowa State University Press, 1974. 151 pp.

Identifies some of the characteristics, entities, and amenities desirable to human life within rural communities. The book covers such topics as quantitative dimensions of decline and stability, social and family adjustment to decline, service structures, enhancing economic and social opportunity, and feasible options for social action and economic development.

Contains items 837, 842, 874, 877.

877. Wilkinson, Kenneth P. "Consequences of Decline and Social Adjustment To It." *Communities Left Behind: Alternatives for Development.* Edited by Larry R. Whiting. (Item 876), pp. 43-53.

Argues that community decline, like community development, is a pervasive process reflected at all levels in a local society--in the demographic and ecological responses through which a population seeks to balance its size with its sustenance organization, in the institutional patterns and organizational structures through which daily social life is lived, in the efforts of groups to alter or improve local conditions of life, and in the feelings people have about the local society. This chapter focuses upon the institutional-organizational level. At that level the author's purpose is to describe the social processes which accompany loss of population, decreased collective viability, and lessening of the collective spirit or sense of community.

878. Young,   John A.,   and Jan   M. Newton.   *Capitalism   and Human
         Obsolescence.* New York: Universe Books, 1980.   253 pp.

         Focuses on   the causes and consequences of   economic decline
         and   unemployment in rural, single-industry communities.   The
         authors   present economic   analyses of the   Oregon lumber
         industry, Hawaiian   plantation agriculture,   copper   mining in
         Arizona, small-scale farming in California, and small business
         in an economically declining region in Washington.

SIA and Specific
Development Types

Mining and Mineral Conversion

879. Arctic Petroleum Operators' Association, and the Canadian Petroleum Association. *Proceedings of the Thirteenth Annual APOA-CPA/OOA Workshop, Frontier Update '84.* Calgary, Alberta, July 1984. Distributed by Pallister Resource Management Ltd, Calgary. 150 pp.

Summarizes panel discussions on the following topics: (1) social and economic considerations in frontier areas, including equity participation, joint ventures, business development, employment and training, community interface, oil spills, safety, and offshore and remote medicine; (2) government research programs and industry, including energy research and development programs and environmental studies revolving funds; and (3) project assessment, including the role of agencies and nongovernmental groups.

880. Arnold, Peter, and Ian Cole. *The Development of the Selby Coalfield: A Study in Planning.* Heslington, Yorkshire, England: University of York, 1981. 157 pp.

Details planning issues brought before the county and district councils resulting from development of the Selby coalfield. Specific issues are the provision of housing, education, health, and social services.

881. Austin, Lynn A., William N. Capener, Lowell B. Catlett, Clyde E. Eastman, James R. Gray, Berry C. Ives, Marie E. Mathews, and Raymond J. Supalla. *Socio-Economic Impacts of Coal Mining on Communities in Northwestern New Mexico.* Bulletin 652. Las Cruces, New Mexico: New Mexico Agricultural Experiment Station, 1977. 118 pp.

Estimates impacts of alternative levels of coal development on selected economic and social variables in two areas of New Mexico: San Juan County and the Cuba area of Sandoval County. In both areas, development was projected to result in substantial increases in employment and income and to inmigration that would increase demands on public services and facilities.

* Baring-Gould, Michael, and Marsha Bennett. *Social Impact of the Trans-Alaska Pipeline Construction in Valdez, Alaska, 1974-1975.* Cited above as item 199.

882. Bennett, Marsha Erwin, Susan D. Heasley, and Susan Huey. *Northern Gulf of Alaska Petroleum Development Scenarios: Sociocultural Impacts.* Tech. Rpt. No. 36. Anchorage, Alaska: Bureau of Land Management, Alaska Outer Continental Shelf Office, 1979. 297 pp.

Provides both a methodology for evaluating sociocultural systems and a detailed information base about two towns located in the Northern Gulf of Alaska--Cordova-Eyak and Seward. The study analyzes the social organization, social conflict, social change, and recent events occurring within these two towns and attempts to place the towns and the effects of Alaska OCS Petroleum Development on them within a regional context while still maintaining a town focus. Attention is thereby drawn to the response capacity of the social system of these two towns to adapt to changes which have already occurred or are likely to occur in the near future.

* Bever, Michael B., and Lawrence E. Susskind, eds. "Special Issue on Assessing the Environmental Impacts of Offshore Oil and Gas Exploration and Development." *Environmental Impact Assessment Review.* Cited above as item 6.

883. Bone, Robert M., and Robert J. Mahnic. "Norman Wells: The Oil Center of the Northwest Territories." *Arctic* 37, No. 1 (March 1984): 53-59.

Discusses changes in the character, size, and functions of the Norman Wells community as a result of recent expansion in petroleum production. Growth in oil production to serve southern Canadian markets is transforming Norman Wells into an important regional center.

* Briscoe, Maphis, Murray, Lamont, Inc. *OIA Monitoring System.* 2 volumes. Cited above as item 517.

884. Campbell, Kimberly A. *NACo Case Studies on Energy Impacts. No. 2, Controlling Boomtown Development, Sweetwater and Uinta Counties, Wyoming.* Washington, D.C.: National Association of Counties, 1976. 43 pp.

Is the second in a series of case studies on energy communities. The purpose of these studies is to familiarize officials in areas having potential energy development with efforts that have been made by counties currently experiencing development. Sweetwater County, Wyoming, had seen its population double in the past five years as a result of the opening of a 2,500-megawatt power plant and the expansion of its trona industry. This growth had not been adequately forecast. There was little preparation for the expected influx of population. Because there was a general expectation that the changes were only temporary, numerous social and economic problems ensued. The county used a variety of approaches to gain control of these problems, but the most significant approach was the development of close cooperation between industry and the local government. Neighboring Uinta County, with no mineral wealth of its own, had become a bedroom community for Sweetwater's industrial and mining workers. With the development of Sweetwater County's mineral resources, Uinta's population greatly expanded. The population increase brought financial and social difficulties to the county and its communities, similar to those experienced in Sweetwater.

See also item 920.

885. Clemmer, Richard. "Hopi Political Economy: Industrialization and Alienation." *Southwest Economy and Society* 2, No.
2 (1977): 4-33.

Discusses the Black Mesa strip mine and other industrial developments affecting contemporary Hopi life. The author contends that (1) alienation characterizes that portion of modern industrial society which impinges upon the Hopi Nation; (2) political decisions in industrial America are responsible for this alienation; (3) political decisions are often made for economic reasons; (4) the agent of alienation is the Department of the Interior; and (5) political reorganization of the Hopi facilitates this alienation.

886. Coddington, Dean C., John M. Gunyou, Keith D. Moore, Edward
F. Harvey, and Ford C. Frick. *Energy Development Impacts on
the Denver Area Economy: Analysis of Past Growth and Future
Growth Prospects.* Denver: Denver Regional Council of
Governments, February 1982. 92 pp.

Analyzes the impact of energy development on the economic base of the Denver, Colorado, area. Specifically, the objectives of the study were (1) to analyze the historic role of energy development on Denver area economic growth; (2) to identify energy-related factors likely to influence future growth; and (3) to examine the Denver area's long-term growth prospects under different energy development scenarios.

 * Cohen, Anthony P. "Oil and the Cultural Account: Reflections
on a Shetland Community." *The Scottish Journal of
Sociology.* Cited above as item 221.

887. Collins, John. "The Social Effects of Development in the
Hunter Valley Region, New South Wales, Australia."
*Proceedings, International Conference on Oil and the
Environment, 1982.* Part A. Halifax, Nova Scotia:
Technical University of Nova Scotia, 1982. pp. 81-88.

Describes the effects of large-scale coal development on the Hunter Valley Region. Effects on the region's socioeconomic structure are discussed in terms of four dimensions: work force, housing, organizations, and status groupings.

* Copp, James H. *Social Impacts of Oil and Gas Developments on a Small Rural Community*. CEMR-MS8. Cited above as item 222.

888. El-Hakim, S. M. "Some Socio-Economic Consequences of the Libyan Oil Discovery on the Zeyadida Nomads of Darfor, Sudan." *Sudan Notes and Records*. Khartoum, Sudan. 1973.

Examines the socioeconomic effects of the discovery of oil in Libya on a remote, rural community in neighboring Sudan, and in particular, the externalities created by the rapid economic expansion on the pastoral Zeyadida tribe of Northern Darfor. The case study illustrates the changes occurring in nomadic-sedentary interactions between the tribe and neighboring communities. Described are the interactions between the pastoral livestock-raising nomads and the cash economy of Sudan resulting in changes in the distribution of wealth. As a result of the Libyan petroleum development, personal income rose rapidly, increasing market prices for livestock and making heretofore unknown luxury goods available in western Sudan. Consequently, new patterns of trade and regional employment emerged, which have produced significant social and economic changes in the Zeyadida tribe.

* Emerson, Craig. "Mining Enclaves and Taxation." *World Development*. Cited above as item 107.

889. *Environmental Impact Assessment Review*. Special Issue on Assessing the Environmental Impacts of Offshore Oil and Gas Exploration and Development. Vol. 4, Nos. 3-4 (December 1983): 265-613.

Begins with two articles, one which points out the risks associated with offshore oil and gas exploration and development, and another which summarizes and evaluates the EIA process for offshore activities in the United States. Five summaries are then presented which outline the information and interpretations found in some recent EISs for offshore leasing in the North Atlantic, the Beaufort Sea, and off the coast of central California. The issue then turns to EIA for offshore development outside the United States, including the North Sea, Norway, the United Kingdom, Ireland, and Canada. The final section addresses environmental negotiation.

890. Galginaites, Michael, Claudia Chang, Kathleen M. MacQueen, Albert A. Dekin, Jr., and David Zipkin. *Ethnographic Study and Monitoring Methodology of Contemporary Economic Growth, Socio-Cultural Change, and Community Development in Nuiqsut, Alaska.* Tech. Rpt. No. 96. Anchorage, Alaska: Minerals Management Service, Social and Economic Studies Program, 1984. 439 pp.

Analyzes Nuiqsut, a traditional Inupiat village on the North Slope of Alaska which was resettled in 1973. The Alaska Native Claims Settlement Act and the formation of the North Slope Borough (NSB) created a fiscal, social, and political environment to make resettlement a viable undertaking. Inupiat perceive oil development as decreasing the availability of subsistence resources, both in absolute terms and in terms of access. However, cash is now absolutely essential for the harvest of subsistence resources. It is recommended that a program to systematically collect information monitoring these changes be implemented. This methodology should and must include the study populations as active participants. Significant variables and potential relationships are proposed, and the question of measurement (operationalization) discussed.

891. Gaskin, M., D. I. MacKay, G. A. MacKay, A. Marr, and N. F. Trimble. *The Economic Impact of North Sea Oil on Scotland.* Final Report to the Scottish Economic Planning Department on a Study Conducted within the Department of Political Economy, University of Aberdeen, 1973-77. Edinburgh, Scotland: Her Majesty's Stationery Office, 1978. 101 pp.

Assesses the overall economic impact of North Sea Oil—exploration, development, and production—on the economy of Scotland. The development phase has had the greatest direct impact on the economy. Net emigration has fallen, incomes have risen, and the unemployment rate has dropped. The petroleum labor force is dominated by native Scots, and there has been a high degree of local recruitment in spite of the comparatively low wages (relative to the industry). A concluding discussion focuses on policy implications of increased involvement in offshore export markets and a substantial downstream oil- and gas-processing industry.

892. Habitat North, Inc. *Socioeconomic Impacts of Selected Foreign OCS Developments.* Tech. Rpt. No. 28. Anchorage: U.S. Bureau of Land Management, Alaska Outer Continental Shelf Office, 1979. 313 pp.

Examines impacts resulting from offshore petroleum exploration and development in the North Sea and in the Canadian Beaufort Sea. The purpose of the study is to determine the nature of impacts that could be expected to result from offshore petroleum development in Alaska, based on the experience in these other regions.

* House, J. D. "Big Oil and Small Communities in Coastal Labrador: The Local Dynamics of Dependency." *Canadian Review of Sociology and Anthropology.* Cited above as item 275.

* House, J. D. "Oil Companies in Aberdeen: The Strategy of Incorporation." *The Scottish Journal of Sociology.* Cited above as item 276.

893. Hutton, John. "Impacts of Offshore Oil on Northeast Scotland." A lecture presented by the MIT Sea Grant Program, 28 April 1973. Cambridge: Massachusetts Institute of Technology, Sea Grant Program, 1975. 29 pp.

Discusses the effects that the exploration for and production of oil and gas from the North Sea has already had on the social and economic life of northeast Scotland. The industry's potential for both the United Kingdom and Scotland is considerable. Hutton outlines the role of the regional development and promotional agency—Northeast Scotland Development Authority—in offshore oil and examines some of the benefits and pitfalls generated by the new industry for the region.

894. Ives, Berry, and Clyde Eastman. *Impact of Mining Development on an Isolated Rural Community: The Case of Cuba, New Mexico.* Res. Rpt. 301. Las Cruces, New Mexico: New Mexico Agricultural Experiment Station, 1975. 16 pp.

Describes the effects of a copper mine on the community of Cuba, New Mexico. Area population, per capita income, and gross business receipts all increased. A few new businesses were established, and many were expanded. Except for the water and sewer systems, community services generally handled the increased population with minimum strain. Local leaders and residents were almost unanimous in their favorable reactions to the mine.

* Jacobs, James J., Edward B. Bradley, and Andrew Vanvig. *Coal-Energy Development and Agriculture in Northeast Wyoming's Powder River Basin.* RJ-178. Cited above as item 129.

895. Jorgensen, Joseph G., Richard O. Clemmer, Ronald L. Little, Nancy J. Owens, and Lynn A. Robbins. *Native Americans and*

Energy Development. Cambridge, Massachusetts: Anthropology
Resource Center, 1978. 89 pp.

Briefly describes postwar changes in the western agricultural economy, then presents a hypothesis for explaining the
twin processes of development and underdevelopment in the
region. The effects of recent energy developments on rural
Anglo populations and Indian tribes are discussed. The report
concludes with personal observations about the responsibilities of social-science research in the context of western
energy development.

896. Jorgensen, Joseph G., and Jean A. Maxwell. *Effects of Renew-
able Resource Harvest Disruptions on Socioeconomic and
Sociocultural Systems Impact Analysis. Unalakleet, Norton
Sound.* Tech. Rpt. No. 90. Anchorage, Alaska: Minerals
Management Service, 1984. 355 pp.

Analyzes the history and contemporary culture of Unalakleet,
the Unalakleet environment and the ways in which it is used by
natives, the political economy of dependency that overlays the
local subsistence economy, the relation between subsistence
and the commercial fishery (and the naturally occurring,
renewable resources on which both are based), the local and
regional social structures (formal and informal), and the wide
networks of kinship and friendship which link Unalakleet
villagers to persons and families in distant locales. Assumptions about the political, social, and economic context in
which Unalakleet villagers are enmeshed, and the likelihood of
changes in this context are delineated. The foregoing serve
to identify the cultural (including social structural) and
economic features of Unalakleet that will be influenced should
disruptions to harvests of naturally occurring, renewable
resources occur. The impacts analysis then defines and
rationalizes harvest disruptions of increasing severity—low,
medium, and high—and offers concluding hypotheses about the
probable consequences of disruptions at each level.

897. Knapp, Gunnar, Ed Porter, and Brian Reeder. *Statewide and
Census Division Demographic and Economic Systems, Navarin
Basin (Sale 83) Impact Analysis.* Tech. Rpt. No. 78.
Anchorage: U.S. Bureau of Land Management, Alaska Outer
Continental Shelf Office, 1983. 368 pp.

Examines economic and population impacts of proposed outer
continental shelf (OCS) petroleum development in Alaska's
Aleutian region. The study begins with historical baseline
analyses of the population and economies of the State of
Alaska and the Aleutian Islands. Next, base case projections
of conditions in the absence of OCS development are presented.
Finally, the projected impacts of OCS development are
examined.

898.   Kruse, John A., Judith Kleinfeld, and Robert Travis. "Energy
       Development on Alaska's North Slope: Effects on the Inupiat
       Population." *Human Organization* 41, No. 2 (1982): 97-106.

       Examines the effects of oil development at Prudhoe Bay on
       the Inupiat population of Alaska's North Slope. Development
       activities occurred 96 km away from the nearest Inupiat
       settlement, and the Inupiat gained local property taxing
       authority by creating a regional government. With a resident
       population of about 4,000, the North Slope Borough had an
       annual budget of $60 million in 1977 and had also launched a
       $511 million capital improvements program. A survey of 290
       randomly selected Inupiat adults indicates that the Prudhoe
       Bay oil development itself had little direct impact on employ-
       ment. The formation of the North Slope Borough, however, led
       to high levels of employment and increased income without
       increasing income inequality.   Subsistence   activities
       continued to play a central economic and cultural role. Oil
       revenues, however, have not led to the growth of a diversi-
       fied, self-sustaining regional economy.

899.   Little, Ronald L., and Lynn A. Robbins. *Effects of Renewable
       Resource Harvest Disruption on Socioeconomic and Sociocul-
       tural Systems: St. Lawrence Island.* Tech. Rpt. No. 89.
       Anchorage, Alaska: Minerals Management Service, Socioeco-
       nomic Studies Program, 1984. 385 pp.

       Analyzes the current and recent uses of renewable natural
       resources by the Eskimos residing on St. Lawrence Island,
       Alaska. Data were collected on family and kinship structures,
       political institutions, economic activities, religious
       affiliations, population, resources utilization categorized by
       species, and a wide variety of topics important to understand-
       ing the potential impacts of offshore oil exploration
       activities on the social and cultural systems of the island.
       The information collected and analyzed in this study provides
       the baseline for determining the magnitude and extent of any
       future disruptions to the naturally occurring resource base
       which presently sustains St. Lawrence Island Eskimos.

900.   MacKay, D. I., and G. A. MacKay. *The Political Economy of
       North Sea Oil.* London: Martin Robinson, 1975. 193 pp.

       Discusses the major economic role of North Sea oil in the
       United Kingdom (UK) and Scotland. Economic benefits include
       the balance of payments to the central government in the form
       of royalties and taxation revenues. The importance of oil to
       the UK economy is underscored and compared to Scotland,
       arguing that the direct benefits to Scotland from the present
       political arrangements are small compared to those accruing to
       the central government. The benefits to the former are likely
       to be insufficient to eradicate the low income and high

unemployment in Scotland. Government policies toward exploration, production, and taxation of oil are presented along with
the extent of North Sea oil and gas reserves and the likely
future production.

901. McMinn, Stuart, John Robertson, and Hassan Rada. "Socio-
Economic Development of the Yanbu Sub-Region, Saudi Arabia."
Third World Planning Review 5, No. 4 (November 1983): 311-
32.

Examines the regional impacts (social, economic, traffic,
housing) of a very large construction work force involved in
building a new industrial city, Marinat Yanbu Al-Sinaiyah in
Saudi Arabia. Primarily based on petroleum processing, Yanbu
is a created economic growth pole in the western region of the
country. The study analyzes the diverse impacts on a region
with strongly traditional culture and values, yet experiencing
rapid oil development. The Yanbu project, begun in 1977, had
a total force of 30,000 workers by mid-1982. Forecasts
indicate that the peak work force has yet to be reached and
construction manpower is expected to remain well above 20,000
until 1986. Over 95% of the work force are foreign and 72%
non-Moslem.

902. Metzger, James E., Pat Wimberley Mosena, and Erik J.
Stenehjem. *Local Socioeconomic Changes and Public Fiscal
Implications of Coal Development in Wayne County, West
Virginia.* ANL/EES-TM-26. Argonne, Illinois: Argonne
National Laboratory, 1978. 140 pp.

Attempts to characterize the economic and societal effects
likely to accompany increased coal mining in and around Wayne
County, West Virginia. The study concludes that population
growth and increased demand for public services will be
minimal as a result of the two new deep mines planned for the
area.

903. Midwest Research Institute. *Economic Impact of the Oil and
Gas Industry in the State of Colorado.* Denver, Colorado:
Independent Petroleum Association of the Mountain States,
January 1982. 58 pp.

Assesses the economic impact of the oil and gas industry on
the Colorado state economy by utilizing an economic base model
and input-output model. Results show that the oil and gas
industry directly employs some 35,000 persons and generates a
direct payroll in excess of $700 million annually. Employment
and income multipliers were estimated to be 3.04 and 2.29,
respectively.

*   Moore, Robert. *The Social Impact of Oil: The Case of Peterhead*. Cited above as item 294.

904.   Morehouse, Thomas A., ed. *Alaskan Resources Development: Issues of the 1980s*. Boulder, Colorado: Westview Press, 1984. 212 pp.

Presents a picture of the realities of and prospects for Alaska's resources development (resource endowments, markets, and policies). Specific areas examined include land policy, petroleum, nonfuel minerals, coal, renewable resources, environmental issues, wealth management, and policy limits.

905.   Nellis, Lee. "What Does Energy Development Mean for Wyoming? *Human Organization* 33, No. 3 (1974): 229-38.

Examines the costs and benefits of energy development on the small town of Hanna, Wyoming. Data came from a survey of Hanna's residents; 78.2% responded. The newcomers were younger, better educated, and were employed in higher-paying jobs. The town had expanded its services and had gone into debt to cover the costs; taxes had gone up drastically. The new population growth was not accompanied by a proportional expansion of the tax base.

906.   Newton, P. W., and R. Sharpe. "Regional Impacts of the Mining Industry in Northern and Western Australia." *Papers of the 5th Australian and New Zealand Regional Science Conference*. Tanunda, South Australia, 1980. pp. 103-23.

Suggests that the contemporary pattern of development in Australia's northwestern regions and the prospects for future but broader-based development will be influenced by two groups of factors common to all peripheral regions. The first involves an amalgam of influences, such as geographical isolation, environmental conditions, presence of minority cultural groups, lack of local entrepreneurship, and lack of confidence in the area's future. The second set of influences originates outside the region in the core nations and capitals of the world. Here, Australia's resource-rich regions are functionally linked with large corporations with a global perspective, not bound by loyalties to place but rather interested in directing international capital to high-return investments.

907.   Olien, Roger M., and Diana Davids Olien. *Oil Booms: Social Change in Five Texas Towns*. Lincoln, Nebraska: University of Nebraska Press, 1982. 220 pp.

Examines the experiences of five Texas communities (Midland, Odessa, McCamey, Wink, and Snyder) during the oil boom of the

1920s. Aspects of social change which receive special attention include population, housing, public services and
education, women and the family, black and Mexican Americans,
crime and vice, spare time and legal amusements, and postboom
adjustments.

908. Petterson, John S., Bruce M. Harris, Lawrence A. Palinkas,
Kathleen Burlow, Will Nebesky, James Kerr, Lee Huskey, Steve
Langdon, and Jeffrey Tobolski. *Socioeconomic/Sociocultural
Study of Local/Regional Communities in the North Aleutian
Area of Alaska.* Tech. Rpt. No. 104. Anchorage, Alaska:
Minerals Management Service, 1984. 531 pp.

Provides a baseline description and analysis of the socioeconomic and sociocultural systems of the North Aleutian lease
sale area (sale 92) in Alaska. Most of this area is located
in the Bristol Bay and lower Kuskokwim regions and includes
twenty-four communities. Most of the analysis concerns
Bristol Bay's two major socioeconomic systems: the cash-based
system, represented primarily by the commercial fishing
industry, and the indigenous, subsistence-oriented system,
represented primarily by hunting and fishing activities and
kin-based patterns of resource distribution.

909. Porter, Ed, and Lee Huskey. "The Regional Economic Effect of
Federal OCS Leasing: The Case of Alaska." *Land Economics*
57, No. 4 (1981): 583-95.

Investigates the hypothesis that OCS development is
characterized by institutional features which disperse the
bulk of net benefits nationally, while leaving a dispropor-
tionate share of costs to be borne locally, and thus imposes a
net economic burden on affected states.

910. Ruffing, Lorraine Turner. "Navajo Mineral Development." *The
Indian Historian* 11, No. 2 (1978): 28-41.

Examines the exploitation of the Navajo Nation's nonrenewable resources. The weak bargaining position of the Nation
and their trustees, the Bureau of Indian Affairs, has resulted
in contracts with inadequate provisions for Indian hiring,
environmental protection, taxation, or changes in royalty
rates. The problem is compounded by uncertainty surrounding
the resource's supply and demand and by a lack of capital
commitment to explore, extract, process, and market the
resources. Solutions lie in the areas of improving traditional mineral agreements, improving existing Navajo agreements,
and implementing new forms of agreements, such as joint
ventures, production sharing, and service contracts.

911. Seifried, N. R. "Economic and Environmental Risks and
      Uncertainty in Frontier Resource Development: Case Study of
      the Athabasca Oil Sands." *Geoforum* 8 (1977): 267-75.

      Uses the Athabasca Oil Sands development (one of the largest
      reservoirs of oil in the world) as an example of resource
      development being pushed ahead while many questions remained
      unanswered. The paper first discusses the economics of oil
      sands exploitation in light of the uncertain nature of extrac-
      tion costs, oil prices, and future demands for petroleum. The
      author then turns to the controversy over the extent and
      nature of land, water, and atmospheric disturbance resulting
      from such extractive activities.

912. Sewel, John, ed. *The Promise and the Reality--Large-Scale*
      Developments in Marginal Regions. Aberdeen, United Kingdom:
      University of Aberdeen, 1979. 198 pp.

      Contains a selection of papers presented at the Fourth
      International Seminar on Marginal Regions, held at Duncraig
      Castle, Wester Ross, Scotland, in July 1977. Fourteen papers
      examine the role of major development projects in stimulating
      economic growth in remote areas of Scotland, Norway, and the
      Atlantic provinces of Canada.

913. Stinson, Thomas F., Lloyd D. Bender, and Stanley W. Voelker.
      Northern Great Plains Coal Mining: Regional Impacts. Agr.
      Info. Bull. No. 452. Washington, D.C.: U.S. Department of
      Agriculture, 1982. 36 pp.

      Examines potential fiscal impacts of large-scale coal
      development in Montana, North Dakota, and Wyoming. In the
      long run, communities gaining population because of the new
      developments, but unable to tax the new mine or powerplant,
      will probably experience financial problems. In the short
      run, most affected communities will probably experience front-
      end cash flow problems due to lags in collecting revenues from
      the new projects. The combined effects of several new mines
      and powerplants in a limited geographic area may exceed the
      capacity of the community to provide services at existing
      levels.

914. Tomlinson, P. "The Agricultural Impact of Opencast Coal
      Mining in England and Wales." *Minerals and the Environment*
      2 (1981): 78-96.

      Identifies significant variations in the impact of opencast
      mining operations, depending largely on the potential for
      reclamation of derelict land and the grade of agricultural
      land affected. Most present mining operations are affecting
      land which is relatively low in agricultural productivity, but

in certain areas operations are entering land of higher agricultural and scenic quality. The quality of reclamation,
while good, can still be improved. The impact on agricultural
productivity is difficult to assess, but it appears to be only
slight in those cases where recent restoration techniques were
used and when lower-grade agricultural land was taken.

915. Wenner, Lambert. *A Survey of the Social and Economic Effects
     of Oil and Gas Development in the Little Missouri National
     Grasslands of North Dakota.* R1-80-28. Missoula, Montana:
     U.S. Department of Agriculture, Forest Service, 1980. 50
     pp.

     Explores the social and economic implications of oil and gas
     exploration and production in western North Dakota. Trends in
     oil and gas activity in the Williston Basin are described, a
     seven-county zone of greatest influence is defined, and the
     challenges that rapid expansion of oil and gas operations pose
     for local communities and their residents are explored.
     Social and economic costs and benefits are examined, with
     special emphasis on the varying perceptions of different
     classes of residents, and potential impact mitigation measures
     are discussed.

916. Wolfe, Robert J., Joseph J. Gross, Steven J. Langdon, John M.
     Wright, George K. Sherrod, Linda J. Ellanna, Valarie Sumida,
     and Peter J. Usher. *Subsistence-Based Economies in Coastal
     Communities of Southwest Alaska.* Tech. Rpt. No. 95.
     Anchorage, Alaska: Minerals Management Service, 1984. 629
     pp.

     Describes and analyzes the systems of subsistence and
     remunerative employment in four traditional Yup'ik communities
     in southwestern and western Alaska. The report examines what
     happens to traditional subsistence activities with an infusion
     of cash through commercial and wage employment opportunities.
     A theory of culture change is developed to account for the
     observed changes occurring in the economy and society of the
     four communities. The theory suggests that only under certain
     sociopolitical organizations is increased cash market partici-
     pation associated with the reinforcement of traditional
     subsistence activities.

*   Wood, K. Scott. "Managing Social Impacts from Large Scale
     Industrial Complexes: Norway's Prospective Oil Exploration
     North of 62° N." *Social Impact Assessment: Theory, Method,
     and Practice.* Edited by Frank J. Tester and William Mykes.
     Cited above as item 330.

Energy Conversion

917. Barone,   Robert N.,   Gano S. Evans, William S. Hallagan, and
      James L. Walker. *Socioeconomic Analysis of the White Pine
      Power Project.* Reno: University of Nevada, Bureau of
      Business and Economic Research, 1979. 240 pp.

      Describes the   probable socioeconomic   effects   of the
      construction and operation of a coal-fired electric power
      generating station located in White Pine County, Nevada. The
      study addresses the impacts of the White Pine Power Project on
      the social and economic well-being of White Pine County,
      including employment, income, public finances, social infra-
      structures, and public attitudes.

  *   Berkes,   F.   "Some Environmental and Social Impacts of the
      James Bay Hydroelectric Project, Canada."   *Journal of
      Environmental Management.* Cited above as item 201.

918. Bjornstad,   David J.   "How Nuclear   Reactor Siting Affects
      Local Communities." *Survey of Business* 11, No. 5 (1976):
      7-10.

      Reviews some of the community impacts of siting a nuclear
      power plant.   The author reviews some of the locational
      constraints affecting impacts, the differing impacts during
      construction and operation, and impacts arising from property
      and in-lieu tax payments.

919. Blomquist,   Glenn.   "The Effect of Electric Utility Power
      Plant Location on Area Property Value." *Land Economics* 50,
      No. 1 (1974): 97-100.

      Estimates the total impact on property values of one amenity
      factor, a power plant in Winnetka, Illinois.   Results reveal
      that within 11,500 feet of the plant, typical property loses
      0.9% of its value for each 10% move closer to the plant.   The
      total disamenity value of the plant is somewhere between
      $200,000 (assuming no nonresidential property damage) to $17
      million (assuming all area property is evaluated and damaged
      as residential property).

920. Campbell,   Kimberly A.   *NACo Case Studies on Energy Impacts.*
      No. 4, *Nuclear Power Plant Development, Boom or Boon?
      County Experiences.* Washington, D.C.: National Association
      of Counties, 1976. 30 pp.

      Is the fourth in a series of case studies on energy communi-
      ties.   The studies were intended to familarize officials, in
      counties where the potential for energy development exists,

with the experiences of other counties that have been affected
by such development. This study, by stressing the effects of
nuclear plant development in several communities, especially
Salem County, New Jersey, gives an overview of the types of
problems such communities face.

See also item 884.

921. Champion, David, and Andrew Ford.   "Boom-Town Effects."
      Environment 22, No. 5 (1980): 25-31.

      Summarizes the results of the Los Alamos Scientific Labora-
      tory interdisciplinary study of the economic, environmental,
      and social consequences of building large, coal-fired power
      plants as compared with the construction of smaller, dispersed
      plants in the West. The studies indicated that small plants
      offer a number of economic and environmental advantages over
      large plants by offering lower-priced electricity to customers
      and spreading their impacts over a greater area.

  *   Cumberland, John H. "The Impacts of a Nuclear Power Plant on
      a   Local   Community: Problems   in   Energy   Facility
      Development." *Energy and the Community.*   Edited by R. J.
      Burby and A. F. Bell. Cited above as item 404.

  *   Faas, Ronald C. *Evaluation of Impact Mitigation Strategies:
      Case Studies of Four Tax Exempt Facilities.* A.E. 82-6.
      Prepared for the Western Rural Development Center.   Cited
      above as item 558.

  *   Fookes, T. W., Project Coordinator.   *Monitoring Social and
      Economic Impact: Huntly Case Study.* Final Report Series in
      13 volumes. Cited above as item 524.

  *   Gilmore, John S. "Boom or Bust: Energy Development in the
      Western United States." *Energy and the Community.*   Edited
      by R. J. Burby and A. F. Bell. Cited above as item 408.

  *   Gilmore, John S., and Mary K. Duff. *Boomtown Growth Manage-
      ment: A Case Study of Rock Springs-Green River, Wyoming.*
      Cited above as item 561.

  *   Goddard, N. J. *The Impact of a Power Project on Local
      Service, Transport and Construction Firms.* Working Paper 4.
      Cited above as item 115.

922.   Goodman, Louis J., and Ralph N. Love, eds. *Geothermal Energy Projects: Planning and Management.* New York: Pergamon Press in cooperation with the East-West Center, Honolulu, Hawaii, 1980. 230 pp.

Assesses governmental initiative, planning, and management in the development of geothermal electric power generation projects through a case history analysis of three projects in New Zealand, Hawaii, and the Philippines. The conceptual framework used in investigating the projects is the integrated project planning and management cycle model. The approach provides a means for analyzing the total process that constitutes the life of a development project. The approach has four distinct phases: (1) planning, appraisal and design; (2) selection, approval, and activation; (3) operation, control, and handover; and (4) evaluation and refinement. The model is a flexible approach underscoring the important role of policymakers.

923.   Herrin, Alejandro N. *The Cagayan Valley Rural Electrification Project: An Impact Assessment.* Working Paper 83-04. Manila: Philippine Institute for Development Studies, 1983. 116 pp.

Presents the results of research aimed at determining the economic and social impact of the Cagayan Valley Rural Electrification Project. Specifically, this research attempts to determine the impact of rural electrification on at least the following areas of development concern: income growth; income distribution; production and productivity; employment; population and fertility; environment; energy; participation, with special emphasis on women's participation; health and nutrition; and education and literacy.

924.   Hoffman, Stephen, and Mary Gray. *The Socioeconomic Impacts of Coal-to-Methanol Plants in Wyoming.* Report prepared for the U.S. Department of Energy, Office of Oil, Gas, and Oil Shale Technology. Bethesda, Maryland: Booz-Allen & Hamilton, Inc., Energy and Environment Division, 1981. 58 pp. plus appendixes.

Estimates the basic socioeconomic effects associated with the peak construction and operation of hypothetical 4,000 and 24,000 bbl per day in-situ coal gasification-to-methanol facilities. The emphasis of the study is on determining the cost of providing major public services to the relocating population. Per capita costs of major public services were estimated and used as the basis for the analysis. Two cities, Rawlins and Casper, Wyoming, were selected as the study locations so that comparisons could be made between the impacts on a small rural town versus a larger urban service center.

925. Johnson, Sue, and Esther Weil. *Social Aspects of Power Plant Siting.* Ohio River Basin Energy Study, Vol. III–D. Washington, D.C.: U.S. Environmental Protection Agency, 1977. 370 pp.

Attempts to assess, using secondary data, what kinds of environmental orientations are likely to be present in counties where power plants, both nuclear and coal fired, are planned or projected. It is a qualitative analysis guided by a theoretical paradigm of environmental orientations which seeks to describe, at the county level, what the authors anticipate the likely impact of a power plant to be. The authors also attempt to relate what they consider to be the prevailing environmental orientation of a county to the probable reaction of the county's residents to this type of developmental change. Selected counties in Illinois, Indiana, Kentucky, and Ohio are examined

926. Jones, James E., Jr., and Harry G. Enoch. *The Kentucky Synfuel Industry: A Basis for Assessment and Planning.* Lexington, Kentucky: Kentucky Department of Energy, Division of Technology Assessment, 1981. 89 pp.

Is intended to provide detailed information regarding the development of a synthetic fuel industry and to serve as a basis for further assessment and planning. National energy supply and demand forces are discussed, and the factors encouraging development of a synthetic fuel industry in Kentucky are described. Four projects which appear likely to be developed in the near future are described in terms of the technologies used, coal requirements, labor demand, and products. Potential social, economic, and environmental problems are identified.

* Justus, Roger, and JoAnne Simonetta. "Oil Sands, Indians and SIA in Northern Alberta." *Indian SIA: The Social Impact Assessment of Rapid Resource Development on Native Peoples.* Edited by Charles C. Geisler, Rayna Green, Daniel Usner, and Patrick C. West. Monograph No. 3. Cited above as item 282.

927. Lebus, Margaret M. *The Synthetic Fuels Industry in Kentucky: An Assessment of Socioeconomic Issues.* Lexington, Kentucky: Kentucky Department of Energy, Technology Assessment Division, 1981. 56 pp.

Describes existing socioeconomic conditions in an eleven-county synfuel impact region in Kentucky and identifies the major issues raised by energy development.

* Leistritz, F. Larry, Norman E. Toman, Steve H. Murdock, and John DeMontel. "Cash Flow Analysis for Energy Impacted

Local Governments--A Case Study of Mercer County, North
Dakota." *Socio-Economic Planning Sciences.* Cited above as
item 416.

* McGuire, A. "The Regional Income and Employment Impacts of
  Nuclear Power Stations." *Scottish Journal of Political
  Economy.* Cited above as item 144.

928. Peter C. Nichols and Associates Ltd. *Overview of Local
     Economic Development in the Athabasca Oil Sands Region Since
     1961.* AOSERP Report 77. Edmonton, Alberta: Alberta
     Environment, 1979. 221 pp.

     Reports that the economy of the Athabasca Oil Sands region
     has been under the predominant influence of oil sands develop-
     ment since 1961. The resultant process of industrialization
     and urbanization has modified existing economic sectors and
     introduced new sectors which have also undergone change and
     development. Research was required to assess both the nature
     and the significance of the changes that have occurred in the
     local economy in the course of the rapid growth associated
     with oil sands development activities. The research results
     are organized into the following sections: regional indus-
     trial development, population, employment, housing, incomes,
     and prices. Other topics covered by the report include
     general impacts of economic growth and the growth of the local
     business sector in Fort McMurray and Fort Chipewyan.

929. Purdy, Bruce J., Elizabeth Peelle, Benson H. Bronfman, and
     David Bjornstad. *A Post Licensing Study of Community
     Effects at Two Operating Nuclear Power Plants.*
     ORNL/NUREG/TM-22. Oak Ridge, Tennessee: Oak Ridge National
     Laboratory, 1977. 115 pp.

     Describes the results of an exploratory assessment of the
     social, economic, and political impacts of two operating
     nuclear power facilities on two New England communities
     through 1975. The study concludes that construction impacts
     were minor due to a dispersed commuting pattern of construc-
     tion workers. The primary impact of the nuclear power plants
     in both communities was an increase in the property tax base.
     Each community chose to maintain or reduce the existing tax
     rate while using the additional revenue to significantly
     increase and enhance public service delivery systems and
     facilities within the community.

930. Rankin, William L., and Stanley M. Nealey. *The Relationship
     of Human Values and Energy Beliefs to Nuclear Power
     Attitude.* B-HARC-411-007. Seattle, Washington: Battelle
     Human Affairs Research Centers, 1978. 84 pp.

Highlights the major findings of a survey concerning individuals' attitudes about the continued development of nuclear power. The purpose of the research was to investigate (1) the relationship of human values to attitudes about the continued development of nuclear power and (2) the relationship of general energy beliefs and beliefs about specific nuclear power issues to attitudes about further nuclear power development. The groups surveyed were (1) a random sample of Washington residents, (2) a random sample of residents located near nuclear pwer plants in the Hanford Reservation region, and (3) a random sample of Washington environmentalists.

* Romanoff, Eliahu, and Stephen H. Levine. *Implications of a Nuclear Facility in South County, Rhode Island.* Vol. 4. *Economic Impact Dynamics.* Cited above as item 171.

931. Sills, David L., C. P. Wolf, and Vivian B. Shelanski, eds. *Accident at Three Mile Island.* Boulder, Colorado: Westview Press, 1982. 258 pp.

Reports some of the findings of the social science research conducted under the auspices of the President's Commission on the Accident at Three Mile Island in 1979. Topics covered in the book include public perceptions of nuclear energy, local responses to nuclear plants, institutional responsibilities for nuclear energy, interactions of social and technical systems, and implications for public policy.

932. University of Denver Research Institute. *Factors Influencing an Area's Ability to Absorb a Large-Scale Commercial Coal-Processing Complex--A Case Study of the Fort Union Lignite Region.* Denver, Colorado: University of Denver Research Institute, 1975. 280 pp.

Identifies and evaluates impacts of a hypothetical large-scale coal processing complex with multiple outputs. Specifically, seven cases of past impacts of large-scale developments in isolated rural areas were examined; the inputs, outputs, and other characteristics of the hypothetical complex were described; economic, social, and land use impacts were analyzed; and recommendations were made for solving potential problems.

Water Development

933. Doughty, Paul L. "Engineers and Energy in the Andes." *Technology and Social Change.* Edited by Harvey Russell Bernard and Pertti J. Pelto. (Item 202), pp. 110-33.

Examines impacts of developing a large-scale hydroelectric facility in Peru.

934. Eshman, Robert. "The Jonglei Canal: A Ditch Too Big?" *Environment* 25, No. 5 (1983): 15-20, 32.

Discusses the controversy related to the joint Sudanese-Egyptian project to divert the Nile in the southern Sudan. Critics argue that the canal will adversely affect the ecology and indigenous cultures of the area, but the Sudanese government maintains that the development is necessary to bolster the country's stagnating economic and agricultural sectors.

935. Findeis, Jill L., and Norman K. Whittlesey. "The Secondary Economic Impacts of Irrigation Development in Washington." *Western Journal of Agricultural Economics* 9, No. 2 (1984): 232-43.

Examines two potential irrigation projects in Washington for their secondary impacts on the state's economy. A major impact of these projects is to increase the energy costs to regional power consumers. The distribution of potential benefits is uneven among sectors of the economy and some sectors will possibly experience substantial decreases in returns to stockholder equity as a result of irrigation expansion.

936. Kneese, Allen V., and F. Lee Brown. *The Southwest Under Stress.* Baltimore, Maryland: The Johns Hopkins University Press, 1981. 268 pp.

Examines various aspects of the development-environment conflict in Arizona, Colorado, New Mexico, and Utah, especially as it relates to possible large-scale development of the energy resources of the region. Emphasis is on policy issues surrounding the conflicts between economic growth and environmental quality in an arid mountainous region that is ecologically, economically, and culturally delicate. The book includes a case study of Page, Arizona, a community which experienced rapid growth resulting from construction of a hydroelectric dam and a coal-fired power plant.

   * McGinnis, Karen A., and Donald A. West. *Community Impacts of Energy Development Projects: The Case of Public Education at Chief Joseph Dam.* A.E. 80-1. Cited above as item 390.

937. Saha, S. K. "Irrigation Planning in the Tana Basin of Kenya." *Water Supply and Management* 6, No. 3 (1982): 261-79.

Explores the reasons why a massive program of irrigation development in the Tana river basin omitted social aspects. As a result the program was of very little benefit to the rural population of the basin.

* Schwinden, Cynthia J., and Jay A. Leitch. *Regional Socio-economic Impact of the Devils Lake Fishery.* Agr. Econ. Rpt. No. 191. Cited above as item 175.

938. Scudder, Thayer, and Elizabeth F. Colson. "The Kariba Dam Project: Resettlement and Local Initiative." *Technology and Social Change.* Edited by Harvey Russell Bernard and Pertti J. Pelto. (Item 202), pp. 40-69.

Discusses the implications of relocating about 34,000 people to make way for development of the world's largest artificial reservoir.

939. Supalla, Raymond J., Glenn Schaible, James A. Larson, Arlen Leholm, Duane Jewel, and Charles F. Lamphear. "Evaluation of Water Management Alternatives: The Nebraska High Plains Study." *The Southwestern Review of Economics and Management* 2, No. 2 (1982): 65-86.

Examines economic impacts of alternative policies regarding groundwater irrigation development in Nebraska. The authors use both a linear programming model to estimate direct (i.e., on-farm) economic effects and an input-output model to estimate secondary (off-farm) effects. Continuation of current water policies would result in a growing agricultural base until at least the year 2020. Alternative policies could prolong the life of the aquifer but at a significant cost in terms of income and employment foregone in the near future.

940. Tahir, A. A., and M. O. El Sammani. *Environmental and Socio-Economic Impact of the Jonglei Canal Project.* Khartoum, Sudan: Executive Organ, National Council for the Development of the Jonglei Canal Area, 1978.

Concerns environmental and socioeconomic studies conducted in preparation for the construction of the Jonglei canal, a major (2,000 mile) canal to enlarge the flow of the White Nile River through a presently unnavigable swamp (the Sudd). The socioeconomic impact assessment was designed not only to improve project planning but also to assist in formulating social and economic policies and to design appropriate development programs to accompany the canal's construction. The affected populations are those of the pastoral nomadic Nilotic tribes. Studies reveal that such social change has

already been occurring in the affected area and that dissatisfied people desire further change, viewing the canal project
as largely beneficial.

Industry

941. Beck, E. M., Louis Dotson, and Gene F. Summers.   "Effects of
      Industrial Development on Heads of Households." *Growth and*
      Change 4, No. 2 (1973): 16-19.

      Examines short-term changes in the socioeconomic character-
      istics of heads of households during a period of industrial
      development in northern Illinois.   Six characteristics were
      examined: age, years of educational attainment, socioeconomic
      status, family's background socioeconomic status, total annual
      income of the head of household, and total annual family
      income.

942. Brady, Guy, Jr. "The Economic Impact of Industrialization on
      a Rural Town Economy: Wynne, Arkansas." Master's Thesis.
      Fayetteville, Arkansas: University of Arkansas, 1974.   104
      pp.

      Examines four aspects of the economic effects of industrial-
      ization on Wynne, Arkansas: (1) the impact on the private
      sector, (2) the impact on city government, (3) changes in the
      quality of public services and utilities offered by city
      government, and (4) the impact on the school systems.   In the
      private sector, the focus is on the primary and secondary
      effects on income, unemployment rates, employment shifts,
      population, in-migration, commuting, and spending patterns.
      Public sector effects of particular interest are revenues and
      expenditures of the city government and the school system.

943. Funk, Herbert Joseph.   "Effects of a New Manufacturing Plant
      on Business Firms in an Eastern Iowa Community." Ph.D.
      Dissertation.   Ames, Iowa: Iowa State University, 1964.
      213 pp.

      Examines demand, cost, and net income effects on business
      firms of a new manufacturing plant in Maquoketa, Iowa. Nearly
      80% of the firms had an increase in demand that was closely
      related to its location, type, and size. Sixty-one percent of
      the estimated increase in total income was attributed to an
      increase in per capita income and 39% to population increase.
      The study indicated that increases in total costs of business
      firms as a result of increases in factor prices due to the new
      plant were relatively small.   With the exception of farm-
      related firms, a majority of firms had an increase in net
      income; smaller firms had a larger percentage increase.   Most

businessmen agreed that the new plant was beneficial for the community.

944. Guedry, Leo J., and Eugene S. Rosa. *The Economic Impact of Industrialization on a Rural Louisiana Economy: La Salle Parish.* D.A.E. Res. Rpt. No. 558. Baton Rouge: Louisiana Agricultural Experiment Station, 1979. 63 pp.

Attempts to provide a more complete assessment of industrial impacts in rural areas. Income, output, and employment impacts of industrial (manufacturing) firms are compared with those of other economic units in a rural economy. In addition, the contribution made by the existence of a manufacturing sector to the economic impacts of other economic sectors in a rural economy are identified and discussed. These impacts are examined via an input-output model developed for the La Salle Parish economy. Manufacturing employees' characteristics and their impacts within the economy are also analyzed. The primary impact of the manufacturing sector resulted from this sector's employment of workers in the local economy and the impacts arising from such employment, rather than from purchases of supplies and raw materials.

945. Pernia, Ernesto M. *Small-Scale Industry Promotion: Economic and Social Impact Analysis.* Working Paper 83-02. Manila: Philippine Institute for Development Studies, 1983. 96 pp.

Examines the effects of small-scale enterprises (defined as manufacturing establishments with less than 100 workers) on a variety of economic and social development concerns. Special attention is given to effects on employment, income growth and distribution, labor force participation, population and fertility, education and literacy, and health and nutrition. A survey of enterprises and households was conducted in Tagbilaran, the capital city of Bohol Province.

946. Poggie, John J., Jr. "Cuidad Industrial." *Technology and Social Change.* Edited by Harvey Russell Bernard and Pertti J. Pelto. (Item 202), pp. 10-38.

Examines the impact of the establishment of three large factories and a new city in a rural area of Mexico.

Transportation

947. Berger, Thomas R. *Northern Frontier, Northern Homeland: The Report of the McKenzie Valley Pipeline Inquiry.* Toronto, Ontario: James Lorimer and Company, 1977. 213 pp.

Considers the broad social, economic, and environmental impacts that a gas pipeline and an energy corridor would have in the McKenzie Valley and the western Arctic. Contains chapters on the cultural, economic, and social impacts.

* Dixon, Mim. *What Happened to Fairbanks?* Cited below as item 237.

* Donohue, Marian, Sallie Edmunds, Ruby Edwards, Jan Hiranaka, Robey Lal, Raymond Oshiro, Harry Partika, Rik Scarce, James Schweithelm, Colleen Wallace, and Jan Yamamoto. *Exploring the Social Impacts of a General Aviation Airport at Waipio.* DURP No. 831402. Cited below as item 238.

948. Hall, Peter. *Great Planning Disasters.* Berkeley: University of California Press, 1982. 308 pp.

Defines *planning disasters* to include any planning process that is perceived by many people to have gone wrong. Such disasters can be of two types: (1) positive disasters-- decisions to take a course of action that was implemented despite much criticism and which was later felt by many informed people to have been a mistake, and (2) negative disasters--decisions to take a course of action, culminating in a physical result that was later substantially modified, reversed, or abandoned after considerable commitment of effort and resources. The author's objective is to examine the pathology of the planning process in order to determine how such decisions are made and then abandoned or continued in the face of criticism. Case studies of London's Third Airport, London's Motorways, the Anglo-French Concorde, San Francisco's BART System, and Sydney's Opera House form the basis for discussion and analysis of such planning problems.

949. Howes, H., and B. Rogers. *An Approach to the Socio-Economic Impact Assessment of Transmission Lines.* Toronto, Ontario: Ontario Hydro, Social and Community Studies Section, 1984. 14 pp.

Presents two case studies to illustrate the socioeconomic impact assessment (SIA) approach used by Ontario Hydro. Both involve current 500 kv transmission line studies. Standard SIA methods were used in each study; however, because of study area, project team, and population dynamics differences, two distinctly different SIA studies evolved. The case studies illustrate the need for flexibility in the SIA approach, the validity of incorporating qualitative information into the decision-making process, and the range of issues that could be covered in an SIA of transmission lines.

* Metzger, John M., and David C. Colony. "Citizens and Project Design: Management Team." *Journal of the Urban Planning and Development Division.* Cited below as item 684.

950. Pelto, Pertti J., and Ludger Muller-Wille. "Snowmobiles: Technological Revolution in the Arctic." *Technology and Social Change.* Edited by Harvey Russell Bernard and Pertti J. Pelto. (Item 202), pp. 166-99.

Examines the social and economic implications of the widespread adoption of snowmobiles in Finnish Lapland and Arctic Canada.

951. Te, Amanda N. *Measuring the Impact of Cagayan de Oro Port Development.* Working Paper 83-03. Manila: Philippine Institute for Development Studies, 1983. 55 pp. plus appendixes.

Evaluates the effects of improving the port facilities at Cagayan de Oro, located on the north coast of Mindanao Island, in terms of changes in a variety of economic and social indicators. Special attention is focussed on effects on employment, income growth, productivity, balance of trade, environment, participation, population and fertility, health and nutrition, and education and literacy.

Other

952. Alberts, T. *Agrarian Reform and Rural Poverty: A Case Study of Peru.* Lund Economic Studies No. 12. Lund, Sweden: Lund University, Research Policy Institute, 1981. 306 pp.

Considers possibilities and problems of agrarian reform and of Peruvian development based on research during the period 1968-1979. The development objectives of the military government, particularly in relation to agricultural development and agrarian reform, are analyzed, and the results of the junta's reign appraised for 1968-1975 and 1975-1980. Government policies toward agricultural growth are discussed, and the extent to which the military junta carried out a successful agrarian reform with respect to social and economic growth objectives is assessed. Finally, Peru's major development options for the years 1980-2000 are considered.

* Albrecht, Stan L. "Community Response to Large-Scale Federal Projects: The Case of the MX." *Nuclear Waste: Socioeconomic Dimensions of Long-Term Storage.* Edited by Steve H. Murdock, F. Larry Leistritz, and Rita R. Hamm. Cited above as item 642.

953. Arong,   Jose R., and Guillermo M. Hagad.   *The Impact of the Third IDA Education Loan Project.*   Working Paper 83-06. Manila: Philippine Institute for Development Studies, 1983. 111 pp.

Assesses the effects of a textbook development project on such socioeconomic dimensions as income and income growth, income distribution, production and productivity, employment, population and fertility, environment, energy, participation, health and nutrition, education and literacy.   The area most directly affected by the project is education and literacy. To some extent, production and productivity together with income growth and distribution were affected by the massive inputs of capital and the consequent development of textbook development and production skills.   Effects on the other areas are mediated through education and literacy.

954. Arroyo,   Gloria M.,   and Mariano San Buenaventura.   *The Economic and Social Impact of Tourism.* Working Paper 83-01. Manila: Philippine Institute for Development Studies, 1983. 97 pp. plus appendixes.

Attempts to analyze the economic and social impact of tourism on the community where the Pagsanjan Tourism Develop- ment Project is located.   One objective is to develop a methodology that can be applied with a minimum of modification to other tourist areas or projects.   Effects examined include those on income, employment, income distribution, labor force participation, and such social dimensions as education and culture.   An input-output model is used to estimate the economic effects.

955. Barnes,   Carolyn.   *Kenya On-Farm Grain Storage Project.* Project Paper 615-0190.   Nairobi, Kenya: Agency for Inter- national Development, East Africa Regional Economic Develop- ment Services Office, 1980.

Provides an example of a social analysis that specifies actions and processes to help ensure a positive social impact from an AID project.   The project aims at reducing grain losses on small-scale farms.   A study will be made prior to the initiation of other field activities in order to better understand determinants of current practices and identify possible entry points and agents for change.   The author recommends that in order for this project to positively benefit the target group, it will be necessary for small holders to play a participatory role in identifying and testing those technologies they deem feasible.   Further, a group approach will increase the extension agent/farmer contact ratio, facilitate public discussion and commitment, and provide for an equitable selection of households to receive materials on a grant basis for trials and demonstra- tions.   The social-economist will investigate the need of

small-scale farmers for financial assistance to adopt the
postharvest technologies and the best delivery system. The
ideal situation would be the identification of economically
feasible technologies which are socially acceptable to the
target group and which are within their financial ability to
adopt.

956. Barrados, M., R. McDowell, and D. Grafstein. *Nuclear Waste
      Management Program: Results of 1980 March Gallup Surveys.*
      TR-19-5. Pinawa, Manitoba: Atomic Energy of Canada Ltd.,
      1981. 75 pp.

      Reports results of a 1980 survey of Ontario residents.
      Respondents were questioned about their knowledge of the
      government's program to study the safe disposal of nuclear
      wastes, their attitudes towards geological research being
      carried out near their community, and their attitudes towards
      the construction of a nuclear waste disposal facility in their
      area.

  *   Baxter, Judith. *Changing Stages of Development: Conse-
      quences for Community Change.* Unpub. Master's thesis.
      Cited above as item 200.

957. Breese, Gerald, R. J. Klingenmeier, H. P. Cahill, J. E.
      Whelan, A. E. Church, and D. E. Whiteman. *The Impact of
      Large Installations on Nearby Areas: Accelerated Urban
      Growth.* Beverly Hills, California: Sage Publications,
      Inc., 1965. 632 pp.

      Consists of case studies of impacts of five large facilities
      on nearby communities. Facilities examined were a steel mill
      located in Bucks County, Pennsylvania; an aircraft plant on
      Long Island, New York; Air Force bases located near Dover,
      Delaware, and in Seneca County, New York; and the Savannah
      River atomic energy plant. The authors attempt to (1)
      identify both the characteristics of impact patterns and the
      devices for anticipating related events and issues and (2)
      suggest procedures or methods for dealing effectively with an
      impact situation, particularly during the critical early
      years.

958. Burby, Raymond J., and Shirley F. Weiss. *New Communities,
      U.S.A.* Lexington, Massachusetts: Lexington Books, 1976.
      593 pp.

      Attempts to provide federal, state, and local officials, as
      well as public and private developers, with (1) an improved
      base of information to use in judging the merits of new
      community development as an urban growth alternative, and (2)
      an indication of the critical factors affecting the success or

failure of new communities in meeting the needs of all their
residents. In pursuing these two goals, the research was
designed to provide answers to the following major policy
questions: (1) Are federally guaranteed new communities
contributing more to residents' quality of life than
nonguaranteed new communities and less planned environments?,
(2) Which characteristics of housing, neighborhood design,
community facilities, and governmental mechanisms contribute
most to the quality of life of new community residents,
including minorities, low-income families, the elderly, and
teenagers?, (3) Which factors in the developer decision
process lead to new community characteristics that contribute
most to the quality of life of new community residents?, (4)
How has the federal new community development program
influenced developer decisions regarding housing, neighborhood
design, community facilities, and governmental mechanisms?,
and (5) How can the federal new community development program
be applied most effectively to produce communities that
promise to improve the quality of life of their residents?
These questions focus on new community housing, neighborhood
design, community facility, and governmental characteristics;
the contributions of these characteristics to the satisfactions and quality of life of new community residents; and the
decision factors that lead to their production.

959. Canlas, Dante B. *Evaluating the Socio-Economic Impacts of an*
      Agricultural College: The Case of Extension Programs.
      Working Paper 83-11. Manila: Philippine Institute for
      Development Studies, 1983. 34 pp.

      Evaluates the effects of some extension activities of an
      agricultural college (Central Luzon State University) on
      variables which serve as indicators of the desired objectives
      of government rural development programs. Emphasis is placed
      on assessing the impacts of agricultural training programs and
      livelihood projects on income and productivity, income
      differentials, and employment.

960. Coon, Randal C., Norman L. Dalsted, Arlen G. Leholm, and
      F. Larry Leistritz. *The Impact of the Safeguard Antiballis-*
      tic Missile System Construction on Northeastern North Dakota.
      Agr. Econ. Rpt. No. 101. Fargo: North Dakota Agricultural
      Experiment Station, 1976. 70 pp.

      Describes the effect of construction of a large military
      installation on nearby communities. The objectives of the
      study were to describe the local economic situation before,
      during, and after the construction project and to evaluate the
      impacts of project development on public services, governmen-
      tal units, and the way of life in the communities involved.

961. Cummings, Ronald G., H. Stuart Burness, and Roger G. Norton. *The Proposed Waste Isolation Pilot Project (WIPP) and Impacts in the State of New Mexico: A Socio-Economic Analysis.* EMD 2-67-1139. Albuquerque: University of New Mexico, 1981. 356 pp.

Reports research concerning the socioeconomic impacts that might be associated with construction and operation of the proposed Waste Isolation Pilot Project (WIPP), a federal nuclear waste repository. The purpose of WIPP is for storage of transuranic waste from the U.S. defense program and to provide a research and development area for experiments concerning all types of nuclear waste in salt.

* Flynn, Cynthia B. "The Local Impacts of the Accident at Three Mile Island." *Public Reactions to Nuclear Power: Are There Critical Masses?* Edited by William R. Freudenburg and Eugene A. Rosa. Cited above as item 248.

* Goldstein, Joan. "The Pine Barrens: A Case Study of the Social Impact of Urban Development Upon Rural Communities." *Social Impact Assessment: Theory, Method, and Practice.* Edited by Frank J. Tester and William Mykes. Cited above as item 261.

962. Kupfer, George, and Charles W. Hobart. "Impact of Oil Exploration Work on an Inuit Community." *Arctic Anthropology* 15, No. 1 (1978): 58-67.

Analyzes the impact of oil exploration work by Gulf Oil Canada in the MacKenzie Delta on the Inuit people of Coppermine in the Northwest Territories, Canada. The effects of the work on the economy, society, and family life and health were examined. Results indicated that cash flow in the community increased by about 75%, and almost all of the income was spent in the community. Residents believed that Gulf employment had a salutary effect on the community and that family life had not been negatively affected.

963. Lindell, M. K., T. C. Earle, J. A. Hebert, and R. W. Perry. *Radioactive Wastes: Public Attitudes Toward Disposal Facilities.* B-HARC-411-004. Seattle: Battelle Human Affairs Research Centers, 1978. 58 pp.

Reports results of a study to more accurately characterize the similarities and differences of opinion of the most strongly pro- and anti-nuclear portions of the public. Overall, the results indicate that pronuclear respondents believe that the hazards of nuclear waste are similar to other industrial risks. Antinuclear respondents, by contrast, are

less optimistic about the prospects for safe storage of
nuclear wastes.

* Macarthur, J. D. "Appraising the Distributional Aspects of
  Rural Development Projects: A Kenya Case Study." *World
  Development.* Cited above as item 143.

964. McGoodwin, James Russell. "The Human Costs of Development."
     Environment 22, No. 1 (1980): 25-31.

     Discusses social and technological problems that arose when
     Mexico developed its shrimp industry.

* MacKay, D. I., and G. A. MacKay. *The Political Economy of
  North Sea Oil.* Cited above as item 900.

* Moore, Craig L. "The Impact of Public Institutions on
  Regional Income: Upstate Medical Center as a Case in
  Point." *Economic Geography.* Cited above as item 156.

965. Murdock, Steve H., F. Larry Leistritz, and Rita R. Hamm, eds.
     *Nuclear Waste: Socioeconomic Dimensions of Long-Term
     Storage.* Boulder, Colorado: Westview Press, 1983. 343 pp.

     Contains seventeen original articles which examine the
     socioeconomic issues associated with developing high-level
     nuclear waste repositories in the United States. Special
     attention is given to problems of communities located near
     potential repository sites and thus likely to be impacted by
     facility siting, construction, and operation. Major sections
     of the book are devoted to (1) ethical, institutional, and
     legal considerations in repository siting; (2) assessing the
     economic, demographic, public service, fiscal, and social
     effects of repository siting; (3) mitigating impacts of
     repository siting, and (4) local community response and parti-
     cipation in repository siting.

     Contains items 642, 676.

966. Murdock, Steve H., F. Larry Leistritz, and Rita R. Hamm.
     "Socioeconomic Impacts of Large-Scale Developments: Impli-
     cations for High-Level Nuclear Waste Repositories." *The
     Environmental Professional* 5 (1983): 183-94.

     Examines some of the potential socioeconomic impacts likely
     to occur in rural areas as a result of high-level nuclear
     waste repository siting and development, and describes some of
     the characteristics of mitigation programs that are likely to
     be necessary, if the impacts are to be addressed. Both

standard impacts, those resulting from the fact that, like many other large-scale developments, repositories will involve a substantial number of new workers and residents (relative to the size of existing communities), and *special* impacts, those resulting from the fact that repositories store radioactive materials, are examined.

* President's Economic Adjustment Committee. *Boom Town Business Opportunities and Development Management.* Cited above as item 163.

* President's Economic Adjustment Committee. *Modeling the Regional Economic Impacts of Major New Military Bases.* Cited above as item 164.

* Roberts, Kenneth J., and R. Bruce Rettig. *Linkages Between the Economy and the Environment: An Analysis of Economic Growth in Clatsop County, Oregon.* Bulletin No. 618. Cited above as item 169.

967. Segura-de los Angles, Marian. *Economic and Social Impact Analysis of Agro-Forestry Development Projects in Villarica, Diadi, and Norzagaray.* Working Paper 83-08. Manila: Philippine Institute for Development Studies, 1983. 154 pp. plus appendices.

Focuses on agro-forestation projects which involve shifting cultivators. The author illustrates methods of analyzing the progress and impact of three pilot agro-forestation development projects. The projects were found to produce impacts primarily in the areas of environment, participation, production, income, and education.

968. Swanberg, K. G. *Institutional Evolution: From Pilot Project to National Development Program--Puebla and Caqueza.* Development Discussion Papers No. 132. Cambridge, Massachusetts: Harvard University, Harvard Institute for International Development, 1982. 47 pp.

Describes two agricultural development projects, Puebla in Mexico and Caqueza in Colombia, which were begun over a decade ago and have now achieved phenomenal local success by more than doubling average maize yields. The projects have also served as the model for large national development programs in their respective countries. The organizational development of the two projects is evaluated, and key elements reviewed.

969. Torres, Amaryllis T., and Rodolfo F. Ventura. *Economic and Social Impacts of the Aquaculture Projection Project.*

Working Paper 83-05.   Manila: Philippine   Institute   for
Development Studies, 1983.   161 pp.

Summarizes   an   economic and   social impact   analysis   of an
aquaculture project   sponsored by   the   Philippine government.
Project   effects   are   evaluated   in   terms   of   changes   in
education, environmental quality, productivity and production,
employment, income   growth, income   distribution,   health   and
nutrition, participation, and energy utilization.

970.   Walker, Charles A.,   Leroy C. Gould, and Edward   J. Woodhouse,
       eds.   *Too Hot to Handle?   Social and   Policy Issues in the
       Management of Radioactive Wastes.*   New Haven,   Connecticut:
       Yale University Press, 1983.   209 pp.

       Provides information about one aspect of nuclear safety--the
       management of radioactive wastes.   In particular, the book is
       designed to   assist the reader in understanding   the following
       topics: the history of radioactive waste management in   this
       country and the role of   nuclear energy   in the future   of the
       United States;   the science   and technology   of   the processes
       that produce   radioactive wastes   and of methods   proposed for
       managing them; the   biological effects   of   radiation; public
       attitudes about   nuclear power; the nature of   risks resulting
       from technological developments and ways of managing them; and
       the   political institutions   and processes that   govern radio-
       active waste management.

Reference Sources

*   Armstrong, Anona F. *First Directory of Australian Social Impact Assessment: Practice and Practitioners.* Cited above as item 52.

971. Barr, Charles W. *Australian Planning and Development: A Selected Bibliography.* No. 505. Monticello, Illinois: Council of Planning Librarians, December 1973. 26 pp.

    Lists 284 titles, including eight bibliographies, by state and region.

*   Brown, M. P. Sharon. *Eastern Arctic Study Annotated Bibliography.* Cited above as item 10.

972. Burg, Nan C. *Economic Development in Nonmetropolitan Areas: Special Socioeconomic Problems of Rapid-Growth Communities-- A Selected Bibliography.* Exchange Bibliography No. 1497. Monticello, Illinois: Council of Planning Librarians, 1978. 24 pp.

    Contains about 260 references dealing with various aspects of population growth in rural areas. The bibliography is arranged by topic area. Sections of special interest include (1) effect of economic development on the quality of life, (2) impacts of community development programs, (3) impacts of rural industrialization, and (4) special problems of rapid growth.

*   Burt, R. S. *Resolving Community Conflict in the Nuclear Power Issue: A Report and Annotated Bibliography.* Cited above as item 649.

973. Canter, Larry W. *Water Resources Assessment: Methodology and Technology Sourcebook.* Ann Arbor, Michigan: Ann Arbor Science Publishers, Inc., 1979. 529 pp.

    Summarizes work done by the author for the U.S. Army Engineer Waterways Experiment Station. It is a comprehensive review and evaluation of methodologies and technologies that are used directly or that have potential application to environmental impact assessment and/or impact assessment and alternative evaluation studies for water resources programs and projects. A total of 254 references published between 1960 and 1978 were examined.

974. Carley, Michael J., and Eduardo Bustelo. *Social Impact Assessment and Monitoring: A Cross-Disciplinary Guide to the Literature.* Boulder, Colorado: Westview Press, 1984. 250 pp.

Consists of a critical review of more than 600 recent publications in social impact assessment (SIA) and related fields. The authors view SIA as falling within the broad range of policy analysis and the policy sciences, and the SIA response to policymaking as tending to be an interdisciplinary effort on the part of political scientists, planners, sociologists, economists, anthropologists, engineers, psychologists, and many others. This guide to the literature clearly reflects the cross-disciplinary aspects of the issues, problems, and methods of SIA. Topics covered include an introduction to SIA, social forecasting, quantification, SIA methodologies, sociocultural effects, communicating and using SIAs, SIA in developing countries, public participation, communitiy preferences, expert preferences, visual and landscape preferences, new and boom towns, energy development risk, environmental impact assessment, monitoring, cost-benefit analysis, decision analysis, periodicals, and other bibliographies.

975. Chang, Raymont J. *The Petroleum Industry in China: Its Planning in the Development of Energy Resources; A Bibliography with Selective Annotations.* No. 1285. Monticello, Illinois: Council of Planning Librarians, May 1977. 28 pp.

Provides about 180 sources which can be used to understand the development of China's energy resources and its future implications. Primary and secondary sources in Chinese, English, and Japanese including reference works, monographs, articles, and documents are listed and annotated selectively.

976. Clark, Brian D., Ronald Bisset, and Peter Wathern. *Environmental Impact Assessment: A Bibliography with Abstracts.* Mansell Publishing, London, and R. R. Bowker Company, New York, 1980. 516 pp.

Lists, selectively abstracts, and critiques works on methods of environmental and social impact assessments, the relationship of EIA to other aspects of planning, and the application of the procedures in different countries. The focus of the work is on assessments in North American and European countries and Australia.

977. Cohen, Phyllis. *The Community Development Process: An Introductory Bibliography.* P-773. Monticello, Illinois: Vance Bibliographies, 1981. 11 pp.

Contains about 120 entries which include many of the key references in the field of community development. The work is directed to community planners and to students of community development, community organization, or related fields.

* *Contact, Journal of Urban & Environmental Affairs.* Special Issue: *New Communities in Canada: Exploring Planned Environments.* Edited by Norman E. P. Pressman. Cited above as item 768.

978. Cortese, Charles F., and Jane Archer Cortese. *The Social Effects of Energy Boomtowns in the West: A Partially Annotated Bibliography.* Exchange Bibliography No. 1557. Monticello, Illinois: Council of Planning Librarians, 1978. 30 pp.

Contains about 180 entries dealing with various social effects of rapid community growth resulting from energy resource development. Most of the references cited were published during the period 1972-76.

979. Dalsted, Norman L., and F. Larry Leistritz. *A Selected Bibliography on Coal-Energy Development of Particular Interest to the Western States.* Agr. Econ. Misc. Rpt. No. 16. Fargo: North Dakota Agricultural Experiment Station, 1974. 82 pp.

Is intended especially for those engaged in research on the economic and social implications of coal development. It contains about 480 references and is partially annotated.

980. Dames & Moore. *Review of the Literature of Cumulative Impact Assessment Methods.* Technical Memorandum Number C1-1. Prepared for the Minerals Management Service (MMS), Alaska OCS Region. Anchorage, Alaska: Minerals Management Service, April 1984. 323 pp.

Reviews literature and provides an annotated bibliography of selected methods, theories, and approaches relevant to cumulative impact assessment of the effects of petroleum development and other industrial development projects. The geographic scope of the review is centered on North America, with a focus on methods developed to assess the impacts of modern industrial or resource development projects on Native American communities. References are reviewed and compared for applicability in Alaskan Arctic sociocultural settings. The first section of the report provides introductory background on the concept of cumulative impacts, their assessment and analysis. The second section reviews nearly 150 reports, articles, and books relating to cumulative impact assessment. Included in the analysis is literature on environmental impact assessment, social impact assessment, the MMS/Alaska OCS Socioeconomic Studies Program, Canada, Native Americans, and international development. The authors recommend that five methodological approaches be further scrutinized: regional area-wide EISs, comprehensive EISs, regional planning studies, longitudinal monitoring, and public inquiries.

981. Davis, Lenwood G. *Migration to African Cities: An Introductory Survey.* No. 1204. Monticello, Illinois: Council of Planning Librarians, January 1977. 21 pp.

Contains a listing of selected articles and books related to migration to African cities, along with a listing of selected African periodicals.

982. Deaton, Brady J., and Kevin K. McNamara. *Education in a Changing Environment: Impact of Population and Economic Change on the Demand and Cost of Public Education in Rural America.* SRDC Synthesis Bibliography Series No. 18. Mississippi State: Mississippi State University, Southern Rural Development Center, February 1984. 78 pp.

Contains 121 entries on the topic.

983. Draper, Dianne. *Public Participation in Environmental Decision-making.* No. 396. Monticello, Illinois: Council of Planning Librarians, May 1973. 28 pp.

Contains approximately 300 entries divided into four sections: environmental concerns, planning and public participation, voluntary interest group studies, and government and environmental quality.

    *   Dunlap, Riley E. *Environmental Sociology: A Bibliography of Conceptual, Methodological and Theoretical Readings.* Cited above as item 240.

984. *Environmental Impact Assessment Review.* March 1980 to December 1983.

Was a quarterly publication for planners, engineers, scientists, and administrators involved in the practice of impact assessment. The journal, in an attempt to bridge the gap between theory and practice, presented summaries of new analytic techniques and environmental decision making. Copies can be obtained through Plenum Publishing Corporation, 227 West 17th Street, New York 10011. The journal may be published again in the near future.

985. Erickson, David L. *Public Involvement in Natural Resource Planning and Decision-making: A Selected Bibliography.* No. 1097. Monticello, Illinois: Council of Planning Librarians, August 1976. 18 pp.

Lists about 200 works pertaining to natural resource planning and decision making in particular and to public involvement in general.

986. Found, William C. *Environment, Migration, and the Management of Rural Resources.* Nos. 1143, 1144, 1145, and 1146. Monticello, Illinois: Council of Planning Librarians, October 1976. 60 pp., 21 pp., 42 pp., and 26 pp., respectively.

Is a series of four bibliographies on the following topics: rural sociology, farm-related decision making, the influence of environment on behavior, interregional migration, farm economics, land use, spatial analysis, and local studies (Ontario, Canada).

987. Fox, William F., Jerome M. Stam, W. Maureen Godsey, and Susan D. Brown. *Economies of Size in Local Government: An Annotated Bibliography.* Rural Development Research Report No. 9. Washington, D.C.: U.S. Department of Agriculture, 1979. 74 pp.

Contains a listing and annotations for 133 papers, reports, and books which test for size or scale economies in producing local government goods and services. Size economies refer to the set of phenomena that cause average costs of providing a good or service to decline with increasing size of the government unit. This report deals solely with the supply side costs of providing services and therefore excludes research on such topics as expenditure determinants of local governments and optimal city size.

988. Frankena, Frederick, and Thomas Kobernick. *Community Impacts of Rapid Growth in Nonmetropolitan Areas: A Cross-Disciplinary Bibliography.* P-560. Monticello, Illinois: Vance Bibliographies, 1980. 27 pp.

Contains 251 entries dealing with various effects of rapid growth on rural communities. A subject index is included.

989. Gill, Dhara S. *A Bibliography of Socio-economic Studies on Rural Alberta, Canada.* No. 1260, 1261, and 1262. Monticello, Illinois: Council of Planning Librarians, April 1977. 206 pp.

Contains over 2,000 books, articles, and reports that relate
to rural Alberta, Canada.

990. Glickfeld,   Madelyn, Tom Whitney, and J. Eugene Grigsby III.
      *A Selective Analytical Bibliography for Social Impact
      Assessment.* Edited by Mary Vance. Exchange Bibliography
      1562. Monticello, Illinois: Vance Bibliographies, 1978.
      85 pp.

      Investigates the research, development, and application of
      social impact assessment by all levels of government in an
      effort to develop a book of theoretical resources which would
      enable practitioners to use SIA as a planning tool. Bibliog-
      raphy is organized into four sections: behavioral science
      theoretical resources, empirical evaluative case studies, SIA
      literature, and SIA predictive case studies.

991. Grayson, Lesley. *The Social and Economic Impact of New
      Technology, 1978-84: A Select Bibliography.* Co-published
      by IFI/Plenum, New York, and Technical Communications,
      Letchworth, Herts, England, 1984. 80 pp.

      Annotates over 700 American, British, and European works on
      the microelectronics revolution. Sections include social
      impacts; economic structure and policy; impacts on business,
      industry, and communications; administrative impacts and
      industrial relations, and national and international
      initiatives, policies, and political manifestos.

992. Gundry, Kathleen. *Public Participation in Planning and
      Resource Management: An Annotated Bibliography.* No. 1551.
      Monticello, Illinois: Council of Planning Librarians, June
      1978. 11 pp.

      Collects thirty-two annotations into three sections:
      theory, research, and case studies; political theory and
      governmental influence on communities; and design processes.

993. Hamilton, Michael S. *Power Plant Siting (With Special
      Emphasis on Western United States).* Exchange Bibliography
      1359-1360. Monticello, Illinois: Council of Planning
      Librarians, 1977. 100 pp.

      Contains about 400 annotated references that constitute a
      selected bibliography of materials concerning issues and
      problems of siting electric power plants in the western United
      States. Most of the titles listed have been published since
      1970.

994. Hansen, Gary B., Marion T. Bentley, Rexanne Pond, and Mark H.
      Skidmore. *A Selective Annotated Bibliography on Plant Shut-
      downs and Related Topics.* Logan, Utah: Utah State Univer-
      sity, Center for Productivity and Quality of Working Life,
      1981. 46 pp.

      Has approximately 120 entries arranged in seven categories:
      (1) General Topics and Case Studies, (2) Alternatives to Shut-
      downs and New Approaches to Work, (3) Job Search and Job
      Finding Activities, (4) Organized Community Programs and Other
      Forms of Assistance, (5) Training and Retraining, (6) Employ-
      ment Problems of Older Workers, and (7) Audio-Visual
      Materials.

   * Hansen, Gary B., Marion T. Bentley, and Mark H. Skidmore.
      *Plant Shutdowns, People and Communities: A Selected
      Bibliography.* Cited above as item 850.

995. Harvey Prentice. *The Social and Economic Consequences of
      Industry in Small Communities and Rural Areas: An Annotated
      Bibliography.* No. 940. Monticello, Illinois: Council of
      Planning Librarians, December 1975. 17 pp.

      Contains forty-four briefly annotated works about the
      desirableness of rural industrial growth in the United States
      and its probable benefits and liabilities. Works also cover
      trends toward industrial decentralization, locational
      patterns, and antipoverty strategies.

996. Honadle, Beth Walter. *Capacity-Building (Management Improve-
      ment) For Local Governments: An Annotated Bibliography.*
      Rural Development Research Report No. 28. Washington, D.C.:
      U.S. Department of Agriculture, 1981. 78 pp.

      Presents 162 annotated references of publications from 1964
      through 1980. *Capacity building* is defined as improving the
      ability of local governments and areas to manage their
      problems. Each citation summarizes the publication's contri-
      bution and determines the type of capacity to which the publi-
      cation refers.

   * Honadle, Beth Walter. *Public Administration in Rural Areas
      and Small Jurisdictions: A Guide to the Literature.* Cited
      above as item 755.

997. Howard, Lynda M., comp. *Issues of Public Interest Regarding
      Northern Development: An Annotated Bibliography.* Edited by
      Lynda M. Howard and Paul Davies. Calgary, Alberta:
      Pallister Resource Management Ltd., 1984. 431 pp.

Identifies source literature relating to public concerns
regarding oil and gas development in northern Canada. Topics
include land and resources, employment, political economy and
land claims, application and approval process, environmental
impact assessment, northern economies and populations, social
and economic conditions, health, culture, community, renewable resources, petroleum and mining, communications and
navigation, and energy and utilities.

998. Hulchanski, John David. *Citizen Participation in Urban and
      Regional Planning: A Comprehensive Bibliography.* No.
      1297. Monticello, Illinois: Council of Planning
      Librarians, June 1977. 61 pp.

      Covers the period from the mid 1940s to the early 1970s and
      includes major U.S. and Canadian literature on citizen parti-
      cipation, including over 500 works on community control,
      advocacy planning, decentralization, community organizing,
      and participation in the U.S. War on Poverty and Model Cities
      programs.

999. Hundemann, Audrey S. *Power Plant Siting (A Bibliography
      with Abstracts).* NTIS No. PS-76/0853. Springfield,
      Virginia: National Technical Information Service, 1976.
      173 pp.

      Abstracts of 173 technical reports pertaining to the siting
      of nuclear, solar thermal, ocean thermal gradient, and coal-
      fired power plants with an emphasis on nuclear plant siting;
      also included are treatment of undergrounding, geologic,
      seismic, social, economic, and environmental factors and the
      siting of power plants in countries other than the United
      States.

1000. *Impact Assessment Bulletin.* 1982 to present.

      Is a journal which presents conceptual, methodological, or
      empirical innovations in impact assessment. Novel applica-
      tions and case experiences are often described. Current
      address is International Association for Impact Assessment,
      c/o Environmental and Ground Water Institute, University of
      Oklahoma, 200 Felgar Street, EL #127, Norman, Oklahoma,
      73019.

1001. Kale, Steven. *The Impact of New or Additional Industry Upon
      Rurally Oriented Areas: A Selectively Annotated Bibliog-
      raphy with Emphasis on Manufacturing.* No. 1148.
      Monticello, Illinois: Council of Planning Librarians,
      October 1976. 28 pp.

Contains 100 works about industrial location and relocation in rural areas, especially in terms of socioeconomic impacts of change in the manufacturing sector of the economy.

1002. Kirkpatrick, Meredith. *Environmental Problems and Policies in Eastern Europe and the USSR.* No. 1491. Monticello, Illinois: Council of Planning Librarians, March 1978. 12 pp.

Lists about 150 books, articles, and government documents.

1003. Krannich, Richard S., and John F. Schnell. *Social and Economic Impacts of U.S. Rural Industrial Development: A Working Bibliography.* No. 1365. Monticello, Illinois: Council of Planning Librarians, October 1977. 12 pp.

Provides an initial listing of about 100 works that address major issues of rural industrial development in the United States.

1004. Levenson, Rosaline. *Company Towns: A Bibliography of American and Foreign Sources.* Exchange Bibliography No. 1428. Monticello, Illinois: Council of Planning Librarians, 1977. 25 pp.

Contains about 280 references categorized by geographic areas. The U.S. areas listed are East, South, Midwest, and West. Entries pertaining to foreign countries are listed under subheads of Canada, England, South America, and Other Countries.

1005. Little, Ronald L., and Stephen B. Lovejoy. *Western Energy Development as a Type of Rural Industrialization: A Partially Annotated Bibliography.* No. 1298. Monticello, Illinois: Council of Planning Librarians, June 1977. 39 pp.

Annotates about 200 works on such specific topics as rural industrialization, rural energy development, and employment patterns, attitudes, rural household economics and family structure, demographic characteristics, environmental impact assessment of energy development, and Native Americans.

1006. Maguire, Robert K. *Socio-economic Factors Pertaining to Single-Industry Resource Towns in Canada: A Bibliography with Selected Annotations.* Chicago, Illinois: Council of Planning Librarians Bibliographies, 1980. 46 pp.

Includes over 300 studies related to resource towns in Canada. A few entries relate to the United States and

Europe. Topics covered include social and economic aspects, housing and health issues, population mobility, and planning.

1007. Morrison, Denton E. *Energy: A Bibliography of Social Science and Related Literature.* New York: Garland Publishing, Inc., 1975. 157 pp.

Is a broadscope, unannotated bibliography with over 2,100 entries on energy from the social science and related literature, with a handy subject index.

1008. Nakamura, Sandra. *Social and Economic Factors Associated With Electric Power Generation, 1978: An Annotated Bibliography.* INFORUM-005. Washington, D.C.: Atomic Industrial Forum, 1978. 111 pp.

Is the second in a series of annotated bibliographies produced from the INFORUM data base on the socioeconomic impacts associated with electric power generation and related energy facilities. The majority of the citations are for specific planned and operating nuclear and coal-fired, steam-electric generating stations and their associated transmission lines. However, there are also citations for other parts of the fossil and nuclear fuel cycles, including mines and mills, fuel transportation, and the breeder reactor. The bibliography is arranged by types of impacts, including direct benefits, indirect benefits, internal costs, and external costs. A state index and an author, sponsor, and plant index are provided.

1009. Napier, Ted L. *Bibliography on Community Development Studies.* Exchange Bibliography 1011. Monticello, Illinois: Council of Planning Librarians, 1976. 47 pp.

Contains approximately 550 entries on the following topics: community development and planning; natural resources development; foreign and international development; social services and government services; community studies; and economic, industrial, and transportation development and planning.

* Nelson, Marlys Knutson. *Socioeconomic Impact Models: An Annotated Bibliography.* ERS Staff Rpt. AGES 850228. Cited above as item 476.

1010. Nilsen, Kirsti. *Bibliography of Bibliographies Prepared by U.S. Government Agencies of Interest to Community Planners.*

No. 527. Monticello, Illinois: Council of Planning Librarians, February 1974. 23 pp.

Includes 153 titles and an index.

1011. Onibokum, Adepoju. *Socio-economic Impact of Highways and Commuter Rail Systems on Land Use and Activity Patterns--An Annotated Bibliography.* No. 815. Monticello, Illinois: Council of Planning Librarians, June 1975. 35 pp.

Is divided into three sections: a discussion of the scope and coverage of publications dealing with impacts of highways and commuter rail systems; annotated previous works (particularly methodology and techniques of analysis); and lists of pertinent books and periodicals. Altogether, forty-two works are annotated, and an additional seventy-seven are listed.

* Pill, Juri. "The Delphi Method: Substance, Context, a Critique and an Annotated Bibliography." *Socioeconomic Planning Sciences.* Cited above as item 305.

1012. President's Economic Adjustment Committee. *Boom Town Annotated Bibliography.* Washington, D.C.: U.S. Department of Defense, Office of Economic Adjustment, 1981. 72 pp.

Contains fifty-five selected references on the subject of planning for and managing rapid, or boom town, growth. Extensive annotations provide an understanding of the material and the source from which each publication can be obtained.

1013. Root, Kenneth. *Companies, Mines and Factories--Shutdowns, Closures and Moves: A Bibliography.* Monticello, Illinois: Vance Bibliographies, 1979. 23 pp.

Contains about 250 entries on plant shutdowns and reloca-tions, and related social change, family crises, and agency programs. Literature relates mainly to the United States and to current research, although some classic and descriptive works date back to the 1930s.

1014. Sanford, Cheryl. *A Bibliography of the Athabasca Oil Sands: Fort McMurray, Alberta Area: Socio-economic and Environ-mental Studies. 1980 Cumulated Update,* 6th ed. and *1982 Supplement,* companion document compiled by Susan Bramm. Edmonton, Alberta: Alberta Environment Library, 1980 & 1982. 341 pp. & 236 pp., respectively.

Provides a comprehensive listing of above 1,900 items
relating to the socioeconomic and environmental aspects of
the development of the Athabasca Oil Sands. Also covers
other Alberta oil sands areas of Cold Lake, Peace River, and
Wabasca.

1015. Schnell, John F., and Richard S. Krannich. *Social and
       Economic Impacts of Energy Development Projects: A Working
       Bibliography*. No. 1366. Monticello, Illinois: Council of
       Planning Librarians, October 1977. 22 pp.

       Contains over 200 policy-oriented, practical research works
       of private and governmental organizations and agencies.

   *   Selby, John, and Lambert Wenner. *Social Analysis
       Bibliography for Forest Service Programs*. Cited above as
       item 42.

1016. *Social Impact Assessment*.

       Is a newsletter solely devoted to the study and practice of
       SIA and published jointly by the Social Impact Assessment
       Center (Box 587, Canal Street Station, New York 10013) and
       the International Association for Impact Assessment.

1017. Swanick, Eric L. *New Brunswick Regional Development During
       the 60s and the 70s: An Introductory Bibliography*. No.
       1122. Monticello, Illinois: Council of Planning
       Librarians, September 1976. 34 pp.

       Lists 382 titles and an index.

1018. Taylor, C. N., C. Bettesworth, and J. G. Kerslake. *Social
       Implications of Rapid Industrialization: A Bibliography of
       New Zealand Experiences*. Canterbury, New Zealand: Univer-
       sity of Canterbury & Lincoln College, Centre for Resource
       Management, 1983. 36 pp.

       Annotates literature pertaining to social change arising
       from rapid industrialization and boom population growth in
       rural New Zealand areas, including hydro towns and develop-
       ments in the coal, oil, gas, iron, steel, and forestry
       industries.

   *   University of Alberta. *Abstract of Papers, The Human Side of
       Energy: Second International Forum*. Cited above as item
       47.

1019. Vidergar, John J. *The Economic and Social Development of Iran.* No. 1380. Monticello, Illinois: Council of Planning Librarians, October 1977. 6 pp.

Contains sixty-three works about petroleum development, industrialization, urbanization, and agricultural reform in Iran.

1020. Vidergar, John J. *Migration Studies of Iraq.* No. 1379. Monticello, Illinois: Council of Planning Librarians, October 1977. 7 pp.

Introduces the planner to the literature on a variety of problems associated with migration and population growth in the Middle East in general and in Iraq in particular. Seventy five works are listed.

1021. Wolf, C. P. *Quality of Life, Concept and Measurement: A Preliminary Bibliography.* P-249. Monticello, Illinois: Vance Bibliographies, 1979. 12 pp.

Contains about 120 references dealing with the conceptual understanding and operational measurement of *quality of life* or *social well-being.*

1022. Wolf, C. P. *Social Impact Assessment of Transportation Planning: A Preliminary Bibliography.* P-250. Monticello, Illinois: Vance Bibliographies, 1979. 35 pp.

Contains more than 400 references that trace the applications of SIA to transportation planning over the past two decades. The literature review indicates that until recently the emphasis has been on highway planning.

1023. Wolf, C. P. *Urban Impact Assessment: A Preliminary Bibliography.* P-251. Monticello, Illinois: Vance Bibliographies, 1979. 65 pp.

Contains more than 700 references and represents a first effort to inventory some of the research and opinion that might be of use in developing and interpreting the substantive side of urban impact assessment. The bibliography focuses mainly on urban communities and places special emphasis on the fields of planning and public participation. Such aspects as growth, alternative futures, quality of life, and social indicators also receive special attention.

1024. *Worldletter: Environmental Impact Assessment.* June/July 1983 to present.

Is an international newsletter for environmental assessment published jointly by the University of Oklahoma, Environmental and Ground Water Institute, Norman, Oklahoma 73019 and the University of Aberdeen, Department of Geography, Old Aberdeen, Scotland, U.K. AB92UF. Coverage of the newsletter is on methodologies, concepts, issues, data acquisition, data bases, resources, networking, postaudit experiences, funding, legislation, people, and literature.

1025. Zinn, Jeffrey. *Socio-Economic Impacts of Rapid Growth Related to Energy Activities in Rural Areas; Overview and Selected Bibliography, 1970-1982.* Report No. 83-42 ENR. Washington, D.C.: Congressional Research Service, 1983. 59 pp.

Contains above 500 references to literature published in the United States since 1970. The overview section indentifies major issues and themes in the literature. Does not include annotations or indexes.

Indexes

Author Index

Subject Index